CONSUMER BUYING GUIDE

CONSUMER GUIDE® MAGAZINE Consumer Information Series is published six times a year, bimonthly.

Cover Photo Credits: American Honda Motor Co., Inc.; NordicTrack; RCA/Thomson Consumer Electronics; Yamaha Electronics Corp.

CONTENTS

INTRODUCTION

Are you finally ready to buy that full-size stereo system with a CD player? Do you know what the difference is between a carousel and magazine disc changer? Is a five-disc changer better than a four?

Looking to replace your aging television set with a spiffy new one? Are you sure you know what "cable ready" means? And did you know that replacing some types of appliances can actually save money in the long run? Today's refrigerators use much less electricity than the decades-old fridge that may be in your kitchen. And modern dishwashers have been designed to use less water than older models.

In short, do you know how to determine what features you'll want in a product? Then do you know how to get the most features for your money?

It takes experience and expert knowledge to spend your hard-earned dollar wisely in every facet of today's marketplace. Intelligent choices become more difficult when you include rapid advances in technology and shifts in the world's economy. These factors can quickly change price, availability, and long-term usefulness, making your buying decisions very confusing.

That's where we at CONSUMER GUIDE® can help. We recognize the challenge in picking a Best Buy, a product that meets your high standards of quality, performance, and value. Our experts in the major product fields have taken the guesswork and confusion out of making major purchases. CONSUMER GUIDE® has no affiliation with any manufacturers or retailers, we accept no advertising, and we are not interested in selling products. Our sole purpose is to provide you, the consumer, with the information needed to make informed, intelligent decisions.

In this publication, we have tried to review a wide variety of products to address diverse consumer needs. We have not limited the choices to lower-end products or top-of-the-line merchandise. We know that a product is only a Best Buy if it meets your needs and budget. Keeping this in mind, we have selected products in a variety of sizes and prices to match the requirements of different shoppers. In fact, this year we have attempted to meet the needs of more consumers than ever.

Many consumers will find they benefit from exercising patience. When a new product first hits the market, it generally demands a premium price. However, if you wait, instead of rushing right out to make the purchase, you will probably observe that not only does the price come down, but changes and improvements will have been incorporated into the product. Prime examples include products such as CD players, personal cassette players, computers, and food processors. These items are much less expensive today than when they first came on the market, and the progression of refinements has been steady.

To make the best use of this book, first review the introductory material at the beginning of each chapter. This introduction contains important information about the product, describes its features, and explains the terminology you need to know when you shop. Determine what features will be most useful to you and those using the product. Once you are acquainted with the criteria we use to select products, go on to our Best Buy selections. These products were chosen for their usefulness, high quality, and overall value. A Best Buy isn't necessarily the least expensive model; it's the highest quality product available at a reasonable price. Recommended selections are also good products, but for one reason or another, they do not measure up to our Best Buy standards. Such a product may carry a high price tag, it may have limited appeal, or it could be so new on the market that we haven't been able to accurately test its performance and durability over a long period of time.

When you shop, compare prices and models. If a dealer quotes a price close to the Approximate Low Price in this publication, then you know that you are getting first-rate value for your money. All the prices listed were accurate at the time of printing. In some cases, prices were not available. All products were checked to make sure that they would be available to consumers in 1996, but product manufacture and distribution is beyond our control.

AUTOS

The auto editors of Consumer Guide® have selected Best Buys and Recommended vehicles in 10 categories of passenger cars, minivans, and sport-utility vehicles. Vehicles are assigned to one of these categories based on their size, price, and market position. That way, a $10,000 subcompact competes against other low-priced small cars, not against $40,000 luxury cars.

At least one Best Buy and one Recommended has been selected in each category. Road-test results play a major role in the selections. Other factors include price, cost of ownership, warranties, reputation for reliability and durability, and safety features.

With new cars being released throughout the year, some 1996 models were not available for testing before this book went to print. As a result, vehicles such as the Acura RL and Hyundai Elantra could not be rated even though they may be available by the time this book goes on sale.

SUBCOMPACT CARS

GEO PRIZM AND TOYOTA COROLLA

✓ BEST BUY

The front-drive Geo Prizm and Toyota Corolla are built from the same design but have different exterior styling and interior features. In addition, Corolla comes as a 4-door sedan and a 5-door wagon, Prizm only as a sedan. Dual air bags are standard, and anti-lock brakes are optional on all models. A 105-horsepower 1.6-liter 4-cylinder engine is standard on all Prizms and the base Corolla. A 115-horsepower 1.8-liter 4-cylinder is optional on the Prizm LSi and standard on Corolla DX models. These cars have roomy interiors for this class, offering ample space for four adults. They also set the subcompact standard for quietness and ride comfort. Prizm, sold by Chevrolet dealers with Geo franchises, is slightly less ex-

Prices are accurate at time of printing but are subject to manufacturers' changes.

pensive with a base price of $12,495 versus $12,728 for the cheapest Corolla. In addition, Corolla is more expensive at the upper end. Both should provide reliable, durable, and economical service.

Approx. retail price	Approx. low price
$12,495–$18,000	$12,195–$17,000

HONDA CIVIC

BEST BUY

A redesigned Civic went on sale in the fall with new styling, two new 1.6-liter 4-cylinder engines, and an innovative continuously variable transmission (CVT) among the key changes. Civic again comes with front-wheel drive in 2-door coupe, 3-door hatchback, and 4-door sedan body styles. A new model lineup includes DX, HX, and EX versions of the coupe; CX and DX hatchback models; and DX, LX, and EX sedans. The CX, DX, and LX models use a new 106-horsepower 1.6-liter engine that is available with a 5-speed manual or a new electronic 4-speed automatic transmission. The HX coupe comes with a new 115-horsepower engine and is available with a 5-speed manual or the CVT automatic transmission. Unlike conventional automatic transmissions, which have three or four forward gears, the CVT has an infinite number of gear ratios and operates like a dimmer instead of a 3-way light switch. The EX models use the same 127-horsepower 1.6-liter engine as last year. It is available with the 5-speed manual or 4-speed automatic transmissions. Dual air bags are standard on all Civics. Anti-lock brakes are standard on the EX sedan and optional on the LX sedan and EX coupe. The new Civic is roomier, more comfortable, and just as lively and agile as the previous model. It shifts much smoother than last year's automatic. Prices have increased slightly this year, and though the LX and EX models are rather expensive, the new versions should continue Civic's traditions for reliability, durability, and high resale value.

Approx. retail price	Approx. low price
$9,900–$17,500	Not available

CHEVROLET CAVALIER AND PONTIAC SUNFIRE

Recommended

Cavalier and Sunfire are front-drive subcompacts that share major mechanical components but have different styling. Both were redesigned last year and come in 2-door coupe, 4-door sedan, and 2-door convertible body styles. Most models use a 120-horsepower 2.2-liter overhead-valve 4-cylinder engine. A new 150-horsepower 2.4-liter 4-cylinder with dual overhead camshafts is offered on more-expensive versions. Base prices start at $10,500 for the Cavalier and $11,504 for the Sunfire, which has more standard features. Both come with standard dual air bags, anti-lock brakes, and useful features such as daytime running lights, 5-year/100,000-mile engine coolant, and 100,000-mile spark plugs. Models with the optional 4-speed automatic transmission this year also get traction control, a safety feature rarely found on cars in this price range. Cavalier and Sunfire aren't as well built, quiet, or comfortable as class leaders such as the Toyota Corolla and Honda Civic, but they're less expensive when comparably equipped and offer good value.

Approx. retail price	**Approx. low price**
$10,500–$18,000	**Not available**

SATURN SEDAN AND WAGON

Recommended

The front-drive Saturn sedan and wagon get a new look for 1996, the first major styling change since these cars debuted for 1990. Dual air bags return as standard. Like the previous generation, all vertical body panels (doors, fenders, and front and rear facias) are made of plastic-like polymer material that resists dings and rust. The roof, hood, and trunk are made of steel. The new bodies are slightly longer and narrower, and the doorways are larger to make entry/exit easier. A 100-horsepower single-camshaft 1.9-liter 4-cylinder is used for the SL and SL1 sedans and the SW1 wagon. A 124-horsepower dual-camshaft version of that engine comes in the SL2 sedan and SW2 wagon. Order the optional anti-lock brakes this year and you'll get traction control whether the car has a 4-speed automatic or

Prices are accurate at time of printing but are subject to manufacturers' changes.

5-speed manual transmission. Saturn's cars aren't perfect, but they're good enough in key areas to be well worth considering. They're also competitively priced, have a good record for reliability, and command high resale value. Saturn's policy is to provide hassle-free treatment before and after the sale, which has helped the company consistently score near the top in customer-satisfaction ratings. Dealers generally charge full retail price.

Approx. retail price	Approx. low price
$10,495–$18,000	$10,495–$18,000

COMPACT CARS

MAZDA 626

✓BEST BUY

The front-drive 626, which is built in Michigan, at a plant jointly owned by Mazda and Ford Motor Co., comes as a 4-door sedan in four price levels: DX, LX, LX V-6, and ES. Dual air bags are standard on all, and anti-lock brakes are standard on the ES and optional on the LX and LX V-6. The DX and LX are powered by a 118-horsepower 2.2-liter 4-cylinder engine. LX V-6 and ES models have a 2.5-liter V-6 with 164 horsepower. All come with a standard 5-speed manual transmission or optional 4-speed automatic. The 626 is roomy, solid, and competent in all areas. The DX starts at $15,495 and the LX at $17,695, with the latter including air conditioning, power windows and locks, and a cassette player. We prefer the V-6 engine to the 4-cylinder, but the LX V-6 starts at $19,895 and the ES, which has leather seats and a power sunroof, at $22,795. The 4-cylinder models have adequate performance and good fuel economy.

Approx. retail price	Approx. low price
$15,495–$22,795	$14,900–$20,950

TOYOTA CAMRY

✓BEST BUY

Since it was redesigned for 1992, the Camry has set the standard among family sedans for refinement and overall quality. It is built from the same design as the more expensive Lexus ES 300, a premium sedan. The Camry benefits

Prices are accurate at time of printing but are subject to manufacturers' changes.

from some of the ES 300's attributes, including smooth, quiet performance; an absorbent, comfortable suspension; and impeccable assembly quality. Camry comes as a 2-door coupe, a 4-door sedan, and a 5-door wagon, all with front-wheel drive. Engine choices are a 125-horsepower 2.2-liter 4-cylinder and a 188-horsepower 3.0-liter V-6. Dual air bags are standard, and anti-lock brakes are available on all models. Now the bad news. Camry prices are high. They start at $16,468 for a base DX sedan and climb to $25,038 for the XLE. An LE sedan, the most popular model, is about $20,500 and includes automatic transmission, air conditioning, power windows and locks, and a cassette player.

Approx. retail price	Approx. low price
$16,468–$26,000	$16,000–$25,000

FORD CONTOUR AND MERCURY MYSTIQUE

Recommended

Introduced last year, the Contour and Mystique are front-drive sedans that differ mainly in styling. Both are based on the European Ford Mondeo but are built at Ford plants in Kansas City and Mexico. Both also have standard dual air bags and optional anti-lock brakes. The base engine is a 125-horsepower 2.0-liter 4-cylinder camshafts. The optional engine is a 170-horsepower 2.5-liter V-6. Both come with a standard 5-speed manual or optional 4-speed automatic transmission. Though the 106.5-inch wheelbase on these cars is longer than some mid-size sedans', interior volume falls in the compact class. They were most criticized last year for their lack of rear seat room. For 1996, Ford has addressed this problem with two changes. First, the backs of the front seats have been scooped out to give rear passengers an additional inch of leg room. Second, the rear seat cushion has been repositioned to provide more rear leg and head room. Despite those changes, Contour and Mystique still aren't as roomy as the Camry. However, both are high-quality, competent sedans that are priced lower than Camry when comparably equipped.

Approx. retail price	Approx. low price
$13,785–$16,170	$13,200–$18,200

NISSAN ALTIMA

Recommended

The front-drive Altima, which is built in Tennessee, comes in four price levels: XE, GXE, SE, and GLE. All have standard dual air bags and a 150-horsepower 2.4-liter 4-cylinder engine. A 5-speed manual transmission is standard and a 4-speed automatic is optional on all but the GLE, which comes with the automatic. Anti-lock brakes are optional on all models. The GXE is the volume model and probably the best deal in the lineup. With the GXE Value Option Package, you get a well-equipped car with automatic transmission, air conditioning, power windows and locks, and a cassette player for a retail price of about $19,000. Intense competition in this price range makes it likely Nissan dealers will be discounting.

Approx. retail price	Approx. low price
$15,649–$20,999	**$14,600–$19,900**

MID-SIZE CARS

FORD TAURUS AND MERCURY SABLE

✓BEST BUY

Taurus, America's best-selling car, and the similar Sable are redesigned for 1996—their first complete overhaul since the originals were introduced a decade ago. Front-wheel drive and 4-door sedan and 5-door wagon body styles are retained, but both cars are larger and more rounded than before, with an elliptical styling theme that carries into the interior design. The wheelbase grows to 108.5 inches—2.5-inches longer than last year. Overall length increases more than five inches on the sedan and nearly six on the wagon. The Taurus GL and Sable GS use an updated version of last year's overhead-valve 3.0-liter V-6 that now makes 145 horsepower, five more than previously. Last year's optional 3.8-liter V-6 has been replaced by the new 3.0-liter V-6 with dual overhead camshafts and 200 horsepower. The dual-cam engine is standard on the Taurus LX and Sable LS. Both engines team with a 4-speed automatic transmission. Dual air bags are standard, and 4-wheel anti-lock disc brakes are optional on all models. The new Taurus and Sable are roomier, more solid, quieter, more comfortable, and

Prices are accurate at time of printing but are subject to manufacturers' changes.

more expensive. The Taurus starts at $18,600 ($1000 more than last year), but Taurus and Sable initially will be built with optional features that will increase the retail price to nearly $20,000. Because we expect high demand for this car, discounts will be hard to come by initially.

Approx. retail price **$18,600–$23,000** | **Approx. low price** **Not available**

HONDA ACCORD

✓BEST BUY

The Accord continues as a Best Buy because it offers good assembly quality, reliable operation, and high resale value in a functional package that's fun to drive. Dual air bags are standard on all versions of the front-drive Accord, which comes in three body styles—4-door sedan, 2-door coupe, and 5-door wagon. The sedan comes in DX, LX, and EX price levels, and the coupe and wagon in LX and EX levels. A 2.2-liter 4-cylinder is the base engine for all price levels, and a 2.7-liter V-6, introduced last year, is optional on the LX and EX sedans. Anti-lock brakes are standard on the EX and optional on the LX. Though the V-6 engine is quieter and more potent, the 4-cylinder Accords are peppy enough and more economical. There also are bigger discounts on the 4-cylinder models. Don't let Honda dealers buffalo you into thinking that Accords still sell for full retail price. It's a great car, but there is too much competition these days for that to continue.

Approx. retail price **$15,100–$25,100** | **Approx. low price** **$14,000–$24,000**

BUICK REGAL, CHEVROLET LUMINA/MONTE CARLO,OLDSMOBILE CUTLASS SUPREME, AND PONTIAC GRAND PRIX

Recommended

All of these cars are built by General Motors from the same front-drive design. They share the same basic structure and most mechanical components but differ in exterior styling and interior features. All come in 4-door sedan and 2-door coupe body styles with a standard 4-speed automatic transmission and dual air bags. Anti-lock brakes are optional on

Prices are accurate at time of printing but are subject to manufacturers' changes.

the base Lumina sedan and the Grand Prix and standard on the others. The base engine for all models is a 160-horsepower 3.1-liter V-6 that provides adequate acceleration and decent fuel economy. A more potent 3.4-liter V-6 is optional on all models except the Regal, which stands apart from this crowd by offering a 205-horsepower 3.8-liter V-6. All have room for as many as six people and ample cargo space. The Lumina is the price leader at $16,355—more than $2000 less than the rival Ford Taurus. The Grand Prix, which has more standard equipment than the Lumina, starts at $17,089. The $17,455 base price for the Cutlass Supreme includes air conditioning, power windows and locks, and a cassette player—a good deal on a mid-size car. The Regal is more expensive (starting at $19,445), but the smooth 3.8-liter V-6 gives it acceleration that rivals V-8-powered cars. Though GM's mid-size cars lack the overall quality of the Taurus and Accord, most models are considerably less expensive when comparably equipped.

Approx. retail price
$16,355–$21,800

Approx. low price
$16,000–$22,000

CHRYSLER CIRRUS/DODGE STRATUS

Recommended

Cirrus and Stratus were introduced last year as Chrysler Corporation's new mid-size front-drive sedans. They share major features and mechanical features and differ in front and rear appearance details, standard equipment, and prices. Both are just 186 inches long overall, which is compact-sized, but they have a 108-inch wheelbase that gives them more interior space than most mid-size rivals. Stratus starts at $14,460 and comes with a standard 2.0-liter 4-cylinder engine and a 5-speed manual transmission. Optional engines are a 2.4-liter 4-cylinder and 2.5-liter V-6, both of which come with a 4-speed automatic. The 2.4-liter 4-cylinder and automatic transmission are standard on the Cirrus, which starts at $17,560, and the V-6 is optional. With either model, you'll be hard pressed to exceed $20,000 (retail price) even with a full load of options. Dealers should be discounting, making these cars even more attractive.

Prices are accurate at time of printing but are subject to manufacturers' changes.

Approx. retail price
$14,460–$20,000

Approx. low price
$14,000–$19,400

FULL-SIZE CARS

BUICK LE SABRE, OLDSMOBILE EIGHTY EIGHT, AND PONTIAC BONNEVILLE

BEST BUY

The Buick LeSabre, Oldsmobile Eighty Eight, and Pontiac Bonneville are front-drive sedans that are built from the same basic design but have different styling and interior features. Dual air bags and anti-lock brakes are standard across the board. All three cars come with a standard 205-horsepower 3.8-liter V-6 engine and a 4-speed automatic transmission. This engine is smooth, quiet, and performs on a par with the V-8s used in rear-drive rivals while returning better fuel economy. For even better performance, a 240-horsepower supercharged version of the 3.8-liter V-6 is optional on the Bonneville and Eighty Eight. All models have ample passenger and cargo space, and they offer a lot of features for a reasonable price. For example, the base Eighty Eight is $20,405 and includes air conditioning, power windows and locks, a stereo radio, and cruise control. The comparable LeSabre and Bonneville models are about $500 more.

Approx. retail price
$20,405–$28,000

Approx. low price
$19,500–$26,500

CHRYSLER CONCORDE, DODGE INTREPID, AND EAGLE VISION

Recommended

The Chrysler Concorde, Dodge Intrepid, and Eagle Vision are front-drive sedans from Chrysler Corporation that have similar styling except at the front and rear. Standard equipment includes dual air bags, while anti-lock brakes are standard or optional on all models. Base engine for all three models is a 161-horsepower 3.3-liter V-6, which provides adequate acceleration. The optional engine is a 214-horsepower 3.5-liter V-6 that delivers more spirited performance. These cars have some impressive credentials: sporty handling, a comfort-

Prices are accurate at time of printing but are subject to manufacturers' changes.

able ride, and modern, spacious interiors. The retail prices are reasonable by today's standards, and discounts should be available on all three models.

Approx. retail price
$18,445–$24,000

Approx. low price
$17,900–$22,700

TOYOTA AVALON

Recommended

Toyota plowed new ground when it introduced the Avalon for 1995 as the first full-size Japanese car sold in the U.S. On the outside, the Avalon has mid-size dimensions (107.1-inch wheelbase and 190.2-inch overall length). However, with 120.9 cubic feet of interior volume it is considered full-size by the federal EPA. The front-drive Avalon is based on the Toyota Camry (a compact car) and is built at the same plant in Kentucky. A 4-inch longer wheelbase gives the Avalon a much roomier rear seat and a bigger trunk. A 3-place front bench seat is available instead of front buckets to give the Avalon 6-passenger seating capacity. A 192-horsepower 3.0-liter V-6 and 4-speed automatic transmission are standard. Avalon is roomy, comfortable, quiet, and well built. The smooth V-6 engine provides brisk performance with reasonable fuel economy. The major drawback is the price, which starts at $23,418—considerably more than domestic competitors. The top-line XLS version starts at $27,448 and can top $30,000 with options.

Approx. retail price
$23,418–$30,500

Approx. low price
Not available

PREMIUM COUPES

CADILLAC ELDORADO

✓BEST BUY

Both the base Eldorado and the sportier Eldorado Touring Coupe (ETC) use Cadillac's Northstar V-8, a 4.6-liter engine with dual overhead camshafts. In the base model, the Northstar makes 275 horsepower and in the Touring Coupe 300. Dual air bags, anti-lock brakes, traction control, and a 4-speed automatic transmission are standard on these front-drive

Prices are accurate at time of printing but are subject to manufacturers' changes.

coupes. We like the base model a bit more than the Touring Coupe because its engine produces more power at lower speeds than the ETC's engine, so you get brisker acceleration and passing response. The base Eldorado also has a more compliant suspension and softer tires. Hefty discounts should be available on both because there isn't much demand for premium-priced coupes.

Approx. retail price
$39,595–$42,995

Approx. low price
$36,500–$41,500

LEXUS SC 300/400

✓BEST BUY

Lexus offers two coupe models, the SC 300 and SC 400, which are the same car with different engines. The SC 300 uses a 3.0-liter 6-cylinder engine rated at 225 horsepower. The SC 400 has a 260-horsepower 4.0-liter V-8. A 5-speed manual transmission is standard on the SC 300 and an electronic 4-speed automatic is optional. The SC 400 comes only with the automatic. Both models have rear-wheel drive, dual air bags, and anti-lock brakes. The Lexus coupes also have the same high quality as the Lexus sedans. The SC 300 isn't quite as fast but offers nearly as much as the SC 400 for about $9000 less.

Approx. retail price
$43,400–54,000

Approx. low price
$41,000–$51,500

BUICK RIVIERA

Recommended

Buick's luxury coupe was redesigned for the 1995 model year, when it gained new styling and a roomier interior. It sports a longer wheelbase (113.8 inches) than all competitors, and—with the standard front bench seat—seats six. Front buckets are optional. Dual air bags and anti-lock brakes are standard. Two 3.8-liter V-6s are available. The base engine produces 205 horsepower, and an optional supercharged 3.8-liter V-6 makes 240 horsepower. The base engine is smooth and delivers adequate acceleration, but the supercharged engine provides a noticeable performance boost. Unlike many coupes, the Riviera's rear seat is usable by adults, though three across in either the front or the back will be a squeeze, so it's really a big 4-seater.

Approx. retail price
$29,475–$32,500

Approx. low price
$28,000–$31,000

PREMIUM SEDANS

CADILLAC SEVILLE

✓ BEST BUY

The front-drive Seville comes in two models, the base SLS (Seville Luxury Sedan) and the sportier STS (Seville Touring Sedan), both of which use Cadillac's Northstar V-8, a 4.6-liter engine with dual overhead camshafts. On the SLS, horsepower is 275 on the STS it is 300. Dual air bags, anti-lock brakes, traction control, and an electronic 4-speed automatic transmission are standard. The Seville is a roomy sedan with commendable acceleration, ride, and handling. We like the SLS better because its engine feels more responsive at lower speeds and it has a softer suspension than the STS. Both should be available at big discounts below suggested retail price.

Approx. retail price
$42,995–$49,500

Approx. low price
$40,000–$48,000

LEXUS ES 300

✓ BEST BUY

The front-drive ES 300, the entry-level model at Lexus (Toyota's luxury division), is built from the same design as the Toyota Camry but has different styling and more standard features. The ES 300 comes with a 3.0-liter aluminum V-6 engine with dual overhead camshafts and 188 horsepower and an electronic 4-speed automatic transmission. Standard equipment on the ES 300 includes dual air bags and anti-lock brakes. On twisting roads the suspension feels soft and allows moderate body roll, but the tires grip well and the ES 300 has a comfortable, stable ride. Leg room is more than adequate front and rear, though head room for 6-footers is marginal with the optional power moonroof. The ES 300 is well-engineered and well-built, and it is a "must see" if you're looking at the lower end of the Premium Sedan segment.

Prices are accurate at time of printing but are subject to manufacturers' changes.

Approx. retail price
$32,400–$36,000

Approx. low price
Not available

LEXUS LS 400

✓ BEST BUY

The second-generation LS 400 debuted last year with new styling, more power, and a roomier interior. Though the current model closely resembles the 1990-94 generation, it is different inside and outside. Lexus retained major styling cues from the previous generation while giving the current one sharper edges and creases. Overall length and body width were unchanged, but the wheelbase was stretched 1.4 inches to 112.2 and the interior was widened by two inches. The rear-drive LS 400 comes with a 260-horsepower 4.0-liter V-8, 4-speed automatic transmission, dual air bags, anti-lock brakes, and a long list of comfort and convenience features. The current LS 400 is faster and quieter than the original and is built with impeccable quality. The base price is $52,900 and optional equipment can push the total past $60,000. Strong resale value and Lexus's excellent customer service will help compensate in the long run.

Approx. retail price
$52,900–$60,500

Approx. low price
Not available

INFINITI I30

Recommended

The I30 is a new model for Infiniti, the luxury division of Nissan, and a competitor for the Lexus ES 300. The I30 is a front-drive 4-door sedan based on the design used for the Nissan Maxima. Both have a 106.3-inch wheelbase, but the I30 is two inches longer at 189.6 overall. The I30 and Maxima use the same 190-horsepower 3.0-liter V-6 engine with dual overhead camshafts. Dual air bags and anti-lock brakes are standard. The main differences between the I30 and the Maxima are styling and price. Base prices for the I30 run from $28,420 to $33,720, while the Maxima is priced from $20,999 to $26,279. The I30's higher prices are justified by additional standard features, such as a CD player, remote keyless entry, a security system, and automatic climate control. In addition, In-

Prices are accurate at time of printing but are subject to manufacturers' changes.

finiti provides a longer warranty and consistently scores near the top in customer satisfaction surveys.

Approx. retail price
$28,420–$34,000

Approx. low price
Not available

MERCEDES BENZ E-CLASS

Recommended

A redesigned E-Class sedan arrives for 1996 with new styling highlighted by four oval headlamps, giving the Mercedes lineup a dramatic new face. From the windshield back, the styling is more evolutionary yet still distinctive from the old E-Class, which was sold in the U.S. from 1986 through 1995. Initially, the new E-Class is available in two versions: the E320 sedan with a 217-horsepower 3.2-liter gas 6-cylinder and the E300 Diesel sedan with a 134-horsepower 3.0-liter diesel 6-cylinder. The wheelbase has grown 1.3 inches to 111.5 and overall length 2.2 inches to 189.4, and the rear seat is much roomier. All models have dual front air bags, anti-lock brakes, and new side air bags mounted in the front door panels. The new E-Class feels more athletic than the old one, with crisper handling and firmer steering. Prices have increased only modestly for 1996: The diesel sedan starts at less than $43,000 and the gasoline model at less than $45,000.

Approx. retail price
$43,000–$48,000

Approx. low price
Not available

OLDSMOBILE AURORA

Recommended

Aurora is a front-drive premium sedan aimed at owners of Japanese brands such as Acura, Infiniti, and Lexus—buyers who normally wouldn't consider an Oldsmobile. Aurora has a 250-horsepower 4.0-liter V-8 with dual overhead camshafts, an electronic 4-speed automatic transmission, dual air bags, anti-lock brakes, and traction control. The engine doesn't snap your head back in hard acceleration, but it delivers brisk acceleration and ample passing power. The transmission shifts so smoothly you hardly notice it. The suspension is firmer than some cars in this category yet never harsh or stiff. The Aurora has a roomy interior with ample space for four

Prices are accurate at time of printing but are subject to manufacturers' changes.

adults. The base price has climbed to $34,360, but that's still thousands less than any V-8 rival. The Aurora is a bargain compared to many premium sedans.

Approx. retail price
$34,360–$37,500

Approx. low price
Not available

SPORTS COUPES

FORD PROBE AND MAZDA MX-6

✔ BEST BUY

These front-drive sports coupes are built in a factory in Michigan jointly owned by Ford and Mazda and share major mechanical components, though each vehicle has its own styling. Probe is a 3-door hatchback and MX-6 a 2-door notchback coupe. Both have standard dual air bags and offer anti-lock brakes as an option. The Probe comes in base and GT versions, while the MX-6 comes in base and LS models. The base models use a 118-horsepower 2.0-liter 4-cylinder engine and the GT and LS versions a 164-horsepower 2.5-liter V-6. Both engines are made by Mazda. The V-6 is the better choice for those who make performance their priority, but the 4-cylinder engine has adequate power and better fuel economy. All versions of these cars look smart, handle competently, and come well equipped. Like most cars in this class, they have tiny rear seats that are too small for adults, but both are well-built coupes that offer good value for the money.

Approx. retail price
$13,930–$21,000

Approx. low price
$13,500–$20,000

ACURA INTEGRA

Recommended

The front-drive Integra is a 3-door hatchback that is the entry-level model for Acura, the luxury division of Honda. There are four price levels: RS, LS, Special Edition, and GS-R, all of which have standard dual air bags. Anti-lock brakes are standard on all models except the RS, where they aren't available. All models except the GS-R come with a 142-horsepower 1.8-liter 4-cylinder with dual overhead camshafts. The GS-R uses a different dual-cam 1.8-liter 4-cylinder with

Prices are accurate at time of printing but are subject to manufacturers' changes.

170 horsepower. A 5-speed manual transmission is standard on all models and a 4-speed automatic is optional except on the GS-R. Integra's base engine lacks enough low-speed torque to perform with any gusto with the automatic transmission, but it provides adequate acceleration. With the 5-speed manual, all models are quick and economical. Though the purchase prices are rather steep, Integra's high resale value and reliability are offsetting factors.

Approx. retail price	Approx. low price
$16,000–$22,500	$15,500–$21,700

SPORTS AND GT CARS

MAZDA MIATA

✓BEST BUY

Miata is a classic sports car that has changed little since it was introduced as a 1990 model. It is a rear-drive, 2-seat convertible with a 133-horsepower 1.8-liter 4-cylinder engine. Standard features include dual air bags, a manual convertible top, and a 5-speed manual transmission. Major options include anti-lock brakes, a 4-speed automatic transmission, air conditioning, power steering, and a removable hardtop. Acceleration is tepid with the automatic transmission and lively with the 5-speed manual. Though you'll feel nearly every bump, the firm suspension absorbs enough of the impact that the car doesn't skitter sideways on rough pavement. Even tall people have adequate working room in the cozy cockpit, but a couple of gym bags fill the small trunk. Prices have risen modestly over the years, so Miata is still an affordable sports car. You should be able to buy one for less than retail price.

Approx. retail price	Approx. low price
$18,500–$22,500	$18,000–$22,500

CHEVROLET CAMARO AND PONTIAC FIREBIRD

Recommended

The rear-drive Camaro and Firebird share mechanical components but have different styling. Camaro comes in base and Z28 versions, while the Firebird is offered in base,

Formula, and Trans Am trim. All models come in 3-door hatchback and 2-door convertible body styles with standard dual air bags and anti-lock brakes. Base models come with a 200-horsepower 3.8-liter V-6, a new engine for this year. The others have a standard 285-horsepower 5.7-liter V-8. This year Pontiac offers an optional "Ram Air" package that boosts horsepower to 305. Camaro and Firebird are long on image and performance, short on comfort and practicality. The V-8 models have outstanding acceleration, but they guzzle lots of gas and are expensive to insure. The 3.8-liter V-6 has more than adequate power and is less-expensive to buy, more economical to drive, and cheaper to insure. If you're interested mainly in performance, the Camaro and Firebird are better choices than the rival Ford Mustang, whether you desire a V-6 or V-8 engine.

Approx. retail price	Approx. low price
$14,990–$28,500	**$14,500–$27,500**

FORD MUSTANG

Recommended

The rear-drive Mustang has new overhead-camshaft V-8 engines this year. Standard on the Mustang GT this year is a single-cam 4.6-liter V-8 with 215 horsepower. The high-performance Cobra model has a dual-camshaft version with 305 horsepower. Base Mustangs return with a 3.8-liter V-6 rated at 150 horsepower. All three models are available as 2-door notchback coupes and convertibles. Dual air bags and 4-wheel disc brakes are standard on all models. Anti-lock brakes are standard on the Cobra and optional on the others. The new V-8s are smoother and quieter, but the 215-horsepower version in the GT model is pretty mild compared to the 285-horsepower V-8 in the rival Chevrolet Camaro and Pontiac Firebird. The Cobra's 305-horsepower engine is much livelier. The V-6 engine in the base Mustang is slower and noisier than the V-6 used in the Camaro and Firebird. Mustang, however, is more user-friendly in day-to-day driving, with a softer suspension, a roomier interior, and a taller design that allows more upright seating and better visibility.

Prices are accurate at time of printing but are subject to manufacturers' changes.

Approx. retail price
$15,180-$26,000

Approx. low price
$14,600-$25,000

MINIVANS

DODGE CARAVAN AND PLYMOUTH VOYAGER

✓BEST BUY

Chrysler Corporation has redesigned the Caravan and Voyager for 1996 and given them more aerodynamic styling, an optional sliding door on the driver's side, and removable seats with built-in rollers. The similar Chrysler Town & Country, a luxury version of this minivan, also has been redesigned, but it is not included as a Best Buy because it has no substantive advantages over the less-expensive Caravan and Voyager. Caravan and Voyager are available in standard-wheelbase (113.3 inches) and long-wheelbase (119.3 inches) body styles that hold up to seven people. Dual air bags and anti-lock brakes are standard. Initially, all models have front-wheel drive; all-wheel drive will be added during 1996. The base engine is a new 150-horsepower 2.4-liter 4-cylinder. Three V-6s are available: a 150-horsepower 3.0-liter; a 158-horsepower 3.3-liter; and a 166-horsepower 3.8-liter. The driver-side sliding door, a first for minivans, is a $450 option. A passenger-side sliding door is standard. The new Caravan and Voyager are even more carlike than the previous models. They ride like big cars, take corners with reassuring grip and stability, and are as quiet as many sedans. The 4-cylinder engine is too weak for vehicles this big. The 3.0- and 3.3-liter V-6s have adequate acceleration. The 3.8-liter V-6 is the best choice for those who usually carry a full load of passengers or cargo. If you're shopping for a minivan, put the Caravan and Voyager at the top of the list.

Approx. retail price
$16,800–$26,000

Approx. low price
Not available

FORD WINDSTAR

Recommended

Windstar, a front-drive minivan that debuted for 1995, gets major changes to its engine lineup for the 1996

Prices are accurate at time of printing but are subject to manufacturers' changes.

model year. Last year the only engine was a 155-horsepower 3.8-liter V-6. The 3.8-liter has been extensively revised to produce 200 horsepower. It is now standard on the LX model and optional on the GL. A 3.0-liter V-6 with 150 horsepower is now standard on the GL. Both models come with a 4-speed automatic transmission, dual air bags, and anti-lock brakes. Windstar comes in one size with a sliding passenger-side door and seats for seven. The 120.7-inch wheelbase is the longest of any minivan, though the new long-wheelbase Chrysler minivans have more interior room. The Windstar has a low step-in height that makes entry and exit easier, an absorbent suspension, adequate power, a functional interior design, and competitive pricing. With the new Chrysler minivans on the market, Ford dealers should be discounting the Windstar.

Approx. retail price	Approx. low price
$19,600–$27,500	**$19,000–$25,000**

MERCURY VILLAGER/NISSAN QUEST

Recommended

Villager and Quest are similar front-drive minivans that were designed by Nissan but are built at a Ford Motor Company plant in Ohio. Both have standard dual air bags, a Nissan 151-horsepower 3.0-liter V-6 engine, and a 4-speed automatic transmission. Anti-lock brakes are standard on all Villagers and the Quest GXE model. They're optional on the base Quest XE. All models come in a single size with a sliding passenger-side door and seats for seven. The main differences between the Villager and Quest are in exterior styling and that Villager comes in three price levels (GS, LS, and Nautica) and Quest in two. Though these minivans aren't as roomy as the Ford Windstar or long-wheelbase Chrysler models, they have adequate space for seven people and adequate power. They also have carlike ride and handling and are easy to get in or out of. Villager and Quest are good choices if you need more space than a mid-size station wagon provides but don't want one of the bigger minivans.

Approx. retail price	Approx. low price
$20,000–$27,500	**$19,000–$26,000**

Prices are accurate at time of printing but are subject to manufacturers' changes.

SPORT-UTILITY VEHICLES

FORD EXPLORER

✓BEST BUY

The Explorer was redesigned last year and gains an optional V-8 for 1996, addressing what many viewed as the Explorer's major shortcoming—not enough power. A 210-horsepower 5.0-liter V-8 initially is optional only on the 2-wheel-drive XLT model and comes only with a 4-speed automatic transmission. Ford expects the V-8 to be available on the Eddie Bauer and Limited models and with 4-wheel drive by next spring. With the V-8, towing capacity increases from 5000 pounds to 6500. All other models use a 160-horsepower 4.0-liter V-6 that comes with either a 5-speed manual transmission or 4-speed automatic. Explorer returns in 3- or 5-door wagon body styles, both available with either 2WD or 4WD. Dual air bags and 4-wheel anti-lock brakes are standard on all models. Ford's Control-Trac 4WD system is standard on 4×4 models. Control-Trac normally operates in 2WD, but when wheel slip is detected the system automatically engages 4WD for improved traction. Explorer's combination of room, comfort, power, quality, and value have made it the best-selling sport-utility vehicle. Unfortunately, because it's so popular dealers don't have to discount the Explorer.

Approx. retail price
$19,600–$36,000

Approx. low price
Not available

CHEVROLET BLAZER AND GMC JIMMY

Recommended

The Chevrolet Blazer and virtually identical GMC Jimmy were redesigned for 1995, when they gained new styling and a revamped interior with a driver-side air bag. Both come as 3- and 5-door wagons with either rear-wheel drive or on-demand part-time 4-wheel drive (not for use on dry pavement). All models use a new 190-horsepower 4.3-liter V-6 engine. A 4-speed automatic transmission and anti-lock brakes are standard. The V-6 engine provides strong acceleration and good passing power, though it's not as potent as the V-8s offered by

Prices are accurate at time of printing but are subject to manufacturers' changes.

Ford and Jeep. Blazer and Jimmy also lag behind their Ford and Jeep rivals in having only one air bag. However, they are priced lower, starting at just under $20,000. You'll have to order virtually every option to get a Blazer or Jimmy up to $30,000.

Approx. retail price	Approx. low price
$20,000–$30,000	Not available

JEEP GRAND CHEROKEE

Recommended

A redesigned dashboard includes a passenger-side air bag, so dual air bags are now standard on the Grand Cherokee, which comes as a 5-door wagon in two price levels, Laredo and Limited. Four-wheel anti-lock brakes are standard on both. The standard engine is a 4.0-liter 6-cylinder engine with 185 horsepower. A 220-horsepower 5.2-liter V-8 is optional. Both models can be ordered with rear-wheel drive, Selec-Trac full-time 4-wheel drive, or Quadra-Trac permanent 4WD. With dual air bags now standard, Grand Cherokee matches the Ford Explorer in that area, but Ford now matches Jeep with an optional V-8 engine. Jeep's 6-cylinder engine should be strong enough for most drivers. The Grand Cherokee is less expensive than the Explorer but more expensive than the Chevy Blazer and GMC Jimmy. Because of competition from those rivals, Jeep dealers should be discounting.

Approx. retail price	Approx. low price
$24,603–$34,000	$23,500–$32,500

Prices are accurate at time of printing but are subject to manufacturers' changes.

TELEVISIONS AND TV-VCR COMBINATIONS

With sales close to 27 million sets last year, the American public has a voracious appetite for color televisions. People seem to want a set in every room—including the bathroom. And a love affair is developing with bigger and bigger screens. Sales of large-screen TVs and projection TVs are exploding, as people in quest of the best picture quality buy the biggest set they can afford.

Television tubes have become flatter. FSTs (flat, square tubes) were initially introduced in 27-inch sets a few years ago. Now sets up to 35 inches are offering reduced-curvature screens. These sets provide more viewing area with less reflections from room light.

An aspect ratio of 4:3 (meaning that the width of the screen is 4 units and the height is 3 units) is standard for a normally square TV screen. In the last few years, wide-screen TVs have appeared on the market that use either 16:9 or Pioneer's 16:10.7 aspect ratios. The 16:9 aspect ratio mimics the shape of your local cinema's screen and is designed to show wide-screen pictures without the letter-box effect (black bars found on the top and bottom of the screen) or greatly reducing the effect. For conventional 4:3-aspect-ratio pictures you will end up with either a cropped picture on the top or bottom or black bars on both sides of the picture. Some projection sets will stretch a standard 4:3 picture to fit the screen, which could result in some distortion. RCA (and its Proscan brand line) offers the 16.9 aspect ratio in direct-view in 34-inch-wide configuration, and JVC, Pioneer, and Toshiba offer it in projection sets. These sets are the harbingers of things to come; broadcasters hope to send the first U.S. HDTV (High Definition Television) signals from the Olympics in Atlanta in 1996. The first consumer HDTV sets are expected to appear by 1997 or 1998 and will become more readily available as we approach the millennium. Those sets will offer wide-screen aspect ratios. Projection TV provides more flexibility in dealing with the considerable variety of aspect ratios, since there is no absolute standard for wide-screen images. Projection TVs have become a mainstream product, with sales of more than 600,000 models in 1994 and predicted sales close to 850,000 units in 1995.

Stereo sound is a significant feature in TV sets today. Many sets offer digital sound processing, Dolby Surround Sound decoding, or other sound enhancement options. More than a third of all TVs sold are stereo models, and all sets 27 inches and larger include stereo as a feature.

The fastest-growing TV/video category is the TV-VCR combination, which combines a television set with a VCR. Initially conceived as a business product, it has definitely found its niche in the home. Sales are expected to top two million units in 1995. Although they are offered in various screen sizes from 2 inches to 35 inches, the 13-inch and 20-inch sets are the most popular sizes. They are equipped with either a two-head or four-head VCR and are great for the bedroom, den, or children's room. Newer models for 1995–96 include a stereo TV and hi-fi VCR. You may not save any money by purchasing a combo, but you gain convenience by not having to deal with cables and wires.

In the rush to reach the new multimedia world, TVs and computer technology are moving closer together. The first example of this is Toshiba's Integrated Multimedia Monitor, or TIMM for short. Capable of receiving 181 channels of stereo television, the set also doubles as a VGA monitor for your IBM-type or Apple computer. We can expect to see more combination models adding features from both the TV and computer worlds in the future.

The coming years will bring increased digital transmissions and signal processing. Digital signals are already being broadcast via direct-to-home (DTH) satellite in the form of DSS (Digital Satellite System). Telephone and cable companies are in the process of outfitting their entire systems with fiber-optic cable in hopes of providing the best possible interactive TV or telecommunications signals. HDTV will also use digital signals, but broadcasters may not rush to convert, because it will cost them millions and millions of dollars to upgrade to new equipment. Instead, it is expected that the first HDTV signals to be sent to your home will be via satellite.

Home theater is no longer a buzzword. It is becoming a way of life for many people in the 1990s. A good home theater system looks and sounds better than your local cinema. The basics of home theater involves marrying your television to better audio, like your stereo system. Many people begin getting into home theater by purchasing a large-screen TV. You will also need a hi-fi VCR. All movies today are hi-fi and encoded with Dolby Surround Sound. For good audio choices, see the chapter "Stereo Components." If you want the best possible picture quality, a laser disc player may also be in your future to round out the package. You can buy each component separately to gradually enhance your listening and viewing experience.

Projection TVs

Projection TVs come in two basic types: front and rear. Though neither type gave good pictures initially, picture quality today verges on exceptional for both types. They offer different advantages for the end user.

Rear-projection models come in sizes up to 70 inches, lines of resolution up to 1,000, and brightness topping 500 foot-lamberts for many models. They use cathode ray tubes (CRTs), mirrors, and complex lens systems to project an image onto a translucent screen for viewing. The sets are so bright that they can be viewed in normal room light without appreciable loss of picture quality. Many models have a tinted transparent plastic screen, which offers contrast as well as protection for the lenticular lens. Models are not as large as they used to be; some are only 20 inches deep. Thanks to casters, these sets are easy to move around the room.

Front-projection TVs project the image from a CRT onto a screen. They need to be viewed in a dark room, which creates what some people feel is a true home theater experience. Units can be either ceiling-mounted or floor-standing. Some floor-standing models are housed in coffee tables. Besides the purchase of the TV itself, a screen is required, which can add up to $2,000 to the set's purchase price. Front projectors range in screen size from approximately 20 inches to 300 inches, in various aspect ratios. To improve picture quality, line doublers and line quadruplers are available from the major brands to enhance the visual element. These can add another $10,000 to $15,000 to the package.

LCD sets have become somewhat sophisticated and an attractive option. These are front projectors that use an LCD wafer and a powerful projector bulb to project an image onto an external surface. The higher the pixel (picture element) count, the more seamless the picture on the screen. LCD projectors are available from only a few brands. They can rival their tube counterparts in quality and high resolution, but they need to be viewed in a darkened room.

Satellite Television

Satellite broadcasting has made a strong comeback recently, thanks in part to many people's dissatisfaction with their local cable service and to the availability of smaller dishes. The introduction of Direct-To-Home (DTH) satellite broadcasting, championed by Hughes' DSS (Digital Satellite System), is revolutionizing the satellite industry. You can now own the means of receiving the best possible television signals via satellite. DSS is characterized by its small, 18-inch dish, superior picture quality, and CD-like sound. Initially marketed to rural areas and secondary cities, it is now taking many suburban neighborhoods by storm. In the span of one year, RCA has sold more than 1 million DSS systems. Since the system is digital, updates and improvements in the system are done at the broadcast center, not through a new set-top box—so your current receiver does not become obsolete. The small dish can be attached unobtrusively anywhere on a dwelling. It only requires a southern exposure free of tall trees to receive signals directly from the satellite 22,000 miles high in the sky. DSS can currently receive up to 175 channels from two programming providers, DirecTV and USSB, at a monthly cost comparable to that of cable. DSS (through DirecTV) also broadcasts 28 channels of commercial-free digital audio for every listening taste. The only downside to DSS is that the FCC has ruled that you cannot receive network programming from the satellite unless you live in a rural area or give up cable for three months. Otherwise, you can use a rooftop antenna or lifeline service from your cable company to receive the networks and local programming. The DSS equipment can be purchased from either RCA or Sony (or Toshiba in early 1996).

Another DTH service is being offered by Primestar, which will rent you a small dish (up to three feet). At this writing, Primestar is still an analog system offering fewer channels than DSS. By 1996 Primestar hopes to be digital and offer a comparable number of channels to DSS. The chief difference will be that you do not have to buy the hardware.

Evaluating a Television Set

The obvious criteria in evaluating a television set are picture quality, brightness, contrast, detail, and lack of signal or video noise. The colors should be pure and lifelike but not lurid. Whenever possible, evaluate a set by looking at programs that offer images you are familiar with for comparison. Black-and-white images will reveal the quality of the contrast and brightness of the set's picture. Dealers often have laser disc players hooked up to various television sets. A laser disc that displays the THX logo has been mastered and duplicated to the highest standards as set by Lucasfilm, Ltd., and will provide you with an excellent vehicle to evaluate picture quality. Ask your dealer to put one of these discs on so that you can evaluate the set that you are thinking about buying.

Other criteria are good sound, a user-friendly remote, and connection options appropriate to your level of use. Since differences in major-brand televisions are slight, manufacturers have added all sorts of special features to their sets in an attempt to differentiate them. Deciding which television to buy is a matter of matching a set's features with your needs. For example, if you don't have children, you will have little use for a set that allows parents to program the set so their small children cannot tune in certain stations, such as cable channels that offer adult programming.

TVs are becoming more automated. Most sets now offer auto-programming, in which you tell it you are attached to either an antenna or cable system. At the flick of a button, it will automatically tune in all viewable channels. Most sets also include a sleep-timer function that lets you nod off to late-night television secure in the knowledge that the set will automatically shut itself off at a preselected interval. Other sets can be programmed to turn themselves on at preselected times, either to wake you up, as a security measure, or to be sure that you don't miss your favorite show. Many sets now include on-screen help for explanation of features.

Screen size is a matter of personal preference and budget. Ideally, you should view a TV image from a distance roughly twice as far from the screen as the screen is high. Sets with screen sizes of two to five inches are portable televisions designed to be carried around. Nine-inch to 13-inch sets are sometimes called decorator models and may come in colors, with white being the most popular color. These sets find themselves in the kitchen and sometimes the bathroom. Sets in the 13- to 20-inch range are being used in bedrooms, dens, and children's rooms. Look for sets that include front A/V jacks, which allow easy hookup of video game systems. Sets 25 inches and larger are now the primary set in most homes.

The majority of sets sold are monitor/receiver or tabletop models. Big floor-standing consoles are quickly diminishing in number, but upright consoles now represent most of this market. Upright consoles take up about the same floor space as a tabletop model and offer built-in storage for a VCR and videotapes. While 27-inch TVs are very popular for the living room or family room, direct-view sets with screen sizes from 30 inches to 40 inches are selling in record numbers.

Cable Terminology

A major cause of confusion for shoppers is the term "cable-ready." Except for a few 13-inch and smaller sets, every TV sold today is cable ready. Many people incorrectly believe that a cable-ready set will allow them to receive cable services free of charge. A cable-ready set merely eliminates the need for a converter box to receive basic cable programming. You still have to pay the initial cable hookup costs and the monthly fee. To receive scrambled premium channels for which the cable company charges extra, such as HBO or Showtime, you will probably need the converter box.

Features and Terminology

The following are some of the terms you should familiarize yourself with before you shop for a television. It is very helpful to decide what options you really want before you begin to shop.

Remote control units come in one of the following types: a basic, standard, unified, universal, or learning remote. A few models have a combination universal-learning remote. A basic remote controls basic functions such as volume or channel up/down and power on and off. A standard remote is an enhanced basic model with a keypad for direct access, plus it allows you to use on-screen menus and displays. Universal remotes come with preprogrammed codes for both VCRs and cable boxes. Most can control from three to eight products, including both audio and video models. A couple of brands can even be programmed by the manufacturer by calling an 800 number. You simply tell them the makes and models of your components plus your zip code and cable company. More sophisticated models will also provide macro keys that will turn on several components simultaneously so that you don't have to press buttons on different components to watch a movie on your VCR. Learning remotes can be "taught" codes from other types of components, for example an A/V receiver. If you are trying to tie all your components together, a learning remote sounds attractive, though at best they can learn only primary functions of each component. A learning remote from an A/V receiver or an aftermarket universal-learning unit might be a better bet for tying all your components together.

Remotes are now user-friendly, with larger buttons of different sizes and in different colors. Some remotes are even illuminated so that the buttons are easy to see in a darkened room. Most 27-inch and larger sets now include universal remotes that will control both a VCR and a cable box or satellite.

Dual antenna inputs can accommodate two antenna sources, such as master antenna and cable box, or master antenna/cable box and DSS decoder. You can then switch easily between antenna sources without using switching devices. Using a signal splitter available from your cable company or an electronics store, you can also split the cable signal before it goes into the cable box so that all unscrambled, basic programming is available on one antenna and the scrambled, premium programming is on the other. This enables your television set's universal remote to control your cable box so that you do not need to rent your cable company's remote.

Horizontal resolution refers to the number of horizontal lines that the TV set can display. Theoretically, the more lines that can be displayed, the better the picture, but this is limited by the picture's source. Broadcast television is 330 lines, VHS tapes are about 240 lines, S-VHS tapes about 400 from a prerecorded video (330 from broadcast), and laser discs about 425 lines. On the other hand, when sources such as DSS with greater resolution become available, a set with high horizontal resolution would be able to receive an enhanced signal.

Comb filter improves resolution and picture quality and reduces objectionable color patterns. Low-end to mid-line TV sets use a glass comb filter. High-end sets use a CCD or digital comb filter, which greatly enhances resolution.

Special picture tubes improve picture quality. Dark-tint or dark glass picture tubes provide greater contrast between black and white. However, those brands that include darkened picture tubes have had to increase brightness levels so that the picture does not appear too dark. Most consumers prefer brightness over color accuracy. Dark-tinted picture tubes now dominate in virtually all sets 13 inches and above. Other advancements include flat screens or flattened picture tubes, which offer less distortion on the outer edges of the picture. Some manufacturers use special coatings to help cut down on glare and dust buildup, giving the appearance of a richer picture. Some manufacturers use a combination of techniques to tweak out the highest performance from their picture tubes.

These sets, while costly, offer the viewer a picture with the highest resolution and provide the most lifelike image.

Invar shadow mask, considered a premium feature, gives the picture more brightness and punch. When sets are very bright, a side effect called "blooming" occurs. To counteract this bleeding of colors, some manufacturers include the invar shadow mask.

PIP (picture-in-picture) allows you to view an image from a second video source in a box in one corner of the screen. Advanced PIP allows you to display multiple channels on the screen (all are frozen except the channel currently being scrolled through) and switch back and forth between the main and PIP image. A handful of high-end models include a second tuner for PIP, thereby eliminating the need to use the VCR tuner as the second video source.

Scan velocity modulation adjusts the rate of horizontal movement of the beam as it "draws" the scan lines, which gives black-and-white picture transitions more punch. This results in a sharper picture.

Notch filter helps remove a small part of the signal that contains excess color information. By doing so, it helps eliminate some objectionable color effects from less than desirable signals. However, a slight loss in picture resolution results.

Stereo television sets include an MTS (multichannel television sound) decoder, which receives and decodes all stereo signals broadcast by the networks or cable channels.

Surround Sound uses a computer chip to decode Dolby Surround Sound signals. However, many manufacturers include matrix surround sound or other psychoacoustic effects to enhance the audio. It may also be called ambiance or extended stereo effects. More and more sets are now including Dolby Pro Logic as a means to greatly enhance the audio quality. You must add rear speakers to obtain the desired effect. Many of these sets do not have the power to produce this much sound on their own, but virtually all sets in this category include variable audio outs for connection to an A/V receiver. Some sets also include a center-channel input, which allows you to use the TV's internal speakers for the center channel.

Audio and video inputs/outputs are outlets for devices you can connect to the set. Normally there are more audio outputs than video ones. However, having more video outputs allows you more versatility in signal switching between multiple VCRs and laser disc players. Depending on how you decide to hook up your A/V system, either the TV or your A/V receiver can be used for video switching. Hooking up a VCR with audio and video input jacks will provide you with better audio and video quality than putting the signal through your RF connector.

S-Video jacks are now included on many components besides S-VHS VCRs. S-Video separates luminance (the brightness portion of the color TV signal) and chrominance (the color portion of the signal), increasing resolution and helping color reproduction when the S-Video jack is used.

Front A/V jacks (usually hidden under a panel) are handy for hooking up a camcorder or a video game.

External speaker jacks allow you to attach separate speakers directly to a TV for improved sound quality or to attach rear speakers for Surround Sound.

Parental lockout or channel block prevents access to specific channels or disables them from being used for a specified time of day or period of hours.

Best Buys '96

Our Best Buy, Recommended, and Budget Buy television sets and TV-VCR combinations follow. In each category the unit we consider the best of the Best Buys is first, followed by our second choice, and so on. At the end of several categories, you will find one or more units listed as Budget Buys. These are models that may not have all of the features of a Best Buy or Recommended product, but they offer a solid value in terms of performance, features, and price. The picture quality of most of the major-brand televisions varies slightly, and differences are highly subjective. Some of this year's choices are included because they offer exceptionally fine picture quality. Many sets, however, were chosen because they offer packages of highly desirable features along with good picture quality.

Although features and styling change from model to model, TV technology is often carried through a company's entire line. This means that many TVs from the same manufacturer offer the same quality picture. The basis for our choice of one TV over another as a Best Buy is the combination of features in addition to the price of the set. For this reason, the Best Buy, Recommended, and Budget Buy designations apply only to the model listed and not necessarily to other models from the same manufacturer or to an entire product line.

35- TO 41-INCH TV SETS

TOSHIBA CN-35E90

✓ BEST BUY

The Toshiba CN-35E90 Cinema Series 35-inch color TV offers the FST Perfect picture tube with an invar shadow mask, which is the flattest and blackest of any 35-inch TV on the market today. The set claims 800 lines of resolution of sparkling color. The colors are vibrant and lifelike with a sharpness, brightness, and clarity not found elsewhere. Designed to be the centerpiece of a home theater setup, it has Dolby Surround Sound and sports three internal (side-firing) and two external speakers so that you don't have to buy extra gear right away. The set features dual antenna RF inputs, two A/V with S-Video inputs, and one A/V/S output. The CN-35E90 also has front A/V/S jacks for the easy hookup of a camcorder or video game. It also features a two-tuner picture-in-picture. Audio output is fixed or variable for the attachment of an A/V receiver. The set features a sleekly designed 51-button universal illuminated remote that will control a VCR, cable box, and one auxiliary component (either an LD player or a piece of audio equipment). Also included is a seven-button mini remote. The on-screen menus are straightforward and easy to use. This is the crème de la crème of 35-inch TVs.

Specifications: height, $30\frac{47}{64}$"; width, $36\frac{39}{64}$"; depth, $25\frac{19}{32}$"; weight, $175\frac{7}{10}$ lb. **Warranty:** 90 days.

Approx. retail price	Approx. low price
$2,600	Not available

Prices are accurate at time of printing but are subject to manufacturers' changes.

SONY KP-41T15

✓BEST BUY

The Sony KP-41T15 is Sony's first offering in the field of tabletop rear-projection TVs in a 41-inch screen size. Designed to compete with Mitsubishi's 40-inch TVs at less than half the weight and a third less cost, the KP-41T15 is a very appealing television product offering the consumer an attractive alternative. The set boasts 760 lines of resolution with a whopping 550 footlamberts of brightness. In turn, it provides a vibrant and rich picture. Colors are natural and lifelike, with a nice balance of hues. The set includes two A/V and one S-Video input and two audio and one video output. The set also features front A/V jacks. The KP-41T15 receives 181 channels from its tuner and comes with a universal remote that controls both VCRs and cable boxes. Optional accessories include a stand with component storage and a high-contrast (dark-tint) protective screen. With the screen in place, the set appears just like a direct-view model.

Specifications: height, 39½"; width, 37½"; depth, 23¼"; weight, 112 lb. 7 oz. **Warranty:** parts and labor, 1 year.

Approx. retail price	Approx. low price
$2,000	**$1,800**

MITSUBISHI CS-40503

Recommended

The Mitsubishi CS-40503 is a 40-inch direct-view TV, which is the largest of its kind on the market. Part of a family of four 40-inch sets, this model is one of the middle siblings and offers exceptional quality and features. Picture quality from its dark-tint black matrix CRT featuring an invar shadow mask is very good to excellent. The set features a dynamic digital comb filter that displays 700 lines of horizontal resolution from a 181-channel tuner. The built-in audio amplifier provides 10 watts per channel both internally and externally (external speaker jacks are included). The CS-40503 features three audio and three video (including two S-Video) inputs and one audio (both fixed and variable) output. A pair of front A/V jacks are also provided for video game or camcorder attachment. Dual antenna inputs are also included. The 52-button universal remote will also control both a VCR and cable box. An optional stand with VCR or component storage is available.

Specifications: height, 31²¹⁄₃₂"; width, 38⅛"; depth, 26¹³⁄₁₆"; weight, 250 lb. **Warranty:** tube, 2 years; parts and labor, 1 year.

Approx. retail price
$3,399

Approx. low price
$2,699

RCA F35760MB

Budget Buy

The RCA F35760MB 35-inch TV provides very good picture quality at an excellent price. Outfitted with RCA's new FDT (Flatter, Darker Tube) with an invar shadow mask, the set will display up to 830 lines of horizontal resolution and receive 181 channels. Housed in a black cabinet with front-firing speakers, the FDT tube displays a very clean picture free of video noise. Audio performance is rated at five watts per channel utilizing SRS (sound retrieval system) to increase the spatial presence of sound. A 16-jack panel on the back of the set provides two A/V inputs with one S-Video input and one A/V output (both fixed and variable). The set also sports a set of front A/V jacks for the attachment of a camcorder or video game using a special plug. Two RF inputs allow the attachment of a TV antenna and cable/DSS satellite to the TV. The F35760MB includes an ergonomically designed 46-button universal remote with color-coded keys for VCR and cable-box control. An optional stand is available for VCR or component storage.

Specifications: height, 32⅝"; width, 34⅞"; depth, 23⅝"; weight, 200 lb. **Warranty:** parts, 1 year; labor, 90 days.

Approx. retail price
$2,199

Approx. low price
$1,769

31- TO 32-INCH TV SETS

PANASONIC CT-31SF31

✓BEST BUY

The Panasonic CT-31SF31 is among the best sets in the category of 31-inch to 32-inch color TVs. Several years ago Panasonic revolutionized the industry by introducing their SuperFlat Data Grade picture tubes that feature a black screen with an invar shadow mask. Into the mix, Panasonic also added a wide-band video amplifier, color noise reduction, luminance noise reduction, velocity scan modulation, and horizontal edge correction. To bring all of these circuits together, they added their AI Picture, which is simply a fuzzy-logic computer chip that features ideal pictures. The end result is one of the finest pictures that money can buy. Picture quality is excellent with little or no background video noise. Edges are crisp. Colors are true and lifelike with no bleeding. The picture itself is very bright with a lot of punch and can display 700 lines of resolution. Included is a color temperature control so that you can adjust the colors from warm to cool. On the audio side, the set features Panasonic's 7-watt-per-channel Dome Sound System, which ports the speaker sound from the back of the set. To enhance the sound further, the CT-31SF31 also includes matrix surround and AI Sound with equalizer that provides more aural spaciousness. The set can receive 181 channels. The two-tuner picture-in-picture allows you to watch two programs simultaneously without having to use your VCR's tuner. The set also features two A/V inputs (including one S-Video) and one variable audio output for hookup to your hi-fi system. The included 30-button universal remote will control VCR, cable box, and a laser disc player using rocker keys. Two optional stands are also available for component storage to complement its all-black cabinet.

Specifications: height, $25\frac{1}{5}$"; width, $30\frac{1}{10}$"; depth, $21\frac{1}{10}$"; weight, 122 lb. **Warranty:** parts, 1 year; tube, 2 years; labor, 90 days.

Approx. retail price
$1,500

Approx. low price
$1,128

SONY KV-32XBR85

✓ BEST BUY

The Sony KV-32XBR85 is a 32-inch upright color TV with its own stand integrated into a one-piece design offering the appearance of a tabletop TV with a special stand. The cabinet is black with midnight maple trim at the base. Part

Prices are accurate at time of printing but are subject to manufacturers' changes.

of a new breed of consoles (sometimes called consolettes), this TV features top-mounted controls for easy access to set functions. Included in the base module are two shelves for component storage plus a bottom-mounted 11-watt superwoofer covered by a glass door. Using a Trinitron picture tube with a deep black screen and the Bi-Cmos video processor, the set produces clean, bright images free of background video noise. The KV-32XBR85 has a digital comb filter along with scan velocity modulation, which sharpens definition detail with reduced dot crawl. The set features a dual-tuner PIP for added convenience. Audio is piped though two side-mounted dynamic-acoustic-chamber speakers, rated at 15 watts per channel, and the 11-watt superwoofer. The set also includes a stand-up universal remote that requires only one AA battery. A side-mounted switch that changes the names of 10 function keys enables the remote to control four video products including DSS. The set also features three A/V inputs (one S-Video), front A/V jacks behind a door, and two audio (fixed/variable) and two video outputs.

Specifications: height, 45 1/16"; width, 33½"; depth, 27⅙"; weight, 199¼ lb. **Warranty:** parts and labor, 1 year.

Approx. retail price
$2,199

Approx. low price
$1,799

MITSUBISHI CS-31505

Recommended

The Mitsubishi CS-31505 is a 31-inch color TV that combines a very good picture with useful features. Capable of displaying 700 lines of resolution with its dark-tint black-matrix picture tube, the set presents warm, natural, and lifelike colors and good contrast in dark scenes. The CS-31505 has a 181-channel tuning capability along with multilingual on-screen menus and displays. A notable feature is the advanced dual-tuner picture-in-picture (PIP). Inputs and outputs include two antenna inputs, two A/V (including S-Video) inputs, fixed stereo audio outputs, and one video output. Stereo is piped through two front-firing speakers that will also produce an enhanced matrix surround sound, providing better aural ambiance. Other features include a universal remote that will control both VCRs and cable boxes. Housed in a dark gray cabinet, the CS-31505 has an optional matching base for component storage.

Specifications: height, 28³¹⁄₃₂″; width, 36¹¹⁄₃₂″; depth, 22¹⁵⁄₁₆″; weight, 130 lb. **Warranty:** tube, 2 years; parts and labor, 1 year; in-home service.

Approx. retail price	Approx. low price
$1,399	$1,299

MAGNAVOX FP3286B

Recommended

The Magnavox FP3286B is a 32-inch color TV that includes VCR or component storage in an all-black cabinet. Picture quality is good to very good, using an invar shadow mask, dark glass, and black matrix to provide very good contrast and brightness. Detail and clarity of picture are quite good, and combined with its comb filter it will display up to 600 lines of resolution. The set has special jacks and circuitry for ghost canceling; if you receive ghosts in your signal, this set could be a possibility for you, although you would still have to buy a special add-on box. It features a 181-channel tuner with automatic programming. Besides providing a good picture and decent sound (12.5 watts per channel), the FP3286B offers some useful features not found on some other sets in this size category. To locate the remote control, press the power button on the TV. The remote will start to chirp until you pick it up and touch any button. The set's smart-sound feature turns down the volume automatically on those loud commercials. Instant replay will play back the last eight seconds of whatever you were watching, courtesy of a memory chip within the TV. It's great for seeing that last play of the game. The set also features one A/V input with S-Video and one variable audio output. It comes with a 40-button universal remote that will control a VCR and a cable box.

Specifications: height, 46⅗″; width, 31″; depth, 21⁷⁄₁₀″; weight, 230 lb. **Warranty:** parts, 1 year; labor, 90 days; picture tube, 2 years.

Approx. retail price	Approx. low price
$1,500	$1,314

Prices are accurate at time of printing but are subject to manufacturers' changes.

JVC AV-31BP6

Budget Buy

The JVC AV-31BP6 is a 31-inch color TV housed in a black cabinet that offers a very good picture. The set features a full-square super-dark-tinted picture tube with black level expansion, a notch filter, and a comb filter that will display up to 700 lines of resolution. Picture quality is good to very good. The set includes a 181-channel tuner with automatic programming. It also includes two front-firing speakers rated at 3 watts per channel and a hyper-surround system that enhances the audio somewhat. The TV includes PIP with freeze-frame capability. Two A/V inputs (including 1-S-Video input) and one variable audio output are included. The 50-button universal remote, which will also control a VCR and a cable box, is among the easiest to use. Fitting easily into your hand, the remote features cursor keys at the bottom so you can move through its on-screen menus and displays with your thumb. Other keys are laid out in group sections by function. The remote is well-designed and easy to use.

Specifications: height, $26\frac{1}{8}$"; width, $30\frac{1}{4}$"; depth, $21\frac{5}{8}$"; weight, $129\frac{3}{16}$ lb. **Warranty:** parts and labor (in-home service), 1 year; picture tube, 2 years.

Approx. retail price
$1,000

Approx. low price
$869

27-INCH TV SETS

RCA F27674BC/F27675BC

✓BEST BUY

The RCA F27674BC or the RCA F27675BC (same set but with a slightly different black cabinet design) takes up very little shelf space. Equipped with a 181-channel tuner, the set sports trilingual (English, French, and Spanish) on-screen menus and displays that are very easy and intuitive to use. Picture quality is very good to excellent, with clarity helped by its comb filter. Colors are very crisp and lifelike, thanks to its optimum-contrast-screen picture tube with a dark tint on its face plate. The tube has a reduced depth of 110 degrees. Because of circuitry that expands the black level, the brightness and contrast are punched up quite a bit. This set features one set of A/V inputs and one set of variable audio outputs. Convenience features include color PIP (you'll need to hook up a VCR to receive a signal) and commercial-skip, which allows you to channel-surf for a specified time—up to 3 minutes—before it bounces back to the original channel that you were watching. The sets also feature a 43-button universal remote that will control your VCR, cable box, DSS, and an audio component. All in all, an excellent value for the money.

Specifications: height, 23″; width, 25⅜″; depth, 18⅞″; weight, 90 lb. **Warranty:** parts, 1 year; labor, 90 days.

Approx. retail price	**Approx. low price**
$599	**$528**

SAMSUNG TXB2735

BEST BUY

The Samsung TXB2735 is a reasonably priced, full-featured 27-inch stereo TV. Equipped with an 181-channel tuner, the model has bilingual (English and Spanish) on-screen menus and displays. Picture quality is very good, the comb filter producing approximately 600 lines of resolution when connected with the S-VHS jack. Colors are very natural and lifelike, with ample brightness levels. The TXB2735 gives 5 watts of stereo power per channel from two side-firing speakers. For added ambiance, the set includes matrix surround. A switch shuts off its internal speakers so that the variable audio output jack can be used, or external speakers can be attached. The set includes three A/V inputs including a front jack pack. It also has an S-Video input for improved picture quality from video sources that include this feature. Linking you to the television is a 51-button universal remote that will also control your VCR and cable box. The remote is simply and clearly laid out with a 10-button numeric keypad.

Specifications: height, 23½″; width, 30″; depth, 20½″; weight, 90 lb. **Warranty:** parts, 1 year; labor, 3 months.

Approx. retail price	**Approx. low price**
$619	**$440**

Prices are accurate at time of printing but are subject to manufacturers' changes.

MITSUBISHI CS-27503

Recommended

The Mitsubishi CS-27503 is a full-featured 27-inch stereo color TV. Utilizing its Diamond View reduced-curvature tube that includes both a black tint and a black matrix, picture quality is excellent, with the capability of displaying 560 lines of resolution. Images are sharp, clean, and crisp, showing very little video noise. Colors are very natural and lifelike. Blooming was kept to a minimum thanks to the set's invar shadow mask. A nice touch is the color temperature control, which allows you to make the images warm (whites are redder) to cool (whites are bluer). This top-of-the-line set includes many desirable features including advanced picture-in-picture and A/V memory by input. This feature allows you to make specific adjustments to video input 1 or video input 2 to optimize viewing of VCRs and laser disc players. Its 181-channel tuner features automatic programming. Mitsubishi continues to provide its TVs and VCRs with exceptional on-screen displays and menus that are easy to use. As with many sets today, the on-screen menu is trilingual. The CS-27503 uses two front-firing speakers rated at 3 watts per channel combined with matrix surround circuitry. The set features dual antenna inputs, two A/V inputs (including one S-Video input), and a variable audio output for hookup to your hi-fi system. Front A/V jacks are also included for video games or a camcorder. Its easy-to-use, 48-function universal remote will also control a VCR and a cable box. This set has an electronic swivel built into its bottom. It adjusts through the remote, allowing viewing of the set from different angles within the room.

Specifications: height, $22\frac{11}{16}$"; width, $27\frac{1}{4}$"; depth, $18\frac{11}{16}$"; weight, 92 lb. **Warranty:** tube, 2 years; parts and labor, 1 year.

Approx. retail price
$1,099

Approx. low price
$915

MAGNAVOX TP2792B

Recommended

The Magnavox TP2792B is a reasonably priced top-of-the-line 27-inch color TV that offers some interesting and unique features. Equipped with a 181-channel tuner, the

Prices are accurate at time of printing but are subject to manufacturers' changes.

set is a versatile performer. It features a dark glass flat square picture tube, a comb filter, and noise reduction circuitry so that it can display up to 600 lines of resolution. Picture quality is good to very good. You can make the picture even better if your signal is prone to ghosts, because jacks on the back of the set allow you to attach an optional ghost canceler box. You can locate a lost remote control by hitting the power button on the TV—the remote will beep until found. This set has advanced PIP; smart sound, which lowers the sound level of loud commercials; and smart picture, which has four settings for optimum picture for video games, sports, movies, and weak station settings. An instant-replay computer chip plays back the last eight seconds of what you were watching. The set also includes two front-firing speakers rated at 3 watts per channel. To improve sound even further, the TP2792B has external speaker jacks for the attachment of outboard speakers. It also has variable audio output so that you can pipe the sound to a separate audio system. The TV has one A/V input with S-Video capability. The 39-button universal remote with cursor keys and numeric keypad will also control a VCR and cable box.

Specifications: height, 22⁹⁄₁₀″; width, 25³⁄₅″; depth, 19⁴⁄₅″; weight, 87 lb. **Warranty:** parts, 1 year; labor, 90 days.

Approx. retail price
$650

Approx. low price
$589

HITACHI 27CX6B

Budget Buy

The Hitachi 27CX6B is a value-priced 27-inch color TV that offers a solid set of features combined with a very good picture. Utilizing Hitachi's UltraBlack picture tube, the set features a dark-tint picture tube and a comb filter to provide up to 600 lines of resolution. The set includes a 181-channel tuner with automatic programming capability. The set includes two front-firing speakers rated at 3 watts per channel. As well, the 27CX6B features its spatially equalized sound system, which provides for better audio imaging. To help correct the annoyance of especially loud commercials, the set has volume-correction circuitry that lowers the volume of loud commercials

Prices are accurate at time of printing but are subject to manufacturers' changes.

or stations. Convenience features include PIP with quick-freeze, a message center that allows you to leave a message for family members that will go on at a specific time, a way to lock out channels from children, on/off timers, and trilingual on-screen menus. The set includes one A/V input with S-Video capability and one variable audio output. The 41-button universal remote features illuminated keys on the bottom half of the unit. The remote will also control a VCR and cable box. A nice touch on the remote is that it separates specific function keys into specific areas for ease of use. Like most 27-inch color TVs today, the 27CX6B is housed in a charcoal black cabinet.

Specifications: height, 23″; width, 26⅝″; depth, 20½″; weight, 91 lb. **Warranty:** parts and labor, 1 year.

Approx. retail price	Approx. low price
$600	$600

20-INCH TV SETS

PANASONIC CT-20G20

BEST BUY

The Panasonic CT-20G20 is a 20-inch stereo color TV. It is a good solid performer offering features and performance found on much more expensive models. It includes a PanaBlack picture tube that provides excellent contrast. The set also features a notch filter and SAW (surface acoustic wave) filter that improves picture quality so that the set is capable of displaying up to 500 lines of resolution. Equipped with a 181-channel tuner, the set will perform auto programming of its channels as well as provide channel captions (logos) for up to 30 channels. It comes in a black cabinet offering a very small footprint. As with many 20-inch color TVs, the set's stereo speakers are front-firing and are located under the screen. Stereo is decoded via its MTS decoder and sent to its internal amplifier, which provides 1.5 watts per channel. SAP is also included. To improve the set's audio, the CT-20G20 also includes AI Sound. Sound can be piped to your hi-fi via the TV's variable audio outputs. A set of audio/video inputs is included. Other features include a bilingual on-screen menu system, on-screen

Prices are accurate at time of printing but are subject to manufacturers' changes.

clock, sleep/on/off timers, and game guard (which protects the set from displaying games on the screen too long). Last, the set's 30-button universal remote also controls VCRs and cable boxes.

Specifications: height, 18⅕"; width, 20"; depth, 19"; weight, 46³⁄₁₀ lb. **Warranty:** parts, 1 year; labor, 90 days; parts for tube, 2 years.

Approx. retail price **$320**

Approx. low price **$287**

SONY KV-20TS32

Recommended

The Sony KV-20TS32 is a full-featured 20-inch stereo color TV that is an able-bodied performer. This set may be a bit pricier than most sets in the 20-inch category, but it has all the advantages of being a Sony. Picture performance is top-notch, with dynamic picture circuitry that constantly adjusts brightness for the amount of light in the room. The KV-20TS32 produces a clean image with excellent contrast thanks to the deep black screen on its Trinitron tube. Featuring a 181-channel tuner with automatic programming, this set sports two complete A/V inputs on both the front and back of the TV as well as a headphone jack on the front for private listening. For improved video quality, the set also includes an S-Video input on the back of the set. It comes equipped with a 27-button remote, and the on-screen menus and displays are clearly written and easy to use with the remote's return and plus-or-minus rocker keys. The KV-20TS32 comes in a dark gray cabinet with front-firing speakers and takes up very little space on your shelf.

Specifications: height, 19¼"; width, 20¾"; depth, 18⅞"; weight, 50⁵⁄₁₆ lb. **Warranty:** parts and labor, 1 year; labor, 90 days; tube, 2 years.

Approx. retail price **$450**

Approx. low price **$352**

TOSHIBA TIMM MM20E45

Recommended

The Toshiba Integrated Multimedia Monitor (TIMM) MM20E45 is the first of a new breed of combination

Prices are accurate at time of printing but are subject to manufacturers' changes.

televisions and computer monitors. TIMM works well as a 20-inch MTS stereo color television capable of receiving 181 channels and featuring a dark-tint FST black picture tube with an invar shadow mask. Thanks to a glass comb filter, TIMM will display 500 lines of resolution in its TV mode. It features one audio input, two video (including S-Video) inputs, and one RGB (for both audio and video) input. It has one set of variable audio output jacks. Because of TIMM's RGB inputs, the multimedia monitor can also be used as a 21-inch VGA computer monitor (the computer industry measures monitors differently) for either a PC or a Mac, with a resolution of 640 × 480 pixels. Picture quality in both modes is very good to excellent. Audio power is rated at five watts per channel from two stereo speakers, which is great for listening to stereo television programs or the many stereo CD-ROMs currently available. While the set may seem pricey for a 20-inch stereo TV, the fact that it can also be used as a VGA computer monitor (priced several hundred dollars less than comparable monitors alone) make this a compelling package for someone desiring both a stereo TV and a computer monitor.

Specifications: height, 24 3/32" width, 26 21/32"; depth, 21 39/64"; weight, 56 1/5 lb. **Warranty:** parts and labor, 1 year; picture tube, 2 years.

Approx. retail price	**Approx. low price**
$999	**$733**

PORTABLE TV SETS

SONY KV-9PT40

✓BEST BUY

The Sony KV-9PT40 is a small, 9-inch portable color TV that has been designed primarily for use in the kitchen. Housed in a sleek and stylish white cabinet, the set rests on a base that either acts as a stand or reverses for hanging from under a cabinet. Picture quality from this set is exceptional, thanks to its Trinitron tube. It comes with its own antenna, but it's ready for cable hookup—its tuner receives 181 channels. Whether attached to a strong master antenna or

Prices are accurate at time of printing but are subject to manufacturers' changes.

hooked up to cable, the set receives excellent signals. One set of audio/video inputs is located on the back for attaching either a VCR or a video game system. Besides channel and volume up/down buttons, the front of the set also features a headphone jack for private listening. A white 25-button remote control includes a sleep timer, TV/video button, on-screen menus, muting, and last-channel recall. The set is monaural with sound coming from one side-mounted, front-angled speaker.

Specifications: height, 9½"; width, 10¼"; depth, 11⅝"; weight, 14 lb. **Warranty:** parts, 1 year; labor, 90 days; tube, 2 years.

Approx. retail price	Approx. low price
$380	$326

GENERAL ELECTRIC 09GP108

✓BEST BUY

The GE 09GP108 Spacemaker is a 9-inch color TV, housed in a white cabinet, that is designed to be placed in the kitchen. Under-cabinet mounting-bracket hardware is included, or the set can easily sit on a countertop. The set offers a built-in FM radio with a weather-band channel. Picture quality is very good for a set of this screen size, with a resolution of about 270 lines. Other features include a 181-channel tuner with automatic programming and a headphone jack. The set also features an on-screen clock, sleep and alarm timers, plus a commercial-skip feature that allows you to channel-surf for a predetermined time before the set jumps back to your originally tuned channel. No A/V inputs or outputs are included on this set. The 09GP108 includes a 23-button remote control that features a numeric keypad.

Specifications: height, 10⅛"; width, 11½"; depth, 12"; weight, 18½ lb. **Warranty:** parts, 1 year; tube, 2 years.

Approx. retail price	Approx. low price
$289	$236

PANASONIC CT-9R20

Recommended

The Panasonic CT-9R20 is a 9-inch AC/DC color television designed to be used anywhere. It can be powered either by 120-volt AC power or a 12-volt vehicle cord, which is included. Picture quality is excellent because of its high-contrast picture tube coupled with a precision notch filter that allows 330 lines of resolution. Also helping to improve picture quality is an SAW (surface acoustic wave) filter that improves picture clarity at the corner edges of the screen. Like TVs of larger screen sizes, this set includes an auto-programming 181-channel tuner and a bilingual (English/Spanish) on-screen menu system. Convenience features include a built-in carrying handle, a built-in bottom swivel, a detachable antenna, and a remote control with a numeric keypad. Audio is piped through a single front-firing speaker. No A/V inputs or outputs are on this television, which has a black cabinet.

Specifications: height, 10⅗″; width, 11″; depth, 11⁹⁄₁₀″; weight, 14⅒ lb. **Warranty:** parts, 1 year; labor, 90 days; tube, 2 years.

Approx. retail price **$350** | **Approx. low price** **$284**

RCA E13335GY

Budget Buy

The RCA E13335GY is a portable 13-inch color TV that can be used at home or in the car with the included vehicle cord. Housed in a flint-colored cabinet, this stunningly designed little set features center top-mounted controls. The set includes a 181-channel tuning capability along with a multilanguage on-screen menu and display. The E13335GY also features an on-screen clock, a sleep timer and alarm, a headphone jack, and a 23-button remote with a numeric keypad. Picture quality is very good for a set of this size. Audio is piped through a single oval front-firing speaker. Sound quality is fair for a mono set. The set has no A/V inputs or outputs. For portability, versatility, and superb design, this set is a winner. Perfect for the kitchen, the bedroom, or the car—something to think about for long car trips with the kids.

Specifications: height, 13⅜″; width, 14⅛″; depth, 14½″; weight, 26 lb. **Warranty:** parts, 1 year; labor, 6 months.

Approx. retail price **$299** | **Approx. low price** **$249**

Prices are accurate at time of printing but are subject to manufacturers' changes.

LCD MINI-TV SETS

SONY FDL-22

✓BEST BUY

The Sony FDL-22 Straptenna WatchMan is a 2.2-inch LCD color mini-TV that features an innovative antenna housed in its neck carrying strap. Supposedly, the human body, along with the strap around the neck, acts as the TV's antenna. A clip on the strap doubles as a stand. Equipped with a 69-channel tuner, it receives all VHF and UHF stations. You change channels with a rocker switch on the right-hand side of the unit. On/off, volume, and brightness controls are on the left side. The TV's shape is triangular, making it look like a futuristic communications device. The LCD TV is located on top of a small speaker. You can also attach stereo or mono headphones (optional). Designed to be carried around, the Straptenna is powered by four AA alkaline batteries, which should last about three hours. An optional AC adapter is available. Like all LCD TVs, it needs to be kept out of direct sunlight, which will wash out the picture entirely. Otherwise, reception is fairly good.

Specifications: height, 6⅛"; width, 3¼"; depth, 1¾"; weight, 10⅗ oz. **Warranty:** parts, 1 year; labor, 90 days.

Approx. retail price	**Approx. low price**
$160	**$137**

CASIO AV-100

Recommended

The Casio AV-100 Freedom Vision mini-TV features a 2.5-inch LCD color screen that displays 118,500 pixels (picture elements). Housed in a black cabinet, the AV-100 can sit easily on your desk or be handheld. The Freedom Vision TV features a 69-channel tuner that will display both UHF and VHF channels. A miniature entertainment center, the model sports an AM/FM radio, a built-in clock with a separate display, and a sleep timer with snooze alarm and wake-up melody. The diminutive unit also includes a complete on-screen calendar display showing the entire month on the 2.5-inch screen. The AV-100 is powered by an AC adapter or six AA batteries (plus three AA batteries for backup). The set's higher pixel count greatly improves its picture quality, which is good to very good for this mini-TV. Like all LCD TVs, it cannot be watched in direct sunlight, and a sun screen is not available. Combining better-than-average picture quality for a 2.5-inch LCD color TV and several useful convenience features, the AV-100 is several notches above the pack.

Specifications: height, 4¼"; width, 7½"; depth, $4\frac{3}{16}$"; weight, 2½ oz. **Warranty:** parts and labor, 90 days.

Approx. retail price	**Approx. low price**
$300	**$210**

REAR-PROJECTION TV SETS

PIONEER SD-P5185-K

✓BEST BUY

The Pioneer SD-P5185K is a 51-inch rear-projection TV featuring the company's exclusive rectangular Cinema Wide 16:10.7 aspect ratio. With a Cinema mode button, you can either reduce or eliminate black bars from letter-boxed movies. Picture quality and clarity are excellent thanks to a three-line digital comb filter displaying 830 lines of resolution, with brightness levels topping 600 footlamberts. Images are sharply focused, due to dual dynamic focus and vertical contour control circuitry. Glare has been reduced through a curved tint panel. The SD-P5185-K also features digital convergence adjustment so that you don't have to manually line up the cross hairs to focus images. The set includes dual antenna inputs, three A/V inputs including S-Video, and front A/V inputs. Outputs include one A/V and two RF. This model sports a newly designed 30-button preprogrammed universal remote that has several hundred functions working off its numeric keypad, function keys, macro keys, and a circular cursor pad. It can control three video products.

Specifications: height, 51¼"; width, $48\frac{13}{16}$"; depth, $25\frac{13}{16}$"; weight, 229 lb. **Warranty:** 1 year.

Approx. retail price	**Approx. low price**
$2,999	**$2,766**

Prices are accurate at time of printing but are subject to manufacturers' changes.

PROSCAN PS 60690

✓BEST BUY

The Proscan PS 60690 by RCA is one of the best examples of a 60-inch rear-projection television. Its exceptional picture quality is due in part to the three 9-inch CRTs housed within the set (most rear projection sets feature either 5.5-inch or 7-inch CRTs). This increases brightness—a crucial picture element in projection TVs. Using a 3-D digital comb filter, the set is capable of producing 800 lines of horizontal resolution. It's ready for TV signals today and tomorrow. Since people's taste in color varies, the set includes a color temperature control that makes the colors either cool, medium, or warm. In any mode, the colors are very lifelike and natural because of its wide-band video amplifier, dynamic beam and magnetic focus, and edge-replacement circuitry. As you make a picture larger, you also blow up the signal's imperfections. These are reduced by special video noise reduction circuitry. Like virtually every set on the market today, the PS 60690 has a automatic-programming tuner capable of receiving 181 channels from either an antenna, cable, or DSS. It has two RF inputs. Audio has been beefed up with a 55-watt amplifier driving a 3-way speaker system featuring a top-mounted center channel. Left and right speakers are housed in side-firing mounts. Audio is enhanced further by the built-in Dolby Pro Logic Surround Sound system. Convenience features include a dual-tuner PIP that allows split-screen viewing or POP (picture-outside-picture), plus a 43-button universal remote with an egg-shaped, 8-button miniremote. The set also features three A/V (including two S-Video) inputs and three audio, one video, and one S-Video outputs. Stunning new on-screen displays and menus feature bit-mapped graphics using a living room setting with Nipper, the RCA dog. The PS 60690 is housed in a beautifully elegant and slightly unusual black pedestal cabinet with a wood-trim base, giving the aura of a motion picture screen.

Specifications: height, 66⅞"; width, 59⅜"; depth, 23"; weight, 448 lb. **Warranty:** parts, 90 days; tube, 1 year.

Approx. retail price	**Approx. low price**
$4,799	**$4,432**

Prices are accurate at time of printing but are subject to manufacturers' changes.

SONY KP-53XBR45

Recommended

The Sony KP-53XBR45 is a 53-inch rear-projection TV that is a breed apart from previous years' models. Using a new CRT with multispot beaming, the new Bi-Cmos video processor produces a superior image from all viewing angles and in all types of light. What separates this projection TV from others in its class is its center-to-corner brightness. Although claiming a brightness of only 250 footlamberts, the set provides excellent contrast and good detail. You can program and use five different video settings for movies, sports events, news, games, and standard use. Included with the KP-53XBR45 is a plastic screen that not only offers protection for the TV screen itself, but also increases contrast and actually cuts down on reflection. Also included in the video package is a 3-D digital comb filter, which could display up to 1,180 lines of resolution with the right video source. This is a PTV (projection TV) that has been designed for the future. The unit is housed in an attractive two-piece cabinet. Included is an 80-watt stereo package that features a Dolby Pro Logic decoder offering 20 watts across the front (left, center, and right) and 20 watts to the rear. Besides Pro Logic, the set includes matrix surround, which enhances sound presence, and Sony's Orchestra Seat Sound Effect, which clarifies the audio signal and centers the audio. The menu systems lets you program your eight most-watched channels into a single on-screen display. Convenience features include two-tuner PIP, dual antenna inputs, front A/V inputs (behind a door), five A/V inputs (all with S-Video), and three A/V outputs. The set includes a universal remote that will control four video components including DSS. The remote also includes an eight-position joystick that controls all on-screen functions.

Specifications: height, 55⅞"; width, 48¾"; depth, 25½"; weight, 222 lb. **Warranty:** parts and labor, 1 year; tube, 2 years.

Approx. retail price
$4,399

Approx. low price
$3,666

FRONT-PROJECTION TV SETS

RUNCO CINEMAPRO 760W

BEST BUY

The Runco CinemaPro 760W is one of the finest examples of a reasonably priced front-projection television. It displays images between 60 inches and 250 inches for either PAL, SECAM, or NTSC TV formats. Its black cabinet can sit on the floor or be ceiling-mounted with the kit included. it holds three 7-inch tubes—one for red, one for green, and one for blue. A screen, available from Runco or other screen manufacturers for up to $2,000, is also needed to complete this package.The 760W features three lens assemblies with high-definition, color-corrected multilayer coatings and hybrid lenses that produce strikingly clear images with very natural color. The 760W will display 650 lines of resolution from a TV signal, or 800 lines from a video source using an S-Video jack, or 1,000 lines using the RGB input (probably HDTV). Brightness is rated at 800 lumens or footlamberts, making this among the brightest front projection models available. The W in the model number stands for wide aspect ratio, meaning that the 760W will properly display images in the 4.3 aspect ratio and in the 16:9 aspect ratio. Images that are more severely letter-boxed at 2.35:1 will show smaller black bars at the top and bottom of the screen. The unit includes one composite video input, one S-Video input, and one RGB video input. It comes with a 12-function remote control for accessing key controls. Front-projection sets are designed for watching movies, videos, or sporting events in a darkened room. This set is designed for anyone wanting a true home theater experience.

Specifications: height, 9⅞"; width, 22¼"; depth, 28⅛"; weight, 77 lb. **Warranty:** parts, 1 year; labor, 90 days.

Approx. retail price
$7,995

Approx. low price
$7,415

SHARPVISION XV-S90U

Recommended

The SharpVision XV-S90U is a front LCD projector that can display images between 25 inches and 200

Prices are accurate at time of printing but are subject to manufacturers' changes.

inches on any white surface. Separate screens from a screen manufacturer can cost up to $2,000. The XV-S90U provides for variable imaging masking, so that it correctly displays 4:3, 16:9, or 21:9 aspect ratios. Aspect ratios can be changed with the remote or the front panel. Using three LCD panels, each rated at 309,120 pixels (or picture elements), the set displays more than 927,000 pixels. This translates into more than 500 lines of resolution. Of any LCD front projector currently on the market, this model has the sharpest and brightest picture. It uses a 250-watt metal halide bulb rated at over 600 lux of brightness. The XV-S90U can be placed on the floor or is ceiling-mountable. Like all front projectors, it needs to be viewed in a dark room. To that end, the remote is illuminated. Because front-projection sets are designed for watching movies, videos, and sporting events, this projector does not have a built-in tuner. To watch regular TV or cable, you have to use the tuner from your VCR. The unit comes with two A/V inputs including one S-Video input and one A/V output. Unlike some front projectors, the XV-S90U features on-screen menus and displays. The projector has a built-in 3-watt amplifier and one speaker, but it cries out to be attached to high-quality audio equipment. This projector is designed for the serious videophile wanting a movie-theaterlike experience.

Specifications: height, $9\frac{1}{16}$"; width, $20\frac{15}{32}$", depth, $17\frac{23}{32}$"; weight, 30 lb. **Warranty:** parts and labor, 1 year; projection lamp, 90 days.

Approx. retail price
$9,995

Approx. low price
$7,995

VIDIKRON VPF 40 SEL

Recommended

The Vidikron VPF 40 SEL is an excellent example of a front-projection television that can display images from 60 inches to 180 inches on any video system: PAL, SECAM, or NTSC. The VPF 40 SEL features a six-element high-resolution, multicoated, dual-focus hybrid lens for each of its three CRTs—one for blue, one for green, and one for red. A screen is also needed to complete this package. Screens are available from

Prices are accurate at time of printing but are subject to manufacturers' changes.

Vidikron starting at $199 and going up to $1,800 depending on the finish and type of grain. Vidikron has added several video circuits to improve picture quality: a chroma decoder that tries to bring the image closer to film quality, a glass comb filter, a color transient circuit that eliminates the bleeding of colors into one another, advanced variable luminance that helps reduce color ghosting, and aperture correction that increases the definition at the edges of darker areas. Like most front projection TVs, this model can be mounted on the ceiling with included hardware. Depending on the video source, the set can display up to 1,200 lines of resolution pumping 600 lumens brightness. The VPF 40 SEL includes two A/V inputs, one S-Video input, two RGB (TTL and analog) inputs, and two audio outputs (one variable). The unit includes a 20-watt audio amplifier for the attachment of speakers. A full-function remote is included. Like all front-projection TVs, it must be viewed in a darkened room.

Specifications: height, 9″; width, 22½″; depth, 29″; weight, 78 lb. **Warranty:** parts and labor, 1 year.

Approx. retail price	**Approx. low price**
$8,895	**$8,747**

TV-VCR COMBINATIONS

TOSHIBA CV27E48

BEST BUY

The Toshiba CV27E48 is the company's second-generation 27-inch stereo color TV-VCR combination, following on the heels of its predecessor, the CV27D48, which may still be available in a few markets. The CV27E48 offers an exceptional picture, derived from Toshiba's FST black picture tube with black matrix and a glass comb filter providing 650 lines of resolution. On its own, it's a great 27-inch TV, but coupled with a four-head hi-fi VCR, the set's a real winner. The VCR uses Toshiba's V3 Chassis, which reduces picture noise and provides clearer sound. This combo sports a 181-channel tuner and allows programming of six events over a one-month period. The CV27E48 offers a unique on-screen analog clock system for programming by turning one knob. Conventional on-screen programming is also available.

Specifications: height, $25\frac{21}{32}$"; width, $26\frac{49}{64}$"; depth, $19\frac{39}{64}$"; weight, $89\frac{3}{10}$ lb. **Warranty:** 90 days.

Approx. retail price	**Approx. low price**
$999	**$749**

PANASONIC PV-M2045

BEST BUY

The Panasonic PV-M2045 combines a 20-inch stereo color TV and a four-head mono VHS VCR. Using Panasonic's PanaBlack picture tube technology coupled with black-level expansion circuitry that further improves and enhances contrast, picture quality is excellent. On its own, this unit stands among the best 20-inch color TVs. Combined with a VCR, it is an impressive package. The VCR section provides for double-fine slow motion, high-speed search, and double-speed playback. The set's tuner is capable of receiving 181 channels, and you can program eight events over a one-month period. The PV-M2045 automatically keeps the correct time and will compensate for daylight savings time. A time signal is continuously being broadcast by your local PBS station, and the set receives it with a special EDS (extended data service) chip. Even after power failures, the VCR will always come back to the right time. The stereo portion of the TV is rated at 1.5 watts per channel from side-firing speakers. Programming could not be easier thanks to Panasonic's proprietary Program Director. You simply roll the thumbwheel on the 41-button universal remote up or down to reach the desired date and times, then press the thumbwheel to enter it into memory. Besides controlling both the TV and VCR portions of the set, the universal remote will also control most cable boxes. Other features found on the PV-M2045 include a real-time tape counter, on/off/sleep timer, bilingual on-screen displays and menus, a one-minute backup for programs, a commercial-skip feature that advances the tape one minute, an earphone jack, and a front A/V input.

Specifications: height, $21\frac{1}{8}$"; width, $21\frac{1}{8}$"; depth, 19"; weight, 54 lb. **Warranty:** parts, 1 year; labor, 90 days.

Approx. retail price $550 — **Approx. low price** $487

GOLDSTAR GCV-1346M

Recommended

The GoldStar GCV-1346M combines a 13-inch color TV and a four-head VHS VCR. Using a dark glass picture tube for improved contrast, its picture quality is quite good. The VCR portion uses four video heads, which allows you to do slow motion and frame-by-frame advancing. Its 181-channel tuner features automatic programming and allows you to record five events over a one-month period with its on-screen programmer. Housed in a black cabinet, the set includes front A/V inputs for easy attachment of a camcorder or video game system. Other features include an automatic head cleaner, a real-time tape counter, an earphone jack, a special switch for rental tapes, trilingual on-screen displays, and VISS (VHS index system). In case of power failures, the GCV-1346M has a 10-minute backup that retains clock and programming information. The 30-button unified remote controls all functions on both the VCR and TV portions of the set.

Specifications: height, 15³⁄₁₀″; width, 16⁴⁄₅″; depth, 16″; weight, 30 lb. **Warranty:** parts, 1 year; labor, 90 days; tube, 2 years.

Approx. retail price $400 — **Approx. low price** $364

RCA T25204BC

Recommended

The RCA T25204BC combines a 25-inch stereo color TV and a four-head hi-fi VCR. Slightly larger than the standard 20-inch TV-VCR combo, the set offers good performance and value on a par with more expensive models. Picture quality is very good, thanks to the dark-tint Optimum Contrast Screen picture tube. Its 181-channel tuner features automatic programming, and you can record five events over a one-month period with its on-screen programmer. Housed in a black cabinet, the set includes front A/V inputs for easy attachment of a camcorder or video game system. The set's 40-button remote will control all of the unit's TV and VCR func-

Prices are accurate at time of printing but are subject to manufacturers' changes.

tions. Since this is a four-head VCR, it includes slow motion and frame-by-frame advancement, plus other features including digital auto tracking, automatic repeat, a quick-start mechanism, a real-time tape counter, a timer backup, and multilingual displays (English, French, and Spanish). Its hi-fi performance is on a par with other hi-fi VCRs. Further, it receives and decodes broadcast stereo reception through its MTS decoder. Since it lacks audio output jacks, you'll have to be content with the set's two front-firing stereo speakers. Where available, you will be able to make use of the set's SAP (second audio program) function.

Specifications: height, 22¾"; width, 24¾"; depth, 20½"; weight, 89 lb. **Warranty:** parts, 1 year; service, 90 days.

Approx. retail price	**Approx. low price**
$799	**$599**

SAMSUNG CXC1912

Budget Buy

The Samsung CXC1912 is a 19-inch TV with a built-in mono VHS VCR. Since it has a front A/V input for the easy attachment of video game hardware, this is an ideal combo for the bedroom or children's room. Another input is on the back of the machine. While resolution is only about 270 lines for the TV and 230 for the VCR, it is more than adequate for this unit. The tuner will receive 181 channels, and you can program eight events over a one-year period. On-screen display is in either English or Spanish, and the unit has a 90-minute sleep timer. The two-head VHS VCR deck is very easy and intuitive to use. The 30-button remote is clearly laid out so that even children can instantly use this combo to watch their videos or tape a program.

Specifications: height, 19⅛"; width, 22½"; depth, 18⅛"; weight, 48 lb. **Warranty:** parts, 1 year; labor, 3 months.

Approx. retail price	**Approx. low price**
$559	**$390**

GENERAL ELECTRIC 13TVR45

Budget Buy

The GE 13TVR45 is a 13-inch color TV-VCR combo housed in a white cabinet that is specifically designed for the kitchen. Not only will it tape the soaps or evening news, it can double as an instructor to whip up new dishes—it's packaged with its own cooking video. The unit has a 181-channel tuner. The two-head mono VHS deck will tape four events over a one-month period. Resolution is about 240 lines. Like the combo itself, the 34-button remote is white and is ergonomically designed with buttons in color-coded shapes. The set is placed on a swivel base for easy viewing from all angles.

Specifications: height, $15\frac{9}{10}$"; width, $14\frac{4}{5}$"; depth, $15\frac{1}{10}$"; weight, 33 lb. **Warranty:** 90 days.

Approx. retail price	**Approx. low price**
$479	**$415**

ACCESSORIES

Univeral Remote Controls

RCA RCU500

BEST BUY

The RCA RCU500 is a universal remote control device capable of controlling five components, including a DSS receiver. Ergonomically designed, the remote features 42 color-coded keys laid out into distinct sections of varying shapes and colors. Some keys (for example the numeric keypad) are common to all components. Others are specific to a particular task. Eight keys are dedicated for picture-in-picture functions for any TV, and six buttons are for recording programs on your VCR. For the home theater enthusiast, an audio control button will turn on and control the volume of the A/V receiver. The RCU500 makes it very easy to progam codes for various components. The manual lists virtually every brand of TV, VCR, audio equipment, and cable/satellite service. Clearly labeled and easy to use, it fits into your hand well and can be used by both right- and left-handed persons. It is powered by four AAA batteries. This is one universal remote that works well in trying to cut down on coffee table clutter.

Specifications: height, 8"; width, 2"; depth, $\frac{3}{4}$"; weight, 2.9 lb. **Warranty:** 1 year.

Approx. retail price	**Approx. low price**
$50	**$25**

Prices are accurate at time of printing but are subject to manufacturers' changes.

ONE FOR ALL URC2099

Recommended

The One For All Lite is an aftermarket universal remote that will control up to four components. All of the keys can be illuminated at the touch of a button and are raised using different shapes, making operation in a darkened room easier. The remote will control a TV plus a VCR, cable box, and one other component, for example a CD player (or any three other devices). Setup is easy and straightforward. You simply press the key for the component first, then the "Magic" key, followed by the code number for the TV, VCR, cable box, or CD player. All codes are preprogrammed into the unit. Designed for one-handed operation, it's convenient for both left-handed and right-handed individuals. The Lite is powered by four AAA alkaline batteries, which should last several months. The instruction booklet leaves space to write down your codes.

Specifications: height, 7"; width, 2"; depth, 1"; weight, 6 oz.
Warranty: 90 days; 30-day double-your-money-back guarantee.

Approx. retail price	Approx. low price
$25	$22

SOLE CONTROL SC-460

Budget Buy

The Sole Control SC-460 is an advanced aftermarket remote capable of controlling up to six devices, including a DSS receiver. It is ergonomically designed with color-coded keys that are placed within different groupings, and it will stand up on your coffee table. The 39 turquoise and gray keys on a black background are clearly labeled and easy to read. The layout seems very uncluttered. It is easy to use by both right- and left-handed persons. Setup is very easy and quick, using the Xtra key, the device key, and the four-digit code for each component, found in a separate code manual. The SC-460 has no memory backup—you'll have to rekey the codes each time you change batteries. Like many universal remotes, it is powered by four AAA batteries. Some keys, for example volume up/down, work in both TV and VCR modes. In each mode, you can get into the devices's on-screen programming and menu system. Thus you can actually program the VCR with this remote instead of just hitting the record button.

Specifications: height, 8″; width, 2½″; depth, ¾″; weight, 8 oz.
Warranty: 1 year, limited; 30-day satisfaction guaranteed.

Approx. retail price	**Approx. low price**
$30	**$23**

VCR Programmer

MAGNAVOX CB1500 STARSIGHT BOX

Recommended

The Magnavox CB1500 is a stand-alone StarSight box that gives you on-screen television listings. It also gives you a way to program your VCR to record any of those listings. The CB1500 works with any TV or VCR that uses an infrared remote control. Setup is easy and straightforward. Your incoming cable signal is routed first to your cable box, then to your VCR, then to the Magnavox CB1500, and last to your TV. Twin emitters from the CB1500 for both your VCR and cable box turn them on and off and change the channels as necessary. StarSight is an innovative on-screen program guide. It lists every channel available on your cable network along with a description of each program. On screen, StarSight gives you a full seven-day program planner. Programs are also listed by themes, such as movies, sports, or comedies. You can scroll by times, by channels, or themes. If you see a program you want to tape, just scroll over to it and press the record button on the remote. The machine will ask you if this is a one-time or a weekly event. That's all there is to programming. A separate screen holds a summary of all the programs that are in its memory, which is not lost by power failure. In total, the CB1500 holds 21 programs in memory. Its 40-button universal remote replaces your TV, VCR, and cable box remotes. Besides having the necessary keys to control those components, the remote also includes special StarSight keys to scroll around the programmer. You can customize the channel lineup by deselecting channels that you never watch and rearranging channels to group your favorites together. StarSight works by receiving a signal from your local PBS station and storing it in the blanking interval between picture images. StarSight's on-screen programmer is available by subscription; it's priced at $4.99 per month, or less if you take a 6- to 24-month subscription. The longer you subscribe for, the lower the monthly service cost.

Specifications: height, 1⅓"; width, 14"; depth, 10½"; weight, 10 lb. **Warranty:** 90 days.

Approx. retail price	**Approx. low price**
$150	**$150**

Digital Satellite System (DSS)

RCA DS2430RW

✓ BEST BUY

The RCA DS2430RW Deluxe System, the company's step-up and most popular DSS system, is capable of controlling two receivers. DSS, or Digital Satellite System, consists of an 18-inch-diameter satellite dish and a receiver. The receiver unit has two antenna inputs—one for the satellite and one for either cable or a rooftop antenna. It has two audio outputs, two video outputs, one S-Video output, and one RF output. The system has been designed to output its signals to a television and a VCR. Picture quality is superb, displaying close to 500 lines of resolution for a seamless picture. Judged by direct comparisons with all types of program signals, including cable TV and rooftop antenna, DSS's color, brightness, sharpness, and clarity cannot be matched. DSS is virtually free of ghosts, halos, and video noise. On top of that, audio quality is on a par with CDs. The 39-button universal remote comes with an ergonomically designed and color-coded keypad that will allow you to control the DSS, your TV, VCR, cable box, and a laser disc player from one remote. The on-screen menu system is very thorough and complete. It lists every program that is being broadcast along with a description of each. Also included is on-screen help along with explanations of each aspect of the system. You can set spending limits on PPV or lock out specific channels with a private code so that the children may not

Prices are accurate at time of printing but are subject to manufacturers' changes.

watch. DSS has been designed for the television viewer who wants the best possible picture and sound plus the freedom to choose many types of programming fare.

Specifications: height, 2⅞"; width, 15"; depth, 11"; weight, 10 lb. **Warranty:** parts, 1 year; labor, 90 days.

Approx. retail price
$899

Approx. low price
$849

DSS Programmer

ABSOLUTE VIDEO ONE TOUCH

Recommended

The Absolute Video One Touch is a special remote control device with macro keys that make DSS easier to use. The current model is RCA-compatible only. Sony and Toshiba variants are in the works. This 55-button remote features 20 preprogrammed keys that enable you to access some stations without punching in the three channel numbers from 200 to 999. It has specific buttons for A&E, Discovery, Disney, HBO, Lifetime, Cinemax, Showtime, TNT, and USA. Eight additional macro keys are programmable so that you can add favorite channels. Other specific macro keys include Info, Select, and View. These eliminate the need to go through several menus to get to those tasks. The remote is powered by four AAA batteries.

Specifications: height, 9¼"; width, 2⅘"; depth, 1"; weight, 7 oz. **Warranty:** parts and labor, 90 days limited.

Approx. retail price
$45

Approx. low price
Not available

VCRs AND LASER DISC PLAYERS

Twenty years ago videocassette recorders (VCRs) were found in only a handful of consumer households. Today they can be found in close to 85 percent of all homes, and 13 million VCRs are sold each year. Although other technologies are also becoming common, VCRs still hold their position as the machine of choice, largely because they alone can record programs unattended.

At this time, the best picture and sound for home video comes from laser disc players. The catalog of currently available discs is extensive, and virtually all films are released on laser disc. Prices of discs are generally competitive with those of videotapes. Discs are far less subject to mechanical failure and wear than tapes. While a high-end laser disc player with dual-sided play and digital time base correction can cost around $800, excellent machines are available for less than $500. For someone who does not do time-shift recording and loves movies, a laser disc player could be a good alternative to a VCR. The imminent death of laser discs has been rumored for many years, but the quality and economy of the laser disc format should insure its place in the market for the future.

A new disc format called DVD (Digital Video Disc) is scheduled for introduction in mid-1996. DVD is expected to be a small, 5-inch CD-like disc that will hold a 135-minute movie on one side of the disc. According to the manufacturers, the players will cost about $499 and the discs about $20. Touted as the future of home video, DVD claims a far superior picture than laser disc (425 lines of resolution), S-VHS (400 lines of resolution), or VHS (240 lines of resolution). According to the movie studios who are backing this format, we can expect an initial release of about 250 film titles at DVD's introduction.

However, with an installed base of more than 7 million households, laser disc releases will continue. Players are selling at a rate of approximately 250, 000 units annually and are expected to continue. While not as widely used as VCRs, laser discs will still be available for those consumers who want an excellent playback system.

Best Buys '96

Our Best Buy, Recommended, and Budget Buy VCRs and laser disc players follow. Within each category, items are listed by quality; the item we consider the best of the Best Buys is first, followed by our second choice, and so on. A Budget Buy describes a less expensive product of respectable quality that perhaps sacrifices some of the performance and/or convenience features of a Best Buy or Recommended product. Remember that a Best Buy, Recommended, or Budget Buy designation applies only to the model listed; unless otherwise noted, it does not necessarily apply to other models made by the same manufacturer or to an entire product line.

VCRs

VCR Formats

The most common format for videocassette recorders is **VHS,** which uses half-inch tape in a cassette shell roughly the size of a paperback book. **Hi-8mm** is a totally digital format that is technically dazzling and uses a much smaller cassette while producing markedly superior pictures and sound. Regular **8mm** tape offers digital images but does not match the technology of Hi-8mm decks. Only a handful of 8mm and Hi-8mm machines are available, because both formats are primarily used in camcorder applications. **Beta,** although in many ways superior to VHS, has virtually disappeared from the marketplace. Sony continues to sell two consumer decks as replacement models for its installed base of approximately 9 million Betaphiles. **S-VHS** VCRs are VHS machines that separate luminance and chrominance signals to give a more detailed image with better definition. Thanks to a lack of prerecorded software, S-VHS never really caught on and represents about 1 percent of total VCR sales. However, with the introduction of DSS (Digital Satellite System), we finally have a medium suited for making S-VHS recordings. For the more than one million people who have already purchased DSS, an S-VHS deck makes a good choice for replacing an aging VCR—it will provide them with the best recorded image currently available.

VHS continues to be the preferred format for consumers, largely due to the wide range of movies and other programming available for either purchase or rental. The future is bound to shift to digital, but VHS should continue to dominate the market until the beginning of the next century.

Choosing Tapes

If you are going to record on a tape only once or twice and not play it back very often, standard-grade tapes are fine. However, if you plan to record and play back the same tape many times, use a high-grade tape. We also recommend that you use brand-name tapes such Fuji, JVC, Kodak, Maxell, Panasonic, Scotch, Sony, 3M, TDK, and so forth, rather than cheaper tapes from unknown manufacturers. Many of the less costly tapes are made so poorly that they can quickly cause extensive and expensive damage to the heads of your VCR.

Most people buy T-120 tapes, which record two hours at the fastest speed and six hours at the slowest speed. The longest tape currently available is a T-210 tape from JVC, which records 10½ hours at the slowest speed—great for a long miniseries.

Features and Terminology

Shopping for a VCR can be a confusing or even intimidating experience. So many features are available, and in so many different combinations, that it can be difficult to make solid comparisons between one machine and another. Since not every consumer needs or wants every feature, it is important to understand what is available and to know what you want.

Hi-fi and stereo sound: Hi-fi is not the same thing as stereo sound. Stereo means that sound is recorded and played back through two channels, as opposed to monaural, one-channel sound. Hi-fi stands for high-fidelity or high-quality sound. If you want the best-quality sound from your prerecorded movies or if you're thinking about home theater, you'll need a hi-fi VCR. All movies and videos are released with hi-fi soundtracks (encoded with Dolby Surround Sound). Prices for hi-fi VCRs range between $350 and $600.

Number of video heads: To record and play back a tape, you need only two video heads. Additional heads are used for special effects such as slow motion, freeze-frame, and clear on-screen searching.

Programmability: If you are buying a VCR primarily to record television broadcasts, programmability is an important consideration. All VCRs can be programmed to record at least one program. The most rudimentary programming uses a built-in clock timer that you set to start and stop within the next 24 hours. More elaborate programming allows you to record several different programs on different channels over a period of 28 days or more. Other program operations let you record the same program every day or every week. Many VCRs include VCR Plus+ , a simple method of programming by entering a number listed in television guides. Some VCR Plus+ models will also change channels on your cable box. Recently some VCRs have come with StarSight programmers included. StarSight is an on-screen program guide available by subscription. It contains all the listings for your area and is updated daily. You simply scroll to the program you want to record on your on-screen guide and press Record. The machine does the rest, since it knows the start and stop times and channel number in your area.

Tape speeds: Virtually all VCRs let you choose between two or three different recording speeds. Playback speed is automatically set, and even VCRs that record in only two speeds play back on all three speeds. The slow speeds allow more recording time on the tape, but the fast speed provides a better-quality recording.

Quick access/quick play: Many VCRs now provide quick play from the stop position. A great number of VCRs provide quick access from fast-forward or fast-rewind to visual scanning and quick access from visual scanning to play.

Index search: Many VCRs record an electronic index code at the beginning of each recording. To scan your recordings on a tape, you press Index Search. The VCR then stops at each index mark and plays back a few seconds of the recording. Some VCRs even let you go directly to a specific index marker and start playback.

Jog/shuttle control: These special-effect tape-advance features allow you to precisely control the speed at which a tape is viewed. Shuttle control allows you to search forward or backward through a tape at a range of fast and slow speeds. Jog control allows you to move the tape forward or backward frame by frame.

Commercial zapper: New decks by RCA this year include commercial-zapper circuitry that senses the beginning and end of commercials in a taped program. Upon playback, it will automatically fast-forward through them and go back into play mode when the program resumes.

Automatic clock set: This new and noteworthy feature is now found on several brands of VCRs. These models set their own clock from a time signal sent from your local PBS station. This means that you never have to set the clock initially, change the time at the beginning and end of daylight saving time, or reset the clock after a blackout. Once power is restored, the VCR will display the right time.

Universal remotes: Many step-up models feature preprogrammed universal remotes with the ability to control TV and cable boxes also. A unified remote will control the same brand of TV as your VCR.

Editing features: Unless you actually plan on editing your camcorder tapes and making dupes (duplicates) for family and friends, stay away from decks with sophisticated editing features such as assemble editing, insert editing, or video dubbing. These features can add up to $100 to the cost of the model and will only make the machine more difficult and intimidating to use.

Hi-fi VHS VCRs

SONY SLV-780HF

✓BEST BUY

The Sony SLV-780HF is a four-head hi-fi VCR. It is among a handful of VHS decks today that produce the finest images at both the slowest and fastest recording speeds. Images from prerecorded tapes are pristine, with very little video noise. Sound quality is excellent. Sony's heritage of technical expertise is represented in the SLV-780HF. Equipped with a 181-channel tuner and programming capability of eight programs over 31 days, the unit is a solid performer with numerous innovative features. Besides VCR Plus+ with cable-box control using a cable mouse, the model features auto clock set to always display the correct time. Cursor keys and an Execute button found on the top of the remote make the on-screen menus and setup easy to use. The remote is a full-featured universal remote that will also control your TV and cable box. Included on this 50-button remote is a recessed jog/shuttle ring you move with your thumb. This ring makes it very easy for either a left- or right-handed person to move the tape forward or backward at varying speeds. The remote uses many small buttons, making it awkward for people with big hands. Other features include automatic head cleaning, commercial-skip (it advances the tape 30 seconds each time you depress it), indexing, and adaptive picture control, which optimizes each tape placed into the VCR.

Warranty: parts, 1 year; labor, 90 days.

Approx. retail price	**Approx. low price**
$499	**$417**

TOSHIBA M-761

BEST BUY

The Toshiba M-761 is a six-head hi-fi VCR. It is also among a handful of models that produce some of the finest images on VHS decks today. Toshiba has been a consistent performer in the VCR arena. The M-761 is a full-featured deck with two extra video 19-micron heads to produce recorded images at its slowest speed (EP) that rival images recorded at its fastest speed (SP). In essence, the 19-micron heads provide steady, natural colors with fine edge detail. The new heads are coupled with the V3 chassis which features a flying preamp that is integrated into the heads, providing less video noise at both playback speeds. To further improve picture quality, this VCR includes color signal enhancement (CSE). CSE makes colors more robust and distinct by reducing color bleed and eliminating multiphase processing. Equipped with a 181-channel tuner and capable of recording six events over a one-month period, the M-761 also sports a universal remote that also controls your TV and cable box. The remote goes one step further by including "Intel-A-Play" keys, which act as macro keys that turn on the TV and VCR and go to the proper video input with one button. To facilitate programming, the VCR includes VCR Plus+ with cable-box control. On-screen programming is very easy to use. Other features include a jog/shuttle dial on the unit, front A/V inputs (besides rear inputs), automatic head cleaner, and a trilingual on-screen display. As with other hi-fi VCRs, the sound quality is excellent.

Warranty: 90 days.

Approx. retail price
$499

Approx. low price
$422

MITSUBISHI HS-U760

✓BEST BUY

The Mitsubishi HS-U760 is a four-head hi-fi S-VHS deck that is truly DSS (Direct Satellite System) ready. This model makes it very easy to tape programs off the DSS satellite as well as making time-shift recordings utilizing both DSS and cable/broadcast channels. Your DSS receiver is attached directly to the S-Video input on the back of the VCR, which in turn is attached to your TV via an S-Video input. The signal passes through, meaning that the VCR does not have to be on to watch DSS. The built-in tuner can tune in 181 channels. By attaching a remote sensor to the infrared "eye" of your DSS receiver from the VCR, it will turn the unit on or off plus change the channels of your DSS. If you reprogram your VCR Plus+ channel guide (accessed through the on-screen menus) within the VCR, you can utilize the Plus+ codes found in television listings for all the DSS channels. This allows you to tape eight programs over a 28-day period. The HS-U760 features Mitsubishi's PerfecTape system, which automatically optimizes the tape in the VCR for the best possible recording and playback. Other features include a childproof locking mechanism to keep fingers and unwanted items out of the VCR, front A/V inputs for the attachment of a camcorder for easy dubbing, and an easy-to-use universal remote with a jog/shuttle dial. Picture quality is excellent, and you get the maximum amount of information out of the signal.

Warranty: parts, 1 year; labor, 6 months.

Approx. retail price	**Approx. low price**
$799	**$666**

RCA VR678HF

BEST BUY

The RCA VR678HF is one of a new breed of four-head hi-fi VCRs that feature the ability to zap out commercials. Called "Commercial Free," it marks the beginnings and ends of commercial breaks. Upon playback, the VCR senses those index marks and quickly fast-forwards to the end of the segment, displaying a blue screen in the interim. The VCR's 45-button universal remote will also control a TV, a second VCR, a laser disc player, DSS, and an audio component. The RCA VR678HF features a 181-channel tuner capable of recording eight events over 365 days. Being DSS compatible, the tuner can record up to channel 999. Other slick features include auto clock set, VCR Plus+ with cable box, and front A/V jacks for the easy attachment of a camcorder. This is a unique and innovative VCR that will set the standard for 1995–96, and picture quality is on a par with the best VHS decks.

Warranty: parts, 1 year; service, 90 days.

Approx. retail price	**Approx. low price**
$499	**Not available**

SAMSUNG VR-8905

Recommended

The Samsung VR-8905 is the first four-head hi-fi VCR that offers StarSight on-screen programming and recording. StarSight offers a daily updated seven-day programmer/planner with times and descriptions of each program. By simply scrolling over to a particular program on the on-screen menu and hitting the record button, the show will be logged into memory for later recording. StarSight carries a monthly

Prices are accurate at time of printing but are subject to manufacturers' changes.

charge of under five dollars depending on the length of the subscription. Picture quality for this VCR is very good on both prerecorded videos and programs taped off the air. Setup could not be easier thanks to its auto clock set feature, which looks for the time signal sent from your local PBS station and instantly sets the time on the VCR's clock. The VCR will allow you to program 10 events over a one-month period from its 181-channel tuner. The very sophisticated but easy-to-use universal remote features a numeric keypad hidden under a top cover and a built-in jog/shuttle dial with cursor keys.

Warranty: parts, 90 days.

Approx. retail price	**Approx. low price**
$550	**$350**

JVC HR-VP720U

Recommended

The JVC HR-VP720U has been designed with some sophisticated editing features for those persons who want to edit their videotapes. Using gold-plated front A/V jacks for signal purity, this model features insert editing (which replaces the picture but leaves the sound), audio dubbing (which replaces just the audio portion of a video), and random assemble editing with audio monitor (which allows you to edit up to eight different scenes at a time, replacing unwanted scenes with desired ones). To make seamless edits possible, the HR-VP720U includes a flying erase head (which provides for good, unnoticeable scene transitions) and jog/shuttle controls on both the deck itself and the remote for precise movement of the tape. The universal remote will also control a TV and cable box. This top-of-the-line four-head stereo hi-fi VCR also produces clean, crisp images from both off-the-air taping and playing back prerecorded videos, thanks to its oval-cut video heads. Hi-fi performance was also quite good. This VCR includes an audio-switching noise-reduction system that further improves on its hi-fi sound reproduction. The model features the ability to record eight programs over a one-year period and can receive up to 181 cable channels. Like many other VCRs today, this model includes VCR Plus+ with a cable-box controller.

Warranty: parts, 1 year; labor, 90 days.

Approx. retail price $550 | **Approx. low price** $407

GENERAL ELECTRIC VG4255

Budget Buy

The GE VG4255 is a budget-minded four-head hi-fi VCR offering features normally found on more expensive models. The tuner can receive 181 channels, and it will allow you to program eight events over a one-year period. Featuring a built-in VCR Plus+ programmer, the VG4255 will allow you to quickly program your VCR by simply punching in the VCR Plus+ codes found in television listings. To assure optimum playback, the deck includes digital auto tracking, which insures correct playback of all tapes, especially prerecorded ones. Picture quality is very good on both prerecorded videos and programs taped off the air. Because the deck has four video heads, it will allow playback in slow motion and variable speeds. Other convenience features found on the VG4255 are an elapsed time counter and VISS (VHS Index Search System) search and time search. Also included with this model is a universal remote that can control over 30 brands of TVs plus a cable box converter.

Warranty: parts, 1 year; labor, 90 days.

Approx. retail price $349 | **Approx. low price** $280

8mm VCR

GO VIDEO GV-8050

Recommended

The Go Video GV-8050 is a dual-deck 8mm/VHS VCR offering the user the luxury of playing back tapes in both formats, editing 8mm tapes, and copying 8mm tapes to the VHS format. Sophisticated decks like the GV-8050 offer advanced editing features normally found on top-of-the-line decks from other manufacturers, but this one has two decks built in. This eliminates having to attach 8mm or Hi-8mm camcorders to your VCR. The GV-8050 has an 8mm deck on the left and a VHS deck on the right, and both decks are hi-fi. Sharing controls and features makes editing a breeze. The unit includes an assemble editor that allows you to put several recorded scenes in a particular order. Once you have finished assembling your video, the built-in titler will allow you to name your new epic and add credits. An extra option is the company's proprietary computer software that turns the GV-8050 into a multimedia edit controller. It guides you through the editing process easily in a step-by-step fashion in clear language. As you edit tapes, an internal memory chip logs them permanently into memory for later retrieval. This option turns the editing process into a manageable task, even for neophytes. The GV-8050's picture is very good in both formats, displaying a consistent 240 lines or better across the board, thanks to four video heads in VHS and two video heads in its 8mm mode. The remote control operates both decks easily by the flick of a switch. As with other hi-fi VCRs, audio quality is excellent. With its 181-channel tuner and an eight-event/100-year programming capability, the GV-8050 is a versatile performer. Although the on-screen programming for taping off the air is somewhat cumbersome, the editing versatility far outweighs its programming shortcomings.

Warranty: parts, 1 year; labor, 90 days.

Approx. retail price
$1,099

Approx. low price
$893

LASER DISC PLAYERS

A laser disc is an optical medium for playing video and digital audio recording. Pits cut in the disc are read by a laser beam. Because information can be read from the discs without any physical contact, the acrylic-coated discs will last virtually forever. Laser discs also produce excellent image quality with ordinary hookups to your television set. They are capable of producing superb images with nearly twice the horizontal resolution of standard videotapes when used with TVs that have

Prices are accurate at time of printing but are subject to manufacturers' changes.

S-Video connections. Most laser disc players are combination players, meaning that they play multiple types of discs, from 5-inch CDs through 12-inch laser discs. Many models today provide a separate drawer for CD-only playback. These models use a CD Direct input that operates the drawer and disconnects the video circuitry for less interference.

Many laser disc players offer dual-sided play, which automatically turns over the disc. This process takes about 12 seconds. The unit will either display a blue screen or freeze the last frame of the video until the next scene starts. There are two types of laser discs: CAV (constant angular velocity) and CLV (constant linear velocity). CAV discs spin at a constant speed of 1800 RPMs with a playing time of 30 minutes per side. All CAV discs can be played back with special effects. CLV discs spin at a speed ranging from 1800 RPMs for the inner tracks to 600 RPMs for outer tracks. This permits a playing time of 60 minutes per side. Special effects with CLVs are possible only with players with digital frame memory.

Because laser disc is primarily a medium for people who love movies, many discs are available in letter-boxed versions. Letter-boxing places black bars at the top and bottom of the screen, retaining the original aspect ratio that the director intended. On videocassette, for example, most movies are panned-and-scanned. This means that the action is centered on one character or thing and information on the left and right sides of the screen are cut off.

FEATURES AND TERMINOLOGY

Random access: All laser disc players have the ability to provide random access, allowing you to quickly find a particular spot on the disc.

Chapter numbers: These numbers are recorded on the discs and are used to indicate sections or chapters, almost like track numbers on music CDs. For example, a movie is divided into distinct sections. For *Forrest Gump,* the sections might be Chapter 1, "Hello, My Name is Forrest. Forrest Gump"; Chapter 2, "Through the Eyes of Forrest Gump"; Chapter 3, "Stupid Is as Stupid Does"; and so forth.

Prices are accurate at time of printing but are subject to manufacturers' changes.

Digital time-base correction: Time-base correction helps reduce jitter at the edges and corners of the picture.

Theater mode: In this mode, several seconds are cut from the turnover time of a disc by skipping over side B's table of contents. It will also dim the front panel's illumination.

Digital Dolby AC-3: Apparently the successor to Dolby Pro Logic, Dolby AC-3 sends discrete audio to all 5.1 channels of a home theater setup (left, right, center, right rear, left rear, and the subwoofer). In the AC-3 mode, distinct sound emanates from each speaker, as opposed to straight matrixed and steered Pro Logic. In our comparisons of the same films in both the Pro Logic and AC-3 modes, the AC-3's circuitry improves the audio over Pro Logic's.

PIONEER CLD-D504

✓BEST BUY

The Pioneer CLD-D504 is part of the next generation of laser disc players, offering many advanced features, including dual-sided disc play. It has the special circuitry digital echo to let you perform karaoke with the supplied microphone. Picture quality is excellent due to its digital time-base corrector, which eliminates noise and jitter from the picture. This allows all 425 lines of resolution to come through, as long as your TV set will display 400+ lines. Direct CD, with its separate CD tray, gives improved audio performance when playing a music CD by disconnecting all video circuitry. The remote is easy to use. The front panel is clear and concise, giving you all the information you need. The deck has two A/V outputs, one S-Video output, and one Dolby AC-3 output.

Warranty: parts and labor, 1 year.

Approx. retail price	Approx. low price
$660	$493

MARANTZ LV-520

Recommended

The Marantz LV-520 is a laser disc player of exceptional quality and design that offers the user many useful and convenient features. It can play dual-sided laser discs with

Prices are accurate at time of printing but are subject to manufacturers' changes.

a turnover time of just a few seconds, and it has a digital time-base corrector to reduce picture noise and jitter. The LV-520 also features direct CD circuits along with a separate CD drawer. When engaged, it disconnects all video circuitry for improved audio performance. In either the audio or video mode, audio performance is right on the money. The LV-520 also includes a remote with a jog/shuttle dial. The deck includes two A/V outputs, one S-Video output, and one Dolby AC-3 output. Moreover, the images displayed are excellent from any viewpoint. The Marantz LV-520 is a superior performer and a welcome addition to anyone's budding home theater.

Warranty: parts and labor, 3 years.

Approx. retail price	**Approx. low price**
$800	**$800**

SONY MDP-650

Recommended

The Sony MDP-650 is among the best laser disc players currently available. Picture quality and product design are excellent. Capable of displaying 425 lines of resolution, the MDP-650 produces crisp images with very little video noise. This is due in part to Sony's tri-digital video processing, which consists of a digital time-base corrector, a digital comb filter, a digital dropout compensator, and a digital noise canceler. The video circuitry clearly improves the player's video performance. This is an auto-reverse model that automatically turns the disc over in about 12 seconds and displays a still image of the last scene until the disc resumes play. Because of its 8-bit digital memory, the unit can conduct both freeze-frame and frame-by-frame advance searches for both CAV and CLV discs. The MDP-650 includes one of the best-designed remotes for a laser disc player. Most laser disc player remotes are clunky, with a bottom-heavy jog/shuttle control. This 51-key Sony remote (RMT-M37A) features phosphorescent basic function keys that don't drain the batteries. Other, less-used keys are hidden under a flip-up door. On the bottom of the remote is a recessed jog/shuttle knob. The MDP-650 also includes two A/V outputs, two S-video outputs and a fiber-optic cable output for attachment to a stand-alone digital/analog converter. Other features include theater mode, which lowers the picture's black level for improved contrast, and digital frame memory, which retains images in memory for showing as a CD plays. Audio and video performance is top-notch.

Warranty: parts, 1 year; labor, 90 days.

Approx. retail price	Approx. low price
$899	$661

PANASONIC LX-H670

Budget Buy

The Panasonic LX-H670 is among the least expensive laser disc players that include the auto-reverse feature and a digital servo for stable playback. Like all laser disc players, the LX-H670 is capable of displaying 430 lines of resolution. Images produced from this player are very good to excellent and are helped by its digital time-base corrector, which reduces jitter on the screen. The player is easily controllable with its standard remote, although the remote lacks a jog/shuttle dial and its buttons all look the same. Nonetheless, the unit turns in a good performance. It includes two A/V outputs and one S-Video output. An optical digital audio output is included for attachment to a separate digital-to-analog converter for improved audio. Other features include a shuttle dial located on the front of the unit, a feature that scans the first eight seconds or so of each track of a CD, and a digital noise canceler. A solid performer at a reasonable price.

Warranty: parts and labor, 1 year.

Approx. retail price	Approx. low price
$549	$476

Prices are accurate at time of printing but are subject to manufacturers' changes.

CAMCORDERS

The camcorder, which combines a video camera and a videocassette recorder in one unit, records live action on tape for near-instantaneous playback on any television.

Now a mature product, even the least expensive camcorders incorporate a variety of useful features with satisfactory performance. As the sales boom of the late 1980s faded, prices for basic models fell, reaching new lows in 1995 even with the rising value of the Japanese yen. Sony, Panasonic, JVC, Sharp, and Hitachi manufacture nearly all camcorders on the market, no matter what brand name is on the unit. Thus you might be able to save a few dollars by comparing two similar (sometimes identical) models sold under different brand names.

Manufacturers use increasingly longer (more powerful) zoom lenses as enticements to buy more expensive models. In reality they serve little purpose. An 8-power zoom lens is the maximum for steady shooting with a compact handheld model, and 12-power is the maximum for shoulder-supported full-size models, or those with effective electronic image stabilization. Only if you have firm support, such as with a monopod or tripod, can you effectively use a zoom lens greater than 12-power. Digital zoom, in which the camcorder electronically magnifies the picture, causes graininess and picture distortion, making it nearly useless for serious shooting with high magnifications.

Many models now come with color LCD viewfinders, which have improved somewhat since they were first introduced a few years ago. While it's nice to see what you're shooting in color, these viewfinders usually are dimmer and lower in resolution than their black-and-white counterparts. If you opt for a color viewfinder, choose a model with at least 100,000 pixels, preferably more. A color viewfinder adds about $100 to the camcorder's cost, which we consider excessive for the benefit derived. A recent feature that replaces the viewfinder is a 3- or 4-inch color LCD screen. This allows shooting from a variety of positions without holding the camcorder directly to your eye. It's also convenient for playback away from a TV set. The drawback is that the LCD screen may wash out in bright sunlight. Sony and Panasonic offer this option without detracting from the functionality of the camcorder. Sony makes the screen a "stealth" option that folds into the camcorder body while you continue shooting using the standard viewfinder. Panasonic offers it as a snap-on optional attachment for several new models.

Whereas picture quality between models in similar categories varies only slightly, the feel and operational ease differ substantially. Shop for a camcorder as you would for a pair of shoes. Try it on for comfort, and try it out for ease of use.

Camcorder Formats

The market share among the three different camcorder formats stabilized in 1994–95, with 8mm at about 44 percent of the market, VHS-C at 41 percent, and full-size VHS at 15 percent.

VHS camcorders have the longest recording capacity of all formats. They can record up to eight hours on a T-160 tape at the slow, extended play (EP) speed. However, picture and sound quality noticeably degrade at the slow speed. The bulky size of the VHS cassette with its ½-inch-wide tape requires a relatively large, often heavy camcorder. Full-size VHS is the only format directly playable in home VHS VCRs. Camcorders without the hi-fi option record low-fidelity audio. An upgraded VHS format, S-VHS (Super VHS), uses a specially formulated, much more expensive tape along with superior electronics. This tape records up to 400 lines of resolution—close to laser discs in video quality—and far outperforms conventional VHS. It also substantially improves the video quality of the slow EP speed, making it more acceptable for ordinary recording.

VHS-C is a variation of the VHS format that uses cassettes about a third the size of the regular VHS cassette. The signals recorded on VHS-C are fully compatible with full-size VHS. This allows VHS-C cassettes to record and play on any VHS VCR when placed in an adapter supplied with nearly all VHS-C camcorders. VHS-C tapes record for a maximum of 40 minutes at standard play (SP) and two hours at the low-quality extended play (EP) speed, twice the time of the original VHS-C tapes. Like full-size-format camcorders, VHS-C camcorders without the hi-fi option record low-fidelity audio.

8mm cassettes are roughly the size of audiocassettes, though slightly thicker, with ⅓-inch-wide tape, narrower than the ½-inch VHS video format. By using metal tape to increase recording density, 8mm tapes reproduce an image comparable to VHS. Camcorders that use this format, like those that use VHS-C, are compact and lightweight, with many models weighing less than 1½ pounds. A standard 8mm camcorder records up to 2½ hours on a single tape.

Hi8 (Hi-Band 8mm) offers the same resolution as S-VHS (about 400 lines), but Hi8 records with slightly less color noise, making the picture quality subtly better than S-VHS's. Standard 8mm tapes will record and play on Hi8 machines, but tapes recorded on Hi8 will not play back on conventional 8mm machines. Hi8 camcorders require special tape formulations: a premium metal evaporated tape (Hi8-ME) and an improved metal particle tape (Hi8-MP). Both are more expensive than standard VHS tape. Hi8-ME offers superior performance, but it is difficult to manufacture, costs appreciably more, and is more difficult to find. New Hi8-MP formulations narrow the performance gap and work as well for everyday shooting. Hi8 camcorders, like S-VHS, include S jacks for maximum signal transfer quality to a TV or an S-VHS VCR. However, most of the Hi8 advantage can still be realized through ordinary cables.

The VHS and 8mm formats are electronically compatible. This allows you, for example, to connect your 8mm camcorder to your VHS VCR and copy your 8mm videos onto VHS tape. Front-panel input jacks for this purpose are becoming nearly standard on VHS VCRs. You can also connect your 8mm camcorder directly to your TV for viewing.

Features and Terminology

Before shopping for a camcorder, you should be familiar with a few terms.

Autofocus describes a feature that focuses the lens and keeps it focused even as the distance between the camcorder and the subject changes. Some camcorders also permit manual focusing. Each company uses a proprietary autofocus system; they have varying degrees of speed and accuracy. Although most companies employ some form of computerized through-the-lens (TTL) system, the simpler infrared system sometimes works better. Be sure to try out the autofocus when evaluating a camcorder.

Aperture designation refers to the maximum opening of the iris—in other words, to the greatest amount of light that can be admitted. The designation is given an f-stop rating, such as f/1.6. The smaller the f/stop number, the larger the aperture and the more light that will pass through the lens. In all camcorders, the iris automatically adjusts. Some camcorders offer a manual adjustment as well.

An **imager (or imaging device)** is the solid-state device that collects light and transforms it into an electrical signal.

A **high-speed shutter** alters the method that the camcorder uses to collect light from its CCD imaging device. This results in the equivalent of allowing less light into the camcorder. A camcorder's high-speed shutter permits operation at speeds up to 1/40,000 of a second. Unless you plan to shoot sports events, this is probably not an essential feature.

Lux is a unit of measurement that gauges the amount of light falling on a photo subject. Many camcorders have a low-light-level rating of around 10 lux, which is the amount of light on a subject about 12 feet from a single 60-watt light bulb. Although sensitive camcorders can deliver a picture with 1 lux, you are most likely to get a good image with 80 lux. The best color and depth of field require several hundred lux.

Minimum illumination tells you the minimum amount of light, stated in lux, necessary to record a clear picture.

Automatic (or continuous) white balance keeps the color of the video image true to life under varying lighting conditions from outdoor to indoor and fluorescent to incandescent. An inaccurate white balance can result in a picture that is too pink or too blue.

Character generators allow you to add the time, date, titles, or other written information to the images you are recording.

A **superimposer** is a digital memory function that can store images or titles. At the push of a button, you can superimpose the stored image over the picture currently being recorded.

Fade in/fade out is a feature that automatically fades the image from or to a black (or white) screen.

CCD (charge-coupled device) is a solid-state imaging device that replaces the pickup tube. CCDs eliminate most image lag, which looks like a streaking highlight on a moving subject. CCDs function well in a broad range of lighting conditions and are rarely damaged by excessive light. All of the CCDs used in camcorders are based on MOS (metal-oxide semiconductor) devices. The CCD is a system by which electrons are collected and moved through the imaging device. The MOS is the type of light-sensitive transmitter that makes up the CCD. References to CCD or MOS in camcorder specifications are arbitrary and bear little relationship to the overall quality of the product.

A **flying erase head** is mounted on the spinning video head drum rather than in a stationary position along the tape path. Because it spins with the other heads, a flying erase head allows you to make smooth transitions when you stop and start the tape between scenes, eliminating noise bursts. The flying erase head is a particularly desirable feature if you want better quality in edited tapes.

Resolution is the ability to produce fine detail in a video picture. It is usually measured in horizontal lines. Vertical resolution, less frequently used, is a more stringent measure. A good video monitor produces more than 500 lines. Television broadcasts have about 340 lines. Conventional VHS reproduces 240 lines, and 8mm yields slightly more.

A **pixel** (short for picture element) is one of the tiny points that make up a video image. A high pixel count produces a more detailed image, but because the size and type of imaging devices vary, comparing pixel counts between different devices doesn't always determine which can yield the more detailed image.

Image stabilization is a generic term for reducing unwanted camcorder motion, such as small shakes and jitters. Some companies use a digital electronic system that fuzzes the picture slightly to reduce the unwanted motion. Others compensate by rapidly moving the lens. Having reviewed a large number of camcorders with this feature, we question the benefit, although effectiveness varies from brand to brand.

Microphones are built into all camcorders, and most can be connected to external mikes as well.

Best Buys '96

Our Best Buy, Recommended, and Budget Buy camcorders follow. They are presented in these categories: 8mm, compact VHS (VHS-C), and full-size VHS. Within each category, camcorders are listed by quality; the item we consider the best of the Best Buys is first, followed by our second choice, and so on. Sometimes differences are minimal. A Budget Buy describes a less expensive product of respectable quality that perhaps sacrifices some of the performance and/or features of a Best Buy or Recommended product. Remember that a Best Buy, Recommended, or Budget Buy designation applies only to the model listed; it does not necessarily apply to other models made by the same manufacturer or to an entire product line.

8mm CAMCORDERS

CANON ES550

✓BEST BUY

The very compact Canon ES550 employs new camcorder technology at a compact price. Align the FlexiZone in the viewfinder with your subject by using a joystick-style button on the back of the camcorder, and no matter where the subject is in the frame, it will be in focus and properly exposed. The 12-power zoom lens also contains a built-in wide-angle adapter—the ability to shoot wide is as important as, or more important than, telephoto power. In the nursery you will shoot better baby videos from close in, made possible with the wide-angle lens. Canon's six-mode programmed auto exposure adjusts the camcorder for a variety of shooting situations, such as sports, portrait, sand and snow, and so forth. The ¼-inch, 270,000 pixel CCD has a minimum light sensitivity of 2 lux.

The built-in titler allows you to create your own titles from its character generator and also choose among three different date and time displays that can be recorded on the tape. High-fidelity mono sound and a flying erase head are standard, as are necessary jacks for editing. Canon supplies a wireless remote control.

Specifications: height, $4\frac{3}{16}$"; width, $4\frac{3}{16}$"; length, $7\frac{5}{8}$"; weight, 1 lb $9\frac{3}{8}$ oz. without tape and battery. **Warranty:** parts and labor, 1 year.

Approx. retail price	Approx. low price
$799	$656

SONY CCD-TR100

BEST BUY

The Sony CCD-TR100 represents one of the best combinations of features in one of the least expensive Hi8 models. This high-performance, modestly featured camcorder delivers the improved resolution of Hi8 along with hi-fi stereo sound for audio impact that matches the video. Its $\frac{1}{3}$-inch, precision 410,000-pixel CCD captures images worthy of the over-400-line resolution of Hi8. That's superior to the broadcast video you normally watch on TV. A variable-speed 12-power zoom lens and the ability to shoot with as little as 3-lux illumination lets you shoot in a wide variety of situations. The CCD-TR100 features Sony's quick-record system, which can start recording in $\frac{1}{5}$ second, and also the ability to automatically record five-second snippets for fast-paced videos. Important indicators and messages appear in the viewfinder and on an LCD panel on the side of the body. The integral lens cover automatically retracts when you turn on the camcorder, a great convenience. The CCD-TR100 includes programmable four-mode automatic exposure so you can fine-tune the automation for specific shooting conditions. More creative users will appreciate the full manual exposure and manual focus using a thumbwheel. Additional bonuses are digital picture effects and a digital fader for giving your videos a custom look. You can automatically record the date and time on your videos from the built in clock/calender. Sony supplies a wireless remote control.

Prices are accurate at time of printing but are subject to manufacturers' changes.

Specifications: height, $4\frac{1}{3}$"; width, $4\frac{1}{2}$"; length, $8\frac{1}{10}$"; weight, 2 lb. without tape and battery. **Warranty:** parts, 1 year; labor, 90 days.

Approx. retail price	**Approx. low price**
$1,099	**$940**

RCA PRO932

Recommended

The RCA PRO932 rates a Recommended rating rather than a Best Buy because it comes with more features than necessary. However, it offers solid performance and a unique benefit: The PRO932 is one of the first camcorders that can operate from standard AA alkaline batteries as well as the supplied rechargeable. Simply moving some tabs in the battery compartment switches from one to the other. The alkalines, which last only about as long as the rechargeable (one to two hours), are an expensive convenience. The PRO932 offers electronic image stabilization that smooths out minor jitters. The $\frac{1}{4}$-inch, 250,000-pixel CCD, coupled with the 24-power digitally enhanced zoom lens, has the ability to instantaneously zoom. The digital circuits also permit smooth digital fades. A two-line, one-page titler allows you to create your own titles with the built-in character generator. The programmable automatic exposure optimizes the camcorder for specialized shooting situations. A flying erase head for near-seamless recording of stops and starts is standard. RCA supplies a wireless remote control. The model PRO942 is the same basic camcorder with a color viewfinder for about $100 more.

Specifications: height, $4\frac{3}{4}$"; width, $3\frac{3}{8}$"; length, $8\frac{3}{8}$"; weight, $1\frac{9}{10}$ lb. without tape and battery. **Warranty:** parts, 1 year; labor, 90 days.

Approx. retail price	**Approx. low price**
$899	**$706**

SONY CCD-TRV40

Recommended

A 3-inch color LCD viewing screen folds out from the left side of the 8mm Sony CCD-TRV40 "Vision" series camcorder. When folded in, it becomes part of the camcorder body, and the standard black-and-white viewfinder operates. This solves the problem of using the LCD screen as a viewfinder in difficult shooting situations, such as outdoors on bright sunny days. This system surpasses the Sharp Viewcams, in which the LCD is permanently affixed to the camcorder body. The Sony screen pivots and tilts, and when folded out it reveals a speaker. The screen permits the camcorder to function as a minimonitor, enabling you to view prerecorded videos. The LCD adds substantial cost, causing this camcorder to fall in the Recommended rather than the Best Buy category. Although the CCD-TRV40 is standard 8mm, rather than Hi8, it stretches conventional resolution to the maximum—it has the ⅓-inch, 470,000-pixel CCD that's used in Sony's Hi8 models. (Model CCD-TRV70 is the Hi8 model nearly identical to this one, but with stereo sound for a $700 premium.) Operationally, the CCD-TRV40 is equivalent to Sony's full-featured "TR" series models, with digital picture effects and fades, SteadyShot picture stabilization, a 12-power digitally enhanced zoom for the equivalent of 24-power, and Sony's virtually instantaneous quick record system. The high pixel count of the CCD allows using the digital effects with pleasing results. The CCD-TRV40 has a low-light sensitivity of 3 lux. The convenient automatic lens cover retracts when you turn on the power. Programmed automatic exposure modes optimize the camcorder for a range of shooting conditions, such as sports, portrait, and night. Like all other camcorders in the 8mm format, it has a flying erase head and hi-fi sound. The CCD-TRV40 contains all the necessary jacks for editing and comes with a wireless remote control.

Specifications: height, 4⅓"; width, 4⅘"; length, 8⅓"; weight, 2³⁄₁₀ lb. without tape and battery. **Warranty:** parts, 1 year; labor, 90 days.

Approx. retail price
$1,399

Approx. low price
$1,132

SANYO VM-PS12

Budget Buy

Among 8mm camcorders, the Sanyo VM-PS12 "EZcorder" comes the closest to the most basic point-and-shoot still cameras. For instance, the viewfinder is optical rather than electronic, like those of the very first 8mm models over a decade ago. However, the VM-PS12's "fuzzy logic" computer circuits that optimize picture taking are strictly cutting-edge. Unlike most computer logic, which makes absolute yes/no judgments, fuzzy logic analyzes the situation and incrementally adjusts accordingly. You have to accept that the camcorder makes all the decisions, since it has very few manual controls. The fuzzy logic operates the six-zone automatic exposure, automatic iris, and white balance. Since the camcorder lacks an electronic viewfinder, you cannot play back your videos and see them until you connect the camcorder to a TV. An LCD screen shows real elapsed tape time, mode, and any necessary warnings. Rather than the sophisticated 10-power autofocus zoom lenses nearly standard on other camcorders, the VM-PS12 comes with a limited fixed-focus 3-power manual zoom lens, so if you plan a lot of long-distance videography, such as on a photo safari, this camcorder may be inappropriate. The $\frac{1}{4}$-inch, 270,000-pixel imager provides good resolution and works with a minimum of 4 lux illumination. Sanyo recommends 300 lux for optimal images. As with all 8mm camcorders, a flying erase head is a standard feature. Eliminating many of the fancy features increases battery life, reduces weight, and lowers the price. We think that's a respectable trade-off for this most compact, simple-to-use camcorder.

Specifications: height, $4\frac{1}{10}$"; width, $3\frac{3}{5}$"; length, $7\frac{1}{5}$"; weight, $1\frac{2}{5}$ lb. without tape and battery. **Warranty:** parts, 1 year; labor, 90 days.

Approx. retail price	**Approx. low price**
$500	**$450**

COMPACT VHS (VHS-C) CAMCORDERS

PANASONIC PV-IQ205

BEST BUY

Though the PV-IQ205 represents the bottom of Panasonic's VHS-C "Palmcorder" line, it performs the same as

Prices are accurate at time of printing but are subject to manufacturers' changes.

the considerably more expensive models in the line. Although these Palmcorders are quite compact, all use a full-size video head drum, the kind found in a home VCR. This fosters more stable tape motion for a clearer picture. The PV-IQ205 includes all the essential features for shooting good videos, and the "IQ" designation means Panasonic designed it to be intelligent for easy use. The camcorder automatically sets recording parameters for optimum videos. The ⅓-inch, 270,000-pixel CCD image provides good pictures and has a low-light sensitivity of 1 lux. The 14-power autofocus zoom lens can be operated in four speed steps from 3 to 15 seconds. Not only will the PV-IQ205 date- and time-stamp your videos automatically if you desire, its clock automatically toggles between daylight and standard time on the appropriate day. The clock comes preset for Eastern Standard Time; all you do is select your time zone from a menu in the viewfinder. The one-touch automatic fade works by simply pushing the fade button once before starting or stopping a recording. A flying erase head virtually eliminates noise when starting and stopping recording, for smoother edits. Graphical tape and battery gauges in the viewfinder, rather than numbers, show tape remaining and charge level. An automatic lens cover opens when you turn on the camcorder. A record indicator light on the record button, in addition to the front tally lamp, reduces the chance of accidentally leaving the recorder running. The camcorder contains a hot shoe for an optional color-enhancement light (it is standard on the step-up model). Panasonic also markets a snap-on color LCD screen for the 1996 IQ models.

Specifications: height, 4⅝"; width, 4⅛"; length, 6⅞"; weight, 1⁹⁄₁₀ lb. without tape and battery. **Warranty:** parts, 1 year; labor, 90 days.

Approx. retail price	**Approx. low price**
$700	**$629**

JVC GR-AX200

✓BEST BUY

The JVC GR-AX200 is another example of a good-performance VHS-C camcorder without the features that appear on the similar but more expensive step-up models. That

Prices are accurate at time of printing but are subject to manufacturers' changes.

said, this is no stripped model. The 12-power variable-speed "hyper" autofocus zoom lens operates very rapidly, taking two seconds from one end to the other. It also has a dual-speed manual focus. Coupled with the ¼-inch, 270,000-pixel CCD, the GR-AX200 needs a minimum of 2-lux illumination. The programmed automatic exposure dial offers six choices, one of which is a twilight setting—usually camcorders take unnatural-looking videos in twilight. A sepia setting will make your videos look like old photos. Most of the camcorder's key functions are grouped into three centrally located buttons that are convenient for your left middle and index fingers. The GR-AX200 incorporates eight "instant titles," such as "Happy Birthday," available at the touch of a button, as well as a character generator allowing you to create your own titles. What separates the GR-AX200 from most camcorders in its price range is its automatic eight-segment random-assemble editing feature. You can mark eight segments of video anywhere on the tape, and the camcorder will dub them in your chosen order to your VCR. The GR-AX200's flying erase head assists smooth recording stops and starts and edits. Unfortunately, it uses the standard low-fidelity, mono VHS sound system. An integral lens cover solves the problem of lost or dangling lens covers. An advantage of limited frills is slightly longer battery life.

Specifications: height, 6 7⁄10"; width, 11¼"; length, 9¾"; weight, 1⅘ lb. without tape and battery. **Warranty:** parts, 1 year; labor, 90 days.

Approx. retail price	**Approx. low price**
$800	**$600**

JVC GR-SZ9

Recommended

At its high price we can't call the JVC GR-SZ9 a Best Buy, but we recommend it for ample performance for the money. Complementing the superior resolution of the Super VHS-C format is a ⅓-inch, 570,000 pixel CCD, the highest pixel number in any consumer model. Hi-fi stereo audio, with the built-in high-quality stereo microphone, provides audio performance to match. A single switch selects three levels of use

Prices are accurate at time of printing but are subject to manufacturers' changes.

from simple point-and-shoot to fully customized operation. An interactive menu system allows you to program the camcorder to your preferences while minimizing the number of buttons. JVC provides dozens of different special effects, automatic exposure programs, and scene transitions such as fades and wipes. Only your own creativity limits the possibilities of this palm-sized studio. Digital enhancement extends the 10-power optical zoom to 100-power. Because of the high resolution of the CCD, this range is more usable than a similar range on many camcorders with digital zoom. The high resolution also improves the performance of the digital image stabilization. The stabilizer can discriminate to some degree between deliberate and unwanted panning and tilting. A one-finger zoom lever, textured coating on the grip, and a unified trigger and power switch reduce hand-induced jitter and unwanted motion. Since the low-light sensitivity of high-resolution CCDs is less than that of standard imagers, JVC uses a very fast f/1.2 lens, comparable to those found on SLR still cameras. This fast lens and low-noise video electronics give this model a 0.06-lux sensitivity in the slow-shutter mode. The automatic eight-segment random-assemble editing feature helps create polished home movies. You can mark eight segments of your video anywhere on the tape, and the camcorder will dub them in your chosen order to your VCR. The GR-SZ9's flying erase head assists smooth recording stops and starts and edits. An integral lens cover solves the problem of lost or dangling lens covers. JVC supplies a wireless remote control. This really is the camcorder that has it all, in a small, light package, yet at under $2,000.

Specifications: height, 6⁷⁄₁₀"; width, 11¼"; length, 9¾"; weight, 1⅘ lb. without tape and battery. **Warranty**: parts, 1 year; labor, 90 days.

Approx. retail price	**Approx. low price**
$1,900	**$1,900**

PANASONIC PV-D705

Recommended

The Panasonic PV-D705 represents the best non-S-VHS-C camcorder for the money, but its myriad features

Prices are accurate at time of printing but are subject to manufacturers' changes.

are reflected in its price, which removes it from Best Buy consideration. It combines a ⅓-inch, 470,000-pixel CCD with a 14-power optical zoom digitally rocketed to a 140-power zoom. The variable autofocus zoom speed increases in four increments, from 3.5 to 15 seconds and from wide to telephoto. Although it's doubtful you can make full use of the 140-power zoom, digital electronic image stabilization (DEIS) does stabilize lower magnifications. The automatic integral lens cover retracts when you turn on the camcorder. Besides using the same size video head drum used on its full-size home machines, Panasonic also gives the PV-D705 its premium metal heads found on its top-of-the-line home decks. This four-head VCR with flying erase head smoothly executes stops and starts and special fast- and slow-motion effects. The factory preset clock/calendar needs only to be told your time zone. It then automatically compensates for the switch between standard and daylight time. The PV-D705 requires a minimum illumination of 2 lux, but a built-in video enhancement light assures well surpassing that minimum. The camcorder offers the usual array of automatic exposure modes to suit various shooting conditions. While we normally find color viewfinders a problem, the 116,150-pixel, brightly lit color viewfinder on this model works better than most, providing a clear image visible on all but the brightest days. Panasonic employs the camcorder's digital circuitry to enhance and clean up the picture for very impressive-looking videos. Unfortunately, it lacks the hi-fi stereo audio to match. Some of the digital gimmicks available include a library of 500 titles, words, phrases, dates, and events, chosen through a menu and easily superimposed on your videos. You can also combine them to store up to ten customized messages. Digital circuitry enables a variety of wipes and fades. The recording indicator on the record button and the tally light reduce the chances of leaving the recorder accidentally recording. A self-diagnostic circuit can reduce repair costs by automatically indicating problems.

Specifications: height, 4⅝"; width, 4⅛"; length, 6⅞"; weight, 1⁹⁄₁₀ lb. without tape and battery. **Warranty:** parts, 1 year; labor, 90 days.

Approx. retail price **Approx. low price**
$1,299 **$1,161**

JVC GR-EZ1

Budget Buy

The VHS-C JVC GR-EZ1 looks as well as functions like a point-and-shoot camera. It uses an optical rather than an electronic viewfinder, which keeps the weight and price down. It automates all shooting decisions for ease of use. The QwikPix mode shoots five-second shots for fast-paced videos. To keep the size small, the GR-EZ1 comes with a limited 3-power zoom. A LCD status panel keeps you informed of settings and necessary warnings. The GR-EZ1 contains many of the convenience features of larger, more expensive models, such as a clock/calendar that can automatically record the date on your videos, instant reshoot, and a real-time tape counter. A flying erase head permits smooth recording stops, starts, and edits. A seek mode automatically locates where to start recording on the tape. This is a neat little camcorder that takes respectable videos at an affordable price. It's also small enough to take along everywhere, even in a purse or pocket. So although it doesn't perform some of the fancy tricks of its bigger, costlier brethren, it just might be used more often.

Specifications: height, 4¾"; width, 6⅝"; length, 2⅞"; weight, 1³⁄₁₀ lb. without tape and battery. **Warranty**: parts, 1 year; labor, 90 days.

Approx. retail price **Approx. low price**
$600 **$450**

FULL-SIZE VHS CAMCORDERS

PANASONIC PV-940

✓ BEST BUY

The Panasonic PV-940 full-size VHS camcorder addresses most of the awkwardness of the full-size format. The centrally positioned hand grip and the viewfinder that flips from one side to the other suits right-handers or lefties, thus earning the camcorder the nickname "Switch Hitter." Its slim width also makes this camcorder more manageable. Acknowl-

Prices are accurate at time of printing but are subject to manufacturers' changes.

edging that you won't dangle it from your neck like a compact model, Panasonic supplies an attaché-style carrying case. The PV-940's ⅓-inch, 270,000-pixel CCD coupled with a 14-power dual-speed zoom requires a minimum of 1-lux illumination. Fully automatic operation assures the best videos in most shooting situations. As with Panasonic's compact models, this camcorder's clock/calendar comes preset—all you have to do is switch it to your time zone. It then automatically switches between standard and daylight time on the correct days. The date and time will automatically be recorded on the tape if you desire. The bookmark search finds the end of the previous recording, eliminating gaps and overlaps before new recordings, even if you remove and reinsert a tape. A flying erase head eliminates glitches when you stop and start recording, which is particularly useful when editing.

Specifications: height, 8¼"; width, 3⅜"; length, 15"; weight, 4$\frac{1}{10}$ lb. without tape and battery. **Warranty**: parts, 1 year; labor, 90 days.

Approx. retail price	Approx. low price
$700	**$625**

MAGNAVOX CVT330AV

Recommended

The Magnavox CVT330AV presents a desirable combination of features at a modest price. A ⅓-inch CCD with 250,000 pixels coupled to a 12-power optical autofocus zoom, digitally boosted to 24-power, requires a minimum illumination of 1 lux. The clip-on video light supplied with the camcorder boosts light levels far above the minimum. The CVT330AV permits manual focusing for aspiring video artists. Since you support this model on your shoulder, your zooms will look pretty steady. This four-head camcorder includes a flying erase head for smooth special effects and transitions when you stop and start recording. For ease of use, the controls on the left side of the camcorder are arrayed in the same arc as your fingers. The electronic viewfinder tilts to further improve operating convenience. It displays a tape-remaining indicator. A two-line titler with built-in character generator can label your videos. You can also add the date and/or time to your videos from the clock/calendar. The camcorder will fade in from or out to black. Multiple shutter speeds, along with auto exposure and white balance, suit every shooting occasion. You must select indoor or outdoor before the auto circuits take over.

Specifications: height, 8⅒"; width, 3⅘"; length, 13⅘"; weight, 4⅗ lb. without tape and battery. **Warranty:** parts, 1 year; labor, 90 days.

Approx. retail price	**Approx. low price**
$700	**$600**

RCA CC414

Budget Buy

The RCA CC414 full-size VHS camcorder takes good videos with a minimum of fuss and frills. Its 12-power autofocus zoom coupled with a ¼-inch, 270,000-pixel CCD needs as little as 2 lux to record a picture. RCA fully automated the camcorder with programmed automatic exposure and automatic white balance for ease of use. It includes a two-page titler to record captions on your videos, and it will record the date and time on your videos if you choose. For convenience, the electronic viewfinder tilts and slides so you can position the camcorder more comfortably. Otherwise, this model is as basic as they come, omitting even a flying erase head. Its main advantage over similarly priced, but slightly fuller-featured, compact models is the ability to use the same VHS tapes as your home VCR does.

Specifications: height, 8⅛"; width, 4½"; length, 12¼"; weight, 4⅖ lb. without tape and battery. **Warranty:** parts, 1 year; labor, 90 days.

Approx. retail price	**Approx. low price**
$499	**$459**

Prices are accurate at time of printing but are subject to manufacturers' changes.

STEREO COMPONENTS

Today's audio and video components come tantalizingly close to recreating the movie theater experience in your home. Any good-quality TV with a 27-inch or larger screen, combined with a Dolby Pro Logic–equipped receiver and a quintet of speakers, can rival the local movie house in many ways. Most manufacturers now design components with home theater in mind. Many receivers control the video as well as the audio signal, and many companies sell packages of the five speakers that are necessary for Dolby Pro Logic Surround Sound. Pro Logic requires the standard left and right front channels, plus a center front channel and a pair of rear (or surround) channels. An optional subwoofer requiring a sixth channel of amplification adds realism to the lowest bass notes and special effects. A stereo hi-fi VCR and perhaps the ultimate video source, a laser disc player, complete the home theater system. These high-fidelity sources, plus stereo TV and digital stereo satellite broadcasts, warrant improved audio for video. The complete shift to CD (compact disc) and the arrival of digital recording systems such as DAT (digital audio tape), MD (MiniDisc), digital VHS, and soon-to-come digital video disc justify a good stereo component system more than ever.

Most audio components mate easily with TVs and VCRs that come equipped with stereo output jacks. Avoid placing speakers too close to the TV unless they were specifically designed for this kind of placement. The magnetic field of regular speakers can distort the TV picture.

Buying stereo components instead of a prepackaged or all-in-one system lets you upgrade your equipment at any time without discarding the entire system. It also accepts new technologies as they come along. If you cannot afford all the components you want, or the quality of components you desire, begin with a stereo receiver (the combination of an amplifier and tuner), a pair of speakers, and a budget CD player. They will provide a high-fidelity AM/FM stereo radio, play prerecorded music, and work with your TV and VCR as a basic home theater system. Later you can add a recording/reproducing system such as an analog cassette or one of the new digital recording systems. The major trends in stereo components today are the popularity of multi-disc CD changers and dual-transport cassette decks.

In 1993 DCC (digital compact cassette) and MD offered new digital alternatives for making high-quality recordings and playing prerecorded software. Although neither has been an overwhelming success in the marketplace, MD shows greater promise, as DCC has fallen by the wayside. MD uses a 2½-inch disc encased in a protective caddy similar to a 3½-inch computer diskette. MD records and plays up to 74 minutes. MD solves the portability problem that plagues the CD format by using memory chips that store ten seconds of sound, so that if you jar the player, the sound will continue without a glitch. The memory also permits nonsequential recording and editing of material on the disc, because the laser can skip around the disc while the sound continues uninterrupted. A limited number of MD titles are at major record stores, rather insignificant when compared with CD. Meanwhile, DAT, which has no prerecorded software, continues with modest success. DAT and MD recorders sell for as little as $500, with some portable players costing slightly less. While DAT sounds identical to CD, there are subtle differences between MD and CD. Most listeners, however, notice little difference between formats.

Over the past 25 years, technology has continuously raised the performance level of audio components while lowering the prices. When CD players were introduced in 1982, they cost $1,000. Now a better-sounding player than the first players can be had for about $150. Most receivers provide five channels of amplification with greater total power than the two-channel models of just a few years ago, and at the same price. When the dollar plummeted in value against the Japanese yen, Japanese companies managed to minimize price increases by increased automation and by manufacturing off-shore in cheaper-labor countries. Rather than raising prices, some companies eliminated features and/or kept models in the line for two years rather than one.

Best Buys '96

Our Best Buy, Recommended, and Budget Buy choices follow. Within each category, stereo components are listed by quality; the item we consider the best of the Best Buys is first, followed by our second choice, and so on. A Budget Buy describes a less-expensive product of respectable quality that perhaps sacrifices some of the performance and/or features of a Best Buy or Recommended product. Remember that a Best Buy, Recommended, or Budget Buy designation applies only to the model listed; it does not necessarily apply to other models made by the same manufacturer or to an entire product line.

LOUDSPEAKERS

Most music lovers consider loudspeakers to be the most important components in the stereo system. It might be advantageous to select your speakers first, because some require more power than others. This will influence your choice of a receiver. Speakers have much more effect on the personality of the system than the electronics do. They are also the most subjective components in a stereo system. Thus the advice of friends, magazine reviews, and the recommendations here should serve only as a starting point. Take great care in choosing them by spending ample time listening.

More than 360 speaker companies flood the market with multiple models. Discerning the sonic differences between two electronic components often requires intense concentration, but the difference between similarly priced speakers comes through loud and clear. Insist on the right to return speakers that fail to meet your expectations. Speakers dramatically interact with room acoustics. What sounds splendid in the store may sound tinny or muddy in your home. The size of the speaker enclosure and the number of individual speakers inside it (woofers, tweeters, and mid-range speakers) do not always correlate with the sound quality. We base our speaker ratings on the quality of construction, reputation, and listening tests.

Features and Terminology

Power requirements: Different speakers apply different laws of physics to produce sound. High-efficiency ported systems—also known as ducted or reflex systems—are the most common among larger speakers. They take advantage of the resonance of the port, allowing the air inside the speaker to move in and out, acoustically amplifying the bass frequencies. Ported speakers use the amplifier of the receiver's power efficiently and require modest power to produce ample sound levels. Low-efficiency acoustic-suspension speakers, sometimes referred to as air-suspension speakers, are most common among bookshelf-size speakers. They seal the enclosure tightly and force the speaker to fight the air within. In a well-designed system, this results in good, tightly controlled bass. Large floor-standing speakers can produce throbbing levels with 24 watts of power, whereas compact bookshelf models require twice that much power.

Too much power can damage speakers, but speaker ratings and amplifier ratings do not always match. Speakers rated at 100 watts maximum may be powered safely by 300-watt amplifiers, but if you force all 300 watts into the speaker, the sound would cause you pain as well as damage the speakers.

Speaker impedance: Speaker impedances are commonly listed from 4 to 8 ohms, with some ranging from 2 to 16 ohms. This is a technical description of the amount of resistance the speaker offers to the flow of electrical signals. Under normal circumstances, impedance makes little difference to sound quality, but many receivers need a minimum of 4 ohms to work properly. A good receiver may work with 2 ohms, but other receivers will automatically shut off or blow a fuse. A 2-ohm load can actually destroy a poorly designed receiver. If you intend to use two pairs of speakers, choose loudspeakers rated at 8 ohms.

Woofers, tweeters, and other speaker elements: The woofer is the largest speaker component. It reproduces bass notes and often the lower mid-range sounds as well. The tweeter is the smallest component and reproduces higher sounds. Some speakers include a mid-range speaker component that reproduces the range of sound between the woofer and the tweeter—the range of the human voice. The point where the dynamic range of an individual speaker component starts and finishes varies from one speaker to another.

The crossover network is a series of resistors, capacitors, and coils that divide the incoming frequencies from the receiver, ensuring that the bass goes to the woofer and the treble to the tweeter. These individual speaker components are "drivers." You cannot tell the actual quality of a speaker just by considering the size of the driver and the material from which it is manufactured. An 8-inch woofer sometimes reproduces more bass than a 12-inch woofer, and paper surpasses some plastics in the quality of the speaker cone.

Home theater speakers: Five or six speakers are placed appropriately in the room for home theater. You can enjoy fairly small speakers when you include a subwoofer in the system to reproduce the deep bass. It's best to buy the entire theater-system speakers from one manufacturer. Ideally, the front three speakers should be a matched set and should be timbre-matched (each having the same sonic "color" and tonal balance) to the surround speakers, which can be smaller. One quick way to determine if the speakers are timbre-matched is to listen to the applause on a CD or music video recorded live in concert. No one speaker should draw attention to itself with a different sound quality.

B&W CDM 2

BEST BUY

The B&W CDM 2 bookshelf speakers pack a punch from their small package. These high-tech speakers incorporate advances originally pioneered in B&W's expensive 800 series but at a much lower price. For example, the 6½-inch mid-range/woofer on this two-way system uses a Kevlar cone. Kevlar radiates sound waves with near-ideal stiffness for accuracy and low distortion. Similarly, the 1-inch tweeter uses a metal alloy formulated for accurate high-frequency reproduction without coloring the sound. Removing the stylish contoured grille, with its acoustically beneficial shape, reveals an unusually well finished front baffle demonstrating conscientious workmanship. B&W surrounds the tweeter with eccentric diffraction rings that reduce the effect of the baffle on the high frequencies. This produces cleaner, more accurate sound. The gently beveled front baffle edges also reduce unwanted reflections from the speaker enclosure itself. Lifting the surprisingly heavy CDM 2 speakers quickly convinces you that these are no ordinary small speakers. The enclosure, covered in real wood veneer in black or red ash, is very dense. This nonresonant design reduces vibrations of the box, which muddy the sound. The quality of the sound, with substantial bass, clarity, and naturalness of voices, makes the speakers' small size almost irrelevant. You will need at least 30 watts per channel of amplifier power. The CDM 2 can be placed on a shelf or on a stand. Gold-plated five-way binding posts simplify connections. These speakers are ideal for uncompromised sound in tight places for people whose budget is between modest and lavish.

Specifications: height, 12¼"; width, 8⅝"; depth, 9½"; weight, 16 lb. each. **Warranty:** parts and labor, 5 years.

Approx. retail price
$800/pair

Approx. low price
$800/pair

POLK AUDIO RT7

✓BEST BUY

The Polk RT7 bookshelf loudspeaker increases versatility over previous Polk models while maintaining an impressively accurate sound. As with other recent new speaker models, Polk upgrades technology while maintaining the price of the previous model. This new RT model employs Polk's Dynamic Balance drivers, which in this two-way system are a 1-inch dome tweeter and a 7½-inch woofer. The high-tech tweeter has stainless steel and aluminum vapors on top of its polyamide dome. Combining materials of dissimilar characteristics cancels resonances. The speaker uses dual ports for improved bass and reduction in air noise. Low-diffraction grilles aid in imaging. Five-way binding posts on the rear simplify connection to other components. One-inch-thick baffles resist sound-muddying vibrations, and the cabinets come finished in black or oak woodgrain vinyl. The RT7 is magnetically shielded so that it can be used close to a video source. Polk collaborated with Johns Hopkins University in acoustical research in designing advanced speakers, and the RT7 represents the second generation of this project. The sound is clear and well-balanced, with good vocal reproduction and stereo image. The RT7 works well for both audio-only systems and home theater systems.

Specifications: height, 19″; width, 9½″; depth, 11½″; shipping weight, 27 lb./pair. **Warranty:** parts and labor, 5 years.

Approx. retail price
$399/pair

Approx. low price
$399/pair

ADVENT LEGACY III

✔ BEST BUY

The floor-standing Advent Legacy III speakers form a large two-way system wrapped in black textured vinyl and grille cloth with real pecan-wood tops and bottoms. Inside each speaker are a 1-inch fluid-cooled soft-dome tweeter and a 10-inch dual voice coil woofer. The dual voice coil offers a choice of impedance from 6 to 8 ohms to improve performance if you decide to power more than one pair of these speakers from your receiver/amplifier. The warm sound of the Legacy III bears some resemblance to the original Advent speakers, with little coloration and a solidity of sound. These speakers magnificently reproduce drums without compromising voices or string instruments. They re-create a good stereo image. These speakers sound comparable to models costing $600.

Specifications: height, 32⅛″; width, 14″; depth, 10½″; weight, 42 lb./pair. **Warranty:** parts and labor, 5 years.

Approx. retail price
$450/pair

Approx. low price
$336/pair

Prices are accurate at time of printing but are subject to manufacturers' changes.

ROCK SOLID SOUNDS SOLID MONITOR

BEST BUY

The Rock Solids, produced by a new division of England's B&W and made in Taiwan, hew true to their parentage. The unconventional speakers sound remarkable. Straight-sided and rounded on the ends, the ported plastic enclosure is available in a variety of colors. Inside is a 5-inch woofer and 1-inch dome tweeter. Since the unusual shape makes it difficult for the speaker to stand on its own, Rock Solid Sounds designed an integral stand connected to the enclosure in the rear with a ball joint. Thus the stand also serves as a wall-mounting bracket and moves to a number of other positions. The magnetically shielded Solid Monitors can be used in close proximity to TV sets and with computers. They come with professional-quality binding posts for easy connections. Their small size limits deep bass, but what bass there is sounds full and natural. An optional subwoofer provides the "boom." Their sensitivity makes good use of modest power. Arrestingly real vocal reproduction, smooth sound, and superb stereo imaging make the Solid Monitor the compact speaker to buy.

Specifications: height, 9½"; width, 6⅖"; depth, $5\frac{9}{10}$"; weight, 10 lb./pair. **Warranty:** parts and labor, 5 years.

Approx. retail price
$299/pair

Approx. low price
$297/pair

NHT 1.1

BEST BUY

The NHT 1.1 represents the descendent of this company's first product, and various refinements during the past several years keep it one of the best-sounding speakers in its price range. NHT (which stands for Now Hear This) is the audiophile/specialty audio division of speaker giant International Jensen, giving it Jensen's research funds and wide distribution. This unconventionally attractive, nonrectangular small bookshelf speaker has an angled front baffle that's responsible for its distinctive appearance. The 6½-inch woofer and 1-inch dome tweeter produce a smooth, natural sound with good bass for such a small box. (A matching subwoofer is available for deep bass.) The NHT 1.1 comes finished in real oak veneer, although other finishes are available. The stereo image is lifelike. The speakers come magnetically shielded, making them an ideal choice for a high-quality video system. NHT also offers them as a part of a complete home theater package.

Specifications: height, 12"; width, 7"; depth, 10"; weight, 12 lb. each. **Warranty:** parts and labor, 5 years.

Approx. retail price
$380/pair

Approx. low price
$343/pair

DCM CX-17

Recommended

The DCM CX-17 continues the DCM tradition of using a less common "transmission line" enclosure but in a small speaker. The transmission line extends bass and reduces distortion by tightly controlling the movement of the woofer. It increases the amount of power the speaker will handle while keeping its sensitivity relatively high. The high-tech polypropylene 6½-inch woofer with a rubber surround delivers full, accurate bass. DCM mounts the ¾-inch dome inside the woofer, which improves the stereo image, since all the sound seems to come from a single point. Special padding on the baffle around the woofer reduces diffraction for a more coherent sound. Although these speakers handle large amounts of power, DCM provides an electronic protection circuit. The CX-17 is magnetically shielded for use in video systems.

Specifications: height, 17"; width, 9"; depth, 10"; weight, 30 lb./pair. **Warranty:** parts and labor, 5 years.

Approx. retail price
$369/pair

Approx. low price
$293/pair

BOSTON ACOUSTICS CR6

Budget Buy

The price of the Boston Acoustics CR6 loudspeakers has increased over the preceding model, but so has the performance. This entry-level model of the Boston Acoustic Compact Reference Series represents a big step forward in budget-priced speakers. Boston Acoustics redesigned the 1¾-inch tweeter's Kortec dome, spinning and weaving the silky fabric and then saturating it with a proprietary stiffening chemical. Boston Acoustics mounts the tweeter very close to the 5¼-inch woofer for a cohesive point-source sound. A redesigned port reduces the possibility of noise from the air moving in and out of the enclosure. The sculpted front panel reduces undesirable diffraction. The magnetically shielded CR6 can be used close to a TV or video monitor. The back of the cabinet even contains a keyhole for wall hanging, and Boston Acoustics offers optional wall brackets. This facilitates using the CR6 for front or surround channels in a home theater system. The CR6 is a very versatile small speaker that delivers sufficient sound for modest money. Boston Acoustics earned its respected reputation building budget speakers, and while the CR6 may not look extravagant, you will probably find its sound quite satisfying.

Specifications: height, 10⅛"; width, 5⅞"; depth, 7⅞"; weight, 7½ lb. **Warranty:** parts and labor, 5 years, limited.

Approx. retail price	Approx. low price
$200/pair	$199/pair

HOME THEATER SPEAKERS

ATLANTIC TECHNOLOGIES SYSTEM 250 ✓BEST BUY

The Atlantic Technologies System 250 was conceived as a complete home theater speaker system rather than just an assemblage of off-the-shelf parts. The six-piece system includes three front-channel speakers, two surround speakers, and a subwoofer. The 251 front left and right speakers and the 253C center speaker are timbre-matched, although the tonal balances of the center speaker can be adjusted for position relative to the TV screen. The speakers are reasonably compact with small baffle areas for flexible placement. The surround speakers are dipoles, which means they radiate in two directions. When the speakers are properly placed, this enhances realism. The fairly low-profile enclosure enhances positioning flexibility. The 252 PBM subwoofer includes its own internal 90-watt amplifier, since most Surround Sound receivers lack an amplified subwoofer channel. When used with a good Surround

Prices are accurate at time of printing but are subject to manufacturers' changes.

Sound receiver and properly installed, the System 250 reproduces smashing movie sound, better than that of many movie theaters. We like the well-conceived nature of the system. The individual parts may be purchased separately, but it's the system that scores high marks.

Warranty: parts and labor, 2 years.

Approx. retail price	Approx. low price
$1,446	$1,350

CERWIN-VEGA SENSURROUND SYSTEM 6

Budget Buy

Cerwin-Vega, best known for providing the most boom for the buck, succeeds admirably with its System 6. Movie sound tracks are most appropriate for systems with pronounced bass, and Cerwin-Vega providés the Sensurround system for movie theaters. Fortunately, Cerwin-Vega doesn't submerge the dialog in the bone-shaking bass. The System 6 contains the six standard surround components: left, right, and center front channels, two surround channels, and a subwoofer. The system saves money by using plain black woodgrain-vinyl-finished enclosures without many frills. The identical front left and right and surround speakers use 5-inch woofers and 1-inch dome tweeters. An electronic circuit protects the tweeters from overload. The subwoofer uses a 10-inch woofer. This is an ideal system for use with a modestly priced Dolby Pro Logic receiver.

Warranty: 5 years, limited.

Approx. retail price	Approx. low price
$1,225	$990

HEADPHONES

Like speakers, headphones are best judged according to how they sound. But unlike speakers, headphones are unaffected by room acoustics, and their sound quality needs to please no one but their owner. The general criteria for good headphone performance include a full bass response with accurate tonal definition and balance from the mid-range frequencies up to the highest frequencies.

A headset must also be comfortable. Weight and fit should be considered carefully. There are three basic designs for headphones. **Circumaural phones** cover your entire outer ear and block out all external sound. **Supra-aural** phones do not completely block out external sound. **Open-air** phones rest lightly against the outer ear and usually have a foam pad that separates the actual phone from your head. This allows almost all outside sounds to be heard while wearing them.

As a general rule, circumaural phones provide the best bass, whereas open-air phones usually provide the least bass. Another style of headphones inserts directly into the ear. These tend to be difficult to keep in the ear and are often uncomfortable. They also tend to have less fidelity than other headphones.

SONY MDR-65

BEST BUY

The lightweight, open-air-design Sony MDR-65 stereo headphones rest comfortably on the ear with their soft ear pads on gimbal-mounted ear cups. The wide molded headband with its gentle cushion further adds to the comfort of these 2.5-ounce phones that feel like they're floating on your head. When it comes to sound, however, the MDR-65 is a heavyweight, with full, well-balanced sound from mid-sized diaphragms using powerful neodymium magnets. For convenience, a sturdy, nearly 7-foot-long, single cord (rather than the cumbersome yoke design) connects the phones to your stereo. That stereo can be either a personal one or home components. The gold-plated miniplug comes with a screw-on adapter for standard ¼-inch jacks.

Warranty: parts, one year; labor, 90 days.

Approx. retail price	**Approx. low price**
$40	**$36**

KOSS PRO/4XTC

BEST BUY

The Koss PRO/4XTC stereo headphones depart noticeably from traditional Koss PRO/4 designs. At 10 ounces

Prices are accurate at time of printing but are subject to manufacturers' changes.

without the cord, they are lighter in weight, and they surround rather than clamp the ears. Instead of sealing out all external sound, the comfortable fabric cushions permit some sound to enter and escape. A well-padded headband and multi-swivel ear cups make the XTC extremely comfortable. These headphones sound as comfortable as they feel. A neodymium magnet reduces weight while increasing the power of the magnetic field, for higher performance. Besides reproducing ample bass, they bring out crisp, clear treble without irritating emphasis. The slightly depressed mid-range frequencies do not muddy or obscure vocals. The sensitivity of the phones makes them suitable for many headphone stereos. A lightweight, 10-foot coiled cord tethers the XTC phones to your stereo. The cord ends in a right-angle, gold-plated miniplug with an integral snap-on, gold-plated, full-size ¼-inch adapter plug for regular stereo components. In reducing weight and bulk, Koss also made the XTC a little more fragile than the old PRO/4 design. This should cause little concern, since Koss is the rare company offering a lifetime warranty, with free repairs or replacement for shipping costs.

Warranty: parts and labor, lifetime limited warranty.

Approx. retail price
$80

Approx. low price
$80

AUDIO-TECHNICA ATH-P9

Recommended

The minimal sound leakage from the backs of the open-air Audio-Technica ATH-P9 belies the good sound within. The ATH-P9 falls between full-size and personal-size phones but weighs a scant 5.1 ounces without its 8-foot cord. Woven cloth cushions rest on the ear, held in place by a springy wide plastic headband with padding at its center. While the ear cups lack any suspension, the headband twists freely, further aiding a comfortable fit. The larger ear cup aids in fuller sound with deeper bass, which is augmented by the use of neodymium magnets. These phones serve nicely for computers and keyboards in addition to personal stereos and stereo components. Their main drawback is the Y-shaped yoke cord from each ear cup, which we find cumbersome. The gold-plated miniplug at the end of the cord comes with a snap-on standard ¼-inch adapter for home components.

Warranty: parts and labor, 1 year, limited.

Approx. retail price	**Approx. low price**
$60	**$53**

AUDIO-TECHNICA ATH-P5

Budget Buy

The Audio-Technica ATH-P5 open-air phones sound great. They're fairly large for personal-size headphones, permitting a good-size diaphragm with neodymium magnets. Their foam cushions rest comfortably on the ear. The plastic headband is just wide enough and springy enough to avoid excessive pressure on your scalp. At 2.5 ounces without the cord, the ATH-P5 seems to virtually hover on your head. Unfortunately, not only do they come with an awkward Y-shaped yoke-style cord, but at only a bit over a yard long, it's too short. So even though A-T supplies a snap-on adapter for use with home gear, the cord is probably too short to take advantage of the adapter. That's the only thing that separates these terrific-sounding phones from a Best Buy.

Warranty: parts and labor, 1 year, limited.

Approx. retail price	**Approx. low price**
$30	**$23**

STEREO RECEIVERS

A receiver combines a radio tuner with a control center and power amplifiers in a single package forming a well-matched system. Most receivers also include a preamplifier (preamp) for phonograph cartridges to play analog records, although some have dispensed with this circuit in this digital age. Through the control center, you select among inputs from other components and adjust volume, balance, and tone. The tone control circuits remain as a vestige of the preamp function. Finally, the amplifiers boost the audio signal to power the loudspeakers.

Traditionally, receivers contained a pair of power amplifiers for the two stereo channels. Home theater systems now require four, five, or six channels of amplification. (On some receivers a single channel powers both of the surround speakers.) All but the most basic models include these extra channels. Premium two-channel receivers are becoming an endangered species.

For optimum effect, the power of each of the three front channels must be the same, and the rear channels should each have at least a quarter of the front-channel power. We suggest they have a third to half of front-channel power.

Video producers encode the surround channels on stereo hi-fi videotapes and laser discs. Surround Sound processors also can extract ambience from many music LPs and CDs, which pleasantly enhances their sound. Dolby Labs, the company that set the standard for noise reduction, also dictates Surround Sound decoding from video. Originally the system required four channels, but Dolby improved it with a front center channel for dialogue reproduction from videos. This keeps the dialogue centered on your TV screen for greater realism. Dolby calls its five-channel system Pro Logic, and including it adds $10 to $20 to the cost of a receiver. In 1996 Dolby will introduce a dramatically improved digital Surround Sound system called AC-3. Some very high-end receivers will also include this feature.

Features and Terminology

Here are some of the terms that you should know before you purchase a receiver.

Power output is stated in watts. Be sure that the wattage applies to each channel and not to the sum of both stereo channels. Most amplifiers deliver higher power when hooked up to 4-ohm speakers than they do when they are driving 8-ohm speakers. When you compare power outputs, make sure that they refer to the same speaker impedances.

Stereo separation is the amount of separation between the left and right channels (or the difference between them). Separation figures vary between sources. Phonograph cartridges provide only 30 decibels (dB) of separation, whereas CD players often claim 90 dB of separation. The amplifier section of the receiver should have a channel of separation of at least 90 dB, and the tuner sections should be more than 30 dB.

Frequency response should be uniform, or "flat," over the entire range of human hearing, from 20 to 20,000 hertz.

Sensitivity is usually stated in microvolts or dBf. Excellent sensitivity figures of 2.0 microvolts or 10 to 12 dBf are typical. Sensitivity concerns you if you are attempting to receive weak radio stations or live in a fringe area.

Selectivity is the ability of a tuner to pick up and isolate stations that are close in frequency to each other. It is quoted in dB; the higher the number the better. Look for at least 60 dB.

Signal-to-noise ratio (S/N) is a measure of how much background noise is present compared with the desired signal. S/N is stated in decibels (dB); the higher the number the better. The stereo FM tuner S/N on a receiver should be about 75 dB; for CD the S/N should be over 100 dB.

Quieting (in dB, decibels) is the amount of signal that is needed at the antenna terminals to provide noise-free, acceptable reception. The lower the number, stated in microvolts (millionths of a volt) or dBf (femtowatts), the better.

Tape monitor (loop) is a set of output and input jacks that allow you to interpose an external audio component in the signal path of an amplifier to monitor recordings as you make them or to process the signal through a device, such as a graphic equalizer.

Two-channel Stereo Receivers

SONY STR-D365

✓ BEST BUY

The STR-D365 shows that Sony has perfected offering value in a low-priced stereo receiver. This two-channel model produces 100 watts per channel. To keep sound quality

Prices are accurate at time of printing but are subject to manufacturers' changes.

high, Sony uses discrete output transistors rather than integrated circuits and even powers the blue fluorescent display separately from the audio section. Although Sony designed the STR-D365 as the centerpiece of an audio system, it does contain a pair of inputs for the audio from video sources. For lovers of LPs, this receiver still includes a phono input. There are a total of six inputs, with facilities for two tape decks. The quality, digitally synthesized tuner in this model matches in most respects the tuner in Sony's more expensive receivers. The STR-D365 makes tuning easy with direct-access tuning. Simply tap in the radio station's frequency on the line of numbered keys below the display or on the numeric keypad of the supplied wireless remote control. Direct access makes setting the 30 possible station presets quick work. The STR-D365 is elegant in its simplicity.

Warranty: parts and labor, 1 year.

Approx. retail price
$250

Approx. low price
$199

ONKYO TX-V940

BEST BUY

Onkyo rates the TX-V940 receiver at 100 watts per channel, but it delivers far more power on musical peaks. It also gracefully powers low-impedance speakers. Onkyo accomplishes this with an oversized power supply in conjunction with high-current discrete output transistors. The digitally synthesized tuner uses Onkyo's automatic precision reception to adjust reception settings for best sound. The tuner's 40 station presets can be divided into six categories, such as rock, jazz, or classical. You can then select and scan each category. Should the power fail, the TX-V940 needs no battery to retain its memory. Direct-access tuning lets you key in the desired station frequency by number. A nice bonus is a sleep timer that automatically shuts off the unit after a set amount of time. The tone controls are more precise than on many receivers and are designed for the way your perception of high and low frequencies varies at different volumes. Onkyo limits the bass boost to the deep bass so as not to muddy the mid-range. The V in the model number means this receiver switches audio and video, with six audio inputs and two video inputs. The TX-V940 comes with a wireless remote control.

Warranty: parts and labor, 2 years.

Approx. retail price $340

Approx. low price $278

YAMAHA RX-595

Recommended

Yamaha improved the RX-595 two-channel, 80-watt-per-channel stereo receiver over last year's model—including boosting its power—without increasing the price. Knobs to adjust most functions grace the rounded front panel. Only tuning the radio requires using buttons. If you really prefer buttons, they are on the supplied wireless remote control. You can select 40 station presets on the excellent tuner section, or the receiver will scan the dial and preset the 40 most powerful stations for you. This tuner is particularly good at separating stations on the crowded FM dial. The amplifier section uses Yamaha's newest approach to amplifier design, which keeps the distances between and within circuits short to reduce noise. For optimum performance, the output uses discrete transistors rather than integrated circuits. The amplifier maintains tight control over the loudspeakers over the entire frequency range—a benefit not engineered into all receivers. This receiver can power virtually any loudspeaker without overheating or added distortion. Pressing a front-panel button bypasses all intermediate circuits before the power amplifier for utmost clarity in the Pure Direct mode. A CD Direct mode provides exceptional signal-to-noise ratio for CD listening. However, the RX-595 retains a phono input for LP lovers. Two of the six inputs accept the audio from video sources. You can record one program while listening to another. We place this receiver in the Recommended category because of its substantial price for its moderate wattage.

Warranty: 2 years, limited.

Approx. retail price $399

Approx. low price $362

TECHNICS SA-GX190

Budget Buy

The Technics SA-GX190 100-watt-per-channel stereo receiver uses the same circuitry as the company's more expensive multichannel surround-sound models. This model acks only minor refinements in sound quality to make it a Best Buy. The SA-GX190 contains Technics' proprietary, efficient Class H+ amplifier circuitry. This provides high power only when necessary, such as on musical peaks from CDs, thus reducing size and cost. The SA-GX190 contains most of the features of more expensive stereo receivers. It has four audio inputs plus an input for the audio from a video source. You can preset 30 stations on the digitally synthesized tuner. Technics makes uning easy with direct access from the keypad and supplies a remote control. You can read the clear, large multifunction display from across the room. The same display also helps eliminate operating mistakes, by alerting you to improper settings. All in all the SA-GX190 provides surprising value for the money.

Warranty: parts and labor, 1 year.

Approx. retail price	**Approx. low price**
$210	**$178**

Multichannel Home Theater Receivers

TECHNICS SA-GX490

✓ BEST BUY

With the Technics SA-GX490, you'll get all the eceiver you need to build a home theater without paying for superfluous features. It produces a solid 80 watts apiece for the hree front channels and 40 watts each for the surround channels. In stereo that increases to 100 watts for each of the two channels. That's enough for a satisfying theater experience, especially with the low distortion from Technics' proprietary Class H+ amplifier circuitry. Class H+ reduces distortion on oud peaks and makes the amplifier circuitry more efficient. The ront-panel LED display shows not only the usual information—source, preset number, and radio frequency—but also a unique "help" function that indicates when you attempt im-

Prices are accurate at time of printing but are subject to manufacturers' changes.

proper operation or forget where you've set the controls. Pushing the "help" button for three seconds returns all settings to normal and selects the FM radio. The SA-GX490 handles four audio sources and two audio/video sources. To optimize home theater use, it includes a Dolby Pro Logic test mode, independent center and rear level controls, and other desirable options. You can preset 30 stations on the digitally synthesized tuner, with direct access making the process easier. Technics supplies a 37-key universal remote control. The step-up models utilize the same basic circuit design, but they supply a few more watts of power and display settings on your TV screen.

Warranty: parts and labor, 1 year.

Approx. retail price	**Approx. low price**
$400	**$284**

ONKYO TX-SV727DSP

✓BEST BUY

The Onkyo TX-SV727DSP breaks new ground among home theater receivers by employing a custom-designed Motorola digital signal processing (DSP) chip. This DSP chip digitally processes the Dolby Pro Logic Surround Sound, as well as digitally synthesizing four acoustic environments—hall, live, and arena, plus a special setting called Pro Logic Theater. Signal processing digitally accomplishes these tasks more effectively and accurately without adding to cost. The TX-SV727DSP produces 80 watts each for the three front channels and 25 watts each for the surround channels. In stereo, each of the two front channels produces 100 watts. Most important, the conservatively designed amplifiers can drive virtually any speaker without endangering either the amplifiers or speakers. Even the massive multiway speaker binding posts instill confidence and provide convenience. The latter attribute is the key to the TX-SV727DSP. Its easy operation makes home theater a pleasure. For example, when you turn on your TV, Onkyo's Intelligent Power Management System switches on the receiver and selects Video 1. The most important area of the programmable universal remote control glows so you can see which key you're pressing, especially useful with the lights dimmed while watch-

Prices are accurate at time of printing but are subject to manufacturers' changes.

ing videos. This receiver also has multiroom and multisource capability, allowing it to serve as the center of a multiroom entertainment system. Multisource also allows taping one source while listening to another, or listening to different sources in different rooms. There are 30 radio station presets that you can organize into three groups that you name. In addition to the four audio/video inputs and six audio inputs, front-panel jacks simplify connecting a camcorder. The TX-SV727DSP will even lull you to sleep with its sleep timer.

Warranty: parts and labor, 2 years.

Approx. retail price	**Approx. low price**
$750	**$633**

SONY STR-D865

BEST BUY

Sony designed the STR-D865 as a true audio/video control center. Even the fluorescent display can be programmed to show not merely the input, such as Video 1, but precisely what you connected to that input. The title can be generic, such as "VCR," or a brand or model number. Considering this receiver has five audio and four audio/video inputs, the display really helps. We really commend this versatility. You can use the same feature to name radio stations. The three front channels of this receiver each produce 100 watts, and the power is the same for each of the two stereo channels. The surround channels each produce 25 watts. Digital signal processing (DSP) synthesizes five acoustic environments: hall, theater, game, stadium, and acoustic. You can then program a sound field to match a source—for example, whenever you select CD, the sound field would switch to hall. The STR-D865 incorporates the same excellent frequency-synthesized AM/FM stereo tuner that has traditionally graced Sony receivers, with good FM sensitivity and very low noise. You can preset 30 radio stations, index them, and then scan only the desired indexes. The 10-key direct access tuning makes selecting stations by frequency quick and easy, or you can scan up and down the dial. To maintain low noise, Sony powers the fluorescent display separately from the rest of this receiver. Auto input balance and automatic sequential test tones simplify Dolby Pro Logic Surround Sound setup. Sony supplies a universal audio/video remote control.

Warranty: parts and labor, 2 years.

Approx. retail price	**Approx. low price**
$450	$330

YAMAHA RX-V490

Recommended

The Yamaha RX-V490 multichannel home theater receiver delivers very good sound, but its modest wattage and limited discounting at retail drop it from Best Buy to Recommended status. The RX-V490 supplies 70 watts to each of the front channels and 15 watts to each of the surround channels. However, these are "honest" watts that will drive most speakers likely to be teamed with this receiver. It does a good job of taming difficult speakers and making them produce their best sound. In addition to Dolby Pro Logic, Yamaha includes its own surround-sound Cinema DSP for a more theaterlike effect. The digital signal processing circuitry also emulates concert hall, rock concert, mono movie, and concert video environments. The RX-V490 incorporates the same outstanding AM/FM stereo tuner that's in Yamaha's more expensive models. You can preset 40 stations, or the receiver will automatically preset stations for you. The receiver comes with four audio inputs and two audio/video inputs. For proper Pro Logic balances, you can adjust the center and surround output levels. Yamaha supplies a remote control capable of operating other Yamaha components.

Warranty: parts and labor, 2 years, limited.

Approx. retail price	**Approx. low price**
$399	$329

JVC RX-717VTN

Recommended

We find the user interface particularly pleasing, with its use of large knobs, on the JVC RX-717VTN multichannel home theater receiver. It uses a jog-dial knob for radio tuning, probably the most natural method on any receiver since tuning knobs disappeared. You can preset 40 radio stations on the good-quality tuner and display the station name for 20 of them. The JVC RX-717VTN produces 105 watts per channel for each of the three front channels and 20 watts for each of the surround channels. We would prefer the surround channels to have slightly more power, considering the high front power. In addition to Dolby Pro Logic, JVC synthesizes a hall surround environment. A flexible equalizer electronically customizes tonal balances with 25 preset equalizations. The manual center tone control is desirable for optimizing dialogue reproduction on videos if you use unmatched speakers or if the video has a muddy soundtrack. The amber fluorescent display shows a moving graph of different sound frequencies, which helps in using the equalizer. The RX-717VTN comes with five audio and two audio/video inputs. JVC supplies a specially designed, ergonomic remote control, shaped to fit the hand and allowing the most frequently used controls to be operated with your thumb.

Warranty: parts and carry-in labor, 2 years.

Approx. retail price
$500

Approx. low price
$335

SHERWOOD RV-4050R

Budget Buy

The Sherwood RV-4050R multi-channel home theater receiver offers good value for money, although we think it may be slightly less reliable than the Technics above. However, it does offer several additional features such as front-panel audio/video inputs for a camcorder, and it has four audio inputs and two audio/video inputs. The RV-4050R produces 50 watts for each of the three front channels and 10 watts for each of the rear channels. The same large knob on the front panel controls volume, balance, and tone, depending on which key you press—an operational novelty. This results in a blissfully uncluttered front panel. The receiver includes all the necessary features and adjustments, including test tone and auto input balance for the Dolby Pro Logic circuits. The good AM/FM stereo tuner has 30 station presets. You

Prices are accurate at time of printing but are subject to manufacturers' changes.

can doze off by setting the receiver's sleep timer. Sherwood supplies a universal remote control.

Warranty: parts and labor, 2 years, limited.

Approx. retail price	**Approx. low price**
$400	**$222**

COMPACT DISC PLAYERS

During the past few years, CD changers have rapidly increased in popularity. The three-, five-, and six-disc carousel models allow you to easily add discs to and remove discs from a large platter, even as one disc plays. This style ideally suits most home situations. The magazine or cartridge changer holds six or ten discs, depending upon the manufacturer, and is most commonly used in automobiles. People with car CD changers benefit from being able to use the same magazine at home or on the road, providing their car changer is compatible with their home changer. The newest trend couples multiple magazines, or jukebox-style individual slots, for changers with 100 discs or more. Unfortunately the magazines are not standardized between manufacturers. In the meantime, the single-disc player becomes increasingly rare, except in the expensive audiophile category.

CD Programmability

CD players differ noticeably in programming capabilities. Programming is a machine's ability to store instructions in its electronic memory and execute them on command.

CDs are divided into tracks. A disc that offers a dozen songs will have 12 tracks, numbered 1 through 12. For classical music, such as a symphony, track numbers denote movements. For added convenience, some CDs further divide selections into index numbers within a given track. For example, index numbers in an opera recording can help you locate your favorite arias.

A programmable CD player can, at the very least, play specific tracks in ascending sequence, while many players also let you program the order in which the tracks will be heard. Some let you specify the tracks you don't want to hear, like telling the sandwich shop to hold the mayonnaise. A few CD players also let you program index numbers. Most machines can store at least a score of instructions in memory; others accept 32 or more.

Most CD players also offer repeat play. Pressing a button plays the disc, selected track, or sometimes even a selected portion of a track until you cancel the command. Most machines will also randomly shuffle the order in which they play tracks. A few players feature permament programming memories of your favorite tracks on a disc. Players with this feature can store a few hundred selections.

Features and Terminology

AAD to DDD: For the first decade of CDs, record companies displayed a code indicating the source of the program material. The letter A stands for an analog source, the letter D stands for digital. The first letter indicates the nature of the original tape. The second letter reveals how the original recording was processed and mixed. The final letter, basically superfluous, confirms the digital nature of the CD. In 1992 record companies began phasing out this code because many recordings go through so many steps that the code became increasingly irrelevant. Virtually all record companies still indicate if the original recording was an analog master.

Digital-to-analog (D/A) converters: These are integrated circuit chips that translate digital numbers back into an analog form. The CD uses 16 bits, meaning that all discs contain blocks of 16-bit information. However, manufacturers encountered great difficulty in producing large quantities of highly accurate 16-bit D/A chips. Thus, some use 18- and 20-bit chips to retrieve information from the disc. They cannot retrieve additional sound, but they do offer a greater margin of error from improved accuracy in the decoding process. A bad 20-bit converter is not always better than a good 16-bit converter.

Engineers developed an alternative to the multibit converters. The 1-bit system, sometimes known by one of its trade names, Bitstream, converts digital information to analog in a rapid stream of single bits. Each company proclaims a proprietary version of this technology, such as MASH, P.E.M., or PWM, along with a number-crunching technique called noise shaping, which shifts what would have been audible noise outside the range of human hearing. One-bit D/A conversion improves sound quality at a lower cost than other methods, a boon to low-cost CD players. However, even among 1-bit conversion systems, there are differences in quality.

Error correction and tracking: Some manufacturers claim that a three-beam laser system surpasses a single-beam system. Both systems use only one laser, which is either split through the use of prisms and lenses into three beams or used as a single beam. Although either system can be effective, various CD players show differences in tracking accuracy and stability irrespective of how many beams are used.

If a CD player cannot read one or more numbers on a disc, an error may result, producing a clicking, or at worst, a crashing sound. Fortunately the CD player automatically mutes major errors to protect your speakers and ears. If several errors occur in a short time, the sound distorts. Developers incorporated error-correction systems in all CD players so that errors will be masked, and you may never hear them. These errors may be caused by a scratch or dirty areas on the disc's surface.

You can best judge a CD player's tracking stability, in addition to its resistance to external vibration and shock, by tapping lightly on the top and sides of the player's cabinet with your hand. Those CD players with superior tracking ability will play through this type of test without skipping a beat.

Single-play CD Players

SONY CDP-XA3ES

✓BEST BUY

The Sony CDP-XA3ES single-play CD player contains most of the same basic technology and features as Sony's top-of-the-line player at one-fourth the price. The difference is that the CDP-XA3ES is not as ruggedly built and does

Prices are accurate at time of printing but are subject to manufacturers' changes.

not use the same hand-selected parts. It's true that the CDP-XA3ES costs more than most single-disc players, but we think people desiring a single-play machine are more interested in high performance than low price. The CDP-XA3ES represents a longer-term investment than players in the $200 to $400 range because of its significantly better construction quality. For example, the CDP-XA3ES uses an antiresonant frame-and-beam construction in a rather substantial chassis. Sony enhances this player with its most advanced technology, such as its proprietary 90-megahertz, single-bit, high-density, linear digital-to-analog converter with 8x oversampling digital filter, and the equivalent of 20-bit resolution from standard 16-bit discs. This translates into crystal-clear, ultra-low-distortion, ultra-low-noise sound. The player skips from tracks at one end of the disc to the other with blazing speed. Conveniences include Sony's Custom File memory system that memorizes your favorite tracks and listening level on up to 172 discs. It also has conventional programming of up to 32 tracks, easily accomplished from the supplied wireless remote control. The simple front panel layout—with large basic function keys, large blue fluorescent display with a music calendar for selecting tracks, and direct track access from the remote—promotes fast, simple operation.

Warranty: parts and labor, 3 years.

Approx. retail price
$700

Approx. low price
$616

DENON DCD-1015

✓ **BEST BUY**

The Denon DCD-1015 feels sturdy, rugged enough to justify its premium price above the majority of single-play CD players. Denon was a pioneer in digital technology and is well known for its digital recordings. The company developed its ALPHA digital data resolution recovery system for its professional machines and has now reduced the price enough to be able to include the system in home players. This coupled with Denon's 20-bit D/A converters delivers impressively good sound. Denon includes an uncommon feature among CD players, a pitch control. While this was easy to implement on analog turntables, it's much more complex on a CD player. People with a serious interest in music will find this useful, since not all orchestras tune to the same pitch. The DCD-1015 features 20-track programming with direct track access via the front panel keypad or supplied remote. The random-play mode shuffles all tracks or just those you've programmed. The player automatically locates the loudest portions of a CD to assist in setting recording levels. You can also fade in and fade out the sound and even program the fades. The player permits searching for index points.

Warranty: 1 year.

Approx. retail price **$550**

Approx. low price **$482**

ONKYO DX-7210

Recommended

The modest price of the Onkyo DX-7210 single-play compact disc player belies its wealth of sound and features. Onkyo's proprietary AccuPulse Quartz System single-bit digital-to-analog converter coupled with its Fine Pulse Conversion System, which includes an 8x oversampling filter, delivers natural sound without harshness. The 20-track music calendar on the blue fluorescent display simplifies the 36-track programming. The display offers a choice of elapsed track time, remaining track time, and disc time remaining. Direct track access on the both the front panel and remote control facilitate listening to your favorite tracks. Once you press the keys, the player locates tracks almost instantaneously. Onkyo designed the DX-7210 to make taping CDs easy. The time edit feature automatically calculates the combination of tracks that will best fill a cassette side, and peak-level search quickly locates the loudest portion of the disc for setting recording levels. Five different repeat modes, including random-shuffle play, offer plenty of listening flexibility. For private listening, there's a headphone jack with volume control.

Warranty: parts and labor, 1 year.

Approx. retail price **$220**

Approx. low price **$219**

Carousel CD Changers

TECHNICS SL-PD987

✓BEST BUY

Technics offered carousel CD changers early, and the SL-PD987 represents generations of refinement and cost savings. An example is the SL-PD987's Quick Disc Rotation, which dramatically reduces the time required to change discs. It complements Technics' lightning-fast ability to skip from the first to last track on a disc. You can swap four discs while one plays. It even has a pitch adjustment, a rarity on CD players. An easy-to-read disc location display clearly shows discs loaded and which is playing. The disc selection buttons have two-color LED indicators. Technics provides a plethora of playing choices including full random play, single-disc random play, or a spiral play that plays all the first tracks from each disc, followed by second, third, fourth, and so forth. You can even program the changer to delete tracks in the random mode. Similarly, the repeat mode can also repeat individual tracks, discs, or programmed sequences. The ID scan mode samples the loudest, and presumably more recognizable, portion of each track. Direct disc/track access keys, logically arrayed on the front panel and the wireless remote, make 32-track programming from any or all of the loaded discs easier. The Edit Guide and Synchro Edit features compute optimum track arrangement for taping. Technics backs up all these features with good sound from its proprietary MASH single-bit digital-to-analog converters. Its advanced digital servo accurately controls the laser pickup, scanning each disc before play to optimize it for each disc, and it resists minor shocks and vibration.

Warranty: parts and labor, 1 year.

Approx. retail price	**Approx. low price**
$270	$227

SONY CDP-C445

✓BEST BUY

The Sony CDP-C445 five-disc carousel CD changer represents another sterling example of performance for value. As with most carousel changers, you can load or swap

Prices are accurate at time of printing but are subject to manufacturers' changes.

four discs while one plays. Sony's hybrid pulse digital-to-analog converter and 8x oversampling, 18-bit digital filter deliver very good sound quality. In addition the Direct Digital Sync circuit cleans up other problems for improved transparency of sound. The digital servo laser control assures accuracy and rapid response of the laser mechanism. The CDP-C445 offers six play modes and six repeat modes, including random-shuffle play. Direct disc access and track access keys are on both the front panel and supplied remote control. These, along with the 20-track music calendar on the display, assist in the 32-track programming from any of the five discs. Even better is the defeatable 400-disc Custom File delete bank, which remembers the songs you like to skip and deletes them when the disc plays. Sony makes taping a breeze: Peak-level search finds the loudest portion of a disc, and time, program, and link edit optimally arrange CD tracks for recording on a cassette. With the timed and manual fader, you can fade in and out at prearranged points or manually. An optical digital output permits direct digital taping to DAT or MD. The CDP-C445 includes a headphone jack with volume control.

Warranty: parts and labor, 1 year.

Approx. retail price	**Approx. low price**
$330	**$236**

ONKYO DX-C320

BEST BUY

Onkyo decided if five discs were good, then six discs were better, so the DX-C320 changes six CDs. In the process, Onkyo's AccuPulse Quartz System single-bit digital-to-analog converters with Fine Pulse Conversion System 8x oversampling digital filters makes them sound very good. You can change three of the six discs while one plays. You can program 40 tracks, assisted by a 40-track music calendar on the display, from among the six discs. Or you can select one of the seven repeat modes or random-play. Playing or programming tracks is easy with direct disc and track access buttons on the front panel and the supplied remote. Not only will the peak-level search find the loudest portion of the disc for setting recording

Prices are accurate at time of printing but are subject to manufacturers' changes.

evels, but it will repeat the segment until you complete the evel setting. You can also choose the next song to play without interrupting the one currently playing. This handsome unit omes with controls logically arranged on the front panel.

Varranty: parts and labor, 1 year.

pprox. retail price	**Approx. low price**
330	$301

ARANTZ CC-65

Recommended

The Marantz CC-65 five-disc carousel CD hanger uses a new 1-bit Bitstream continuous calibration digtal-to-analog converter that delivers the equivalent of 18-bit ound. Philips, the parent company of Marantz, invented the itstream converter and now has developed it to near perfecion. The CC-65 also uses premium parts in its analog sections. o reduce noise, Marantz powers the analog and digital portions f this player separately and somewhat isolates the D/A conerter. You can swap three discs while one plays on this unit. he laser mechanism quickly jumps between tracks. Features for aping include peak search for locating the loudest point on a isc and tape edit for arranging the tracks optimally to fill a casette side. The CC-65 allows programming of 30 tracks, which s made easier with direct disc and track access from the front anel and the remote control. This model also has random-shufe play and a few repeat modes. Although this player's features natch most others in its class, we chose it for its fine sound qualy. Because it costs significantly more than other players in its lass, however, it is Recommended rather than a Best Buy.

Varranty: parts and labor, 3 years.

pprox. retail price	**Approx. low price**
400	$368

Magazine CD Changers

VC XL-M417TN

✓ BEST BUY

Even after you've loaded the six-disc magazine f the JVC XL-M417TN, it will still function as a single-CD player. Its automatically loading single tray means it reall holds seven discs. You can program 32 tracks from any of thos seven discs, aided by a 20-track program chart on the amber an red fluorescent display. Program and play are quick and eas with the direct disc access keys on the front panel and direc disc and track access keys on the supplied remote control. Th remote will even allow you to eject the magazine from acros the room. The player stores 48 disc titles in memory, entere by using a novel jog dial on the front panel. You can the search discs by title. The player has four repeat modes and ran dom play. The magazines are compatible with some of JVC's ca changers. The XL-M417TN uses JVC's proprietary 1-bit P.E.M digital-to-analog converter with advanced noise shaping alon with an 8x oversampling digital filter for low distortion an very low noise. The combination of features and performanc makes this player very attractive.

Warranty: parts and carry-in labor, 1 year.

Approx. retail price	**Approx. low price**
$330	**$218**

PIONEER PD-M603

Recommended

Pioneer offers an unusual feature on the six-disc magazine PD-M603 changer. You can classify magazine into six different music types that the player identifies and dis plays when you load the magazine. Pioneer's 1-bit Pulseflov D/A converter delivers good sound. Pioneer's unique Automati Digital Level Controller (ADLC) complements the sound qual ity by automatically matching the levels between discs, so yo won't be blasted by some and straining to hear others. It doe this without compression or distortion. When programmin the 32 tracks, the display prompts you to enter the correct data To assist in recording from the changer, it will automaticall arrange discs and tracks for optimal tape usage. The PD-M60 will automatically fade out music at a specified time. Hi-Lit Scan plays ten seconds from each track on any or all discs. Yo can directly access discs and tracks from the front panel. A re mote control is supplied.

Warranty: parts and labor, 1 year.

Approx. retail price	Approx. low price
$270	$265

Multiple CD Changers

FISHER STUDIO 24

✔ **BEST BUY**

As its name implies, the Studio 24 changes 24 discs with neither carousel nor magazine. Simply load the discs into a slot in the front of the player, and they are stored juke-box style. Fisher calls it a compact disc management system. The player comes with seven preset music categories to group CDs for playback, and you can program your own as well. This makes it easier to keep track of the discs you've loaded. Simply assign a new disc a category at the push of a button when loading. You can intermix play between categories or program the Studio 24 to play discs within a single category. It's amazingly versatile in its programming possibilities. The Studio 24 uses a 1-bit D/A converter for good sound quality. Even though the player holds 24 discs, it still fits into a normal-size stereo component system.

Warranty: parts and labor, 1 year.

Approx. retail price	Approx. low price
$400	$268

SONY CDP-CX153

✔ **BEST BUY**

The Sony CDP-CX153 100-disc changer manages to store and play all those discs in one cabinet, but the unit will still stack with other audio components. Its Custom File lets you assign a 13-character name to each of the 100 discs. The disc's name is then displayed on the front panel while it's playing, and the name also flashes in memo scan as the disc tray turns. The front-panel jog dial rotates through the 100 discs and also scans the alphabet for storing disc and group file names. The Custom File Group File permits designating seven different types of music for classifying the discs, whether it be a music type like rock or classical or the names of family members. One disc can belong to multiple groups. Sony provides direct access of discs, tracks, and groups. This simplifies the 32-track programming, which allows you to choose 32 tracks in any order on any of the 100 discs. A 20-track music calendar further aids programming by showing tracks programmed, tracks played, and tracks remaining. The CDP-CX153 offers six play modes and six repeat modes, including random shuffle on play and/or repeat. If 100 discs are not enough for you, the CDP-CX153 can be chained with two additional 100-disc changers and a Sony controller. Sony pays ample attention to technical quality with its pulse digital-to-analog converter coupled with an 8x oversampling 18-bit digital filter combined on a single integrated circuit chip. Direct digital sync further reduces digital anomalies for cleaner sound. The digital servo control accurately and rapidly positions the laser. An optical digital output allows either direct digital taping to DAT or MD or processing through a digital signal processing receiver. A supplied remote control duplicates all front panel controls. Sony packs this unit with impressive sound quality and versatility for the money.

Warranty: parts and labor, 1 year.

Approx. retail price	**Approx. low price**
$600	**Not available**

JVC XL-MC301

✓ BEST BUY

Not only does the two-piece JVC XL-MC301 change 100 discs, but a loading drawer on the control unit allows it to function as a single-disc player as well. The sleek control unit stacks with other components, while the disc storage unit can be hidden several feet away. JVC permits chaining two additional 100-disc storage units, and there's no need for modifying the controller. The user file feature permits creating ten user files, each holding up to 32 discs in memory. The delete file feature removes tracks from up to 300 discs for playback of favorite tracks only. You can program 32 tracks from any of the 100 to 300 discs, and the random play shuffles through as

Prices are accurate at time of printing but are subject to manufacturers' changes.

many discs as you've loaded, up to 300. That means you could have weeks of unrepeated music in random sequence. The player also has a four-mode repeat function. JVC created a special remote control to command this monster jukebox. The remote contains a memory bank for titles of 300 discs and a memory for user file names, which it displays on its LCD. The disc title index and search are also on the remote. The front panel keypad directly accesses discs and tracks. JVC incorporates its proprietary single-bit P.E.M. digital-to-analog converter with its advanced noise-shaping 8x oversampling digital filter for clear, smooth sound. This unit justifies its price because basically it's two CD players in one with plenty of versatility.

Warranty: parts and carry-in labor, 1 year.

Approx. retail price
$1,000

Approx. low price
$850

CASSETTE DECKS

The original cassette decks played and recorded on a single cassette tape. If you wanted to copy tapes, you needed two machines. More and more people wanted to copy tapes but didn't want to spend the money to buy two decks or fuss with interconnecting them. In the 1980s a single box was developed with two transports: the dual deck. This offered three advantages: one-button tape copying, double-speed copying, and lower cost than two separate decks. The dual transports of the double deck share many parts, reducing their cost by 30 to 50 percent of that of two separate decks of comparable quality. Initially only one deck of the dual-transport pair could record, so their main utility was copying. In this decade more and more dual-recording, dual-transport decks have appeared. This opens the possibilities of making two copies of an external source (such as a CD or an FM broadcast) simultaneously. It also enables making a virtually uninterrupted recording of nearly four hours if both transports auto-reverse, and most do. Dual recording adds between 15 and 20 percent to the price of a dual-transport cassette deck, depending on the manufacturer's marketing strategy. The ultimate quality cassette decks remain single-transport models. Below the ultimate, single-transport models are disappearing in favor of the overwhelmingly popular dual-transport models.

Before you shop for a single- or dual-transport cassette deck for your stereo system, read through this brief explanation of the major specifications.

Frequency response, distortion, and signal-to-noise ratio are closely related. Frequency response is sometimes improved at the expense of distortion and signal-to-noise ratio. But achieving the true hi-fi range of 20 to 20,000 hertz many not mean the overall quality is better, since most humans (especially as they get older) cannot hear much above 15,000 hertz and few instruments other than a grand pipe organ produce tones that go much below 30 hertz. When comparing the frequency responses of two machines, be sure the response of each is accompanied by a tolerance, usually stated as plus or minus a certain number of decibels (dB); otherwise the frequency response statement is meaningless.

Distortion is quoted by tape deck manufacturers as a percentage at a -20 dB recording level, lower than the level most people record at. (A few specs quote a more realistic 0 dB level.) Many manufacturers advise recording peaks as high as +5 dB. This specification depends on the type of tape, but distortion should be no higher than 1 percent.

Signal-to-noise ratios (S/N) often use the -20 dB recording level as a reference. Choose a deck with better than 60 dB S/N when the Dolby noise reduction is switched off. To enjoy the best sound from the tape deck you have selected, use the brand and type of tape recommended by the manufacturer, or have a technician adjust the machine for your favorite brand and type of tape. Avoid bargain-brand tapes; not only will they lower sound quality, they can potentially damage the machine.

Wow and flutter is a measurement of tape-speed fluctuation. It is usually listed as a percentage, followed by the acronym WRMS. For example, a wow-and-flutter specification might read 1/10 percent WRMS. Look for the lowest percentage available within your budget limitations.

Bias, equalization, and level-setting adjustments are not available on all cassette decks, but some tape decks offer fine-tuning controls that let you adjust for slight differences in the bias of recording tapes. Other decks control adjustments with microprocessor chips. These circuits test the tape and adjust for the optimum bias, equalization, and sensitivity to provide the best performance from a tape.

Three-head cassette decks have one head for erasing, another for recording, and a third for playback. This arrangement provides the same sort of rapid off-the-tape monitoring capability found on professional open-reel machines. Using a separate head for each function also improves performance by permitting the use of specialized heads for record and play.

Noise-Reduction Systems

Even with the very best cassette tape used in a superior cassette recorder, you will probably notice some tape hiss, or noise, when playing back your recordings. Hiss, which occurs where the human ear is most sensitive, in the upper mid-range and treble, is especially noticeable during playback of softer musical passages. Although several noise-reduction technologies competed during the cassette's early days, Dolby noise reduction proved the most viable. Different levels of noise reduction from Dolby Laboratories are now standard on all cassette decks. Dolby A is a very expensive professional noise-reduction system not used in consumer cassette decks.

Dolby B reduces high-frequency (treble) noise by 5 to 10 decibels; this is equivalent to perceiving about a 50 percent reduction in high-frequency noise. Tapes recorded in Dolby B can be played back on non-Dolby players with only a slight sonic aberration.

Dolby C reduces both mid-range and high-frequency noise by about 10 decibels, but it sounds as if it reduced noise twice as much as Dolby B. It also slightly lowers distortion on high-frequency peaks. While Dolby C–encoded tapes can be played back with some success using Dolby B, they sound unpleasant when played back on machines lacking any Dolby decoding.

Dolby S reduces noise throughout the audible range and as much as 20 decibels in the high frequencies. It also significantly reduces distortion. Dolby S is the consumer version of the Dolby SR professional noise-reduction system. Dolby requires a basic standard of quality for cassette decks equipped with Dolby S. Tapes recorded on these decks approach digital sound quality, with their dramatically low noise and distortion. Dolby S cannot eliminate speed variations such as flutter and wow. Dolby S tapes can be played back through Dolby B or C with reasonable success. Although its full benefits won't be realized, the sound quality is acceptable.

Dolby HX-Pro is a headroom expansion (HX) system that, unlike noise-reduction systems, is single-ended. That means it works only during recording and needs no decoding on playback. Dolby HX-Pro adjusts the recording current, or bias, to allow higher levels of high frequencies on the tape while lowering distortion. A by-product of this is a subtle reduction of noise. A cassette deck with HX-Pro will greatly assist your efforts to make superior tape recordings. It is now becoming standard in all but the least expensive models.

Single-Transport Cassette Decks

SONY TC-RX606ES

BEST BUY

The Sony TC-RX606ES single-transport cassette deck combines auto-reverse convenience with high performance. We think superior performance is the hallmark for anyone choosing a single-transport deck. The TC-RX606ES is also one of the lowest-priced decks with the highly desirable Dolby S noise-reduction system. It also includes Dolby B, C, and HX-Pro. Sony loads this deck with most of its performance-enhancing technologies such as laser amorphous tape heads, ceramic cassette holder, and 160 kilohertz super bias (which eliminates conflicts between the audio and recording bias). To maximize performance from each individual tape, the deck automatically calibrates to that specific tape. This noticeably improves sound quality. The deck auto-reverses rapidly, barely missing a beat. A real-time linear tape counter lets you know where you are on the tape in minutes and seconds. The automatic music search (AMS) feature skips forward and back on the tape to locate your favorite selections. Power loading smoothly accepts the cassette and closes the door as it loads the tape into the transport. For ruggedness, fast and smooth tape handling, and long life, Sony endows the TC-RX606ES with three motors. The deck also comes with microphone inputs, a rarity these days. Convenience and performance of this class would have cost three times as much a decade ago.

Warranty: parts and labor, 3 years.

Approx. retail price	**Approx. low price**
$500	$483

ONKYO TA-R410

Recommended

The Onkyo TA-R410 two-head cassette deck uses two motors for smooth, reasonably fast tape handling. Full-logic, feather-touch controls, which use a computer chip to operate the motors, contribute to smooth operation and tape motion. The TA-R410's quick auto-reverse functions with impressive speed. The deck includes Dolby B and C noise reduction plus HX-Pro. The large, dual-color fluorescent display with peak level indicators and four-digit electronic tape counter is easy to read, although we miss having a real-time tape counter. The manual AccuBias system allows you to fine-tune the deck to the specific tapes you plan to record on. If you have the time and patience to do this, you may noticeably improve recording quality. You can specify a section of tape you'd like to replay, and the deck will repeat the block up to eight times. The controls operate easily and are logically laid out.

Warranty: parts and labor, 1 year.

Approx. retail price	**Approx. low price**
$280	$243

Double-Transport Cassette Decks

TECHNICS RS-TR575

✓BEST BUY

The Technics RS-TR575 stands out as an exceptional value among dual-transport cassette decks. All that's missing on this high-performance deck is a headphone jack. Its forte is sound quality, made possible not only from proper design, but also from one of the most accurate automated tape-calibration circuits on the market. The RS-TR575 precisely adjusts its electronics for whatever tape you place in the machine. This noticeably improves fidelity. This deck plays and records on both transports, for parallel or serial recording. It loads tape automatically, like a VCR, and handles tape rapidly and smoothly. Each transport's dual-motor design contributes to making it one of the fastest-winding decks on the market, at nearly twice the speed of many others. (Rewinding a C-60 takes 50 seconds.) The full-logic, feather-touch controls quickly translate your commands to accurate responses. The deck includes Dolby B and C noise reduction as well as HX-Pro. The twin electronic tape counters display real tape time. Sound quality and operation are exemplary for a deck in this price range.

Warranty: parts and labor, 1 year.

Approx. retail price
$270

Approx. low price
$232

SONY TC-WA8ES

✓BEST BUY

The Sony TC-WA8ES dual-transport, dual-auto-reverse, dual-record cassette deck records nearly as well as the best single-transport decks while maintaining a reasonable price. Sony bestows each transport with two heads and two motors, for sure, smooth operation over an extended time period. Full-logic, feather-touch controls further ensure graceful operation with minimal effort on your part. The TC-WA8ES records on both transports for parallel and serial recording. To ensure the utmost fidelity from each individual tape, this deck has an automatic-calibration tape-matching

Prices are accurate at time of printing but are subject to manufacturers' changes.

feature that functions on both transports. Dolby S further elevates recording quality. The deck also incorporates Dolby B and C noise reduction as well as HX-Pro. The programmable automatic music search (AMS) feature will locate more than one music selection on either transport. Ceramic cassette holders keep the tape rigidly in place with minimum vibration to maintain sonic clarity. Although the deck features twin electronic tape counters, they read out arbitrary numbers rather than real tape time.

Warranty: parts and labor, 3 years.

Approx. retail price $550 | **Approx. low price** $533

PIONEER CT-W704RS

✓ BEST BUY

The Pioneer CT-W704RS dual-transport auto-reverse cassette deck represents one of the least expensive double decks to incorporate Dolby S noise reduction along with Dolby B and C and HX-Pro. Both transports record and play, permitting parallel and serial recording and play. To complement Dolby S, Pioneer incorporates its own third-generation automated custom tape calibration circuitry, Super Auto BLE (Bias-Level-Equalization) XD. Pioneer's proprietary FLEX (Frequency Level Expander) circuit further improves the naturalness of treble sound. FLEX calculates the amount of treble lost in the recording process, most common for tapes made on inferior decks and old tapes, and adds it back into the playback. The dual tape counters on the amber- and-red fluorescent display show real elapsed tape time in minutes and seconds. Full-logic, feather-touch controls assure smooth, sure operation. The music search feature will wind forward or back to find your favorite song. The CT-W704RS includes microphone inputs, a rare feature, as well as a headphone jack.

Warranty: parts and labor, 1 year.

Approx. retail price $365 | **Approx. low price** $272

Prices are accurate at time of printing but are subject to manufacturers' changes.

JVC TD-W217TN

Recommended

The JVC TD-W217TN dual-transport, auto-reverse cassette deck provides all the necessary features for good recording and tape copying at a modest price. The three-motor design is the same one used in JVC's most expensive dual deck. One transport records and plays, the other only plays. Both incorporate Dolby B and C noise reduction, and the recording transport also records with Dolby HX-Pro. When used with a JVC CD player, the Dynamics Detection Recording Processor will automatically set optimum recording levels. Full-logic control with light-touch keys keeps the deck operating smoothly with minimal effort on your part. Silent mechanisms driven by separate motor actuators load the tapes. The amber-and-red fluorescent display has dual tape counters showing arbitrary numbers, not real tape time. For people who don't need dual recording and the ultimate sound quality of Dolby S, this deck provides very good value.

Warranty: parts and carry-in labor, 1 year.

Approx. retail price	**Approx. low price**
$220	**$161**

SONY TC-WR465

Budget Buy

The price of the Sony TC-WR465 dual-transport auto-reverse cassette deck may be low, and the features limited, but it makes good recordings with enough features to do the job. Twin motors operate the transports commanded by full-logic, feather-touch controls. One deck plays and records, and the other only plays. Both include Dolby B and C noise reduction, and the recording deck also has Dolby HX-Pro. Dual electronic tape counters appear on the blue- and-red fluorescent display. The counters show arbitrary numbers, not real tape time. The headphone jack lacks a volume control. Like all other dual-transport decks, the TC-WR465 copies tapes at double speed and offers relay play. Since both decks auto-reverse, you can enjoy three hours of uninterrupted music.

Warranty: parts and labor, 1 year.

Approx. retail price	**Approx. low price**
$170	**$165**

Prices are accurate at time of printing but are subject to manufacturers' changes.

DIGITAL AUDIOTAPE (DAT) DECK

Digital audiotape (DAT) is to the analog cassette as CD is to the analog LP record. It records digitally using a system nearly identical to the CD system. DAT records using 16 data bits, but with a choice of sampling rates of 48,000 hertz for recordings originating on DAT, 44,100 hertz for copies from CD, and 32,000 hertz for long-play and special applications—at the cost of some fidelity. Because it is digital, DAT requires no noise-reduction system.

The record industry fought DAT's arrival because the system is capable of recording with fidelity virtually identical to the source material. Whereas each generation of copies of regular tapes lose a bit more fidelity, you can digitally copy from one DAT to another DAT to another, and so on, and the final copy will sound like the original. DAT decks can also make unrestricted copies with their analog inputs and outputs, but the results are not as perfect as when using digital inputs and outputs. This is because the signal must first go through a D/A converter and then back again through an A/D (analog-to-digital) converter.

The record industry and DAT manufacturers reached a compromise in 1989. Dutch electronics giant Philips—inventor of the analog compact cassette—developed a microchip that would limit digital copying without affecting sound quality. This chip, called Serial Copy Management System (SCMS), allows you to make a digital copy from a digital source. For example, you can copy a CD onto DAT, but you can't make digital copies of that copy. You can copy that same CD as many times as you like onto DAT. You can also copy DAT to DAT digitally one time. Analog sources such as LPs or radio broadcasts can be recorded on DAT and then digitally copied from DAT to DAT once only.

DAT not only far surpasses the fidelity of conventional cassettes, it also offers superior tape handling. Any selection on a tape can be located within a minute by the touch of a button.

SONY DTC-60ES

Recommended

Because the DAT format met limited acceptance and the price of the Sony DTC-60ES DAT recorder is so substantial, we can give it only a Recommended listing, no matter how incredible its sound quality. There are less expensive DAT decks, but we think someone choosing this format desires ultimate sound quality, which the DTC-60ES provides. This deck can record and play with a quality equal to or superior to most CDs. It uses a proprietary Sony technique called Super Bit Mapping (SBM) to provide the equivalent of an 18-bit digital system, an improvement over the 16-bit standard. Yet the DTC-60ES remains compatible with all other DATs. The deck records and plays at all three DAT sampling frequencies, which includes the CD sampling frequency, simplifying digital dubs and pressing a CD from tapes recorded on this deck. In the long-play mode, you can record for four hours with fidelity slightly better than FM radio. The deck uses single-bit analog-to-digital and digital-to-analog converters. The D/A is Sony's proprietary pulse converter. Including three motors suggests durability. Automatic and manual ID subcodes mark selections during or after recording for easy programming and recording. SCMS prevents serial copying of digital tapes, but it permits individual digital copies and serial copies from the deck's analog inputs/outputs. The DTC-60ES sounds better than an analog consumer recording system.

Warranty: parts and labor, 3 years.

Approx. retail price	**Approx. low price**
$1,300	**$1,300**

MINIDISC (MD) DECK

MiniDisc is a revolutionary digital recording system. It stores up to 74 minutes of sound on a 2½-inch disc encased in a caddy like a 3½-inch computer diskette. Like DCC, it compresses the digital data, using an algorithm to discard inaudible sound. Prerecorded MDs are pressed the same way as CDs and cost about the same. Like CDs, MDs are immune to wear.

The recordable/erasable MDs use a laser and a magnetic head similar to a tape head to record on the disc. Blank recordable/erasable MDs cost $12 to $14. MD matches CD in ease of use, with nearly instant access to desired tracks and programming capability. Recordable MDs offer the advantages of computer diskettes, permitting nonsequential recording on any blank space on the disc. You can also reorder selections on the MD without rerecording or programming.

MDs are nearly indestructible and resistant to heat. The caddy makes them less susceptible to damage than CDs. They fit easily into a shirt pocket.

All MD players incorporate a "shock-resistant memory." These memory computer chips store ten seconds of sound. When the player is jarred or shaken, you hear no interruption of sound because of this memory. This makes MD a more effective portable medium than CD. Sony, the inventor of MD, intends it mostly as a portable/automotive format rather than a home music format. Because of the extraordinarily high price of MD, it does not qualify as a Best Buy.

SONY MDS-JA3ES

Recommended

Although there are less expensive home MiniDisc decks than the MDS-JA3ES, this machine unlocks the full potential, in features and sonics, of MD. We think people investing in this specialized technology do so for the features found on the MDS-JA3ES. This deck brings the sound of MD extremely close to CD with features such as its single-bit pulse analog-to-digital converter, its special 20-bit playback digital filter, and the third generation of improvements to MD's ATRAC compression circuitry. MD provides all the convenience features of CD, such as 25-track programming with 25 tracks displayed on the music calendar on the fluorescent display, random shuffle play, and three repeat modes. However, MD goes beyond CD because it records. You can customize each disc you record with the name, music type, artist, and other information, up to 1,700 characters per disc. The information then scrolls across the front panel display. This information is stored on the disc, not in the player. Because MD uses a "table of contents" like that found on a computer disk, with the MDS-JA3ES you can combine, divide, reorder, move, and remove tracks without actually recording or rerecording. When recording, after 30 seconds of silence, the deck automatically goes into pause mode. It also automatically marks recordings with the date and time of the recording, which can also be shown on the front panel display. This deck offers several other fascinating features available only from the MD format on a machine of this caliber. The MDS-JA3ES also has microphone inputs and a headphone output. Sony supplies it with a remote control that includes 25-key direct-access track selection and the ability to enter titles.

Warranty: parts and labor, 3 years.

Approx. retail price
$1,200

Approx. low price
$1,200

STEREO SYSTEMS

Stereo systems, sometimes called rack systems, are audio components from a single manufacturer that are grouped together to offer optimum value and performance. Some companies also use this arrangement to optimize profit. A stereo system provides the assurance that the matched components will work well together and that little wiring will be required on your part.

Over the past few years, stereo systems have been undergoing an evolution. Mini- and microsystems have surpassed full-size systems in popularity. Many of these small systems reproduce sound faithfully, with output comparable to that of the bigger systems. An added attraction is that the mini- and microsystems often offer more features, such as integral clock/timers.

When shopping for a stereo system, consider what components it includes and its sound quality. Just as compact disk players replaced turntables in most systems available today, CD changers are replacing single-disk players. Features you may want to consider are wireless remote control (giving you full control of the system from across the room) and logic connections between the components. Logic connections mean, for example, that the CD player will shut off when you select the tuner, or vice versa. Most systems now interconnect the CD player and the tape deck to simplify tape copying.

In full-size package systems, the weakest link is usually the speakers. Most electronics manufacturers do not make good loudspeakers. If possible, attempt to convince the dealer to allow you to substitute different speakers for the ones supplied with the system. If not, you could upgrade the speakers at a later date.

The stylish minisystems come with specially engineered small speakers that are important to the overall sound of the system. The amplifiers are special bass enhancement circuits matched to the supplied speakers to reproduce impressive bass from such small boxes.

For additional information about stereo components, please refer to the preceding chapter.

Best Buys '96

Our Best Buy, Recommended, and Budget Buy stereo systems follow, in three categories: complete home theater systems, full-size systems, and compact stereo systems. Within each category, systems are listed by quality; the item we consider to be the best of the Best Buys is listed first, followed by our second choice, and so on. At the end of a category you may find a Budget Buy. A Budget Buy is a less expensive product of respectable quality that sacrifices some of the performance and/or features of a Best Buy or Recommended product. Remember that a Best Buy, Recommended, or Budget Buy designation applies only to the model listed; it does not necessarily apply to other models made by the same manufacturer or to an entire product line.

COMPLETE HOME THEATER SYSTEMS

MAGNAVOX MX931 AHT

✓BEST BUY

Think of the Magnavox MX931 AHT as a budget home theater Surround Sound system that's worthy of being a Best Buy. Team the MX931 AHT with any 27-inch or larger TV and a VHS hi-fi stereo VCR, and you'll understand what home theater is about. While the sound is not audiophile quality, the MX931 AHT sounds better than all but the best surround systems packaged in or with TV sets. Unlike some budget Surround Sound receivers, this Magnavox incorporates genuine Dolby Pro Logic. A full-featured AM/FM stereo receiver forms the heart of the Magnavox system. The front panel's large fluorescent display even scrolls instructions when you invoke certain functions. Numeric keys permit tuning a radio station by tapping in its frequency, a most convenient feature. You can then enter the call letters of your favorite stations into memory. In addition to Pro Logic, the receiver synthesizes pseudo-stereo from mono and synthesizes acoustic environments such as hall, stadium, and theater. The amplifier portion

Prices are accurate at time of printing but are subject to manufacturers' changes.

f the MX931 AHT produces 50 watts each for the left and right 'ont channels and 10 watts for the center channel. The rear hannels share 10 watts. Current practice, and our recommen-ation, is for the three front channels to produce the same 'attage, since the center channel reproduces the dialogue. Vhen used in two-channel stereo mode the MX931 AHT pro-uces 50 watts per channel. The modest bookshelf-size left and ght speakers fit nicely next to a 27-inch TV, or they can be used n stands. The center channel speaker perches perfectly on top f the TV, or it can be placed below, in front. The small, unob-usive surrounds come with the appropriate eye holes and crews for wall mounting. A headphone jack is included. A re-note control controls all functions and will operate other Mag-avox components.

Varranty: carry-in parts and labor, 1 year.

pprox. retail price	**Approx. low price**
500	**$367**

OSE LIFESTYLE 12 HOME THEATRE SYSTEM

BEST BUY

The Bose Lifestyle 12 Home Theatre System is) elegant, so easy to install, and so sonically pleasing that we st it as a Best Buy regardless of its high price. It includes a good M/FM stereo tuner and a CD player. Bose has included a sur-ound-sound decoder, five channels of amplification, and five airs of its nifty cube speakers. The sleek, brushed-aluminum nusic center is smaller than most coffee-table books. A mod-st fluorescent display and a few buttons occupy a long oval utout along the top front left. A hidden button raises the lid f the CD player. Bose expects you to operate the system from ne white, uncluttered, finger-friendly remote control. The ifestyle remote works via radio waves rather than the infrared ght used by most remotes. This means you can conceal the nusic center or even operate it from another room. This mi-rosystem gives you big sound for music playing, which Bose emonstrates by providing a superb-fidelity CD sampler. The peakers represent the ultimate refinement of a concept Bose

Prices are accurate at time of printing but are subject to manufacturers' changes.

innovated about a decade ago. The woofer (or bass module, as Bose calls it) uses Bose's Acoustimass design for thundering bass from a relatively small enclosure. The bass module, about the size of a carry-on suitcase, also includes all the power amplifiers and bass and treble controls. Because of the unique amplifier and speaker designs, Bose does not rate the system's power. The five pairs of speaker cubes can be placed on a shelf (the center channel on top of the TV) or, with their built-in threaded adapters, attached to optional stands or wall brackets. Each cube of the pair twists, so they can be aimed at right angles or even opposite directions. Aiming one of the cubes toward you and the other at the wall creates a more spacious sound and improves the effect of the surround channels. You can set up the complete system in less than hour, even if you consider yourself technologically impaired. All the wires terminate in plugs or tinned leads that easily go into spring-clip speaker inputs, so you won't even need a screwdriver. Bose uses its own VideoStage surround decoding system rather than the industry standard Dolby Pro Logic. While not identical to Pro Logic, VideoStage works admirably.

Warranty: parts and labor, limited, 1 year.

Approx. retail price	**Approx. low price**
$2,200	**$2,000**

FULL-SIZE STEREO SYSTEMS

SONY R-2500

BEST BUY

The Sony R-2500 full-size stereo system may be basic, but it delivers solid performance at a very attractive price. Sony packages a 100-watt-per-channel stereo amplifier with a built-in five-band graphic equalizer, a five-disc carousel CD changer, an AM/FM stereo tuner, and a dual-transport cassette deck in a simple imitation-maple cabinet flanked by floor-standing speakers. The equalizer puts on quite a light show with its spectrum analyzer display, which shows you the relative level of seven frequencies adjusted by the equalizer. The CD changer uses Sony's single-bit pulse-type digital-to-analog con-

Prices are accurate at time of printing but are subject to manufacturers' changes.

erter with digital filter. The changer provides direct disc access.
'ou can program 32 tracks for any of the five discs, aided by
he 20-track music calendar on the display. The changer offers
hree play modes and two repeat modes. A useful feature is cus-
om edit, which helps you optimize track order for copying
nto cassettes. The cassette deck plays on both transports and
ecords on one, both using Dolby B noise reduction. Operation
s easy with the full-logic feather-touch controls. You can pre-
et 30 radio stations on the tuner. Sony supplies a full-function
emote control for the system. The three-way speakers each
onsist of a 10-inch woofer, 3⅛-inch mid-range, and 2-inch
weeter in an imitation-maple finish that matches the cabinet.
'his system is refreshing because it supplies what you need
vithout unnecessary frills, and it supplies very good sound for
he money.

Warranty: parts and labor, 1 year.

Approx. retail price	Approx. low price
700	$599

VC GX-8330

The JVC GX-8330 full-size stereo system offers **✔ BEST BUY**
ll the sound-system essentials at a rational price. It combines
receiver, five-disc carousel CD changer, dual-transport cassette
eck, and 5-band graphic equalizer in a black audio rack, plus
pair of floor-standing three-way speakers. The receiver pro-
uces 110 watts per channel, a substantial amount of power.
ou can preset 40 AM and/or FM radio stations. The tuner sec-
ion performs impressively for a system of this type. The CD
hanger permits swapping four discs while one plays, and it also
rovides direct disc and track access on the front panel. The
hanger uses JVC's P.E.M. single-bit digital-to-analog converter
ith digital filter for clean, smooth sound. You can program 32
racks or set the player for random play. The dual-transport
uto-reverse cassette deck records on one transport and plays
n both, with Dolby B noise reduction. It has easy-to-see amber-
nd-red level indicators, but the mechanical tape counter is
mall and difficult to read. The large tower speakers consist of

12-inch woofers, 4-inch mid-ranges, and 3⅛-inch tweeters. JVC designed the speakers to make full use of the receiver's high power. The supplied remote control also powers on JVC TVs and VCRs. The well-chosen combination of desirable features, performance, and a nice price explains our choice of this system as a Best Buy.

Warranty: CD player and tape deck, parts and carry-in labor, 2 years; receiver, parts and carry-in labor, 2 years; speakers, parts and carry-in labor, 3 years; rack, parts and carry-in labor, 1 year.

Approx. retail price	Approx. low price
$900	$775

ONKYO AV-F3030/3040

Recommended

The Onkyo AV-F3030 full-size stereo system offers the best of both worlds. It's a custom-matched group of components, consisting of Onkyo's respected separate components combined at a discount, with an audio cabinet. Onkyo supplies five speakers with this audio/video system to further increase its value. The A-SV210 AV integrated amplifier has five audio and two audio-from-video inputs. In two-channel stereo the amplifier produces 100 watts per channel. Dolby Pro Logic provides full Surround Sound decoding. In surround mode the amplifier produces 60 watts for each of the three front channels and 15 watts for each of the surround channels. The T-4010 quartz-synthesized AM/FM stereo tuner automatically chooses optimum reception settings. You can preset 40 radio stations and save them in six categories. The DX-C120 six-disc carousel CD changer uses Onkyo's proprietary AccuPulse Quartz System single-bit digital-to-analog converters in conjunction with 8x oversampling digital filters for excellent sound. You can program 40 tracks and choose from six repeat modes. Direct disc and track access keys make programming or finding your favorite tune fast and easy. The TA-RW111 dual-transport auto-reverse cassette deck plays on both decks and records on one with Dolby B and C noise reduction. The floor-standing left and right front speakers consist of 12-inch woofers, 4-inch mid-ranges, and ¾-inch dome tweeters. The considerably smaller center speaker tonally matches the left and right speakers with dual 4-inch mid/low-frequency drivers and a ½-inch dome tweeter. The surround speakers use the 4-inch driver. A single remote operates the system as well as other Onkyo components. Onkyo offers the attractive audio cabinet in black Zeldawood (AV-F3040) or blond Appalachian wood (AV-F3030).

Warranty: CD and cassette player, 1 year; tuner and amplifier, 2 years; speakers, 2 years.

Approx. retail price
$1,680

Approx. low price
$1,179

PIONEER SYSCOM D-2170K

Recommended

The Pioneer Syscom D-2170K full-size stereo system includes a 100-CD changer. We found this most impressive, considering the system's $1,310 price and complement of components. The changer's rolling rack system facilitates loading and unloading, allowing you to swap up to 75 of the discs while one is playing. The built-in custom filing function lets you divide the 100 loaded discs into three custom groups, in classifications such as type, artist, or family member. A disc can be assigned to more than one file, and you can reclassify discs without physically moving them. You can program 36 tracks and choose among eight different play/repeat modes. The player uses Pioneer's single-bit Pulseflow digital-to-analog converter with a digital filter for good sound. The amplifier produces 100 watts per channel. The tuner and cassette deck offer basic, unexceptional performance. You can preset 24 radio stations on the tuner. The auto-reverse cassette deck records on one transport and plays on both, with Dolby B noise reduction. A five-band graphic equalizer allows you to adjust tonal balances to your preference. The floor-standing speakers contain 12-inch woofers, 4¾-inch mid-ranges, and 2½-inch tweeters. The audio cabinet and the speakers come finished in black.

Warranty: parts and labor, 1 year.

Approx. retail price	Approx. low price
$1,310	**$1,021**

COMPACT STEREO SYSTEMS

ONKYO PCS-103

BEST BUY

The Onkyo PCS-103 compact stereo system will grab you not only with its great sound but also with its good looks. PCS stands for "personal component system," and it lives up to its billing. Onkyo combines a 20-watt-per-channel amplifier with a preprogrammed equalizer, an AM/FM stereo tuner, a three-CD changer, and a dual-transport cassette deck into a package not much taller than an LP record jacket, along with matching speakers. You can set the amp for what Onkyo engineers assume to be the best tonal balance for jazz, pop, rock, or classical music, or for flat, unadulterated sound. The tuner permits 16 FM and 8 AM radio preset stations and adjusts its setting for optimum reception. The CD changer does all the things the big changers do. You can swap two discs while the third plays, program 32 tracks, or choose one of the four repeat modes, which includes random play. The changer works along with the cassette deck to calculate and arrange disc tracks for the best fit on a cassette side. The auto-reverse cassette deck with full-logic controls plays on both transports and records on one, with Dolby B noise reduction. The amber fluorescent displays on the amp/tuner and CD player clearly let you observe the status of the system. Dancing lights of the 5-band spectrum analyzer show relative frequency levels—an eye-pleasing frill. The controls feel solid, belying the Best Buy price of this system. Onkyo supplies a remote control for further convenience.

Warranty: parts and labor, 1 year.

Approx. retail price	Approx. low price
$570	**$456**

Prices are accurate at time of printing but are subject to manufacturers' changes.

YAMAHA CC-75

✓BEST BUY

The Yamaha CC-75 compact stereo system features the latest generation from the company that gave this category sonic credibility almost a decade ago. The key to the sound is Yamaha's innovative "active servo technology," in which the amplifier and speakers work together as a team. The amplifier reacts to feedback from the speakers to correct errors in the sound. This results in unusually low distortion and big sound from small speakers. The CC-75 system consists of an AM/FM stereo receiver, a three-CD changer, and a dual-transport, auto-reverse cassette deck. The receiver incorporates Yamaha's DSS (Digital Super Surround), a derivative of its acclaimed digital-sound field processing technology. DSS synthesizes, through the CC-75's two speakers, the ambience of a hall, disco, church, jazz club, and something called Relax, supposedly for New Age music. The receiver even custom-tailors the sound should you decide to switch off the speakers and listen through headphones. Although the CC-75 probably contains everything you'll ever need for good listening, Yamaha supplies the CC-75 with several extra inputs, including one for a turntable to play phonograph records. The three-disc carousel changer permits swapping two discs while the third plays. It uses Yamaha's "S-Bit" single-bit digital-to-analog converters. Unlike most compact systems, it even has a digital output. The dual-transport cassette deck records on one transport and plays on both, with Dolby B and C noise reduction.

Warranty: parts and labor, 1 year.

Approx. retail price
$799

Approx. low price
$783

PIONEER CCS-590

Recommended

The Pioneer CCS-590 compact stereo system includes a 50-disc CD changer in the same space occupied by the average compact system. Furthermore, it looks stunning in its high-tech silver finish (also available in black for traditionalists). Besides the 50-CD changer, the system includes a 70-watt-per-channel stereo amplifier, AM/FM stereo tuner, and dual-transport, auto-reverse cassette deck. This monster of a minisystem is a lot more than most people need, and fairly pricey, so we Recommend it rather than listing it as a Best Buy. One of the nice features of the changer is that you can still load and play a single disc from the front panel. Pioneer supplies a booklet to store the liner notes in, with numbered stickers to complement the changer. You can organize the discs into three "custom files" by music type or family member. The player permits 32-track programming. There are multiple play and repeat modes, including random shuffle. Of course, Pioneer endows the changer with its high-density single-bit Pulseflow analog-to-digital converter and digital filter for good sound. The changer works in conjunction with the cassette deck for ease of taping, including a feature that optimally arranges tracks for each side of the cassette and starts copying with the touch of a single full-logic button. The dual-transport cassette deck plays on both transports and records on one, with Dolby B and C noise reduction. The amplifier can synthesize three sound fields: disco, hall, or movie. It has Pioneer's power bass feature for bass fanatics. A nine-band spectrum analyzer provides an entertaining light show of displaying relative frequency levels. You can preset 24 radio stations on the tuner. Pioneer supplies a full-function remote control.

Warranty: parts and labor, 1 year.

Approx. retail price
$1,215

Approx. low price
$756

SONY LBT-D260

Budget Buy

The Sony LBT-D260 compact stereo system gets down to basics without excluding good performance. The 50-watt-per-channel amplifier produces plenty of power for a system this size, especially with its three-way ported speakers. The speakers consist of 6¼-inch woofers, 2-inch tweeters, and ¾-inch supertweeters. Dynamic bass feedback compensates for compact speaker size for richer, fuller bass response. Five preset equalizer (tone) settings may match your musical preferences, and you can watch the relative frequency levels on the

Prices are accurate at time of printing but are subject to manufacturers' changes.

nine-band spectrum analyzer. The tuner permits 20 FM and 10 AM radio station presets. The five-CD carousel changer uses Sony's pulse-type single-bit digital-to-analog converter coupled with an 8x oversampling, 18-bit digital filter. The 20-track music calendar on the fluorescent display aids in programming up to 30 tracks. The dual-transport cassette deck plays on both transports and records on one, with Dolby B noise reduction. The time-edit computer on the CD player works with the cassette deck to arrange CD tracks for optimal recording on cassette. A sleep timer turns off the system after a specified amount of time that you select. Sony supplies a remote control.

Warranty: parts and labor, 1 year.

Approx. retail price
$450

Approx. low price
$384

Prices are accurate at time of printing but are subject to manufacturers' changes.

PERSONAL STEREOS

The personal stereo revolutionized music listening. For the first time, people could enjoy their music anytime and anywhere with high-fidelity sound. The personal stereo forever altered the music industry, boosting the cassette and FM radio to new prominence. It has become as ubiquitous as the telephone. Although the personal stereo revolves around the analog cassette, some versions offer only DAT (digital audio tape), DCC (digital compact cassette), MD (MiniDisc), or radio. Sony invented the personal stereo category in 1979 and still offers the widest array of models. Sony's trademark name of Walkman has become almost generic for a category alternatively known as headphone stereos and personal portables. Some of these models easily fit in a shirt pocket.

Recent years have brought major changes in personal stereos. Prices for basic models hit rock bottom, while full-featured models increased in price or entirely vanished. Companies expunged most of the sleek, super-small models from their catalog pages. Moreover, features disappeared from midprice models: Auto-reverse is no longer common on $50 models, and Dolby noise reduction is absent from $70 models.

Another kind of personal stereo, which followed on the heels of the Walkman craze, is the boom box. This all-in-one portable stereo system can be as small as a car battery or as large as a suitcase. The personal headphone stereo can combine radio, tape player (and recorder), or CD player; the more versatile boom box can combine radio, tape player/recorder, CD player, and even tape-dubbing dual-cassette transports.

Various portable models offer a variety of the following features: Dolby B and Dolby C noise reduction, auto-reverse, automatic music search (AMS), graphic equalizer for fine-tuning frequency response, bass booster, water resistance, and recording capability. Portables may also supply integral rechargeable batteries, solar power, TV sound (on units with radio tuners), and digitally synthesized tuning. Many of these features are marketing ploys rather than performance enhancements. However, you may find auto-reverse and digitally synthesized tuning with preset station buttons a great convenience.

Choosing a Portable

Most major brand-name portable stereos perform impressively under ideal conditions, but the true test of a portable is how it performs in motion. Listen for tape skewing (a varying amount of treble) and wow and flutter (warbling or off-speed sound) while you shake and vibrate the unit to simulate jogging or cycling.

The critical test of FM reception occurs in cities, where the unit may overload from nearby transmitters. This is often compounded by multipath distortion caused by signals bouncing between tall buildings. A stereo/mono switch or a local/distant switch helps in these situations. Some FM models use automatic stereo/mono blending to assist in smoothing out the rapid and distorting change between stereo and monaural sound that can occur when you are in an urban setting.

Another test of reception occurs inside steel and concrete buildings. These structures shield the stereo's antenna from radio signals. The length of the headphone cord determines the quality of FM reception in units that use the cord as the FM antenna. A few inches of cord more or less than the ideal 31 inches makes a great difference.

Upgrading Your Portable System

Even though electronics used in portable stereos are constantly being improved, many units come with inferior headphones. The only remedy is to purchase better phones. You may also want to consider small, powered speakers that allow you to share the music with others in the room.

Best Buys '96

Our Best Buy, Recommended, and Budget Buy personal stereos follow. Within each category, systems are listed by quality; the item we consider the best of the Best Buys is first, followed by our second choice, and so on. At the end of some categories, you will find a Budget Buy. A Budget Buy is a less expensive product of respectable quality that perhaps sacrifices some of the performance and/or features of a Best Buy or Recommended product. Some categories may not have a Best Buy listed because the price, features, and specifications for the top items are not up to Best Buy standards; Recommended items are the best in those categories. Remember that a Best Buy, Recommended, or Budget Buy designation applies only to the model listed; it does not necessarily apply to other models made by the same manufacturer or to an entire product line.

PORTABLE CD PLAYERS

PANASONIC SL-S290

✓BEST BUY

The Panasonic SL-S290 personal portable CD player plays for nine hours on a pair of alkaline AA batteries and reproduces great sound. We think this long playing time is essential for portable CD players. Panasonic builds three seconds of electronic shock protection into the SL-S290, which it calls Anti-Shock Active Use Memory. This compensates for minor bumps and bounces so that you continue to hear uninterrupted music. It also reduces battery life and can be switched off. The player uses Panasonic's single-bit MASH digital-to-analog decoder for good-quality sound. For convenience, the SL-S290 offers 24-track programming with four play/repeat modes. The small, centrally located backlit LCD clearly shows mode, track number, timings, and low battery, and it is an aid in programming. The resume mode picks up precisely where you left off playing a disc. We particularly like the ergonomics of this unit. The one-touch, full-open mechanism makes the disc easy to grab, and to make it still easier, pressing on the center spindle pops the disc off. The XBS (Extra Bass System) boosts bass for those in quest of pronounced low frequencies, while a high-cut filter reduces the shrillness heard on some discs. A wide plastic headband holds the comfortable on-the-ear headphones in place. The same player equipped with accessories for car use, the SL-S291C, costs $30 more.

Specifications: height, $1\frac{3}{16}$"; width, $5\frac{1}{16}$"; depth, $5\frac{11}{16}$"; weight, $9\frac{9}{10}$ oz. without batteries. **Warranty:** parts and labor, 1 year.

Approx. retail price **$150**

Approx. low price **$126**

AIWA XP-200

Recommended

The Aiwa XP-200 personal portable CD player performs as well as top-of-the-line players of several years ago. Aiwa keeps the price low by dispensing with frills such as electronic shock protection. Yet it still provides eight hours of play from a pair of alkaline AA batteries. An optional rechargeable battery provides three more hours of play. The unit acts as a recharger with the optional rechargeable battery pack. The XP-200 uses single-bit digital-to-analog converters for good sound quality. Aiwa's Dynamic Super Linear Bass boosts bass response. A wide plastic headband makes these impressive-sounding headphones comfortable on the ear. You can program 24 tracks, aided by the small LCD that shows tracks and timings. A LED indicator shows battery condition. The repeat function offers a choice between one track or all tracks. The XP-200 is available with a car adapter kit as the XP-C207 for $30 extra.

Specifications: height, $6\frac{3}{4}$"; width, $5\frac{9}{16}$"; depth, $1\frac{5}{8}$"; weight, $12\frac{1}{3}$ oz. without batteries. **Warranty:** parts, 1 year; labor, 90 days.

Approx. retail price **$110**

Approx. low price **Not available**

MAGNAVOX AZ683217

Budget Buy

The Magnavox AZ683217 is one of dozens of personal portable Magnavox CD players that have multiple configurations of several units. We chose this particular one for its combination of features at a budget price. The AZ683217 has car accessories, including a cigarette-lighter power adapter and a cassette radio adapter. The headphones are the on-the-ear type. An AC power adapter also comes with this CD player. The player operates about 10 hours on four AA batteries. Although it lacks electronic shock protection, the mechanical design re-

Prices are accurate at time of printing but are subject to manufacturers' changes.

duces shock for use in a moving car. You can program 20 tracks, aided by the multifunction LCD that shows tracks, timings, settings, and low battery. Random play shuffles the tracks. The dynamic bass boost feature lives up to its name. The AZ683217 uses 16-bit digital-to-analog converters, which are somewhat less accurate than the more contemporary single-bit converters. However, on a portable the difference in sound quality should not be a major problem.

Specifications: height, $1\frac{1}{5}$"; width, $5\frac{1}{5}$'; depth, $6\frac{1}{5}$"; weight, $10\frac{1}{5}$ oz. without batteries. **Warranty:** 1 year free exchange warranty.

Approx. retail price	**Approx. low price**
$130	**$105**

PERSONAL RADIO–CASSETTE PLAYER–RECORDERS

AIWA HS-JS445

✓BEST BUY

The HS-JS445 personal radio–cassette player–recorder is far from the least expensive model of its type, but it combines desirable features at a reasonable price. It records in stereo on standard or high-bias tape from the tuner or from the supplied one-point stereo microphone. The digital tuner permits six AM and 12 FM radio station presets. An LED indicates the condition of the two AA batteries powering the unit. Aiwa supplies exceptionally good-sounding, comfortable on-the-ear headphones supported by a wide plastic headband. Aiwa's Super Bass circuit adds extra bass for those who enjoy it. The anti-rolling mechanism reduces warbling tape distortion. The multisound processor optimizes the sound on playback for different types of music such as classic, pop, rock, and jazz, although many listeners may prefer their music without the processor. The HS-JS445 autoreverses only in the playback mode, and the Dolby B noise reduction functions only during playback. A belt clip allows convenient attachment to your belt for music while you're in motion. Aside from its many features, the HS-JS445 sounds very good and operates reliably.

Specifications: height, 3½"; width, 4 11/16"; depth, 1½"; weight, 5⅓ oz. without battery. **Warranty**: parts, 1 year; labor 90 days.

Approx. retail price	**Approx. low price**
$145	**$116**

SONY WM-GX302

Recommended

The Sony WM-GX302 radio–cassette player–recorder records as well as plays your tapes in stereo. It records from the built-in AM/FM stereo tuner or the supplied one-point stereo microphone. The tape reverses automatically on playback and shuts off automatically at the end of each side in record mode. You can monitor tapes in mono from a small monitor speaker or listen through the stereo headphones. A narrow metal headband that might prove uncomfortable to some people supports the good-sounding on-the-ear phones. Sony's Mega Bass pumps up the bass for listeners who can't get enough of it. The FM local/distant switch optimizes the tuner for reception locale and conditions. The Automatic Volume Limiter System adjusts dynamic range to protect hearing while increasing audibility in a noisy environment. The WM-GX302 operates on a pair of AA batteries. The recording quality is adequate for school classes and business meetings and will do for live music in a pinch. Playback quality is very good.

Specifications: height, 3⅜"; width, 4¾"; depth, 1⅜"; weight, 8 oz. with batteries. **Warranty**: parts, 1 year; labor, 90 days.

Approx. retail price	**Approx. low price**
$90	**$79**

PERSONAL RADIO–CASSETTE PLAYERS

SONY WM-FX401

BEST BUY

The Sony WM-FX401 personal radio-cassette player features a digitally synthesized AM/FM stereo tuner with 10 radio station presets, directly accessible from five keys. The digital liquid crystal display not only doubles as a clock but also works as an alarm that will wake you with a tone from

Prices are accurate at time of printing but are subject to manufacturers' changes.

the unit as well as the headphones. The FM local/distant switch optimizes reception depending on location and reception conditions. The Automatic Volume Limiter System adjusts dynamic range to lower distortion and protects your hearing while improving audibility in noise environments. The auto-reverse tape player also has automatic shutoff after both sides have played. The on-the-ear headphones sound quite good, but they are supported by a single thin metal band. Large push buttons operate the tape player. A switch optimizes playback for standard or chrome/metal tapes. The WM-FX401 contains all the features and sound for enjoyable music on the go, including a belt clip.

Specifications: height, $3\frac{5}{8}$"; width, $4\frac{1}{2}$"; depth, $1\frac{1}{2}$"; weight, $7\frac{1}{2}$ oz. with batteries. **Warranty:** parts, 1 year; labor, 90 days.

Approx. retail price	**Approx. low price**
$60	**$57**

AIWA HS-TX356

BEST BUY

The Aiwa HS-TX356 is unusually elegant for an inexpensive radio-cassette player. It features a digital tuner with six AM and 12 FM radio station presets. Six keys make it easy to immediately access the presets. The digital display doubles as a clock with multiple time zone settings. In contrast, the basic tape player does not automatically reverse, but it does shut off automatically at the end of the side. Large mechanical buttons operate the player. It has settings for both standard and chrome/metal tapes. The on-the-ear headphones, though not Aiwa's best, sound good and are comfortable with their wide plastic headband. The Super Bass setting boosts the bass. A belt clip makes it convenient to attach the HS-TX356 to your waist and go. The unit operates on a pair of AA batteries.

Specifications: height, $3\frac{11}{16}$"; width, $4\frac{11}{16}$"; depth, $1\frac{5}{8}$"; weight, $6\frac{7}{10}$ oz. without batteries. **Warranty:** parts 1 year; labor, 90 days.

Approx. retail price	**Approx. low price**
$50	**$43**

Prices are accurate at time of printing but are subject to manufacturers' changes.

SONY WM-FX435

✓BEST BUY

The Sony WM–FX435 personal radio–cassette player adds luxury to our Best Buy list. It incorporates all the necessary features for ideal reproduction without superfluous gimmicks. As in our other Best Buys, a digital AM/FM stereo tuner brings in strong reception and tunes easily. The WM-FX435 gives you five AM and five FM radio station presets. It also receives VHF TV sound and allocates five TV sound presets. Having TV sound on the go can keep you current with your favorite show, even without the picture. You quickly access the presets from the five buttons on the cover of the unit. An FM local/distant switch optimizes reception for location and listening conditions. The auto-reverse tape player, operated by large mechanical buttons, shuts off after playing both sides of the tape. Dolby B noise reduction improves tape sound quality when playing Dolby-encoded tapes. A switch chooses between standard and chrome/metal tapes for optimum tonal balance. The Automatic Volume Limiter System protects your hearing and reduces distortion while making music more audible in noisy environments. The Mega Bass circuit offers bass boost for the bass-hungry listener. The liquid crystal radio display also functions as a clock. A particularly outstanding feature is the extended battery life, about 18 hours from a pair of alkaline AA batteries. The on-the-ear headphones deliver good sound, but are supported by a thin metal headband. A belt clip comes with the WM-FX435 for on-the-go convenience.

Specifications: height, 3⅛"; width, 4⅜"; depth, 1¼"; weight, 7⅜ oz. without batteries. **Warranty:** parts, 1 year; labor, 90 days.

Approx. retail price
$80

Approx. low price
$80

PANASONIC RQ-V197

Recommended

The Panasonic RQ–V197 personal radio–cassette player includes all the expected features, but with a twist. Panasonic developed a way to not only produce audio from the headphones but also make them vibrate for tactile low bass.

Prices are accurate at time of printing but are subject to manufacturers' changes.

Panasonic calls this the Virtual Motion Sound System (VMSS). However, Panasonic no longer includes Dolby B noise reduction on most of its personal stereos, which is why this model, at this price, is Recommended rather than a Best Buy. The digital AM/FM stereo tuner cleanly snares radio stations, aided by a local/distant switch to optimize reception. You can preset 20 radio stations (10 AM and 10 FM) in four groups, accessed by five preset buttons. A liquid crystal display shows frequency and preset number. The auto-reverse cassette player operates reliably. To provide continuous music, the player does not automatically stop at the end of the second cassette side. A switch selects between normal and chrome/metal tapes. In case the VMSS doesn't rattle your earlobes enough, Panasonic includes its standard XBS extra bass system. The excellent on-the-ear headphones sound good and are supported by comfortable dual headbands. Push buttons control mechanical functions. The RQ-V197 operates on two AA batteries.

Specifications: height, 3⅜"; width, 4½"; depth, 1⅜"; weight, 6⅖ oz. without batteries. **Warranty:** parts and labor, 1 year.

Approx. retail price
$90

Approx. low price
$83

AIWA HS-TA153

Budget Buy

The Aiwa HS-TA153 personal radio cassette player is a basic value. It's as small and compact as the expensive models but has minimal features. It tunes AM/FM stereo the old-fashioned way on a small slide-rule dial. A switch selects the proper treble balance for standard or chrome/metal tapes. It automatically stops at the end of the cassette side. The super-bass setting boosts the bass. The on-the-ear headphones are the budget type, but they nonetheless sound good, and their wide plastic headband is fairly comfortable. A belt-clip makes the HS-TA153 easy to take along. Though it's short on frills, it performs quite competently. Two AA batteries power the HS-TA153.

Specifications: height, 4⅝"; width, 3¹¹⁄₁₆"; depth, 1½"; weight, 5⁹⁄₁₀ oz. without batteries. **Warranty:** parts, 1 year; labor, 90 days.

Approx. retail price	Approx. low price
$30	$27

PERSONAL HEADSET RADIO

SONY SRF-H2 ✓BEST BUY

The SRF-H2 AM/FM stereo headset radio stays on your head because of its double headband. You won't mind the tenacity, because it's extremely lightweight and has reasonably comfortable on-the ear cushions. A flexible short-whip antenna resists breaking, yet it pulls in stations loud and clear. The reflective yellow tip on the antenna is a safety feature that increases visibility, which is especially useful when jogging at night. The SRF-H2 has a local/distant switch for optimizing FM reception. Radio reception is quite good, although an overload is possible in the immediate vicinity of powerful transmitters. The unit operates for about 70 hours on a single AAA alkaline battery (about 25 hours on a regular battery).

Specifications: weight, 4⅛ oz. with battery. **Warranty:** parts, 1 year; labor, 90 days.

Approx. retail price	Approx. low price
$35	$30

PERSONAL RADIOS

SONY SRF-85 ✓BEST BUY

Although this sports model Sony SRF-85 personal radio carries a premium price for its bright yellow water-resistant case, we think it's convenient to own at least one all-purpose, nearly indestructible radio that brings in good reception. This AM/FM stereo model has a local/distant switch to optimize FM reception. It includes Sony's Automatic Volume Limiter System to protect your hearing, reduce distortion, and improve audibility in noisy environments. In this radio, Sony's ultra-light, in-the-ear headphones make sense, since they tend to stay put better than the over-the-ear kind when you're active. A belt clip and swiveling armband/handgrip keep the SRF-

85 glued to you whether you're relaxing or jogging. It operates on a single AA battery. We prefer the old-fashioned mechanical tuning of the SRF-85, because the feather-touch buttons of the digital models accidentally activate when you put the radio in a pocket or purse.

Specifications: height, 3⅞"; width, 2⅝"; depth, 3¹⁄₃₂"; weight, 3⅖ oz. without battery. **Warranty:** parts, 1 year; labor, 90 days.

Approx. retail price	Approx. low price
$40	$39

SONY SRF-39 Budget Buy

The Sony SRF-39 AM/FM stereo personal radio brings in reasonably good reception under most conditions. Its large tuning wheel with slide-rule dial makes it easy to use. A local/distant switch optimizes FM reception. The light, on-the-ear headphones are supported by a thin metal band. Sony supplies a belt clip, but this radio is easily pocketable. It operates on a single AA battery.

Specifications: height, 3⅝"; width, 2½"; depth, 1"; weight, 2⅓ oz. without battery. **Warranty:** parts, 1 year; labor, 90 days.

Approx. retail price	Approx. low price
$20	$19

BOOM BOXES
Boom Boxes with CDs

SONY CFD-626 ✓BEST BUY

The Sony CFD-626 is a new product that blends portable stereo features (single cassette deck and AM/FM radio) with hi-fii enhancements. Two notable additions to this hot new design are higher power outputs—the CFD-626 pounds the sounds with 4.5 watts per channel—and a six-CD changer. The CD changer scans and automatically plays the first track of each disc loaded, so you can sample all the music and then program your choices for full play. The sound system has a remote recording feature that pauses the recording operation while the CDs are changing for a seamless taping job. It also allows unattended recording of random tracks. This unit can operate with eight D batteries or the included AC line cord.

Specifications: height, $10\frac{1}{8}''$; width, $23\frac{1}{4}''$; depth, $12\frac{5}{8}''$; weight, 19 lb. $1\frac{1}{4}$ oz. **Warranty:** parts, 90 days; labor, 1 year.

Approx. retail price
$340

Approx. low price
$279

OPTIMUS 13-1268

Budget Buy

The Optimus 13-1268, made by Radio Shack, is also called the Optimus Micro Music System. It includes an AM/FM tuner, cassette player, CD player, twin speakers, and remote control. The sound quality is good but lacks any special circuitry to enhance the output from the dual four-inch speakers. The only sound aids are the three-band equalizer that lets you adjust the tone and sound and the Bass Boost feature. The CD player can program 21 tracks, and the Automatic Search Music System lets you quickly find any track on a CD. The only other CD controls are repeat play and random play. The tape deck's auto-stop feature stops the tape when it reaches the end. An automatic level control adjusts the recording level to compensate for low sounds. An auxiliary input jack lets you hear an external audio source through the system. This unit is powered by two AAA batteries.

Specifications: height, $10\frac{5}{8}''$; width, $17\frac{1}{8}''$; depth, $5\frac{11}{16}''$; weight, $6\frac{4}{5}$ lb. **Warranty:** 90 days.

Approx. retail price
$200

Approx. low price
$200

Boom Boxes Without CDs

PANASONIC RX-FS470

✓BEST BUY

The Panasonic RX-FS470 is a compact portable stereo with a big boom-box sound. The two-way, four-speaker system has Free Edge Woofers for great low-frequency range

Prices are accurate at time of printing but are subject to manufacturers' changes.

reproduction. The bass sounds are enhanced with the Extra Bass System's on/off switch and level control. An FM stereo/mono mode selector gives optimum sound quality depending on the type of signal selected. The tape deck has one-touch recording and a soft eject system. The unit is powered by six D batteries or an included AC power cord and has a built-in condenser microphone and a headphone jack. Although it has no built-in CD player, you can use the RX-FS470 as an amplifier system by plugging a mini CD player into the external CD jack.

Specifications: height, 5⅞"; width, 18⅛"; depth, 5 5/16"; weight, 5 5/16 lb. **Warranty:** parts and labor, 1 year.

Approx. retail price
$80

Approx. low price
$65

PANASONIC RX-FT570

Recommended

The Panasonic RX-FT570 is a feature-laden portable stereo with dual cassettes. The two play/record tape systems give this model lots of flexibility. Both cassette decks have the automatic stop feature. Deck 1 has a reverse mode selector and forward/reverse direction control. Deck 2 has cue and review controls and one-touch and follow-up recording. The built-in condenser microphone works on either tape deck. A very useful feature for serious taping work is the high-speed and synchro-start editing and the automatic replay playback functions. The two-way, four-speaker system has Free Edge Woofers for great low-frequency range reproduction. The bass sounds are enhanced with the Extra Bass System's on/off switch and level control. An FM stereo/mono mode selector gives optimum sound quality depending on the type of signal selected. This unit is powered by six D batteries or an included AC power cord. It has a headphone jack and a jack for plugging in an external CD player.

Specifications: height, 5¾"; width, 22 5/16"; depth, 6 5/16"; weight, 6⅜ lb. **Warranty:** parts and labor, 1 year.

Approx. retail price
$100

Approx. low price
$90

GENERAL ELECTRIC 3-5620

Budget Buy

The GE 3-5620 offers good basic portable stereo convenience. It has an AM/FM stereo tuner and a cassette deck. The two-speaker system has three-inch woofers and Bass Boost to enhance low volume. The built-in microphone lets you record "live," or you can push one button to record from the radio. The tape system features include cushion eject and automatic shut-off. The GE 3-5620 has a stereo headphone jack and operates on six C cell batteries or the included AC line cord. The optional rechargeable battery sticks provide greater usefulness and reliability.

Specifications: height, 5¼"; width, 16⅖"; depth, 4"; weight, 3½ lb. **Warranty:** 1 year, limited.

Approx. retail price
$40

Approx. low price
$32

CLOCK RADIOS

Clock radios have been around for years and can be found in most households. Standard clock radios—offering features such as radio and tone alarms, digital- or analog-style clock face, and AM/FM radio reception—are inexpensive and found everywhere. These days you can also purchase a more complex, feature-laden clock radio that can double as an entertainment system in the bedroom. Some of these models have multiple alarms, cassette record and playback features, and CD players. The two models reviewed this year offer advanced features not found on the inexpensive standard models.

PANASONIC SL-PH2

✓BEST BUY

The Panasonic SL-PH2 is an AM/FM stereo clock radio with compact disc player that gives great sound quality. The sound system uses built-in three-inch speakers, a digital-to-analog converter, and an adjustable bass boost for good sound quality at low volumes. For an alarm, choose CD, AM/FM radio, or a buzzer. The doze/snooze feature lets you sleep a few more minutes before sounding the alarm again. A

Prices are accurate at time of printing but are subject to manufacturers' changes.

sleep mode automatically turns off the radio after playing for up to 59 minutes. The CD player has 24-track random accessing for programming, repeat mode, track skip, forward and reverse searching modes, and memory recall. The AM/FM radio has seven preset frequencies for each band. The unit can be powered by an AC power adapter or six C batteries.

Specifications: height, 2⅞"; width, 13⅜", depth, 6⅛". **Warranty:** parts and labor, 1 year.

Approx. retail price	Approx. low price
$260	$225

SONY ICF-CD833

Recommended

The Sony ICF-CD833 is a new product packaged in a space-saving design. The sleek case fits well on any night table or dresser. This unit is a combination clock radio and CD player. Its features include a digitally synthesized AM/FM stereo tuner, five preset stations, and the Mega Bass sound system, with a three-position switch for adjusting low harmonic bass tones. This electronic design adds a rich, deep sound to the two 3-inch speakers. A special memory feature lets you set the alarm to play any track on the CD, select your favorite radio station, or sound the buzzer. The Dream Bar programs the alarm to allow a few extra minutes of sleep. Sleep Timer mode shuts off the sound system after a preset time.

Specifications: height, 7"; width, 6¹⁵⁄₁₆"; depth, 7⁹⁄₁₆". **Warranty:** parts, 90 days; labor, 1 year.

Approx. retail price	Approx. low price
$160	$155

CAMERAS

Every year around the world some 60 billion pictures are taken. Today at least 85 percent of them are taken with color negative film. This is due partly to the rapid growth of minilabs, but another reason is that you no longer have to be an expert to operate a camera. Many cameras will automatically focus the lens, meter the available light, set the correct aperture and shutter speed, and even activate the built-in or attached flash for you if the light level is too low for a good exposure. More sophisticated models give you a choice: You can use them as fully automatic cameras, or you can take control to make your own picture-taking decisions. Fully manual cameras still exist for those who always want to be in control of their photographs.

Photography is an enjoyable way to record the many things that please you. Consider the type of pictures you want and take care to choose a camera that will help you get them. Camera manufacturers have turned their attention to producing high-quality lenses, accurate exposure systems, and wide-ranging exposure controls even in less expensive models. The result is a wide range of choices to suit your personal needs.

Types of Cameras

With a **single-lens reflex (SLR) camera,** you view the subject of your picture through the lens that takes the picture, so that you see exactly what the camera sees.

With a **viewfinder camera,** you see the image you are going to photograph through a window, or viewfinder, in the camera's body. The 35mm autofocus and compact cameras listed in this section are viewfinder cameras.

With a **rangefinder camera,** you view your subject through a viewfinder, and the rangefinder projects a second image of the subject in the viewfinder: The lens is in focus when the two images coincide.

A **zone-focus camera** is a viewfinder camera that uses symbols or a distance scale to focus the lens. You estimate the distances and set the lens accordingly. Some autofocus cameras use zone-focus symbols in the viewfinder to indicate where the camera is focused.

A **fixed-focus camera,** usually called a point-and-shoot camera, is a viewfinder camera that has its focus fixed at a certain point. With this type of camera, everything from a specified minimum distance to infinity is in focus.

An **autofocus (AF) camera** focuses the lens automatically when you touch the shutter release button. Any of several methods can be used to do this.

A **single-use camera** comes with a roll of film in it. When the roll is finished, you bring the camera to your lab, which returns the processed film and prints to you but sends the camera parts to a recycling plant. Single-use cameras are handy, especially if you don't want to expose your own camera to damage from the elements. Special camera designs also allow you to take pictures that you could not take with your own camera. If you don't have an underwater camera, you can buy a single-use camera for a few dollars that can be taken underwater to depths of up to ten feet. Underwater models are available from Fuji, Kodak, Konica, and Vivitar. Agfa and Kodak have introduced shirt-pocket-size models with or without flash, while Polaroid has a talking camera. Of the panorama cameras, Konica's 17mm lens has the widest sweep.

Features and Terminology

The **aperture,** or **f-stop,** is a ratio of the diameter of the lens opening to the focal length of the lens. All lenses are identified by their focal length and their largest aperture. A standard, or normal, lens for a 35mm camera is usually listed as a 50mm f/2 lens. (A normal lens produces a picture that approximates the perspective and degree of magnification that is seen by the human eye, excluding peripheral vision). The f-stop is a function of the lens aperture setting. The standard series is f/1.4, f/2, f/2.8, f/4, f/5.6, f/8, f/11, f/16, f/22, and f/32. The smaller the number, the larger the aperture and the more light that will strike the film: An f/1.4 aperture allows twice as much light to pass through the lens as does an f/2 aperture. Most lenses do not cover the full range of settings, and some may extend higher or lower.

A **focal-plane shutter** uses curtains or blades that travel either vertically or horizontally across the film plane to make an exposure. Almost all 35mm SLR cameras use this shutter because it allows the camera to use interchangeable lenses.

A **leaf shutter** uses a series of blades arranged in a circle that open and close to make an exposure. Compact 35mm cameras with fixed lenses use leaf shutters.

Exposure value (EV) compensation is used to correct the automatic exposure of subjects that are either very light or very dark. One EV is equivalent to one full f-stop.

Viewfinder information is a visual display in the camera's viewfinder of the exposure information you need to take good pictures. Autofocus SLR cameras also have signals that indicate when an image is in focus, and some signal out-of-focus conditions. Most cameras also provide flash signals that tell you when the flash is needed for a good exposure.

DX coding imparts information about the film directly to the camera. Metal strips on the 35mm film cassette make contact with pins in the camera and tell the camera the film speed, exposure latitude, and number of exposures on the roll. Most SLRs offer both DX coding and manual film-speed settings, but compact 35mm cameras offer only DX coding.

The **International Standards Organization,** or **ISO,** is a numerical system that indicates the film's relative speed or sensitivity to light. The higher the ISO number, the faster the film is in recording the image and the less light it needs to record the image. To take photographs in low light, you use a high-speed film.

A **dedicated hot shoe** is a shoe, or clip, found on most 35mm SLR cameras. It interfaces accessories such as electronic flashes with the camera's electronics. Some dedicated systems provide through-the-lens-off-the-film (TTL-OTF) flash control.

A **self-timer,** found on most 35mm cameras, is a switch that delays the operation of the shutter for about ten seconds, allowing the photographer to get in the picture.

Best Buys '96

Our Best Buy, Recommended, and Budget Buy cameras follow. They are presented in five categories: 35mm manual-focus SLR cameras, 35mm autofocus SLR cameras, 35mm autofocus cameras, 35mm compact cameras, and instant-print cameras. Within each category, products are listed according to overall quality. The best of the Best Buys is first, followed by our second choice, and so on. At the end of a category, you may find one or more products listed as Budget Buys. These products may not have all the features of a Best Buy or a Recommended product, but they are still a good, solid value. Remember that a Best Buy, Recommended, or Budget Buy rating applies only to the model listed and not to other models in the same product line or from the same manufacturer.

35mm MANUAL-FOCUS SLR CAMERAS

The 35mm SLR (single-lens reflex) camera is probably the most widely used professional camera. Newspaper, combat, and sports photographers use 35mm SLRs, as do fashion and nature photographers, scientists, and doctors. Manual-focus SLR cameras are particularly suitable for amateur photographers who want to be the master of the images they create through the focus and exposure controls. Our selections have built-in metering with both automatic and manual exposure controls.

MINOLTA X-9

The Minolta X-9 is a microcomputerized SLR **✔ BEST BUY** with aperture-priority autoexposure (AE) and metered manual exposure. A very welcome feature is the X-9's diagonally oriented split-image rangefinder. Diagonal orientation means that you can easily focus on either horizontal or vertical subjects. The viewfinder also provides you with complete exposure information: The lens aperture appears in a window below the image area, and LEDs along the right side give you mode and shutter-speed information. The top two LEDs tell whether you

Prices are accurate at time of printing but are subject to manufacturers' changes.

are in manual-exposure or AE mode. Below the mode LEDs are listed shutter speeds from 1/1000 second to one second, and B for long exposures, with an LED next to each one. In auto, an LED lights up next to the shutter speed selected by the camera's microcomputer, whereas in manual, the correct shutter speed flashes until you select the correct setting. An AE lock button allows you to take a reading of your subject, lock in your exposure, then recompose and make the exposure. The meter couples with all films from ISO 12 to ISO 3200. A safe-load signal on top of the camera monitors the film transport by advancing as you advance the film. Other features are a depth-of-field preview button and a self-timer. With its full-information viewfinder and the handy location of all its controls, the X-9 is a well-balanced and comfortable SLR.

Warranty: parts and labor, 1 year.

Approx. retail price	**Approx. low price**
$325	**$210**

RICOH XR-X 3 PF

✓BEST BUY

The Ricoh XR-X 3 PF is a compact 35mm SLR with a built-in flash and a built-in motor drive that can advance the film up to two frames a second. All popular K-mount lenses from wide-angle to telephoto can be used in manual and aperture-priority exposure modes. The XR-X 3 PF has an electronic shutter speed from 32 seconds to 1/3000 second in AE modes and 16 seconds to 1/2000 second plus B for long exposures in manual. Along with the TTL center-weighted and spot metering for ambient light, the camera also has TTL flash metering for the built-in pop-up flash and dedicated Ricoh flashes. The XR-X 3 PF has two mode-selection buttons next to the LCD panel that let you select exposure modes, exposure meter mode, motor drive mode, red-eye reduction mode, multiexposure mode, depth-of-field preview mode, auto-bracketing mode, exposure compensation, flash exposure compensation, and manual film-speed setting. Other features include a self-timer, an AE lock button, and both automatic and manual rewind. Housed in the well-designed finger grip are the four AA alkaline batteries that power all camera functions. The XR-X 3 PF is a very versatile manual-focus SLR that can handle virtually any photographic situation.

Warranty: labor, 1 year.

Approx. retail price **$500**

Approx. low price **$313**

VIVITAR V50

Recommended

The Vivitar V50 is an SLR with aperture-priority auto-exposure and match-LED-metered manual exposure; an SPD cell provides center-weighted metering. We tested it with the 50mm f/1.8 lens and case. The viewfinder displays shutter speed: LEDs along the right side give you mode and shutter-speed information. The top two LEDs tell whether you are in the manual exposure or AE mode. Below the mode LEDs are the shutter speeds, from 1/1000 second to one second, and B for long exposures, with an LED next to each one. In auto, an LED lights up next to the shutter speed selected by the camera's microcomputer, while in manual, the correct shutter speed flashes until you select the correct setting. An LED arrow between one second and B glows if the metered speed is between one and four seconds, and it blinks if the shutter speed needed is below that range. An AE lock button allows you to take a reading of your subject, lock in your exposure, then recompose and make the exposure. The meter couples with all films from ISO 12 to ISO 3200. A safe-load signal on top of the camera monitors the film transport by advancing as you advance the film. A self-timer provides a 10-second delay. The V50 is a well-balanced SLR that uses the popular Minolta M and MD bayonet lenses.

Warranty: parts and labor, 1 year.

Approx. retail price **$338**

Approx. low price **$186**

PENTAX P30T

Recommended

The Pentax P30T is a basic manual-focus SLR that has an electronically controlled shutter with speeds from one second to 1/1000 second, plus B for long exposures. The P30T

Prices are accurate at time of printing but are subject to manufacturers' changes.

has four exposure modes: programmed AE, aperture-priority AE, shutter-priority AE, and metered manual. The full-aperture TTL metering is center-weighted via a GPD cell. The viewfinder screen has a diagonally oriented split image for easy focusing on both horizontal and vertical subjects. Next to the viewing screen is an array of LEDs, and the shutter speed will light up in use; in manual, the recommended shutter speed blinks. Film advance is by a thumb-operated lever, and film is rewound with a crank. Manual film transport allows the P30T to be powered by two 1.5-volt button batteries. DX-coded films from ISO 25 to 1600 can be used. Other features are a hot shoe with dedicated operation for Pentax electronic flashes, AE memory lock, depth-of-field preview, and a self-timer with a 12-second delay. The P30T is a solid manual-focus SLR that uses all Pentax bayonet mount lenses, including autofocus lenses that can be manually focused.

Warranty: parts and labor, 1 year.

Approx. retail price	**Approx. low price**
$323	**$173**

35mm AUTOFOCUS SLR CAMERAS

Autofocus, or AF, SLR cameras have charge-coupled-device (CCD) sensors that use subject contrast to achieve the correct focus. Some CCDs are so sensitive that they can focus on low-contrast subjects in light so low that you can hardly see the AF frame in the viewfinder. Many AF SLRs now have built-in near-infrared AF illuminators that automatically project a focusing pattern so that the camera can focus on subjects with no contrast—and even on subjects in total darkness. Highly efficient microprocessors and micromotors have made autofocusing very fast and accurate, even with long telephoto lenses.

The zoom-lens reflex (ZLR) is a new type of AF SLR. The ZLR is so named because it is a single-lens reflex with a permanently attached zoom lens. A ZLR gives you the best of both worlds: viewing through the lens in a compact, unified camera/lens design. ZLRs produce quality images equal to or better than those of other SLRs.

MINOLTA MAXXUM 700SI

✓BEST BUY

The Maxxum 700si employs unique technology to make perfect flash exposures using off-camera flashes without wires. Wireless TTL flash photography uses the 700si's built-in flash, the optional remote flash controller, or an optional attached flash to send out stroboscopic codes that fire from one to ten remote flashes. When the camera's meter senses the correct exposure, a second set of codes stops the remote flashes from emitting light. The stroboscopic flashes are so fast that the eye sees only one burst of light. This feature is controlled by the Maxxum's underlying expert intelligence system, a fuzzy-logic microcomputer that emulates the way a knowledgeable photographer thinks. This system also controls autofocus, autoexposure, and autozoom. The multisensor autofocus system uses four sensors in the horizontal position and three sensors in the vertical—fuzzy logic determines which of the sensors are seeing the main subject and focuses the lens. You can manually select any one of the four sensors for special situations. The 14-segment honeycomb metering pattern is tied into the autofocus system so that it can center the exposure around your main subject. Spot metering is available for difficult lighting situations. The 700si has a number of convenience features: Often-used settings can be stored for instant recall with the memory function; the viewfinder gives eyeglass wearers full view; auto eye-start can be used to activate AF and AE operation when you bring the camera to your eye; and the pop-up flash, with red-eye reduction, is very convenient when quick flash fill is needed. The 700si uses the unique Maxxum creative card system to perform many specialized operations, ranging from exposure and flash bracketing to multiple exposures and fantasy effects. The Minolta Maxxum 700si is among the very best AF SLRs and has no peer when it comes to wireless TTL flash operation.

Warranty: parts and labor, 1 year.

Approx. retail price	**Approx. low price**
$1,111	**$637**

Prices are accurate at time of printing but are subject to manufacturers' changes.

:ANON EOS ELAN IIE

✓ BEST BUY

The Canon EOS Elan IIE has an improved ver-ion of eye-controlled focus (introduced in the EOS A2E) that ıow works for vertical as well as horizontal compositions. 'hree autofocus areas are outlined on the viewing screen. The ıF sensor nearest to where you are looking when you depress he shutter release button halfway is the AF sensor that does he focusing, insuring that the camera focuses on your main ubject. The Elan IIE can be calibrated for up to three different hotographers. The depth of field mode is also eye-activated, y looking at the box in the upper-left-hand corner of the 'iewing screen. Standard autofocus operation is also selec-able. The six-zone evaluative metering is linked to the three-oint AF system so that light metering emphasizes the main ubject for both ambient light and flash exposures. Partial spot) metering and center-weighted metering are also avail-ble. The motor drive is very quiet and provides up to 2.5 rames per second of continuous shooting. The command dial ıas a creative zone for photographer control and a picture one with programs that automatically set the camera for por-raits, landscapes, close-ups, and sports photos. Along with he standard autoexposure and manual exposure modes in the reative zone, the Elan has depth-of-field AE that sets the roper aperture for sharp pictures of foreground and back-round. The other creative-zone settings include manual film-peed setting and custom function settings for personalized amera operation. Other exposure controls are automatic ex-osure bracketing, exposure compensation, and multiple ex-osures. There is TTL AE for the built-in pop-up flash, which lso has red-eye reduction. An AF-assist beam automatically ghts up in low light. Autofilm-speed settings for DX-coded lms range from ISO 25 to ISO 5000, with manual settings pos-ible from ISO 6 to ISO 6400. The EOS Elan IIE is a very versa-le AF SLR with superior autofocus operation.

Varranty: parts and labor, 1 year.

pprox. retail price	**Approx. low price**
800	**$523**

Prices are accurate at time of printing but are subject to manufacturers' changes.

NIKON N70

✓BEST BUY

The Nikon N70 has a command-input control system and a quick-recall (QR) function that provides wide photographic control and a quick method of setting your chosen operation modes. The QR function allows you to preset three different sets of modes, then quickly recall any one set whenever needed. The LCD panel on top of the camera displays the eight functions of the command-input control system, which cover all variable camera operations from motor drive, and focus operations to exposure bracketing, metering, and flash operations. Displayed above the LCD panel are the eight vari-program modes of the programmed AE mode, which automatically make the proper settings for such things as portraits, macro photography, and sports or night scenes. The built-in pop-up flash, which has a red-eye reduction mode, performs most of the same functions as Nikon dedicated speed lights: rear-curtain sync, slow sync, flash exposure compensation, and flash exposure bracketing. Eight-segment 3-D Matrix metering, which includes distance information from subject to camera, is performed with all Nikon D lenses; with non-D lenses, Advanced Matrix metering is performed. Spot metering and 75-percent weighted metering are also available. The N70 has two autofocusing areas: Wide-area AF is for general shooting, while spot-area AF is for difficult focusing situations such as small objects, through fences, and backlit subjects. Both focus on horizontally and vertically oriented subjects. Film from ISO 6 to ISO 6400 can be manually set; DX coding is accepted for ISO 25 to ISO 5000. The N70 sounds complicated but is actually user-friendly and very easy to operate, right down to its multimode flash operation.

Warranty: parts and labor, 1 year.

Approx. retail price	**Approx. low price**
$945	$637

OLYMPUS IS-2 ZOOM-LENS REFLEX

Recommended

The Olympus IS-2 is an AF ZLR with a 35mm-to-135mm f/4.5–5.6 lens. One of the lens elements is made of

Prices are accurate at time of printing but are subject to manufacturers' changes.

xtraordinary dispersion (ED) glass, specially formulated to ring the focus of all light rays closer together than ordinary lass, thus producing sharper images with more accurate colrs. The IS-2 is L-shaped, a unique, natural design for a solid nd comfortable hold. The autofocus system is highly sensitive nd fast, with an autofocus indicator for accurate focusing even vith low-contrast subjects. Focusing is from 3.9 feet to infinity verall and 2.0 feet to infinity from 35mm to 100mm. Life-size nacro is possible with an accessory macro converter. The four rogram AE modes—standard, sports, portrait, and night cene—use fuzzy-logic ESP to meter even very subtle differnces in light for accurate exposures. Spot metering is also vailable for special situations. Center-weighted metering is sed with aperture-priority AE and metered manual exposure. unique pop-up intelligent variable power (IVP) flash has two ash tubes to cover macro, wide-angle, and telephoto situaions, including red-eye reduction. All films from ISO 25 to 200 can be used, and +/-4 EV compensation can accommoate most non-DX-coded film. The built-in motor drive can adance the film up to two frames per second. The accessory G40 ash adds more power, bounce lighting, rear-curtain sync, and nultiexposures and can be used with the built-in flash for ounce lighting plus fill light. Accessory converters extend the ange of the zoom lens to 28mm and 200mm. The Olympus S-2 is a uniquely designed SLR with a permanently attached D glass zoom lens. Physically, it's the most comfortable to hold f all cameras reviewed here.

Varranty: parts and labor, 1 year.

pprox. retail price	**Approx. low price**
800	**$430**

35mm AUTOFOCUS CAMERAS

The 35mm leaf-shutter AF camera is popular because it proides an easy way to shoot high-quality 35mm film. An AF camra does more than focus the lens automatically. It loads the lm, advances it after each exposure, and rewinds the film after

Prices are accurate at time of printing but are subject to manufacturers' changes.

the last exposure. Many AF cameras have a sophisticated meter that activates a built-in flash in difficult lighting situations, such as backlighting, to produce a well-lighted subject that is balanced with the background exposure. Some models, called dual-lens cameras, have both a normal and a moderate telephoto lens. Others have a zoom lens that gives you a variety of focal lengths. Many cameras now have special flash operations that reduce or eliminate red eye, a problem caused by the flash being too close to the film plane. The trend toward ultracompact design has reached the zoom cameras, and the panorama format has come to the autofocus field.

PENTAX IQZOOM 140

✓BEST BUY

The Pentax IQZoom 140 with its 3.68x, 38- to-140mm power zoom lens has the greatest range of any compact camera. A six-segment metering system, based on the metering system used in Pentax AF SLRs, ensures well-exposed images under a wide variety of lighting conditions. Phase-matching five-point autofocusing is from 2.4 feet to infinity at 38mm and 3.3 feet to infinity at 140mm. A focus-aid illuminator is emitted in low light or on hard-to-autofocus subjects. Spot AF can be used on particularly small or difficult-to-focus-on subjects. A landscape mode fixes the focus at infinity for sharp scenic pictures, even through windows. Slow-shutter-speed-with-flash-off and slow-speed-with-flash modes use shutter speeds down to two seconds, and bulb and bulb-with-flash provide exposures up to five minutes. A separate mode button activates red-eye reduction in any flash mode. Other modes provide self-timer operation, remote-control shooting, and multiexposure operation. Whenever a mode button is pressed, the LCD panel on top of the camera is illuminated for easy viewing—even at night. The real-image zooming viewfinder has an adjustable diopter for perfect viewing of your subjects; when you switch to the panoramic format, the viewfinder changes to frame out the panoramic composition. The IQZoom 140 has a wide range of features and the longest reach of any autofocus camera.

Warranty: parts and labor, 1 year.

Prices are accurate at time of printing but are subject to manufacturers' changes.

Approx. retail price
$560

Approx. low price
$310

KONICA BIG MINI ZOOM TR BM-610Z

✓BEST BUY

The Konica Big Mini Zoom TR BM-610Z is a unique and cleverly designed autofocus compact that has its own tripod as an integral part of its design: The folding flatbed lens cover becomes the front leg of the tripod when the two legs are unfolded from the base of the camera body. Behind the folding flatbed lens cover is a wide-angle-to-portrait 28mm-to-70mm zoom lens that focuses from three feet to infinity. At 70mm, the autofocusing goes down to 23.6 inches for sharp close-ups of small subjects. The automatic flash fires when the center-weighted metering system detects strong backlighting as well as when the light level is too low for good natural-light exposures. Red-eye reduction is available for good flash portraits. The night-view and flash-off modes can take advantage of the camera's slow shutter speeds down to 3.5 seconds. A TV mode produces accurate exposure from television screens, while an infinity mode lets you shoot landscapes even through windows. The self-timer gives you 10 seconds to get into the picture. The wireless remote, which operates over a distance of about 16 feet, is supplied with the camera. Other features include a real-image zooming viewfinder, motorized winding and rewinding, and midroll rewinding. DX-coded film from ISO 25 to 3200 can be used. The Big Mini Zoom TR BM-610Z is a unique autofocus camera that can be mounted on a tripod and can also stand on its own three legs.

Warranty: parts and labor, 1 year.

Approx. retail price
$380

Approx. low price
$217

OLYMPUS INFINITY STYLUS ZOOM

✓BEST BUY

The Olympus Infinity Stylus Zoom is a sleek, shirt-pocket-size AF compact with sophisticated autofocus, exposure, and flash operation. The weatherproof Stylus Zoom has a clamshell cover that becomes a comfortable finger grip

Prices are accurate at time of printing but are subject to manufacturers' changes.

when open; weatherproof means that you can even take pictures in a downpour. The 2x 35-to-70mm zoom lens has 200 focus zones for accurate focusing from two feet to infinity. The two-zone light metering system reads the central and surrounding areas of the image separately, then makes the best exposure for the lighting ratio, including firing the flash in backlit situations; for small subjects and tricky lighting situations, you can switch to spot autofocus/metering. The Stylus Zoom also features the Olympus S-flash operation, which sends out a rapid series of low-level flashes that closes down the iris of the eye before the exposure is made, thus virtually eliminating red-eye. Other modes are fill-in flash, which fires the flash regardless of the lighting; flash-off for natural light pictures; and night scene with flash. The programmed electronic shutter has speeds from four seconds to 1/500 second. The autofocus indicator in the real-image zoom viewfinder lights up when the shutter release is depressed halfway and blinks when your subject is closer than two feet. DX-coded film from ISO 50 to 3200 can be used. The Infinity Stylus Zoom, with its sculptured design, black finish, and clamshell lens cover, is as attractive as it is easy to use.

Warranty: parts and labor, 1 year.

Approx. retail price	**Approx. low price**
$325	**$188**

KONICA BIG MINI HG BM-300

Recommended

The Konica Big Mini HG BM-300 is an ultra-compact autofocus camera with a 35mm lens that completely retracts into the camera body when the power is turned off, making it easy to carry in pocket or purse. The Big Mini HG has a continuous-focusing range of 13.9 inches to infinity; at 13.9 inches, the 35mm lens produces excellent close-up pictures of small subjects. The flash automatically adjusts its output according to the focus distance so that you get well-exposed close-ups even when flash is used. The HG also has a choice of exposure control settings: In the flash-off mode, you can choose no exposure adjustment, plus 1.5 EV for very bright subjects, and minus 1.5 EV for very dark subjects. In the flash-on and flash-off modes, shutter speeds down to 7.5 seconds will be used, with the flash firing at the end of the exposure time in the flash-on mode. There are two autoflash modes, one with red-eye reduction preflash operation. There is also an infinity mode for scenery pictures and a self-timer mode. The HG handles all films from ISO 25 to ISO 3200. Autowind and rewind are available, and midroll rewind is also possible. The Konica Big Mini HG is a fine, pocketable camera with a center-weighted meter system that produces accurate exposures.

Warranty: parts and labor, 1 year.

Approx. retail price	**Approx. low price**
$260	**$141**

MINOLTA FREEDOM ZOOM EXPLORER

Recommended

The Minolta Freedom Zoom Explorer is sophisticated in its operation and style, with a smooth, pocketable, pebble-shaped design. All its corners are rounded, and there are cleverly shaped oval finger and thumb grips on front and back. The round, solid lens cover protects the lens even when the camera is put in a bag with keys and other hard objects. The 28-to-70mm zoom lens autofocuses from 1.6 feet to infinity in standard shooting modes, and 1.3 to 3.3 feet in its close-up mode; a landscape mode sets the lens to infinity for shooting sharp scenery photos even through windows. The multibeam autofocus system has about 300 focus zones (including the close focus mode). The pop-up soft flash produces the right amount of light for each subject distance so that you will never get overexposed pictures of close subjects; other flash modes are red-eye reduction, fill flash, and flash off, which uses the Explorer's slow shutter speed that goes down to eight seconds. A night portrait mode uses both flash and long exposures to produce good exposures of both close subjects and background. The built-in motor provides automatic film transport and 1.2-frames-per-second shooting in its continuous drive mode. DX-coded film from ISO 25 to 3200 can be used. The

Freedom Zoom Explorer is a good-looking camera that takes good-looking pictures.

Warranty: parts and labor, 1 year.

Approx. retail price	**Approx. low price**
$325	**$240**

RICOH R1

Recommended

The Ricoh R1 is the thinnest autofocus camera available, being no thicker than a roll of film, except for the finger grip, behind which the battery and film cassette are housed. Amazingly enough, this ultraslim camera has a 30mm retractable lens. The R1 has two panorama formats: one at 30mm and one at a wide-angle 24mm. A multiple LCD display in the viewfinder marks out the lens setting, including close-up corrections down to the close-focusing distance of 1.1 feet. Also in the viewfinder is a three-point LCD display of the seven-zone multi-AF operation: At least one of the AF indicators will stay on when you depress the shutter button part way, showing you the subject the camera is focused on. For special focusing situations, there is the single AF mode; the infinity mode sets the lens at infinity for landscapes and shooting through windows. The flash-off, slow synchro, and super night modes have shutter speeds down to two seconds. The slow synchro mode shows the shutter speed and fires a soft flash as the exposure begins; the super night mode makes the exposure for the available light, and if it senses a subject within 13 feet, it refocuses on that subject and makes a flash exposure. In the auto backlight mode, the camera's meter will sense contrast situations, such as backlighting, and fire the flash to illuminate the main subject. Red-eye reduction is also available when shooting in the dark. DX-coded films of ISO 50 to 3200 can be used, and when the film is loaded, the camera prewinds the film, with the LCD frame numbers counting down as each exposure is made. The R1 is ultraslim and offers a wide panoramic view.

Warranty: parts and labor, 1 year.

Approx. retail price	**Approx. low price**
$300	**$181**

Prices are accurate at time of printing but are subject to manufacturers' changes.

KODAK CAMEO AUTOFOCUS

Budget Buy

The Kodak Cameo Autofocus is a basic shirt-pocket-size 35mm autofocus camera with a two-zone autofocus system that provides focusing from 2.5 feet to infinity for the 28mm lens. The flip-up lens cover, which is also the camera's on/off switch, contains the flash at its tip to keep the flash high above the film plane to minimize red eye; the flash automatically fires when the light level is too low for good pictures. Color negative film of ISO 100 to 1000 can be used. When you load the film, the camera advances the film to the last frame; after each exposure, the exposed frame is wound into the cassette and the LCD frame counter counts down one frame. Depressing the shutter release button partway locks the focus so that you can recompose your picture before making the exposure. Other features are a midroll-switchable panorama format and a self-timer. The Cameo Autofocus is a simple, pocketable camera designed for snapshots and holiday pictures.

Warranty: parts and labor, 1 year.

Approx. retail price	**Approx. low price**
$130	**$38**

35mm COMPACT CAMERAS

The 35mm compact is a relatively inexpensive camera with a fixed lens. Many 35mm compact cameras are point-and-shoot cameras with simple exposure systems designed for color negative films. Some compacts are more versatile and take high-quality photographs; these cameras demand more input from the photographer than point-and-shoot and autofocus compacts, but they often produce excellent results.

MINOLTA F20R

✓BEST BUY

The Minolta F20R is a point-and-shoot camera with a 28mm wide-angle lens, a focus range of 4.9 feet to infinity, and a three-position flash-control switch. Opening the sliding lens cover activates the camera's electronics, which power the flash and the motor drive that advances and rewinds the film. When the light level is low, the flash automatically fires; a lamp just below the flash illuminates when the shutter-release button is depressed partway, which reduces red eye; the flash can be activated in bright light to fill in shadows or turned off in low light. Film is advanced to the next frame after each picture and rewound via a switch on the bottom of the camera. A safe-load signal on top of the camera confirms that the film is being properly transported. ISO 100 to 400 film can be used. The F20R is an ideal snapshot camera for landscapes, group photos, and picturing people in front of interesting backgrounds.

Warranty: parts and labor, 90 days.

Approx. retail price	**Approx. low price**
$63	**$52**

KONICA U-MINI

✓ **BEST BUY**

The Konica U-mini is a shirt-pocket-size focus-free camera with a 28mm wide-angle lens with a focus range of three feet to infinity, the closest focus of the 35mm compact cameras reviewed here. The flash system includes a red-eye reduction light that lights up about one second before the flash exposure is made. The autoexposure sensor also activates the flash system when the light level is low. A micromotor provides automatic film advance at one frame per second and auto-rewind at the end of each roll of film. An LCD panel on top of the camera displays the frame number, flash-ready signal, and condition of the lithium battery. The U-mini is a fine, ultracompact camera for snapshots of scenery and group shots.

Warranty: parts and labor, 1 year.

Approx. retail price	**Approx low price**
$76	**$74**

VIVITAR EZ1 BIG VIEW

Recommended

The Vivitar EZ1 Big View has the largest viewfinder of any point-and-shoot camera, giving photographers an easy look at their subjects. The 34mm lens has a focus

Prices are accurate at time of printing but are subject to manufacturers' changes.

range of five feet to infinity. The built-in autoflash system has a red-eye reduction light located below the flash; the red eye reduction light is activated when the shutter-release button is depressed partway; the autosensor activates the flash in low light levels and controls the shutter speeds of 1/60 to 1/250 second. ISO 100 to 400 films can be used. Two AA alkaline batteries power the flash and the winder, which automatically loads, advances, and rewinds the film; midroll rewind is also possible. The EZ1 Big View is the perfect snapshot camera both for eyeglass wearers and for those who like to have a good look at their subject.

Warranty: parts and labor, 1 year.

Approx. retail price
$96

Approx. low price
$44

CANON SNAPPY LX

Recommended

The Canon Snappy LX is a point-and-shoot camera with a red-eye reduction lamp and a shooting range of 2.18 feet to infinity. The white lamp lights up whenever the meter determines that the flash is needed for good exposure. There are two push buttons on the front of the camera—one for flash off and the other for fill flash. A self-timer is also included. The sliding lens cover is also the on/off switch for the camera's power. The Snappy LX uses color negative film DX-coded ISO 100 to 400; the film is automatically advanced after each exposure and automatically rewound after the last exposure; a rewind switch is included for midroll rewind. The Snappy LX is a snapshot camera with a large viewfinder that gives you a good look at your subjects.

Warranty: labor, 1 year.

Approx. retail price
$115

Approx. low price
$59

KODAK STAR MOTOR DRIVE

Budget Buy

The Kodak Star Motor Drive is a 35mm focus-free camera with a built-in flash and a red-eye reduction lamp located just below the flash. The 34mm lens has a focus range

Prices are accurate at time of printing but are subject to manufacturers' changes.

of four feet to infinity. An autosensor activates the flash indoors—or outdoors when the light level is low. When you depress the shutter-release button partway, the red-eye reduction lamp lights up until the picture is taken; to bypass the red-eye light, depress the shutter-release button all the way in one smooth motion. The lens cover switch also turns the flash system on and off. Two AA alkaline batteries power the flash and the motor that winds and rewinds the film. An indicator on the back turns on when the film is being correctly transported. Midroll rewind is possible. ISO 100, 200, 400, and 1000 film can be used. The Kodak Star Motor Drive is a reasonably priced, compact point-and-shoot camera that takes good snapshots.

Warranty: parts and labor, 1 year.

Approx. retail price	**Approx. low price**
$70	$32

INSTANT-PRINT CAMERAS

Instant-print cameras produce a finished black-and-white or color print in anywhere from 15 seconds to a few minutes. Instant-print cameras provide immediate gratification for those who can't wait to see the pictures they have taken.

POLAROID SPECTRA (AF) SE ✓BEST BUY

The Polaroid Spectra is a versatile instant-print camera with many features that give you both image control and creative control. A three-element Quintic lens produces sharp, rectangular pictures with an image area that measures 3⅝ × 2⅞ inches. On the back of the Spectra are the LCD information panel, system-control buttons, and flash-status LEDs. Autoflash mode, with a normal shooting range of two to 15 feet, can be turned off for available-light pictures, with exposures down to 2.8 seconds. The sonar autofocus system can be switched off for taking pictures through windows, as the sonar autofocus system would set the focus at the glass. The audio signals for focus, self-timer, and empty film pack can be turned on or off; autoexposure can be adjusted to lighten or darken the picture. The normal shooting range of the Spectra is two feet to infinity, and the flash has a range of two feet to 15 feet. A yellow warning symbol in the viewfinder will flash along with the number 1 when your subject is closer than two feet; flashing with the numbers 16 through 20 means your subject is beyond the flash range. The Polaroid Spectra is a fine instant-print camera that produces quality images.

Warranty: parts and labor, lifetime.

Approx. retail price
$186

Approx. low price
$111

POLAROID ONE STEP

Budget Buy

The Polaroid One Step is an instant-print point-and-shoot camera that produces 3⅛×3⅛-inch pictures on Polaroid 600 High Definition instant film. The camera has a normal picture range of four feet to infinity and a close-up range of two feet to four feet. To use the close-up feature, you slide the close-up lever on the front panel to the close-up position, which sets both the lens and the flash for sharp pictures within the range of two to four feet; in the close-up mode, an oval frame enters the viewfinder that is used to frame a face for a head-and-shoulders portrait. Lowering the flash, which acts as a lens cover when closed, will return the close-up mode to the normal shooting range if you forget to return the switch yourself. The flash range is four to ten feet (two to four feet in close-up); the flash always fires, but there is a nonflash button that is used when shooting through windows.

Warranty: parts and labor, 1 year.

Approx. retail price
$30

Approx. low price
$29

POLAROID CAPTIVA SLR

Recommended

The Polaroid Captiva SLR is an instant camera with viewing through the taking lens so that you see the actual image that will be made on the film. After the exposure is made, the film is automatically transported to a storage area in the back. A window allows you to see the last picture taken, and you can remove the picture at any time. The storage area holds up to ten pictures, which is one pack of Polaroid Captiva 95 instant film. Autofocusing is from two feet to infinity, and the built-in full-time flash has a range of two to ten feet. The camera has only two controls: a self-timer and a lighten/darken control. The latter will automatically be returned to its normal position when the camera is closed so that you cannot forget to reset the exposure control. The Polaroid Captiva SLR is an easy-to-use folding instant-print camera with an ingenious print-storage area.

Warranty: parts and labor, 5 years.

Approx. retail price
$100

Approx. low price
$100

Prices are accurate at time of printing but are subject to manufacturers' changes.

TELEPHONES AND ANSWERING MACHINES

Technological developments in the telephone industry continue to amaze us. Cellular advancements make carrying "cell" phones more convenient for everyday use. The number of features on basic and feature phones keeps increasing, as well. Mute buttons, speakerphones, call screening, last number redial, and phone-number memory have made cellular, portable, and feature models more attractive and easier to use. Answering machines, too, have improved greatly in the last year. Some models now use digital technology. The latest models double as both telephone and answering machines to provide what amounts to a communications center in your home.

Familiarize yourself with these telephone features so you can make an informed purchase. Different models use a variety of feature combinations, so compare features carefully. There is no standard set for all models.

Telephone Features

Automatic last-number redial. If the last number called was busy, the phone keeps redialing until a preset number of attempts is reached. The redial efforts continue every 45 or 60 seconds until a connection occurs.

Flash. This works like a switch hook and is used with customer-calling services like call waiting and conference calling. It sends a half-second signal through the line to activate these services.

Hearing-aid compatibility. These telephones provide distortion-free conversation for people who wear hearing aids. Most telephones have this feature.

Last-number redial. The last number dialed is temporarily stored in the phone's memory so that it can be redialed by pushing one or two buttons.

Speed-dialing memory. Phone numbers are stored so that they can be dialed by pushing one or two buttons. Base models store ten or more numbers, while feature phones can keep up to 100 numbers.

Mute. By pressing the mute button, you can have a second conversation in the same room without being heard by the person on the other end of the line.

Pause. This inserts a pause between numbers in the memory-dialing sequence to allow for switchboard delays encountered by long-distance phone equipment.

Speakerphone. A button on the base of the phone activates a microphone and a speaker so you can make and receive calls without picking up the handset.

Best Buys '96

Our Best Buy, Recommended, and Budget Buy choices follow. We have listed our reviews for telephones by category. Our answering-machine reviews are found after the telephone reviews. Within each category, the unit we consider the best of the Best Buys is listed first, followed by our second choice, and so on. Remember that a Best Buy, Recommended, or Budget Buy designation applies only to the model listed. It does not necessarily apply to other models made by the same manufacturer or to an entire product line.

FEATURE TELEPHONES

GENERAL ELECTRIC 2-9390

✓BEST BUY

General Electric's GE 2-9390 is a full-featured telephone with speakerphone and Caller ID features. Caller ID usually requires a separate device attached to your phone line—but this model provides that equipment as an integrated unit. The speakerphone feature is activated with one touch; there is also a speaker volume control, as well as a mute button to silence the microphone for privacy. You can dial a number by pressing one of the 20 one-touch memory buttons or keying in the number. Once your connection is made, you can pick up the handset and begin speaking. The phone also has a built-in timer, useful for controlling long-distance charges or keeping track of customer billing. Other features include a temporary tone; ringer control; hold, flash, and pause functions; an LCD screen and 61-number or 22-name memory for Caller ID; and a priority ring selector.

Warranty: 1 year, limited.

Approx. retail price
$120

Approx. low price
$100

SOUTHWESTERN BELL FM890A

✓BEST BUY

There aren't many features you won't find on the Southwestern Bell FM890A feature phone. The memory lets you store 16 phone numbers. The display screen shows a confirmation of the number dialed and the stored number pressed—and doubles as a clock and call timer. Speaker volume is controlled easily with a control knob on the side of the phone. Other phone features include flash (for call waiting), hold and pause buttons, a pulse/tone switch, a ringer control, and a low-battery indicator. The Caller ID display, which shows ten characters on a single scrollable line, identifies name and phone number, time and date of call, and whether the incoming call is from out of the area or is a blocked call. Other features include three-language operation, call counter, and message erase.

Warranty: 1 year, limited.

Approx. retail price
$80

Approx. low price
Not available

PANASONIC KX-T3175

Recommended

The KX-T3175 is the ideal two-line phone for the home office worker or small-business owner. The console shows separate LEDs to help you keep track of which line is in use, and each line has a distinct ringer. The speakerphone feature allows hands-free operation; a mute button shuts off the speaker for privacy. Volume is controlled electronically, and a 12-digit LCD window displays a clock. The phone has one-touch dialing for 24 numbers and last-number redial. Other features include electronic hold, timed flash memory, automatic pause, and three-way conference calling.

Warranty: 1 year, limited.

Approx. retail price	Approx. low price
$120	$103

PANASONIC KX-T3185

Recommended

Busy households and offices with multiple phone numbers might well need a three-line feature phone. Besides offering all the features found in the two-line model (above), the KX-T3185 is especially easy to use. Separate distinctive rings readily identify which line has an incoming call. In addition, LEDs light up to tell you which button to push to take the call. The only option you might miss in this model is additional memory for more stored phone numbers (this unit stores 24 numbers).

Warranty: 1 year, limited.

Approx. retail price	Approx. low price
$200	$172

AT&T 832

Recommended

Multiline feature phones usually have similar features. The AT&T 832 is a two-line phone with a bit more to offer, though. The LCD display shows date and time and the number dialed. Its memory capacity lets you program 16 auto-dial and 16 speed-dial numbers. A programmable pause feature makes it easy to set up numbers that will work with business trunk lines and international dialing. The speakerphone produces crisp vocal sounds. The phone has all the expected standard features, including three-way teleconferencing, a distinctive ring pattern, line-in-use LED indicators, automatic redial, hold/flash/mute buttons, and adjustable ringer and volume controls.

Warranty: 2 years, limited.

Approx. retail price	Approx. low price
$110	$99

Prices are accurate at time of printing but are subject to manufacturers' changes.

CORDLESS TELEPHONES

Think of cordless phones as portable extension phones. They keep you from missing calls when you are outside or away from an extension phone. In addition to mobility, today's cordless phones offer more features than ever before. They use a special radio for transmissions between base and handset, and the latest technology has produced excellent sound quality: Multichannel scanning lets your phone send and receive on various frequencies so your conversations are clearer. Some models even let you select high or low channels to improve performance as you move about the house. New noise reduction features further help lessen interference and improve reception. Late last year, the Federal Communications Commission authorized the use of 25 different channels in the frequency range used by cordless phones. (Until now, the maximum number of channels was ten.) This is good news because more channels means clearer reception. As you consider your purchase, look for upgraded models with this 25-channel feature. At press time, many manufacturers were still planning which of their 1996 models would be redesigned with the 25-channel circuits. You may find models with slightly different model numbers but with exactly the same features as those listed in this section, except for the 25-channel upgrade.

When shopping for a cordless phone, be sure to consider other options besides voice clarity. Check how long battery charges last. A cordless phone that has to be frequently recharged isn't much of a convenience. Two other important features are intercom and paging: Intercom allows you to speak between the base and the handset, while paging lets you send a tone signal between base and handset. The paging function comes in handy when you're trying to locate a misplaced handset.

SONY SPP-2000

✔BEST BUY

The Sony SPP-2000 is a ten-channel cordless telephone with the advanced features you would expect to find on high-end models. A unique power feature, though, makes the SPP-2000 a real winner: Its dual-battery system lets the phone operate during a power failure. One battery powers the handset while the second is charged and stored in the base. This stand-by battery powers the base when the house current fails. During normal use, there is always a fully charged battery to keep the handset working without an overnight recharge. The combination of two batteries gives this unit a 30-day battery reserve. Other features include seven-number speed-dialing, three-number one-touch memory dialing, a battery status indicator, base-to-handset paging, and out-of-range alert.

Warranty: parts and labor, 1 year.

Approx. retail price $120

Approx. low price $129

UNIDEN EXP 901

Recommended

The Uniden EXP 901 cordless phone operates at 900 MHz for exceptional long-range service, hence its Extend-A-Phone logo. This multichannel cordless produces unusually clear, crisp voice communication. A speakerphone feature lets you operate the phone from the base unit without using the handset. A mute button turns off the microphone for private conversations. The two-way switch lets you leave the intercom feature on as a convenient room monitor. Other features include last-number redial; ten-number memory; tone/pulse dialing; three one-touch memory buttons; a hold button; and handset, base, and ringer volume control. Another useful feature is Call Monitor, which lets you hear the dialing and connect sequences from a built-in monitor speaker. A flash button sends a timed signal for use with call waiting and other phone-company options. An optional second NiCad battery can be used as a battery backup to extend the handset's usability.

Warranty: parts and labor, 1 year.

Prices are accurate at time of printing but are subject to manufacturers' changes.

Approx. retail price
$229

Approx. low price
$170

AT&T 4725

Recommended

The AT&T 4725 is part of a new line of cordless telephones. This model is designed so that the cordless handset stands vertically in the base unit. It includes circuitry that gives the cordless the same sound quality as corded phones. The 4725 has automatic ten-channel selection, two-way paging and intercom features, and a flexible antenna that stays at one length and resists snapping. Both the antenna and the battery can be replaced easily. The phone's memory holds up to nine numbers. There is no provision for an optional battery as a backup, but the single NiCad battery in the handset lasts about three days without recharging. The temporary tone feature can be useful if you have only rotary pulse service, letting you use services that require tone signaling. The 4725 also can be used with either tone or rotary service via its selectable dialing feature.

Warranty: 1 year.

Approx. retail price
$100

Approx. low price
$79

PANASONIC KX-T3908

Budget Buy

The Panasonic KX-T3908 is a cordless phone with only a few extras, but it produces acceptable sound using Panasonic's Sound Charger Plus technology and ten-channel autoscanning system. The base unit has only a green indicator light showing when the phone is in use. The battery, which has a 30-day standby life, is more durable than those in similar units. Features included are one-touch tone switching, last-number redial, a hi/lo volume setting and ringer volume on the handset, a battery-strength indicator, ten-station speed dial, and one-way paging.

Warranty: 1 year, limited.

Approx. retail price
$70

Approx. low price
Not available

Prices are accurate at time of printing but are subject to manufacturers' changes.

CELLULAR MOBILE, PORTABLE, AND TRANSPORTABLE TELEPHONES

Cellular phones have become enormously popular since their introduction in 1983. Once a status symbol for business executives and professionals, cellular phones now are the personal communication device of busy family members, allowing them to stay in touch while commuting or traveling. Cellular phones are so popular that they have invaded American homes at a faster pace than any other consumer electronic product, including color TVs and VCRs. There are more than 10 million users in the United States, and the cellular-phone market continues to grow by thousands every day.

Pricing varies widely. Near major cities, consumers often have a choice of carrier. The Federal Communications Commission, which regulates cellular services, allocates cellular licenses to two carriers in each major metro area. As competition expands, you will probably find an independent carrier and cellular service provided by your regional phone company.

Approximate retail and low prices have not been included in this section because, as so often happens, pricing depends on available service. Many cellular companies offer a number of free calling hours and other discounts. Fees are billed monthly. A typical service fee includes the company's service charge plus toll calls. You will pay for air time on calls you originate and ones you receive.

Because the industry is still new and in flux, terminology does tend to change. We've divided cellular phones into three categories. **Cellular portable phones** fit in a purse or coat pocket and operate from rechargeable batteries. They are unsurpassed in convenience, but because of their small battery size, cellular portable phones have the fewest features and shortest talk time. Depending on the type of battery, you can expect several hours to a full day of continuous battery power before recharging. Features are usually limited to memory dialing. **Cellular mobile phones** are slightly heavier and more cumbersome. Lately, the line between the portable and mobile categories has become somewhat blurred.

Cellular transportable phones are larger, heavier, and come in a case. They often have car adapter kits. With their larger batteries, transportable phones have a greater range, longer time between recharging, and more features than portable and mobile phones. Features can include memory, last-number redial, and a speakerphone.

One of the biggest concerns about using cellular phones is the issue of security. Eavesdropping can occur: Radio-frequency scanners can pick up your conversations. Cellular-phone users should be careful about giving out information—credit card and phone numbers, addresses, and details about long absences from home could fall into the wrong hands. To improve security, consider buying a digital phone, which makes it impossible for scanner operators to listen in. The drawback here is that digital phone technology is relatively new, making digital models costlier than analog units.

A word to the wise: There's potential danger in using any cellular phone while driving a motor vehicle in traffic. It's easy to become distracted while engaged in a phone conversation.

Cellular Portable Telephones

ERICSSON AH-320

✓ BEST BUY

The Ericsson AH-320 is a featherweight model you can carry easily in a pocket or purse. The flip design contributes to the phone's compact size. The mouthpiece portion of the phone folds closed over the number pad. With the slimline battery, talk time is 50 minutes (the unit weight is 7.5 ounces); with the high-capacity battery, talk time is boosted to 120 minutes (and the unit weight to 9.4 ounces). The memory holds 109 speed-dialing numbers with ten-number secured-memory and memory-scrolling features. Other features include a five-number scratch pad, four call timers, an easy-to-use menu, and alphanumeric name tagging. (Incidentally, Ericsson also makes cellular phones under the General Electric label.)

Warranty: 1 year.

MITSUBISHI AH-5000

Recommended

The Mitsubishi AH-5000 is one of the smallest, lightest cellular phones around, weighing 6.5 ounces with its slim-line battery and 7.7 ounces with the extended-life battery. Only 6.1 inches long and 2 inches wide, the AH-5000 is barely an inch longer than a flip phone and still tiny enough to fit in a pocket. The slim-line version gives 60 minutes of talk time and 12 hours of reserve; the extended battery provides 130 minutes of talk time with 28 hours of reserve. The large LCD display shows 20 digits with a clock readout and viewing-angle control. Memory features include 99 speed-dial locations, a one-touch dialing button, ten private memory locations, five last-number-redial locations with time stamp, a scratch pad, and memory scan. The AH-5000 also offers call timing, a voice mute button, selectable ring tone, a pager mode with time stamp, and a function menu in English, Spanish, and French.

Warranty: 3 years.

Cellular Mobile Telephones

MITSUBISHI AH-4500

✓BEST BUY

The Mitsubishi AH-4500 offers superior functionality. Using the extended-life battery, the 9.9-ounce unit gives you 130 minutes of talk time and 19 hours of standby. (The slim battery lightens the load to 8.8 ounces but shortens talk time to 60 minutes, with eight hours of standby.) The display screen shows 14 characters and has a viewing-angle control for greater visibility. You can store up to 99 phone numbers and redial the last three. The electronic security lock allows emergency dialing without first dialing the unlocking code. The number pad uses large oval digits that simplify dialing. Other features include a call timer, voice muting, fax/data compatibility, and multilevel call restrictions. The three-year limited warranty makes the AH-4500 a solid value.

Warranty: 3 years.

TOSHIBA TCP-1000

Recommended

At 8.5 ounces, the TCP-1000 is a lightweight cellular phone that's ideal for the heavy user. It offers 100 minutes of talk time and up to 20 hours of standby using the phone's standard battery. Its large, clear display window is easy to see at a glance. The 15-character screen has a signal-strength indicator above the dialed number. The send and end keys are also large, making for quick and easy operation, and volume can be adjusted to nine levels. Other features include one-touch dialing, automatic answering, secret-number memory, silent alert, and automatic lock.

Warranty: 1 year, limited.

Cellular Transportable Telephones

MOTOROLA MC480

✓BEST BUY

The Motorola MC480 provides the benefits of more sophisticated features with the convenience of easy carrying. This model weighs 3.1 pounds without a battery (most batteries add about 1.5 pounds) and has a rugged vinyl carrying case with extra room for a notepad and business cards. The MC480's operating power—a full 3 watts—provides greater coverage in fringe areas, and the unit has a large, seven-character LCD display. Besides the standard cellular phone features, the MC480's added power allows features not possible in lighter, smaller models. For example, it lets you tag a seven-letter name to a phone number for added memory reference; there are also 102 memory locations and an option for name-only entries. Other features include memory autoload to store a new number in the next available location, incoming-call screening, and auto answer for hands-free operation.

Warranty: 1 year, limited.

MITSUBISHI AT 1000

Recommended

The lightweight AT 1000 (2.06 pounds with battery, 1.65 pounds without) is a small, short telephone—but it's long on convenience. You can conserve the 60 minutes of talk time and eight hours of standby time by selecting one of three output-power selections. Depending on the signal area you're in, you can choose 0.6, 1.2, or 3.0 watts of power. The LCD display shows two lines of 14 digits and is large enough for easy viewing of the function menu. The AT 1000's memory will hold 114 numbers, with 99 name and number locations, two one-touch dial locations, three last-number-redial spots, and ten private-number locations. Alphabet scan and memory scan help you find desired phone numbers quickly. Other features include emergency dialing when locked, multilevel call restriction, hands-free operation, and auto-store.

Warranty: 1 year.

ANSWERING MACHINES

Answering machines are more a necessity than a luxury these days. In the home, they provide a simple and inexpensive way to screen calls, and they keep family and friends in touch. Although the business world is increasingly relying on computerized voice mail, answering machines—especially the two-line variety—are still preferred by many homes and small businesses.

Answering machines are easy to install: Just connect the cords to a modular phone jack and an electrical outlet. Some models use digital technology to record messages on a voice chip instead of a cassette or microcassette tape, but others continue to rely on one or two audiotapes to record outgoing and incoming messages. One major drawback to machines with digital storage is the recording time: Voice chips allow fewer—and shorter—messages.

Consider your needs in selecting an answering machine. Smaller and cheaper machines designed for a low volume of calls put outgoing and incoming messages on a single audiotape. A tape must be changed occasionally, as wear and tear tends to hurt voice quality.

Integrated answering machines do double duty as telephones and message centers. These units are equipped with a handset and are ideal when phone jacks are in short supply.

Features and Terminology

Announce only. You set the machine to deliver only an outgoing message. This setting does not allow recording of incoming messages. It's useful for a business wishing to announce hours of operation or directions.

Autodisconnect. This lets you pick up the telephone and automatically stop the answering machine. On some models, this feature works with any extension phone.

Beeperless remote. This allows you to call in for your messages from any push-button phone. The answering machine is accessed by a personal security code.

Memo. You put a message on your machine for someone who is expected to arrive after you leave.

Remote turn-on. This lets you turn on your machine when you are away from home.

Room monitor. You can monitor sounds in a room while you're away via your beeperless remote.

Time/day stamp. The machine indicates the time and day a message was received.

Toll saver. This is a money-saving feature. The machine rings four times before answering the first call but rings only once to answer subsequent calls. Thus, you can call your number and know by the second ring that there are no messages, then hang up to avoid a toll charge.

VOX. This allows incoming calls of any length, up to the tape's capacity. The machine records as long as the person continues to speak, deactivating within a few seconds after the caller hangs up.

Basic Answering Machines

GE 2-9863

BEST BUY

General Electric's GE 2-9863 is a full-featured answering machine using a single microcassette to record incoming messages and a voice chip to store the recorded outgoing message digitally. The separate cassette is often preferred, since it allows users to save messages for future reference. An indicator light blinks to show how many unheard messages are waiting, and messages can be marked with a voice time and day stamp. The GE 2-9863 lets you screen calls with a built-in speaker that also doubles as a remote room monitor. With the memo function, you can leave a voice message for others in the household. This answering machine has exceptional remote control features: Among other things, you can access messages and change the outgoing message while away from your home or office as part of the one-touch-tone remote function. The unit has a special feature protecting against power failure, plus an autodisconnect option.

Warranty: 1 year, limited.

Approx. retail price	**Approx. low price**
$50	**$50**

SOUTHWESTERN BELL FA981

Recommended

The Southwestern Bell FA981 is a digital system with tapeless recording of announcement and messages. The digital audio circuitry tags each message with a date and time stamp. This model is wonderfully easy to use, with controls clearly labeled and five easy-to-reach buttons on top of the unit. You can skip or repeat messages, stop playback, save a message, and change the outgoing message by pressing a single announce button. There is also a separate volume control on the side of the machine. A display window shows the number of messages recorded and indicates when the backup battery is low. Additional handy features are remote access and a branch interrupt feature that cuts off the outgoing message whenever you pick up an extension phone connected to the same line.

Prices are accurate at time of printing but are subject to manufacturers' changes.

Warranty: 1 year, limited.

Approx. retail price $50

Approx. low price $50

SOUTHWESTERN BELL FA945G

Recommended

The Southwestern Bell FA945G is a compact, easy-to-use answering machine weighing only 8.5 ounces. It uses a single microcassette to store outgoing and incoming messages. It will place a time/day stamp on each incoming message so you can keep track of messages. The machine also has a variable-announcement-length feature that lets callers talk without being cut off by a beep. There is even a memo record feature that lets you leave messages on the machine for others to hear. The FA945 stops its outgoing announcement when you pick up any extension phone on the same phone line as the answering machine. Other features include volume control and toll saver.

Warranty: 1 year, limited.

Approx. retail price $40

Approx. low price $40

Integrated Answering Machine

GE 2-9896

✓BEST BUY

General Electric's GE 2-9896 is a full-featured integrated telephone and answering machine. It combines the best options of a feature phone with the high-end features of an answering machine. The telephone has a 12-number dialing memory. Three of these memory areas are reserved for one-touch emergency phone numbers, and the remaining memory stores nine other phone numbers. The base holds a list of memory numbers. Other features include power-failure protection by battery backup, tone/pulse-switchable dialing, one-touch redial of last number dialed, ringer-volume control, temporary tone, and flash function. The answering machine uses digital recording (voice chips) of the outgoing message, which can be up to 20 seconds long, and a single microcassette to store incoming messages. You can access messages and change the outgoing message remotely as part of the ten push-button remote functions. The GE 2-9896 also offers autodisconnect, a voice time/day stamp, a message-counter indicator light, and toll-saver and remote room-monitor functions.

Warranty: 1 year, limited.

Approx. retail price
$70

Approx. low price
$70

COMPUTERS

Buying your first computer or upgrading your current system can be an overwhelming experience—even for veteran computer users—because of the wealth of products on today's market. To make the process easier, we've compared dozens of computers and then chosen the best values. In this section, you'll find detailed reviews for a variety of computers. We've also determined approximately how much you can expect to pay for each product. Although prices vary according to market conditions, our price information will help you be more prudent with your computer investment.

The Ratings

At the end of each review, you'll find ratings based on a scale of 1 (worst) to 10 (best).

The **overall value** rating compares the product's price to its performance, ease of use, and features. Accordingly, an overpriced item won't have a very high overall value rating, even if it is an excellent product.

The **performance** rating tells how well the product performs its various functions. Keep in mind that the performance ratings of different items can't always be fairly compared unless the products are similar.

The **expandability** rating is determined by the availability of and capacity for add-ons or peripherals. Portable computers (also called **laptops** and **notebooks**) are given an expandability rating because most of them have provisions for adding more memory, a fax/modem board, and additional floppy drives. Most have a parallel port that lets you add on more than just a printer. Several companies market an SCSI (Small Computer Systems Interface)—pronounced "scuzzy"—module that plugs into the parallel port and lets you daisy-chain up to seven peripheral devices, such as hard-disk and floppy drives, tape drives, and CD-ROM drives.

The **documentation** rating judges whether or not the manuals and on-line help are effective and well organized.

Understanding Computer Terminology

Although computers have become much easier to use over the years, a basic understanding of computer terms is still useful.

The computer's "brain" is the **central processing unit,** or **CPU;** an equivalent term is **microprocessor.** The CPU resides on a chip or tiny silicon wafer with thousands of electronic parts. Encased in plastic or ceramic, a chip uses tiny metal "legs" as electrical connectors. The CPU and the operating system regulate the flow of data between the computer's parts, as well as between the computer and its printer, monitor, and other peripherals.

The CPU usually receives data from an input device such as the disk drive or keyboard; sometimes data will come from a mouse or trackball. A **mouse** is a small device that you move around on a desktop or pad to move the cursor, or on-screen pointer. The button or buttons on a mouse let you access on-screen functions. **Trackballs** also have buttons, but instead of moving the mouse on a level surface, you merely spin the trackball in its socket to position the cursor.

The CPU manipulates data and software programs in random-access memory (RAM). Read-only memory (ROM) might store an operating system, a utility program, or an application like a word-processing program, so it can be sent into RAM. When the computer is turned off, RAM usually loses its contents; ROM retains its memory. RAM changes constantly; in most cases, ROM never changes. Printers use internal RAM buffers to store data received from the computer. Because such data are received much faster than they can be printed, without a buffer the computer would be unusable until printing is completed.

RAM and ROM are measured in bytes, which are made up of bits. A **bit** ("binary digit") is the smallest unit of data. Its value is either one or zero (yes or no). A **byte** is a group of bits, usually eight, that stand for one character (it could be a letter, number, or symbol) and is treated as a unit of data. A **kilobyte** (Kb) is roughly a thousand bytes, while a **megabyte** (Mb) is about a million bytes. A **gigabyte** (Gb) equals 1,000Mb.

With more RAM, a computer can run more powerful programs faster. You can increase the amount of RAM in a computer by adding chips or expansion cards.

Programs and data can be saved to magnetic disks. Floppy lisks are circular, 5.25 inches in diameter, and flexible, although hey are packaged in square, stiff housings. Compared to the loppy disks, the more popular **microfloppies** are smaller (3.5 nches in diameter), have sturdier plastic housings, and are nore durable. **Hard disks** are normally fixed in place, holding nuch more data than floppies, sometimes a hundred times nore. Hard disks work at high speeds, so they can load soft-vare into RAM more quickly and make programs run much aster than floppies can.

High-density disks are the most common; they hold between .2 and 1.44Mb of data. When shopping for disks, avoid the nexpensive no-name variety. Considering the amount of in-outting that could be lost if a disk fails, buying poorly made disks aves very little money—and could end up costing a lot of time nd anguish. For the same reasons, most people use a second lisk to make backup copies of important information.

A **disk drive** transfers data and programs back and forth be-ween a disk and RAM. There are different sizes of floppy and ard-disk drives. The disk drives differ in diameter (usually 5.25 nd 3.5 inches) and height (there are full-height, half-height, nd even third-height drives). Disk drives also differ in the av-rage speed at which they randomly access data from the disk. his access time is measured in milliseconds (ms). A good hard lrive should have an access speed of between 10ms and 18ms.

An operating system that stores data on a disk is called **disk perating system (DOS).** The most common is Microsoft's OS, or MS-DOS, and its IBM version, PC-DOS. IBM personal omputers, or PCs, are copied by other firms more than any ther system. These IBM-compatible computers can use most eripherals and software designed for IBM-type computers. ther operating systems include IBM's OS/2, introduced in 987, and the highly popular Microsoft Windows, which em-loys a graphical user interface, or GUI (pronounced "gooey"), hat involves selecting on-screen icons with a mouse instead of yping lengthy text commands. Apple Macintosh computers se a different operating system, which also has a graphic user nterface.

When the CPU finishes its work, it sends data to an output device, such as a disk drive, monitor, printer, or modem. A modem, in turn, sends data over telephone lines to another computer. The CPU, RAM, ROM, connecting circuits, and other parts are found on the main circuit board, called the **motherboard.** This board often has slots for expansion cards, which are circuit boards that increase a computer's functions, speed, or memory.

The number and type of ports (connectors) and the kind of operating system employed by a computer often limit the peripherals and programs it can use. Application software (such as a spreadsheet or database program) is commonly sold for only one operating system. Similarly, an RS-232C port can communicate only with devices that have RS-232C interfaces (software and hardware that permit the transfer of data). The application software must also be able to use that port.

Prices

We have tried to provide accurate prices in this chapter. However, the release of new products, the withdrawal of older models that are thought to be outdated, and strong competition in certain markets cause prices to change constantly. Manufacturers occasionally offer special prices or add "free" items to their packages. Prices also vary across the nation. To complicate matters further, the availability of dynamic RAM (DRAM) chips (the kind supplied with computers, peripherals, and many electronic devices) often varies, which might cause prices to change. Furthermore, the fluctuating U.S. dollar produces price changes as well.

All this means that the retail and low prices in this buying guide might differ from what you find at your local store. Be sure to contact several dealers and compare their prices. Also, check newspaper and magazine ads for sales. Low profit margins or a lack of direct competition might make discounts hard to find on some items.

Best Buys '96

Our Best Buy and Recommended choices follow. They are broken down into the following categories: home and small-business computers, high-powered computers, and portable computers. Personal Digital Assistants (PDAs) are covered in the Home Office Products chapter. The unit we consider to be the best of the Best Buys is listed first, followed by our second choice, and so on. Remember that a Best Buy or Recommended designation applies only to the model listed. It does not necessarily apply to other models by the same manufacturer.

HOME AND SMALL-BUSINESS COMPUTERS

GATEWAY 2000 P5-75 (PROFESSIONAL VERSION)

✓BEST BUY

The professional version of the Gateway 2000 P5-75 offers the best value for the home office of any computer reviewed. If you can get along without much technical support, this is the computer for you.

Gateway 2000 sells its computers strictly by mail order. The company builds each computer to your specifications, so ordering a customized configuration does not slow down delivery or increase the cost, other than the extra expense of the additions you want.

The P5-75 comes with an excellent instruction manual that shows you how to connect everything. The pictures are clearly labeled. The ports are marked using icons. They are easy to see but sometimes hard to interpret. However, the setup manual will clear up any problems you have.

The P5-75 is well equipped for expansion. It has lots of slots, extra drive bays, and a large power supply. The setup guide has photographs of the inside, with everything clearly labeled so you can quickly find the memory, slots, or power cable. It comes with 16Mb RAM, so there is room in memory for all the Windows programs you might want to run. (The extra memory also makes this an excellent OS/2 machine.) It has a 730Mb Enhanced IDE hard disk, so there is room for all the programs and data you might want to store.

The display is a 1,280 × 1,024 noninterlaced 15-inch monitor that is crystal clear. The only drawback to the hardware is

Prices are accurate at time of printing but are subject to manufacturers' changes.

that the 3.5-inch floppy drive is mounted sideways, which takes some getting used to. Gateway 2000 does not include a bunch of games to make the computer appeal to the kids. Rather, the company packs it with software designed for the office—Microsoft Office, that is. Fortunately, this is the most popular high-powered business suite available. Also bundled with the professional version of the P5-75 are Microsoft Money and Microsoft Bookshelf. All in all, this system will handle just about any business need without your having to purchase additional software.

The P5-75 ships with all the software preinstalled on the hard disk. A master CD-ROM disk is also provided. No floppy disks or printed manuals are included for most of the software. If you want them, most are available for an extra charge. However, you can probably find better substitutes at a cheaper price at your local bookstore.

Thanks to the inclusion of an optional 16-bit sound card and Altec Lansing speakers, the P5-75 is multimedia-ready right out of the box. The CD-ROM drive is a quad-speed unit with motorized eject; it does not use a caddy. The CD-ROM drive playing through the Altec speakers gives crisp, satisfactory sound. The keyboard is programmable—you can change its layout or program keyboard macros.

In our tests, the P5-75 proved to be very fast at all Windows and MS-DOS programs. Even the biggest and slowest programs loaded and ran with surprising agility. Everything about the Gateway 2000, from its 16Mb RAM to its 10ms 730Mb hard drive to its 75MHz Pentium processor to its Vivitron monitor with 32-bit PCI graphics accelerator, oozed speed and power.

The Gateway 2000 Telepath internal fax modem comes with Triton Technologies' CoSession remote diagnostic software. This enables technical support to log onto your system (with your permission, of course) and remotely diagnose problems. It can edit system files, run diagnostics, and load new drivers and other support files as required.

The Gateway 2000 modem and the included FaxWorks software can turn your computer into a voice-mail server. It supports multiple mailboxes and remote-message pickup. Incoming calls can be routed to either voice mail or fax by the modem, so one line can support both fax and voice. This can save you a lot of money in phone-line charges. It also supports fax on demand, where users call and request documents to be faxed to them. The fax-back service can be publicly available or require a password.

This machine is an excellent value with enough powerful software to keep you out of the store for a long time. If you are looking for a business computer for your home office, the professional version of the P5-75 (or its 60MHz or 100MHz sister) deserves to be at the top of your shopping list.

Specifications: operating system, Windows 95; RAM (std./max.), 16Mb/128Mb; CPU/MHz, Pentium/75; floppy drive, 3.5″; hard drive/speed, 730Mb/10ms; storage bays, 7; expansion slots, 4 16-bit ISA, 2 32-bit PCI, 1 PCI/ISA; ports, 2 serial, 1 parallel, 1 keyboard, 1 monitor, 1 audio, 1 mouse; monitor, 15″ Vivitron. **Warranty:** 1 year on-site; parts, 3 years; 30-day money-back guarantee.

Ratings: overall value, 10; performance, 10; expandability, 10; documentation, 9.

Approx. retail price
$2,399

Approx. low price
$2,359

PACKARD BELL MULTIMEDIA PENTIUM PC

✓ BEST BUY

For readers looking to balance the need for a home-based business computer with the demands of a family, the Packard Bell Multimedia Pentium PC may be the perfect choice.

For the business, it offers a large hard disk, lots of speed and memory, an advanced telephone system, a 14.4 Kbps fax modem, and out-of-the-box multimedia support. For the family, it comes with a lot of games, reference material, and educational software. In addition, the design is stylish enough to fit into a living room or office decor.

Packard Bell sells its computers through retail stores to typically less-knowledgeable consumers than those who buy from

Prices are accurate at time of printing but are subject to manufacturers' changes.

mail-order vendors. This shows in their attention to the details of getting your computer up and running. Everything except the monitor is packaged in a single, surprisingly small box. That way, there is little chance of your leaving the store without something you need.

When you open the computer box, the first thing you find is poster-size instructions on how to put everything together. These full-color directions are excellent. Ports are clearly labeled using icons, not words. Some, like the printer and mouse, are understandable. Others, like the COM and video port, are not. No matter, the installation instructions will handle any confusion, and cables are all color coded.

The speakers are designed to bolt onto the side of the monitor and wrap around it much like a large pair of ears. Installing them requires a screwdriver. Their design prevents using them as freestanding equipment. With the speakers designed to attach to the monitor, building them as part of the monitor would have made more sense. It would prevent the user from having to bolt them on and avoid the tangle of speaker wires wrapped around the monitor.

The Packard Bell Multimedia Pentium PC is not designed for expandability. It does not have any additional externally-accessible drive bays for a tape drive or second floppy-disk drive. There is no internal bay for adding a second hard disk. The power supply provides only 150 watts. There are two PCI slots and three ISA slots, with one taken up by the fax modem.

The 75MHz Pentium we reviewed was very fast and capable. It would be acceptable for anyone running even the most demanding applications. (The computer is also available in speeds of 60MHz and 100MHz.) With 8Mb RAM standard on the machine, Windows will run much faster than it does on 4Mb computers.

When you turn the computer on, it boots into the Packard Bell Navigator, a Windows front end. Navigator tells you what to do by talking to you over the speakers. The main screen can be configured to look like a house. As you click on different "rooms," they light up and give you access to different features.

The kids will love it, and you can quickly switch from the Navigator to Windows.

The 14.4 Kbps fax modem also functions as a telephone answering system with multiple mailboxes. It offers all the features of a business phone, including redial and call screening. You can use it to record important telephone conversations (be sure to tell the other person). It also functions as a full-duplex speaker phone and can record these conversations as well.

The answering machine portion of the Packard Bell solves a nagging problem. It gives the sender the option of leaving a fax or voice message, so one phone line can easily accommodate voice, voice mail, and fax.

The most noticeable feature is the computer's dual CD-ROM drives. While the need to access two different CD-ROM disks at once is fairly rare, this arrangement does allow you to play music while working with a CD-ROM-based program.

Not reviewed here, a Packard Bell card can turn the Packard Bell Multimedia Pentium PC into a television. It also allows you to capture video images for use in other applications.

The Packard Bell Multimedia Pentium PC comes with almost no floppy disks. Everything is delivered on CD-ROM. A special CD-ROM disk allows you to restore your hard disk to its factory condition (should that become necessary) by booting off a special floppy disk, which is included.

Hardware documentation and documentation for a few of the programs are printed. However, the documentation for the major programs (MS-DOS, Windows, Microsoft Works, and the like) is included only in an electronic version. The ability to search the document is nice, but a printed copy to read away from the computer would be even nicer.

The Packard Bell Multimedia Pentium PC includes an impressive list of software, including MS-DOS, Windows, Software Toolworks World Atlas on CD-ROM, and Sports Illustrated Multimedia Sports Almanac on CD-ROM. Much of this software is aimed at kids. The major productivity software bundled with it includes Microsoft Works, Microsoft Money, and FaxWorks. Microsoft Works is an integrated package offering word processing, a spreadsheet, and a database. While adequate for term papers and the like, Microsoft Office would be much more useful for the home office, and Quicken would have been a wiser choice than Money.

The Packard Bell Multimedia Pentium PC offers an intelligent mix of features and software for both the home and home-based office. Its fax modem with built-in answering machine gives you a head start on setting up your office. Its low price will leave you enough money to look at printers. And its educational and entertainment software will certainly make the kids happy.

Specifications: operating system, MS-DOS 6.22, Windows 95; RAM (std./max.), 8Mb/128Mb; CPU/MHz, Pentium/75; floppy drive, 3.5"; hard drive/speed, 1.275Gb/12ms; storage bays, 2 CD-ROM, 1 floppy disk, 1 hard disk (none available for expansion); expansion slots, 3 ISA, 2 PCI; ports, 1 serial, 1 parallel, 1 keyboard, 1 monitor, 1 audio, 1 mouse, 1 phone jack; monitor, none. **Warranty:** 1 year on-site (hardware only). **Ratings:** overall value, 10; performance, 10; expandability, 8; documentation, 10.

Approx. retail price	Approx. low price
$2,000	**$1,860**

IBM PC 350

Recommended

The PC 300 series is one of IBM's lines for the home office. IBM has a reputation for making some of the best computers on the market, and the PC 350 is no exception. It is rock solid, and with IBM quality, it's a machine you can depend on for years to come.

The IBM PC 300 series includes the entry-level 486DX2 50MHz, a traditional 486DX2 66MHz, a fast clock-tripled 486DX4 100MHz, and a very fast 60MHz Pentium. They are all upgradable using a ZIF socket. There are two case models to choose from—the small-footprint PC 330 series with three expansion slots and three bays, and the PC 350, which gives you five expansion slots and five bays in a larger case. We reviewed the PC 350 486DX4 100MHz.

You cannot make a wrong decision regarding bus architecture with the PC 300 Series 486 systems, thanks to the SelectaBus feature. You can elect VESA or PCI—both give you the option of using an ISA riser for economical system expansion. There is also a PCI/ISA riser. These provide investment protection for whatever adapters you already have, and they support the architecture decisions you will want to make in the future. (The Pentium-based systems come with PCI only.)

The case comes off without tools—just press one tab and it pulls right off. A sliding panel covers the power switch and the drive bays on the front when they are not in use. The panel and the cover lock into place with a single key. This added measure of security allows you to lock up the disk drive and case along with the keyboard. Ports on the back are marked with icons, not words.

The only end-user software included with the IBM is the preinstalled PC-DOS and Windows 3.1 (or OS/2 Warp). This makes sense if you are upgrading, since you wouldn't want to pay for software you already have. If you are buying your first computer, you must factor in the cost of the software that other makers bundle with their systems. The IBM does include a number of utilities. There's Welcome, providing new users with a get-acquainted multimedia presentation. In addition, there's NetFinity to allow LAN administrators to remotely gather system configuration details, plus QAPlus diagnostic software, Online Housecall to allow technical support to log onto your computer, AnyView to dynamically change screen resolution, FaxWorks to control a fax modem, and Reprint for sending desktop publishing output directly to commercial copying centers.

Documentation is good but sparse. One guide shows you how to set up the computer. A second shows you how to install options, while a third gives you an overview, and a fourth explains PC-DOS and Windows.

IBM does offer solid toll-free technical support. In our test, the phone was answered right away, and the delay before reaching a technician rarely exceeded one minute. We found the technicians quite knowledgeable.

The base price of the PC 350 does not include a monitor. Our review system came with a 17-inch IBM display (list price:

$1,199) that was the highlight of the system. It was easier to read than the smaller monitors on the other systems, and it certainly made working with Windows at higher resolutions much more pleasant.

As for performance, we could not find anything to complain about. Running most programs, the 486 DX4/100 performed admirably and was comparable to a 60MHz Pentium system.

The PC 350 comes with Rapid Resume, an especially nice feature that saves your work if there is a power fluctuation or if you turn the computer off while running an application. When you turn the computer back on, it restores everything to the status just prior to the loss of power. Rapid Resume does this by having enough backup power to take a snapshot of memory (which, of course, will also save you time booting your machine in the morning).

The machine also has a standby mode that complies with Energy Star guidelines. This puts your monitor and disk drive into idle mode if no activity occurs for a specified time. The feature is integrated with Rapid Resume so that when you begin using your computer again, it returns to full power at the exact point in your application where you left off.

If you elect to buy the optional fax modem, your PC 350 also has a wake-up-on-ring mode so the fax machine activates when a call comes in. This also allows you to access your system remotely, even if it is turned off. The Scheduler wraps it all together with time-specified command initiation. For example, you can instruct your system to be up and running at the same time every morning, with updated E-mail and faxes ready for review.

The low price of the IBM PC 350 is deceptive. In its base configuration, it lacks a monitor and has only 4Mb RAM, a 270Mb hard drive, and very little software. A fully configured model is likely to be similar in price to other systems reviewed here. Nevertheless, IBM is synonymous with quality, and the PC 350 is a well-built system deserving a closer look.

Specifications: operating system, PC-DOS and Windows 3.1, or OS/2 Warp; RAM (std./max.), 4Mb/128Mb; CPU/MHz, Intel

DX4/100; floppy drive, 3.5"; hard drive/speed, 270Mb/12ms; storage bays, 5 (3 available); expansion slots, 4 ISA, 1 VL; ports, 2 serial, 1 parallel (Extended Capabilities Port), 1 keyboard, 1 mouse; monitor, none. **Warranty:** 1 year on-site; parts and labor, 3 years. **Ratings:** overall value, 9; performance, 9; expandability, 9; documentation, 8.

Approx. retail price	Approx. low price
$1,231 (4Mb)	**$1,231 (4Mb)**

APPLE POWER MACINTOSH 6100/66

Recommended

The first generation of Macintosh PowerPC computers were some of the most eagerly awaited machines in recent history. They took the Macintosh line to new heights of power and performance and at the same time were the most affordable Apple computers ever. The 6100/66 is part of the second wave of Power Macintosh computers, offering more power and speed for even less money.

The 6100/66 is this second wave's entry-level machine. It sports a 601 chip running at 66MHz. Like all the new Power Macs, the 6100/66 includes 256Kb of CPU cache memory. This significantly speeds up many operations by reducing the time needed to retrieve information from memory. The average speed increase is 15 percent.

The 6100/66 is well equipped for the home office. It has 8Mb of memory, a 350Mb SCSI hard drive, a double-speed CD-ROM drive, a 3.5-inch floppy-disk drive, built-in audio capabilities, built-in LocalTalk and high-speed Ethernet connections, AppleTalk networking software, and System 7.5, all for just a little over $2,000 (keyboard and monitor are not included). Expect to pay about $2,600 for a complete system.

The 8Mb of memory means that even such RAM-demanding applications as QuarkXPress will run without a memory upgrade. The 350Mb hard drive means there's space to store large applications. The built-in SCSI support makes adding an external drive quick and easy.

The computer is built inside a small, pizza-box-shaped cabinet. Its footprint is no larger than the monitor, so it can fit almost anywhere that you have room for a monitor and keyboard. However, its tiny size does limit expansion. The only expansion slot is one 7-inch NuBus slot. The 6100/66 has three drive bays, and if you order the CD-ROM, all three of them will be full.

The good news is that lots of the things you might want to add to your computer are already built in, such as network capabilities. The 6100/66 has a monitor port to which you can attach a 12-inch to 16-inch monitor. It uses a nonstandard connector, but an adapter is included. Using this built-in video saves money, but it uses 600Kb of main memory as system memory. Also, the number of colors you can see is somewhat limited: You can see thousands of colors on the smaller monitors but only 256 on the largest 16-inch display.

If you are new to computers or have never set one up, you will find the 6100/66 a joy. Apple computers generally are very easy to set up. The ports on the case have tiny pictures of what is to be connected; in many cases, connectors cannot fit into the wrong port because different sizes are used.

The documentation is very clear on how to set up the 6100/66. Apple developed the first graphical, user-friendly personal-computer operating system. The latest version that comes with the 6100/66—System 7.5—continues that tradition. New users will be up and running in no time. (The 6100/66 includes no other software than the operating system.)

If you are running an older Macintosh application not designed specifically for a Power Mac, the computer will run it in emulation mode. On the 6100/66, these applications run at about the speed of an LC III. The emulation is rock solid, and almost everything runs fine. Applications that require a floating-point unit, such as most 3-D modeling programs, will not run in emulation mode; however, most of these have been upgraded to run in native PowerPC mode.

If you want to adopt a Macintosh but you occasionally need to run a Windows program, the 6100/66 can accommodate you; but you will need to upgrade RAM to 16Mb and purchase a copy of SoftWindows from Insignia Solutions. Once you do, the 6100/66 runs Windows applications at about the speed of a slow 486/SX computer. It would not be comfortable for everyday use but it is acceptable for occasional work. If you need the ability to run Windows, you may want to consider one of the faster Power Macs, since they already come with 16Mb RAM and SoftWindows installed.

System 7.5 has also improved its support for MS-DOS. Now, DOS disks mount without a translation program, exactly as a Macintosh disk would. That makes it easier to transfer data between a PC computer and the 6100/66—especially if you are using a program like Word or Excel that can directly load data files that it creates on other platforms.

Overall, the 6100/66 is extremely attractive to someone with an older Macintosh looking for an upgrade to a Power Mac, or attractive as an entry-level machine to someone new to computers. However, seasoned users may be turned off by its limited expandability.

Specifications: operating system, System 7.5; RAM (std./max.), 8Mb/72Mb; CPU/MHZ, PowerPC 601/66; floppy drives, 3.5" 1.4Mb SuperDrive; hard drive/speed, 350Mb/speed not available; storage bays, 3; expansion slots, 1 NuBus; ports, 1 16-bit stereo I/O port, 1 high-speed asynchronous SCSI interface, 1 Ethernet connector, 1 high-density display port, 2 DMA serial ports compatible with LocalTalk and GeoPort cables; monitor, none. **Warranty**: 1 year on-site service, toll-free technical support. **Ratings:** overall value, 9; performance, 9; expandability, 7; documentation, 10.

Approx. retail price	**Approx. low price**
$1,818 (CD-ROM)	**$1,699**
$2,029 (no CD-ROM)	**$1,899**

HIGH-POWERED COMPUTERS

DELL DIMENSION XPS P100C

BEST BUY

The Dell Dimension XPS line has a long and proud history of excellent value complemented by superior performance and product packaging. The Dimension XPS P90 has been a desktop standard for the last year, and Dell seems

Prices are accurate at time of printing but are subject to manufacturers' changes.

well on its way toward continuing that tradition with the Dimension XPS P100c.

Besides its superfast Intel Pentium 100MHz CPU (which Dell loudly asserts is the updated bug-free version of the chip), the Dimension XPS P100c has the added performance advantage of the only 128-bit video card currently available on the market. Number Nine Visual Technology's Imagine128 video card includes a whopping 4Mb VRAM standard and is expandable up to 8Mb.

While this certainly pumps up the Dimension's performance numbers, especially under graphics-oriented operating systems like Windows, Dell didn't shirk its responsibilities in other areas of system configuration.

The XPS P100c comes with all the trimmings, including 16Mb EDORAM, a 256Kb pipeline burst secondary processor cache, and a 1Gb Enhanced IDE (EIDE) hard disk. (EIDE is a more powerful, faster version of IDE that's still backward compatible for your old hard disk but offers better speed and higher capacities for new hard disks. It even supports other peripherals like tape or CD-ROM drives.)

Speaking of CD-ROM drives, Dell includes an EIDE quad-speed multisession CD-ROM drive standard, as well as a SoundBlaster 16 sound card, which is wired to some very sweet Altec Lansing ACS 31 speakers. Altec Lansing pretty much sets the standard for PC speakers, and while the ACS 31s aren't quite top of the line, they certainly offer better-than-average sound quality.

And while you're listening to all your favorite multimedia applications and games, you'll not only be running them at a superfast rate via the Imagine128, but you'll also be seeing them on a wonderful 17-inch Dell UltraScan 17LS monitor. This display is basically a flat-screen monitor with a 0.28mm dot pitch that provides truly crisp images with even color distribution. Its controls are digital, and it even has memory so you can store your own preset video settings. It's also fully VESA-compliant, meaning it supports all the necessary refresh speeds to keep its image clean and flicker-free, thus saving you eye strain.

While the display's maximum resolution is 1,280 × 1,204, we found it most pleasing to the eye to keep things running at

800 × 600 with a 70Hz refresh rate. (On the downside, the review model did take quite a long while to warm up and sometimes needed to revert to black-and-white mode while it was still running cold. That's a fairly minor problem, though, since the display always went into full color once it warmed up.)

Inside the full-tower case, things were roomy and uncluttered. The Intel-manufactured motherboard holds five 16-bit ISA expansion slots and three 32-bit PCI slots. The PCI controller is Intel's latest Triton chip set, which supports all the most up-to-date features of the PCI bus, including plug-and-play support for the Windows 95 operating system. The motherboard also holds one high-speed bidirectional parallel port and two high-speed serial ports, as well as an integral mouse port. The only drawback we found here was that, although you can expand RAM up to 128Mb, the 256Kb pipeline burst cache can't be enlarged after it's been installed (although a 512Kb cache is a factory-installed option). There's also only the single 3.5-inch 1.44Mb floppy-disk drive, but no one distributes anything on 5.25-inch disks anymore anyway.

The only complaint we have here is Dell's use of a standard "space-saver" keyboard. For those who suffer from carpal tunnel syndrome or who are at risk of developing the painful condition, we feel the Microsoft ergonomic keyboard should always be offered. (It is available through the DellWare catalog.)

Setting up the Dimension is very simple. Not only is there enough paper documentation to satisfy even the most discriminating user, but you also get a software tutor that comes up as soon as the system boots automatically in Windows. Here, you're given a choice of whether you'd like to continue setting up configuration parameters, operate the machine under Dell's own Windows shell, or dispense with the shell and move directly to the Windows operating system. While this may be annoying to the experienced user, it's very helpful to the novice—and computer veterans can disable the whole thing with a single mouse click. If you purchased the Dimension XPS P100c with a modem installed, this introductory screen will even register your purchase with Dell automatically.

Under performance testing, the Dimension XPS is a very fast mover. Bolstered by its speedy CPU and the greased lightning of its video card, it's a machine to reckon with—although it would be nice if Dell offered, as standard, a three-year warranty, instead of the one-year warranty that comes with the PC.

Specifications: operating system, MS-DOS 6.22, Windows for Workgroups 3.11; RAM (std./max.), 16Mb/64Mb; CPU/MHz, Intel Pentium/100; floppy drive, 3.5" 1.44Mb; hard drive/speed, 1Gb/10ms; storage bays, 6; expansion slots, 4 ISA, 4 PCI, 1 ISA/PCI; ports, 2 serial, 1 parallel, 1 mouse, 1 keyboard; monitor, 17" Dell UltraScan 17LS. **Warranty:** parts and service, 1 year on-site. **Ratings:** overall value, 9; performance, 9; expandability, 9; documentation, 10.

Approx. retail price
$3,549

Approx. low price
$3,352

APPLE POWER MACINTOSH 8100/110

Recommended

The race for the fastest processor reached a new level with Intel's introduction of the 120MHz Pentium and its long-awaited P6. To keep pace, Apple announced upcoming additions to the PowerPC chip line and shipped a 110MHz version of the original PowerPC 601. The folks at Cupertino then placed the extremely fast CPU in an upgraded Power Macintosh to arrive at the $6,379 Power Macintosh 8100/110.

While a 10MHz improvement over the 8100/100 may not seem like such a big deal, Apple, IBM, and Motorola also added a few other speed enhancements, including an improved NuBus interface. In its original implementation of the NuBus with the PowerPC, Apple left a small bug in the NuBus controller chip, which caused slower performance for such applications as high-end video editing and multimedia authoring—two of the Mac's most important customer types.

The 8100/110 finally contains some fixes for these problems for which the Macintosh-based video folks have been howling for quite some time. First, the company improved the bus's ability to handle third-party (non-Apple) NuBus video cards by redesigning the NuBus controller. The chip now supports burst-mode data transfers—useful for video-editing hardware—and also takes care of most of the bus-timing errors that can happen during large data transfers (like 24-bit color TIF files).

If you're worried about these flaws in the PowerPC chip, here's the scoop. The Power Macintosh 6100/66, 7100/80, and 8100/100 all contain the NuBus flaws. In practical terms, this just means that in some instances where people are using high-end video-editing tools, Power Macintosh/NuBus performance has fallen below that of the older Macintosh Quadra machines. If you bought your Power Macintosh to do high-end editing, you may find that some of your NuBus cards won't work properly with your new Power Macintosh. It's best to test these out before making a purchasing commitment. (Just so you know, Apple does not see this as a pervasive problem, and the company has no plans to do a corrective redesign or offer a chip trade-in program, as happened with the Intel Pentium blooper).

While the 8100/110's raw processor speed is tantalizing, be aware that the speed of the NuBus implementation may throw you. Since the 8100/110's PowerPC 601 is a clock tripler, its NuBus runs at 36.7MHz. The 8100/80, meanwhile, has a NuBus that cranks along at 40MHz, but this CPU is a clock doubler. The important thing to remember is that, even though the bus is slightly slower, in combination with the 110Mhz PowerPC 601, the pair actually work faster than either the 8100/80 or the 8100/100.

While that may seem like a lot of talk about the new processor, there really isn't that much to say about the rest of the system. For one thing, Apple is offering it in only one configuration, which includes 16Mb RAM, a 256Kb cache, a 2x CD-ROM drive, an HPV card with 2Mb VRAM (expandable to 4Mb), and a hard disk that will store 2Gb. While you might certainly want to increase the RAM complement here, you'll also want to rethink the 256Kb cache. This seems awfully small for a PC designed for moving large data files across its bus. You can upgrade the cache to 512Kb or even 1Mb, and, if you've got the money, it's definitely worth a look.

On the inside you'll also find three NuBus expansion slots and a dual-channel SCSI configuration. With these you can add more SCSI devices than ever, using the Fast-SCSI-2 channel for your internal high-speed data transfers and the external port for your typical SCSI peripheral daisy chain.

On the back, the Power Macintosh 8100/110 carries the usual array of I/O ports, including sound in, sound out, two serial ports (GeoPort compatible), one ADB port, and an Ethernet jack. A potential inconvenience is that the 8100/110 requires a special version of System 7.5. This comes both preinstalled as well as on a bootable CD.

With its upgraded NuBus support, the 8100/110 is definitely the fastest Power Macintosh available—and will continue to be until Apple and IBM start releasing systems combining the PowerPC with the PCI bus. But so far there's little but rumors of such systems.

Earlier this year, production snafus led to a major slowdown in manufacturing the Power Macintosh 8100/110. By the time you read this, the problems will undoubtedly have been resolved. However, with its steep list price, this is one Power Macintosh you'll find only on the desks of those who really need it.

Specifications: operating system, System 7.5; RAM (std./max.), 16Mb/264Mb; CPU/MHz, PowerPC 601/110; floppy drive, 3.5" 1.44Mb; hard drive/ speed, 2Gb/10ms; storage bays, 3; expansion slots, 3 NuBus; ports, 2 serial (GeoPort compatible), 1 SCSI, 1 ADB, 1 sound in, 1 sound out, 1 video, 1 Ethernet jack; monitor, none. **Warranty:** parts and labor, 1 year. **Ratings:** overall value, 8; performance, 8; expandability, 6; documentation, 9.

Approx. retail price	**Approx. low price**
$6,379	**$4,099**

PORTABLE COMPUTERS

APPLE POWERBOOK 540C

✓BEST BUY

The Apple PowerBook 540c is the notebook equivalent of a sports car—a spiffy Italian two-seater with racy curves and raw power under the hood. It goes from zero to 66MHz in just seconds and runs for nearly six hours on its two-battery tank. With a list price of $4,999, the 540c may give you sticker shock, but when you see its active-matrix color screen, ample 500Mb of hard-disk space, and state-of-the-art keyboard, you'll be driving it off the lot with a grin from ear to ear.

This is Apple's top-of-the-line PowerBook, equal in performance to the high-end Quadra desktop models. As such, this power-user's dream machine is equipped with a host of innovative features and loads of expansion options. This could very easily be the ultimate PC for the road, office, and home.

Based on a Motorola 68LC040 processor, the 7.3-pound 540c incorporates a high-density disk drive, a 9.5-inch backlit active-matrix color display, a 500Mb internal hard drive, and dual NiMH batteries.

It's not lightweight for a notebook, but you can't fault the 540c's other features. The screen is gorgeous—bright and colorful from any angle. The hard drive is roomy for a desktop PC, let alone a notebook. The 3.5-inch disk drive is able to read and write to MS-DOS and Windows disks. Also, according to Apple, the two batteries are good for three hours each, so the extra weight is well worth it. Of particular merit is Apple's unique finger-controlled trackpad pointing device, which is embedded in the palmrest.

The 540c also features 16-bit stereo sound, two built-in speakers, and a built-in microphone for on-the-road recording. Expansion options include an SCSI port for adding up to six external devices, a high-speed Ethernet port for instant networking, a processor-direct slot for connecting an optional PCMCIA adapter, and a video-out port compatible with most Apple and SVGA monitors. Of particular importance, the 540c is upgradable to PowerPC-chip technology, so it's well protected from obsolescence. (An upgrade card should be available by the time you read this.)

Our evaluation unit came with two optional upgrades installed, both of which account for a fair portion of the 540c's price. The first was an upgrade from the 540c's standard 4Mb RAM to 12Mb—necessary for running any significant applications. The second was a Global Village fax modem capable of data transfer at 19.2 bits per second (bps) and fax transmission at 14.4 bps.

Although Apple's software bundles change often, our unit came with the award-winning ClarisWorks 3.0—an integrated package featuring word processing, spreadsheet, database, and other software—plus Claris's Power To Go, a collection of power-saving and hard-disk-compression utilities. Neither package was preinstalled.

As always, Apple's documentation is outstanding. The 540c is backed by toll-free technical support and a one-year overnight-replacement warranty. You get what you pay for: We called the 800 number and immediately spoke to a live human.

Except for a slightly flimsy hinge on which the 540c's screen rotates, there's nothing about this muscle machine not to like. It's expensive, but for power users with power needs, the 540c is the only way to drive.

Specifications: operating system, System 7.5; RAM (std./max.), 12Mb/36Mb; CPU/MHz, 68LC040, 66/33MHz; floppy drive, 3.5" 1.44Mb; hard drive/ speed, 500Mb/speed not available; storage bays, none; expansion slots, 90-pin processor-direct slot, internal modem, RAM slot; ports, 1 Apple Desktop Bus, 1 Serial/LocalTalk, 1 Ethernet, 1 SCSI, 1 power adapter, 1 stereo input jack, 1 stereo output jack, 1 video out port. **Warranty:** overnight replacement, 1 year; toll-free technical support. **Ratings:** overall value, 10; performance, 10; expandability, 10; documentation, 10.

Approx. retail price	Approx. low price
$4,999	**$3,699**

COMPAQ CONTURA 410CX

✓BEST BUY

Although notebook manufacturers will try to dazzle you with an array of exciting features, the new 5.9-pound Compaq Contura 410CX properly accentuates the important stuff.

The Contura employs an 8.4-inch active-matrix color display, which makes up for being a bit small by delivering gorgeous, vibrant color. Even in direct sunlight, it's very readable.

The keyboard is also a plus. Notebooks often suffer from cramped, shrunken keys that lack the feel of a true keyboard.

Not so the Contura, which provides a comfortable, full-size set of keys—almost as good as the real thing.

Equally important is the pointing device. There's no substitute for the mouse, and the Contura does have an external mouse port. You can also use the built-in trackball, which is embedded in the palmrest just below the keyboard. The design isn't unique, but it is well implemented.

Compaq says that the typical user can expect at least 3.5 hours of operation from a single battery, as long as the Contura's power-saving features are enabled. The machine's prominent LED display panel keeps you apprised of remaining battery life.

In other areas, the Contura features a 486-DX2/50 processor, a 350Mb hard drive, a 3.5-inch disk drive, a PCMCIA expansion slot, 4Mb of memory (expandable to 20Mb), and preinstalled copies of MS-DOS and Windows. Compaq also includes TabWorks, which replaces the usual Windows interface with something akin to a three-ring binder with tabbed "pages"—great for novices. There's also a wealth of on-line documentation. On the downside, Compaq includes no application software other than Lotus Organizer, a personal information manager.

When you first power up the Contura, it runs through a one-time software installation procedure. This takes about 15 minutes, which gives you time to peruse the various instruction manuals.

At just under $3,000, the Contura is a bit on the pricey side—but in this case you get what you pay for. Compaq provides 24-hour technical support seven days a week, plus a three-year warranty.

Specifications: operating system, MS-DOS, Windows 95; RAM (std./max.), 4Mb/20Mb; CPU/MHz, SL-enhanced 486DX2/50; floppy drive, 3.5" 1.44Mb; hard drive/speed, 350Mb/14ms; storage bays, none; expansion slots, PCMCIA slot (supports 1 Type III or 2 Type II), port for docking station; ports, 1 serial, 1 parallel, 1 external SVGA, 1 PS/2 mouse/keyboard. **Warranty:** overnight replacement, 3 years. **Ratings:** overall value, 9; performance, 10; expandability, 10; documentation, 10.

Approx. retail price	Approx. low price
$2,999	$2,973

TWINHEAD SLIMNOTE 5100T

Recommended

Our first reaction to reviewing a laptop with a touchpad was, "It can't be any good." Despite some reserva tions, though, we found that the Twinhead Slimnote 5100T' touchpad is often better than the alternatives.

Controlling the touchpad, which is located in the three-incl palmrest, is easy and natural. Touchpad software requires th use of special gestures; for example, a double tap ending wit the finger down starts a click-and-drag. On the other hanc menu selections are a breeze. After a few minutes outside on sunny, pleasant day, the touchpad became unusable. Back ir doors, the problem cleared up quickly without rebooting (trackball is also available).

Just a bit bigger than notebook size (8.8 × 11.6 × 1.9 inches) and weighing 6.2 pounds, the 5100T includes an Inte DX4/100 processor and an active-matrix display—perfect ir doors, but often hard to see in sunlight. The 640 × 480 × 25 resolution display hinges 180 degrees. External support goe up to 1,024 × 768 × 256.

Battery life is great, surviving two hours and 37 minutes wit one battery on our toughest rundown test. Take off the remo able floppy drive, insert an additional battery, and you could g more than five hours without needing AC. You must reboot t swap, but you can alter power management without this.

Along with hot-key power, the Slimnote can Suspend and Su pend-To-Disk. The AC adapter is small and light. The Slimnote full-size 85-key keyboard has an excellent layout, with inverte T cursors and dedicated Home, End, PgUp, and PgDn keys.

The 5100T has the usual ports and two upgradable memor slots for up to 32Mb (be sure you get at least 8Mb). The r movable hard drive is available in 340Mb, 500Mb, and 800M capacities.

Two speakers on either side of the palmrest provide cle audio from the included 16-bit sound card. The notebook h a built-in microphone plus microphone and stereo in and ou

Prices are accurate at time of printing but are subject to manufacturers' changes.

jacks. An optional I/O Slice device provides an extra serial port, separate PS/2 mouse/keyboard ports, a Type III PCMCIA slot, a game/MIDI port, and a SCSI-2 interface. An optional docking station provides one 3.5-inch and one 5.25-inch drive bay, plus two full-length 16-bit ISA expansion slots.

Unfortunately, the Slimnote could have been named for its documentation—slim notes. The laptop does come with sufficient preinstalled software and installation disks, but nothing fancy.

Overall, the Twinhead Slimnote 5100T is an impressive laptop with excellent video performance and very good disk and memory access scores. With built-in 16-bit sound and excellent active-matrix video, it makes a great portable presentation machine. If you want a fast laptop with a nice display at a low price, the 5100T is worth considering.

Specifications: operating system, MS-DOS 6.22, Windows 3.1; RAM (std./max.), 8Mb/32Mb; CPU/MHz, Intel DX4/100; floppy drive, 3.5″ 1.44Mb; hard drive/speed, 340Mb/15ms; storage bays, 2 (on docking station); expansion slots, 2 full-length 16-bit ISA (on docking station); ports, 1 16550 serial, 1 EPP/ECP parallel, 1 SVGA, 1 PS/2, 1 mouse/keyboard, 1 expansion. **Warranty:** parts and labor, 1 year; replacement parts within 48 hours. **Ratings:** overall value, 9; performance, 9; expandability, 10; documentation, 8.

Approx. retail price	**Approx. low price**
$3,599 (8Mb/340Mb/active)	**$3,599**

HOME OFFICE PRODUCTS

Home office equipment is designed and priced for a fast growing market of home business owners, students, job seekers, and employees who spend part of their week working at home.

Americans today are buying home office products in record numbers. These products are capable of delivering the reliability, productivity, and many of the same features as their high-priced counterparts in commercial offices. However, products made for the home often are not designed for the heavy use that commercial office equipment must endure.

BEST BUYS '96

Our Best Buy and Recommended home office products follow. They are categorized into word processors, desktop copiers, scanners, desktop fax machines, personal digital assistants, and electronic organizers. Within each category, the product we consider to be the best of the Best Buys is listed first, followed by our second choice, and so on. Remember that a Best Buy or Recommended designation applies only to the model listed. It does not necessarily apply to other models made by the same manufacturer.

WORD PROCESSORS

A word processor is a specialized computer designed primarily for creating and printing professional-looking reports, manuscripts, letters, and other documents. Some word processors can also produce spreadsheets and perform other tasks that are usually functions of a personal computer. Some models interface with computers and printers. Word processors are different from electric typewriters in two major ways. First, electric typewriters cannot duplicate computerized page formatting functions the way word processors do. Second, electric typewriters cannot store documents for later retrieval and editing.

Features to be considered while shopping are print quality, memory, page display, and merge functions. Look for a word processor that produces high-quality documents. As for memory, word processors can vary widely in their ability to store information internally or on disk. Page display is the number of lines or parts of documents that can be displayed on the screen. Merge functions allow you to automatically generate individual letters to names on a mailing list.

BROTHER WP-7550J WHISPERWRITER

✓BEST BUY

The Brother WP-7550J is one of the most sophisticated portable word processors available. It has a 14-inch monitor and a built-in ink-jet printer, which sprays ink onto the paper for print quality that closely resembles that of a laser printer. The very quiet WhisperWriter lets you combine five type sizes (10 point, 12 point, 18 point, 24 point, 36 point), seven printing styles (bold, underline, strike-out, italic, outline, shadow, shading), and five fonts (Helsinki, Brougham, Tennessee, U.S., Calgary) plus special characters and symbols. It also prints five types of charts and graphs. The WP-7550J has a 3.5-inch floppy disk drive that stores up to 1.44 Mb of documents, Lotus 1-2-3–compatible spreadsheets, and address book files. The files can be converted for use by a DOS computer. This model also has 198 letter templates for fast document creation, as well as layout and page view features and dual screen and multicolumn printing features. The word processor has a 114,000-word spelling checker and a 45,000-word thesaurus. Another handy feature is the abbreviated phrase memory that fills in complete words for partial spellings as you type. The unit comes with a modem port that lets you attach a modem to a telephone line to log onto CompuServe.

Specifications: height, $5\frac{4}{5}$"; width, $16\frac{1}{10}$"; depth, $17\frac{9}{10}$"; weight, 11 lb. (monitor excluded). **Warranty:** labor, 90 days; parts, 1 year, limited.

Approx. retail price $449 **Approx. low price** $433

SMITH CORONA PWP 5500

Recommended

The Smith Corona PWP 5500 is a quiet-printing system with a 14-inch flat screen that shows 24 lines by 80 characters. Like many computers, it uses a graphical interface with pull-down menus and comes with a mouse for clicking icons to load programs. There's also an on-screen help-manager module, and a screen saver program protects the monitor from getting a burned-in image. Programs included are an address database, spreadsheet, calendar/schedule, calculator, desktop reference, grammar checker, and the word processor. You'll also get 100 sample letters for all occasions on disk, a 90,000-word spelling checker, and a 96,000-word thesaurus. This model comes with three changeable print wheels: Regency 10, Orator 10, and Presidential 12. The printer supports three-column text and bidirectional printing. Spreadsheet files can be converted to Lotus 1-2-3 for Windows, and word processor documents can be converted to WordPerfect for Windows.

Specifications: height, 5″; width, 16¾″; depth, 16¼″; weight: 14⅕ lb. (monitor excluded). **Warranty:** labor, 90 days; parts, 1 year.

Approx. retail price $424 **Approx. low price** $370

BROTHER WP-5600MDS

Recommended

The Brother WP-5600MDS is a new, improved model. Its major enhancement over last year's model is the high-density 3.5-inch 1.44Mb floppy disk drive. It has a 14-inch monitor that shows 20 lines by 90 characters. The printing carriage is 12.8 inches and takes paper up to 9 inches wide. This model prints only in one type style, since it has a built-in impact, or typewriter-style, printer. The WP-5600MDS has a 95,000-word spelling checker and a 45,000-word thesaurus and grammar checker. The address book has data merge for printing individually addressed letters from a master document.

Other functions include a dual screen feature, abbreviated phrase memory, and a spreadsheet program. As a bonus, you also get the Tetris arcade game. The data saved on floppy disk can be used on a DOS computer. A file conversion program lets you transfer ASCII word processing files and Lotus 1-2-3 spreadsheet files between the word processor and a DOS computer.

Specifications: height, 5⅖"; width, 16⅖"; depth, 19⅕"; weight, 12³⁄₁₀ lb. (monitor excluded). **Warranty:** labor, 90 days; parts, 1 year, limited.

Approx. retail price	Approx. low price
$329	**$300**

DESKTOP COPIERS

Desktop photocopy machines used to be considered a luxury item in the home office. Today, with improved design and affordable pricing, copy machines have become a regular part of the home office. The latest designs combine printing and faxing features so that one machine takes over the work of several. One of the best features of desktop copiers is a user-friendly design that makes them easy for the owner to service. New models are built to take up very little space. They are also time- and cost-effective when compared to the inconvenience and expense of using a print shop or coin-operated copier. Before you buy any copier, test a floor model in the store to ensure that it produces clear copies. The major upkeep on photocopy machines is related to the toner, a powdery substance used to re-create the image being copied. Some models require replacement of a toner cartridge; others have a refillable toner reservoir. Toner cartridges vary in price depending on the manufacturer and the suppliers. A few companies recycle empty cartridges. Proper disposal of an empty toner cartridge may be inconvenient.

HEWLETT-PACKARD HP OFFICEJET

✓ BEST BUY

The Hewlett-Packard OfficeJet is more than a desktop copier; it's also a high-quality printer and a full-featured fax. It prints 600 by 300 dots per inch using HP's latest

Prices are accurate at time of printing but are subject to manufacturers' changes.

ink jet technology. The printing engine makes up to 99 copies for each original and is capable of image reductions to fit more detail on a single page. The document feeder holds 20 pages. A 40-character display on the front panel simplifies operating procedures. This is the perfect document device for any small business or home office. It takes up little desk space and handles paper sizes ranging from letter and executive to legal, as well as transparency film and envelopes, all using the 100-sheet paper tray. The OfficeJet prints up to three pages per minute, which isn't very fast compared to other desktop copiers. But the combination of fax, computer printer, and copier may make this slower printing pace an acceptable trade-off. Many extras in the area of fax and printer functions make the OfficeJet the ideal office companion. If you don't have to constantly supply a large distribution of multiple copies, this combination copier will replace two other essential office tools quite nicely and give you improved service.

Specifications: height, 11³⁄₂₅"; width, 17¼"; depth, 15½"; weight, 21 lb. **Warranty:** overnight express exchange, 1 year.

Approx. retail price	Approx. low price
$860	

XEROX 5305

Recommended

The Xerox 5305 isn't intended for heavy office use. Its mission is to provide fast, reliable copies for personal or small-office purposes. It handles up to 300 copies per month without showing signs of strain. If your regular needs won't exceed this recommended usage, this desktop copier may give you worry-free service. The 5305 prints about three copies per minute, taking some 19 seconds to push out the first copy. It handles paper from four by six inches to 8½ by 11 inches. The toner cartridge life varies depending on the type of documents and the paper size used. The copy cartridge or drum produces about 10,000 copies before needing replacement. The warranty is itself a strong reason to buy the Xerox 5305. Xerox guarantees the unit's reliable service for three years. If you have trouble, the manufacturer will ship an exchange unit within 48 hours.

Prices are accurate at time of printing but are subject to manufacturers' changes.

Specifications: height, 4″; width, 15″; depth, 14″; weight, 15½ lb. **Warranty:** 3 years; 48-hour exchange or ship-in.

Approx. retail price
$349

Approx. low price
$349

SCANNERS

A scanner is a personal computer input device that lets you transfer printed text to the computer without rekeying the material. It also lets you transfer graphics directly into the computer. Scanners can be either hand-held or flatbed. Flatbed scanners are often more convenient because they capture an entire page more easily. But they are much more costly. Hand-held scanners have software that seams several passes together to make a completed page.

In shopping for a scanner, be sure to select one that is designed to work with the operating system of your computer—DOS, Windows, or Macintosh. Some manufacturers offer an optional OCR (optical character recognition) software package for scanning text. Retailers may offer a variety of OCR software at a variety of prices as part of a scanner package. Scanners require lots of memory, so be sure your computer has enough memory for the scanner's needs. Scanners come in two basic types—gray-scale and color. Color models are much more expensive.

LOGITECH SCANMAN EASYTOUCH

✓BEST BUY

Logitech's hand-held ScanMan makes copying small graphics and full pages simple and efficient. It copies images and text using 256 gray-scale shades to produce resolutions from 100 to 400 dots per inch. The "autostitch" feature seams each pass of the page or graphic together on the screen. The ScanMan includes OmniPage Direct AnyFont OCR software, which recognizes text from 6 to 72 points in English and 10 other languages. The scanner cord plugs into a parallel port via an included pass-through connector that also connects the printer, so installation is done without opening the computer's case. There are no IRQ or DMA settings to make. Operation is simple. ScanMan works with DOS 3.3 or higher and Windows 3.1 or higher and is both TWAIN-compliant and OLE-compliant. It needs a mouse, hard drive, and at least a 386 computer with four Mb RAM and VGA or better graphics. You'll get a better price and a 30-day money-back guarantee if you purchase this model directly from the manufacturer.

Specifications: height, 1⅘"; width, 5⅗"; depth, 4⅕"; weight, 10½ oz.; cord length, 6 ft. **Warranty:** parts or replacement, 2 years; lifetime technical support.

Approx. retail price	**Approx. low price**
$249	**$193**

HEWLETT-PACKARD SCANJET 3C

Recommended

The ScanJet 3C is a flatbed color and monochrome scanner for IBM AT–compatible computers. It produces scanned images of 16 gray-scale levels. The unit includes a power cord, SCSI cable, and adapter, and comes with HP DeskScan II scanning software, OCR software, and other software needed for various graphics programs. There are several scanning speeds, including preview mode (which takes 4 seconds, 200 dpi gray scale), letter size (3.3 seconds, 300 dpi black and white), letter size (7.5 seconds), and 600 dpi color letter size (30 seconds). The scanner software produces scaling from 3 to 400 percent in one-percent increments at 600 dpi. The maximum document size is 8½ by 14 inches. The TWAIN-compliant feature lets you scan directly into an application. The HP Copy utility lets you make copies with your printer. The one-pass scanning mechanism offers much more convenience than hand-held scanners. Related models work with the IBM Micro Channel architecture and the Macintosh, producing 1,024 gray-scale levels and one billion colors, respectively. Though this model is considerably more expensive than its predecessor, the IIcx, it has double the speed and improved shadow detail, with over three times the level of gray. The 30-bit color internal capabilities also provide increased control in maintaining original image quality when scanning and enlarging images. If speed and quality images are your need, this unit might justify its cost.

Prices are accurate at time of printing but are subject to manufacturers' changes.

Specifications: height, 4$\frac{1}{10}$"; width, 14½"; depth, 23"; weight, 21$\frac{8}{10}$ lb. **Warranty:** overnight express exchange, 1 year.

Approx. retail price	**Approx. low price**
$1,179	**$1,026**

DESKTOP FAX MACHINES

Fax is the commonly used term for "facsimile machine" or the electronic facsimile transmission of documents. It is now considered a must-have item in the home office. In fact, many families are bringing them home for personal use. Prices for fax machines bundled with features are steadily coming down, and most models now include an attached phone so the fax machine can double as an extension phone in the household or home office. Other useful features include built-in answering machines and the ability to make copies of single-sheet documents. Many models also have a small LCD (liquid crystal display) screen. Some fax machines use heat-sensitive paper to print transmissions and copies of personal documents, but plain-paper fax machines are becoming increasingly popular. Fax machines transmit and receive over ordinary telephone lines, and no special skills are needed to connect a fax machine. It is not necessary to have a separate phone number, although it is often more convenient and productive to have a dedicated fax line if the machine is used in a home office. Sending and receiving faxes can be done manually or automatically, and most machines can be programmed for delayed transmission to take advantage of low nighttime phone rates. Most machines also have various reproduction modes for transmitting different types of documents, and many have halftone settings for transmitting photographs.

HEWLETT-PACKARD FAX-700

✓ BEST BUY

The Hewlett-Packard 700 fax copier has a full set of advanced features and a special front panel design that walks you through any feature and makes it easy to get the most out of your fax machine. This unit produces plain-paper copies that don't curl or fade. The printing engine uses HP ink-jet technology to make printed pages that resemble high-quality laser print. It prints at a rate of one page every nine seconds. The 20-page automatic document feeder provides almost double the capacity of most other fax machines. You can autodial up to 50 numbers: Ten are stored in one-touch key memory; 40 are speed-dial keys. This unit can also hold 12 pages in memory, which is handy if the machine runs low on paper during a transmission. The Hewlett-Packard 700 is more expensive than other brands, but the price is worth it, especially when you consider the iron-clad warranty, a one-year overnight express exchange that provides next-business-day replacement.

Specifications: height, 8⅗"; width, 13⅗"; depth, 13"; weight, 19 lb. **Warranty:** overnight express exchange, 1 year.

Approx. retail price	**Approx. low price**
$675	**$560**

BROTHER INTELLIFAX-725M

Recommended

The Brother IntelliFax-725M is loaded with features that make it a good choice for business or home office use. One of its most striking features is the 14.4-Kbps high-speed fax modem, which lets you complete transmissions about 40 percent more quickly than standard 9,600-bps-speed fax machines. This can pay off nicely in reducing long distance phone bills. Another useful feature is the Super CoverPage, which lets you select up to six programmable messages to introduce your documents. The Enhanced Remote Activation feature lets you transfer a fax call from any phone extension in the office or house. The FAX/TEL switch and TAD interface let you share the same phone line with an answering machine, telephone, and computer modem. The IntelliFax-725M has an automatic 15-page document feeder, an automatic paper cutter, and a 16-digit LCD display with on-screen programming. A nice feature not found on most fax machines is the 256Kb memory capacity that stores up to 10 pages for quick-scan, broadcast faxing, multicopy with sorting, and error correction. One small drawback: This is not a plain-paper fax machine.

Prices are accurate at time of printing but are subject to manufacturers' changes.

Specifications: height, 4⅘"; width, 14⅘"; depth, 12"; weight, 7½ lb. **Warranty:** parts and labor, 90 days.

Approx. retail price	Approx. low price
$314	Not available

PANASONIC KX-F550

Recommended

The Panasonic KX-F550 provides good-quality faxes and copies and easy operation. A help function gives you instructions on setting up, programming, and using the fax machine. Just press the help key to get a printout of simple instructions. This is a handy unit for a single line that shares a voice line. The system detects the type of incoming call (voice or fax) and sounds a distinctive ring pattern. If you use the Silent Ring feature, the machine will ring only for incoming phone calls, staying silent when faxes are received. The Absence mode lets you set the system to automatically switch between the answering mode and facsimile mode. The KX-F550 has a 40-station dialer, automatic redial, and a hands-free speakerphone (an especially useful feature not found on many models). The paper well, which has an automatic paper cutter, holds 164-foot paper rolls, making fewer changes necessary. The unit uses a super thermal paper grade that resists fading and takes highlighting without smearing. The automatic document feeder holds up to 15 sheets of paper.

Specifications: height, 4$\frac{13}{16}$"; width, 14¼"; depth, 11⅝"; weight, 8⅗ lb. **Warranty:** parts and labor, 1 year limited.

Approx. retail price	Approx. low price
$430	$300

BROTHER INTELLIFAX-625

Recommended

The Brother IntelliFax-625 has many of the same features as the IntelliFax-725M reviewed above. However, it lacks the high-speed modem and memory capacity features. The Electronic CoverPage lets you select up to four preprogrammed messages to introduce your documents. Enhanced Remote Activation lets you transfer a fax call from any phone extension in the office or house. The IntelliFax-625 has an au-

Prices are accurate at time of printing but are subject to manufacturers' changes.

tomatic 15-page document feeder and automatic paper cutter. It also has a FAX/TEL switch and TAD interface. This lets you share the same phone line with an answering machine, telephone, and computer modem. Other features include a 16-digit display with on-screen programming, 40-station number memory (20 one-touch and 20 speed dial), automatic redial up to three times in 5-minute intervals, large paper roll capacity (164 feet), distinctive ring detection, and 32-shade gray-scale reproduction.

Specifications: height, 4⅘"; width, 14⅘"; depth, 12"; weight, 7½ lb. **Warranty:** parts and labor, 90 days.

Approx. retail price
$249

Approx. low price
Not available

ELECTRONIC ORGANIZERS

Electronic organizers are fast becoming the preferred way to keep track of schedules and information for busy executives and students. These devices resemble computers in thier operation but are so small that they fit in your purse or pocket. They typically have an LCD (liquid crystal display) screen and special programs that help you keep track of important telephone numbers, appointments, bank account numbers, and other information. Electronic organizers usually have date and time displays, calculator functions, and time alarms. Some models have enough memory to include calendars, to-do lists, spreadsheets, and electronic notebooks. They often have two long-lasting batteries so you can change one without losing all your stored data. Some electronic organizers come with software and cables so you can move data between a desktop computer and the electronic organizer.

CASIO SF-7900 EXECUTIVE BOSS BUSINESS ORGANIZER SCHEDULING SYSTEM

✓ BEST BUY

The Casio SF-7900 is a powerful data manager that lets you transfer information from the organizer to a computer with a single cable and special software. It can also transfer data from many popular software programs. This lets you take data files on the road, make changes, and avoid manually updating your computer files when you return. This model comes with 128Kb of memory and a large display showing 16 characters by 8 lines. It includes programs to track expenses and maintain telephone lists and business cards. It also has a built-in calculator, event scheduler, calendar, and a reminder alarm you can set to sound for different events stored in the calendar. A memo feature lets you type in and save detailed notes or diary entries that can be used as a work log. The password feature protects you from unauthorized viewing of details in the various program functions.

Specifications: height, 1⅟₁₆″; width, 5¾″ (folded); depth: 3⅛″; weight, 8³⁄₁₀ oz. **Warranty:** 1 year.

Approx. retail price
$190

Approx. low price
$113

SHARP WIZARD OZ-6500FX

Recommended

The Sharp Wizard OZ-6500FX is a compact, reliable pocket organizer with lots of storage power. It comes with 512Kb of memory. That's almost as much as full table-model personal computers used to pack. This unit gives you a big advantage over a full-size PDA (see next section) but sacrifices little. It comes with a feature few, if any, other organizers have: telecommunications. The OZ-6500FX has a 9,600/2,400 bps fax/modem. You can use the built-in communications software and an RJ-11 phone cable to connect the unit to a standard telephone line to send and receive faxes and electronic mail. Use its infrared port to swap data with similarly equipped desktop computers. A $100 cable kit lets you connect the organizer to computers and printers without the infrared device. The OZ-6500FX's features include all the expected organizer tools: calendar, appointment scheduler, to-do list, phone book, notebook, and outliner. It sports a liquid crystal display screen of 14 lines by 40 characters. The phone directory, which for some people is the primary use for pocket organizers, stores 7,670 phone numbers.

Specifications: height, ¾"; width, 5⅘"; depth, 3½"; weight, 10 oz. **Warranty:** 1 year.

Approx. retail price	**Approx. low price**
$600	**$293**

PERSONAL DIGITAL ASSISTANTS

Personal Digital Assistants (known as PDAs) are small hand-held computers used to write notes, track appointments, and help you computerize other daily chores to keep your life in order. Early models, which are still quite popular, required data input by pressing small keys on a tiny keyboard. The newest models use a combination of pen-based input and character recognition software. This method lets you write notes, much like you would on a paper notepad, and press areas on the screen with the pen device to use various programs. The distinction between a feature-laden electronic organizer and a low-end PDA are often blurred. In general, PDAs have more memory and larger LCD (liquid crystal display) screens. PDAs often come with internal modems and fax features that allow users to perform many computer tasks associated with palm-top computing. PDAs usually have more computing features and complete operating systems that make them more compatible with computers.

When selecting a PDA, consider the screen size, memory expansion capabilities, and availability of add-on programs through plug-in cards. With the array of built-in programs and other features, a PDA can be a good alternative to lugging around a larger, heavier laptop computer and cost at least 50 percent less.

HEWLETT-PACKARD HP 200LX PALMTOP PC

✓BEST BUY

The HP 200LX is a personal digital assistant loaded with enough features to merit its name, Palmtop PC. If you fancy the Windows interface on a full-fledged computer, this unit will take some getting used to because it lacks a graphical interface. It also doesn't have a pen device. But for near-

Prices are accurate at time of printing but are subject to manufacturers' changes.

pocket-sized portable computing, its DOS 5.0-based power offers many features. It's packed with one Mb of RAM, which leaves plenty of computing space for more than a dozen built-in programs. These include Quicken, Lotus 1-2-3, and cc:Mail, among others. The software also includes an appointment book, phone book, financial calculator, memo editor with outliner, note taker, database, card filer, and an applications manager; all are accessed by pressing application keys. The display is a giant 80 columns by 25 rows. The unit can be plugged into a CGA monitor. The keyboard, though tiny, is in the familiar QWERTY layout with a separate keypad and 10 function keys. Other programs are added via a PC card slot.

Specifications: height, 1″; width, $6\frac{3}{10}$″; depth, $3\frac{2}{5}$″; weight, 11 oz. **Warranty:** labor and parts, 1 year; express exchange policy.

Approx. retail price	Approx. low price
$549	$496

SHARP ZAURUS ZR-5000

Recommended

The ZR-5000 personal digital assistant is a 16-bit palm-sized computer that runs fast. It has its own graphical operating system that manages up to 4Mb of software. The keyboard is small but functional, especially with lots of practice to get used to your fingers touching each other when you type. The unit has a pen-based interface as well. Using it is awkward on the fold-up screen, but the handwriting recognition is nearly flawless. The 4 by $2\frac{3}{5}$-inch screen is smaller than other models. The built-in applications include a word processor, notepad, outliner, flat-file database, calculator, drawing application, and phone number index. The unit has an infrared device for transferring data to other computers. A $7 optional utility converts Zaurus data into formats used by many popular Windows and Macintosh programs. A PCMCIA card (extra) provides remote communications.

Specifications: height, 1″; width, $6\frac{7}{10}$″; depth, $3\frac{9}{10}$″; weight, $13\frac{3}{5}$ oz. **Warranty:** 1 year.

Approx. retail price	Approx. low price
$500	$500

PERSONAL CARE APPLIANCES

Perhaps you're happy with your old faithful razor, iron, or electric toothbrush. Or maybe 1996 will be the year you decide to buy a new model. If so, you've chosen a good time to shop for personal care appliances. Today's models are available in an unparalleled array of functions, forms, styles, and colors.

These products meet more needs with their added-value features than ever before. Ultra-technology makes the electric toothbrush a real revelation; ironing becomes an experience tantamount to having your very own dry cleaner steaming service in house. A newer player in the field, home health care equipment is less painful (and quicker) than a trip to the doctor's office.

The newest products are designed for maximum use whether you're at home or traveling internationally (where U.S. appliances require dual voltage). If you can't bring yourself to part with an old, tried and true standby, or if you're not in the market right now for yourself, then by all means keep our suggestions in mind for future gift giving.

Best Buys '96

Our Best Buy, Recommended, and Budget Buy selections for 1996 follow. In each category, the product we consider to be the best of the Best Buys is listed first, followed by our second choice, and so on. Remember that a Best Buy, Recommended, or Budget Buy designation applies only to the model listed. It does not necessarily apply to other models by the same manufacturer or to an entire product line.

HOME HEALTH MONITORING SYSTEMS

If you have diabetes or low blood sugar, getting the best home health care available is essential. Since most people have no desire to wait hours for a readout or undergo painful bloodletting, home care kits have focused on quick, easy, painless monitoring. They have succeeded beyond most people's wildest dreams with simple-to-perform tests that only take minutes to administer.

LIFESCAN ONE TOUCH BASIC BLOOD & GLUCOSE MONITORING SYSTEM

✓ BEST BUY

The medical assistant who tested this simple, portable home health monitoring system for diabetes couldn't believe how easy it was to use. It literally takes just one touch. Simply turn on the power, insert the test strip, apply the sample, and get a readout. No wiping or blotting is necessary. The easy-to-use Penlet automatic blood sampler helps make the process virtually painless. The best part is that the monitor displays accurate blood sugar results in only 45 seconds. Check strips and a control glucose solution are included in the package so that you can periodically test the unit's functioning. The complete package includes the One Touch Basic Blood Glucose Meter, ten Genuine One Touch Test Strips, One Touch Normal Glucose Control Solution, PENLET II Automatic Blood Sampler, ten Lancets, a Check Strip, carrying case, logbook, owner's booklet, and size J battery. Lifescan offers generous rebate and trade-in programs, so the price you pay may be considerably lower than the approximate retail price below.

Warranty: 3 years; 30-day money-back guarantee.

Approx. retail price	**Approx. low price**
$50	$50

LIFESCAN PROFILE DIABETES TRACKING SYSTEM

Recommended

The Lifescan Profile is the Rolls Royce of home health care testing. The portable diabetes monitoring system comes with many more features than the Basic model. This system is especially useful for the diabetic who needs careful record keeping; it boasts a 250-test memory, including easy-to-set date and time. It also provides an automatic 14-day and 30-day test average, as well as an event marker, to organize test results. The

Prices are accurate at time of printing but are subject to manufacturers' changes.

system works just like the Basic model, giving accurate results in only 45 seconds. The prompts (which are set for English) can be programmed for 18 other languages. It also lets you know when the meter must be cleaned. The package includes the One Touch Profile Blood Glucose Meter with 250-test memory, 25 Genuine One Touch Test Strips, One Touch Normal Glucose Control Solution, PENLET II Automatic Blood Sampler, 25 Lancets, a Check Strip, carrying case, logbook, owner's booklet, and size J battery. Lifescan offers generous rebate and trade-in programs, so the price you pay may be considerably lower than the approximate retail price below.

Warranty: 5 years, extendable to 10 years; 30-day money-back guarantee.

Approx. retail price	**Approx. low price**
$110	**$94**

SCALES

HEALTH O METER ELECTRONIC STRAIN-GAUGE SCALE 840KLD-30

✓ BEST BUY

This electronic strain-gauge digital scale is constructed with superior electronics and an advanced, springless mechanism that makes for a quick, easy, automatic readout, up to 300 pounds. Its twin load-beam construction gives the scale consistent accuracy with no servicing required for the life of the scale. After you step on the scale, it takes only seconds for your weight to appear in a bright, 1½-inch, bold-stroke display (double the width of standard readouts) that reads weight to the half pound. It automatically recalibrates to zero after use. The scale, though compact enough to fit in even the smallest bathroom, has a wide base for lots of extra feet room. Two attractive features not usually seen in strain-gauge scales are a selector switch to set at either pounds or kilos and a low-battery indicator on the display. Cleaning is easy, with a soft cloth and detergent. The 840KLD-30 requires four AA alkaline batteries to operate (not included) and is available in white or platinum.

Warranty: 5 years.

Approx. retail price $50 | **Approx. low price** $40

HEALTH O METER 150N-41 DOCTOR +PLUS

Recommended

Health O Meter has been building medical-quality scales for 75 years. The 150N-41 is a precision-engineered scale built with a professional rack and pinion mechanism for consistent accuracy, even on carpet. It has a spacious, heavy-gauge, galvanized steel platform design that's moisture resistant. The scale, which can handle up to 330 pounds, has an extra-large, 7½-inch dial with extra-bold, widely spaced numbers. Also included are five color-coded weight reminders that slide around the dial to any position you choose. Built for stability, this model has a white platform and base with an exclusive safety-grip textured mat in black.

Warranty: Lifetime, limited.

Approx. retail price $70 | **Approx. low price** $65

ELECTRIC TOOTHBRUSHES

Brushing your teeth just isn't what it used to be. Nowadays you have a range of electric toothbrushes to choose from, some of which benefit from amazing innovations. New breakthroughs in technology have made the rotations of the bristles faster and more effective than ever before (just like a visit to the dentist's office), and manufacturers have responded to customer requests by making the newest brushes lightweight and easy to handle. Next to these transformations, a regular toothbrush looks boring and inefficient.

BRAUN ORAL-B 7025

✓BEST BUY

Braun has introduced this new plaque remover to its highly successful oral care line, which has been awarded the American Dental Association's seal of approval. The Oral-B 7025, which is shaped just like a dentist's cleaning instrument, features a lightweight, easy-to-handle design. The unit's small size makes it perfect for travel. The two Indicator brushes included in the package have soft, end-rounded bristles to effectively but gently remove plaque. The Indicator bristles also alert you when it's time to change brushes, and they can even help you determine whether you are brushing properly. The brush rotates at 2,800 times a minute (a little above standard for this type of device), and the bristles are cup-shaped to clean between teeth and below the gumline. Up to four brushes can be stored in the brush container, which is ventilated for faster drying. This model is cordless and rechargeable.

Warranty: 1 year; 30-day money-back guarantee.

Approx. retail price	Approx. low price
$80	$70

TELEDYNE SENSONIC SR100W

Recommended

Most electric toothbrushes use noisy gears and motors to produce only 2,000–3,000 brush strokes per minute. The SenSonic SR100W uses sonic technology (up until now available only in a dentist's office) and a quiet, gearless operation to generate 30,000 precision brush strokes per minute to clean teeth. Although its technology is powerful, the SenSonic works gently (all you hear is a low hum) to remove plaque without making you feel that your whole mouth is vibrating. The action of the brush massages your gums, and the contoured bristles are designed to reach between teeth. The vibration turns toothpaste into a bubbling foam that penetrates hard-to-reach areas in the mouth. A built-in electronic feedback system automatically adjusts speed to maintain peak performance while brushing. Included in the package are two toothbrushes with a compact brush head design and contoured bristles. The SenSonic must be charged for 24 hours before using, but once charged, it provides a week's worth of brushing. Also in-

Prices are accurate at time of printing but are subject to manufacturers' changes.

cluded in the package are screws and instructions for easy wall-mounting.

Warranty: 1 year; 30-day money-back guarantee.

Approx. retail price	Approx. low price
$130	$110

WOMEN'S SHAVERS

Recent innovations have made women's shavers much more convenient and easy to use. This year's models have wet/dry flexibility for shaving in the shower; slimmer, easy-grip shapes with textured fingerhold areas for gripping in soapy water; and specialty features such as underarm and bikini-line trimmers. Most 1996 models have durable cases that are perfect for travel. These days, customer service increasingly comes down to function, form, and fair price.

REMINGTON "SWIRL" WRR-6000

BEST BUY

This cordless, rechargeable rotary shaver is the only one of its kind on the U.S. market today. Instead of the usual foil method of shaving (foil and a straight blade) the shaver's dual-track, dual-head rotary shaving system uses two rotating heads for precise dry-skin shaving (this shaver should not be used on wet skin). The swirling action helps cut hair in the natural direction of growth, and the shaving action feels light, especially on sensitive areas of the skin. Testers found that the cutting action worked especially well on longer leg hairs. The reason: The dual-head technology features 60 precision sharp cutting blades mounted on two floating heads, each of which is individually mounted to adjust to body contours for beautiful, smooth, and nick-free legs. A convenient pop-up trimmer is helpful for the bikini line. A unique plus, the "Swirl" has a protective head shield that can be placed over the shaver to keep the outer cutting blades from pinching underarm skin. This model has a locking on/off switch and indicator lights, and comes with a soft pouch, perfect for travel.

Warranty: 1 year.

Approx. retail price $40 | **Approx. low price** $38

REMINGTON LWD-1000 WET/DRY RECHARGEABLE SHAVER

✓BEST BUY

This wet/dry cordless rechargeable shaver performs well in or out of the shower. The Remington LWD-1000 uses foil shaving technology for the closest, most comfortable shave. As you glide the razor across the skin's surface, dual intercept trimmers on the angled head painlessly catch and cut longer hairs. Remington's "Swirl" model is preferred for dry shaving, but the LWD-1000 compares well to other models on the market for wet shaving. The head is hinged for easy cleaning, and the shaver includes a cleaning brush and head/cutter guard. It has a locking on/off switch and a convenient overnight charging stand. Because of its worldwide voltage with automatic conversion, it's also perfect for travel.

Warranty: 1 year.

Approx. retail price $45 | **Approx. low price** $33

WINDMERE LADY WINDMERE WET & DRY SHAVER LWD-1C

Budget Buy

The Windmere LWD-1C is your basic battery-operated wet/dry shaver, with an easy-to-handle grip and curved foil cutter for the closest, nick-free shave. This cordless shaver is very versatile—you can use it with lather in the shower or dry, when you're in a hurry. A convenient bikini trimmer is included. The compact size and clear protective cover make this model perfect for travel, and it cleans up easily under running water. This unit has a safety lock on/off switch and operates on two AA batteries (not included).

Warranty: 1 year.

Approx. retail price $15 | **Approx. low price** $15

Prices are accurate at time of printing but are subject to manufacturers' changes.

WINDMERE LADY WINDMERE TRAVEL SHAVER LTS-1C

Budget Buy

This tiny shaver has cordless convenience for shaving any time, anywhere. Its compact size makes it perfect for travel and quick touch-ups (even bikini trims). The Windmere LTS-1C is so small it will hardly take up room in your pocketbook. The shaver features dual cutting action, a straight head for shaving legs, and a curved radius trimmer for underarms. A protective head cover is included, and the head pops out for easy cleaning. This unit operates on one AA battery (not included).

Warranty: 1 year.

Approx. retail price	Approx. low price
$10	$9

MEN'S SHAVERS

High on the list of what a shaver must offer is convenience. The shaver that travels well is likely to be found not only in the drawer of an executive's desk, but also in a student's locker or in a gym bag.

Function is the other crucial consideration. As anyone who shaves will testify, you don't want a shaver that pulls, scrapes, or nicks the skin or leaves stubble behind. Whether you're shopping for a shaver for yourself or to give, consider the degree of skin sensitivity, beard texture (fine or coarse), and how heavy the growth of hair is overall. Shaving frequency has a bearing on your selection, as does maintenance of a beard, mustache, or sideburns. And keep in mind that most manufacturers, anxious to do well in the customer service area, have free 30-day trial offers.

BRAUN PRECISION SERIES 155

✓BEST BUY

For the price, this rechargeable dry-only shaver (part of Braun's Presicison Series) is an excellent buy, with many of the features of higher-cost models in a compact

Prices are accurate at time of printing but are subject to manufacturers' changes.

package. The fixed head with ultra-thin, platinum-coated, single foil does an excellent cutting job even for men with curly beards or sensitive skin. The shave is close and comfortable. Like more expensive models, the Braun 155 has a conveniently located pop-out mustache/sideburn trimmer. The design is sleek and contemporary, the platinum gray color looks classy, and the shaver is easy to handle. The built-in recharger gives it the capacity for either a quick five-minute charge (for one shave) or a one-hour charge (good for up to 30 minutes of cordless shaving, easily one week's worth). Some of the more expensive models feature only 20 or so additional minutes of shaving time per electric charge. You may find that the sharing time provided by this model gives you enough shave for the buck. The Platinum 155 also has overcharge protection and automatic worldwide voltage adjustment.

Warranty: 2 years, limited; 30-day money-back guarantee.

Approx. retail price	Approx. low price
$50	$40

PANASONIC WET/DRY RECHARGEABLE SMOOTH OPERATOR ES 718

BEST BUY

The Panasonic ES 718 is versatile, is easy to handle, and gives a close, comfortable shave. It matches the closeness of a warm, wet shave with the no-nick comfort of an electric shaver. Twin independently floating heads with micro-thin dual steel foils easily hug facial contours for a painless shave. The trimmer feature can be set on three positions for stray neck hair, sideburns, or mustache grooming. The shaver must be fully charged for eight hours before first use. A full charge supplies enough power for 14 shaves (three minutes per shave). An added feature is the low-battery indicator light. The shaver cleans easily under running water and comes in its own travel pouch. Automatic voltage conversion for international travel is a nice plus.

Warranty: 1 year, limited; 30-day money-back guarantee.

Approx. retail price	Approx. low price
$116	$70

Prices are accurate at time of printing but are subject to manufacturers' changes.

BRAUN FLEX INTEGRAL 5510

Recommended

The Braun 5510 is the newest model in the company's top-of-the-line Flex Integral series of cordless rechargeable shavers. Its three-phase integrated shaving system makes this shaver stand out from the rest. It has a platinum-coated twin foil cutting system with pivoting heads for the closest, most comfortable shave. The pivoting heads follow the contours of the face for easy cutting of both long and short hairs, or they can be locked for precision shaving. The trimmer has three extended positions for easy, convenient mustache and sideburn trimming. The five-minute charge capability, good for three minutes of shaving, is perfect when you're in a hurry; the one-hour charge gives you up to 70 minutes of cordless shaving. This model has overcharge protection, as well as a low-charge indicator light. One-button release makes for easy cleaning. The easy on/off switch lock is a nice feature, and the universal voltage adjustment is great for international travel. This unit has an attractive black matte finish and comes with its own travel pouch.

Warranty: 2 years, limited.

Approx. retail price	Approx. low price
$110	$93

IRONS

Nowadays, nearly everyone must wield an iron from time to time. With the rising popularity of natural, easily wrinkled fabrics, you might even find yourself ironing more than you once did. Fortunately, today's irons boast a number of features that make this common chore much easier. Touch controls regulate features such as variable heat, steam, mist, and even automatic shutoff (so if the phone rings and the iron tips over you won't ruin that fancy blouse). Other benefits include lightweight construction, water-filling features, soleplate choices, steam options, cord storing facilities, and smooth stick-free glide, to name only a few. To meet the varied demands of different people and fabrics, modern irons come in numerous sizes, weights, and shapes.

ROWENTA DE-263 CLIP-UP

✓BEST BUY

The number-one reason consumers say they don't iron is that they don't have a good iron: one that doesn't stick to fabric, make water stains, and drip scalding water on their fingers. With the Rowenta DE-263 Clip-Up, the search is over. The popular clip-up feature allows you to detach the water-fill compartment and then reattach it without getting water on the rest of the iron. This feature also keeps water from leaking and scalding clothing and hands. The soleplate glides easily over all clothing surfaces, and the steam button gives a burst of steam to smooth every wrinkle, even in the hardest-to-press garments. A button also controls spray (you can choose a spray jet or a spray mist). A popular feature of this iron is that it automatically shuts off after 30 seconds if left standing on its soleplate, after 8 minutes if left standing on its heel, and after 30 seconds if it falls over on either side. The back of the iron pulls out for easy cord storage.

Warranty: 1 year.

Approx. retail price	**Approx. low price**
$80	**$75**

ROWENTA PROFESSIONAL IRON DE-87

Recommended

Rowenta's large top-of-the-line stainless-steel soleplate is the DE-87's outstanding feature. This wide soleplate covers a lot of fabric territory and is easy to handle. The iron has ten excellent steam options, including variable steam control, burst of steam, constant steam, and a cool spray of atomizing mist. The water tank is transparent and part of the body of the iron. When the iron is left in the vertical position for 8 minutes or if it is tipped over for 30 seconds, the automatic shutoff kicks in, keeping the DE-87 safe. The center-pivoting cord stores conveniently on the iron's heel base.

Warranty: 1 year.

Approx. retail price	**Approx. low price**
$110	**$80**

Prices are accurate at time of printing but are subject to manufacturers' changes.

BLACK & DECKER SURGE EXPRESS 895

Budget Buy

The Surge Express 895 is easy to use, with many convenient features, such as a surge steam button, adjustable steam control, auto shutoff (if not used for ten minutes), and self cleaning. The water tank is transparent, making it easy to check water level. The Silverstone GlideXpress soleplate provides a nice, gliding touch on a variety of fabrics. When the surge button is pressed, water is quickly heated and then comes out the soleplate steam vents at four times the velocity of other Black & Decker models to quickly remove even the toughest wrinkles. You can also use the spray button for a light mist. A handy booklet of ironing tips is included.

Warranty: 2 years.

Approx. retail price	**Approx. low price**
$65	**$48**

Prices are accurate at time of printing but are subject to manufacturers' changes.

HOME FITNESS EQUIPMENT

Fitness isn't a state of mind alone, it's a way of life that's increasingly hard to integrate with the pace of modern life. Family responsibilities and longer work hours cut into personal time. With so much to do, people wonder, how does anyone find time to work out? The solution for many singles and families is to create a fitness area at home, cutting out the daily commute to a gym or health club.

If you're considering bringing your workouts home, deciding what machines to invest in can be quite confusing. Experts and professionals agree that you should start with the best aerobic fitness machine you can afford and a set of basic weight lifting equipment. While some companies have promulgated the idea that an aerobic workout must be "total body," others reply, "Why mess up an otherwise enjoyable exercise?" Total body exercise may burn up more calories (in general), but will not necessarily promote muscular growth and strength improvement. So if you don't particularly enjoy a total body aerobic workout, it may not pay to force yourself to do one.

What's more important in choosing an aerobic exercise machine is picking one you will use regularly, not one that's trendy, cute, popular, or new. The best aerobic exercise, regardless of the machine, is one you do day after day. Thoroughly try the machine at the store or get a money-back guarantee.

The latest innovation in fitness is the inclusion of heart rate control of exercise. Polar Electro makes heart rate transmitters and receivers and currently has the greatest market share. Many machines—steppers, treadmills, rowers, ski machines, and bicycles—have built-in receivers. Some take the next step and directly control exercise level using instantaneous transmission of your current heart rate. This helps you keep working at your optimum heart rate.

Another popular category of home exercise equipment is the home gym. These affordable units rival club equipment for quality, versatility, and specificity. And home gyms are self-spotting, a comforting thought when you or your children exercise alone. A home gym is a great investment if you're serious about toning muscles and improving strength.

Best Buys '96

Our Best Buy, Recommended, and Budget Buy home fitness equipment products follow. In each category, the best of the Best Buys is listed first, followed by our second choice, and so on. Remember that a Best Buy, Recommended, or Budget Buy rating applies only to the model listed; it does not necessarily apply to an entire product line or to other models made by the same manufacturer.

EXERCISE CYCLES

When buying an exercise bike, be prepared to do a lot of testing. You not only need to find a bicycle that is comfortable and will fit you and other users in your home, you'll also have to sift through all the bicycle-exercise options to find the machine that best combines the specific options you like.

The standard upright models are, of course, still available; several offer upper-body workouts as well. The newest designs use recumbent seating. Recumbent bicycles support your lower back with an upright lounge-chair seating style. Reucmbents also leave your hands and arms free to use dumbbells for upper-body exercise. Test the seat for comfort before buying. Also, look for a bike that is comfortable to pedal and has pedals with foot straps. Some favorite exercise cycle accessories are reading racks, water bottle holders, and personal stereo holders.

Upright Models

LIFECYCLE 5500

✓BEST BUY

Lifecycles are the stationary bicycle of choice in most health clubs. Though smaller than club models in every

Prices are accurate at time of printing but are subject to manufacturers' changes.

way, the Lifecycle 5500 has similar features and virtues. Its smooth stroke on the pedals and quiet operation make it a pleasure to use. Changing exercise levels requires only the touch of a button. A variety of built-in programs will challenge any rider. They include cardiovascular improvement, a hill course, a race, a random series of hills and valleys, and manual control. All programs have 13 levels of difficulty. The computer console shows elapsed time, rpm, level or miles, calories, and an LED exercise difficulty profile. This unit can also accurately assess your fitness level by measuring your Maximum Oxygen Uptake. A large, well-padded seat features coil suspension, and posture is upright for comfort. Seat height adjustment is easy, but the handlebars are not adjustable. This machine is self-powered and requires no electrical hookup. Casters make it easy to move and store.

Specifications: height, 52"; width, 20"; depth, 41"; weight, 65 lbs. **Warranty:** electrical and mechanical, 3 years.

Approx. retail price **$988**
Approx. low price **$919**

SCHWINN AIRDYNE EVOLUTION

✓BEST BUY

The Schwinn Airdyne Evolution is among the most rugged and long-lasting stationary bikes ever produced. Airdyne's patented synchronized arm/leg movement is a benchmark in total body fitness. Featuring a wide seat and upright posture, the bike has two sticklike grips connected to the drive mechanism. Pedal the bike and the handlebars move back and forth. You can rest your arms or push and pull on the handles for upper-body exercise. A fully enclosed fan provides resistance (and cooling). The fan and mechanical links are not exactly silent but not overwhelmingly loud. A small readout provides information on time, distance, workout level, calories, calories per hour, and rpm.

Specifications: height, 48"; width, 25"; depth, 44"; weight, 80 lbs. **Warranty:** machine, lifetime; electronics, 2 years.

Approx. retail price **$799**
Approx. low price **$499**

Recumbent Models

CYBEX SEMI

✓BEST BUY

The Semi from Cybex is among the finest full-featured commercial recumbent bikes made. Seat position is comfortable, leg extension easy to adjust. Six preset workout programs have 15 levels of difficulty. Included among the programs are a race (against the computer) and both aerobic and anaerobic test modes for fitness evaluation. Of course, you can also select manual mode. With the optional Polar heart rate transmitter, you can adjust your workout according to your desired heart rate. The readouts show work rate in calories per hour, watts, or Kg; your speed displays in mph, kph, or rpm; the distance display shows miles or kilometers traveled, calories consumed, or heart rate. Pedal effort is smooth, with a realistic "gear" feel provided by a large chain and gear-driven flywheel. Cybex has a functional seat that positions you to use all lower body muscles, not just the quadriceps. Although the cost is high, with a Semi you can exercise comfortably for long periods and expect years of hard use.

Specifications: height, 51"; width, 22"; depth, 59"; weight, 215 lbs. **Warranty**: 2 years.

Approx. retail price	**Approx. low price**
$2,690	**$2,493**

TUNTURI ECB F570

✓BEST BUY

Tunturi's flagship recumbent stationary bike uses eddy current or magnetic resistance to vary the load and is completely silent in operation. Easy to adjust, the front flywheel unit is connected to the seat with a large metal tube that collapses to accommodate users of any height. The seat holds you quite upright, assisting you into a posture that engages most prime mover muscles. The electronic control panel to the left includes simple controls to select from various programs or manual operation. Resistance is easy to set via push buttons. Program mode offers you a choice of five programs of varying duration. The level of difficulty can be adjusted. Like other recumbents, this ma-

Prices are accurate at time of printing but are subject to manufacturers' changes.

chine emphasizes different muscle groups from those a moun- tain bike or racing bike addresses. With a modest price and sounc construction, this unit earns a Best Buy rating.

Specifications: height, 32⅘"; width, 23"; depth, 69⅒"; weight not available. **Warranty:** structural components, 10 years other parts, 2 years.

Approx. retail price	Approx. low price
$699	$682

ROWING MACHINES

Rowing machines are the least popular of all home fitness ma chines, and no one is sure why. Better models accurately ech the catch and pull of rowing and provide a true total body ex ercise. The action is weight-supported and zero impact. Row ing's motion is fluid, and the lengthy stroke works both ab dominals and back.

If you're considering a rower, look for a smooth gliding sea and sturdy glide rail that's long enough for your legs. Air resis tance models have been the most popular and cool you as yo work. If the noise bothers you, try an electronic model that use silent magnetic resistance.

CONCEPT II INDOOR ROWER MODEL C

BEST BUY

Concept II has the most realistic feel of rowers tested, with highly accurate "catch" and "recover." The mode C is tough, smooth, and sturdy, with adjustable effort levels an advanced workout display. Other features include a large deeper, more comfortable seat; larger, wider, and stronger ra for greater stability; and an enclosed fan with variable discharg to adjust the "feel of your boat." Foot rests are deep and easil adjustable with a heel cup that grips your foot. A strap capture your toes, and the plastic foot cups permit your heel to rise na urally while firmly retaining the foot. The monitor display time for 500 meters, calories per hour, duration of work, ave age stroke rate, heart rate (optional), total calories, on/off, an memory recall. You can preset rest or work intervals and distance or adjust your effort to stay in the training zone (if you purchase the optional Polar heart rate transmitter). And no matter how hard you work, you stay seated.

Specifications: height, 35"; width, 24"; depth, 95"; weight, 61 lbs. **Warranty:** materials and workmanship, 1 year.

Approx. retail price **$725**
Approx. low price **$700**

TUNTURI 701R

Recommended

Similar in appearance to a Concept II, this model's advantage is a folding design. Folded, the unit can easily slide into a closet. This fan-equipped unit creates minimal noise, particularly at long-duration effort levels—when sprinting, noise becomes more noticeable. Action is smooth at all phases of the stroke, making the Tunturi 701R a comfortable machine to use. The seat is stable, but resistance at all-out effort can cause some rise out of the seat. The rowing handle is large and well padded. Foot pegs are large, with straps to secure feet. This model provides a small LCD readout to track load, tempo, calories, calories per minute, strokes, and time. Controls are simple: on/off, stop/start, reset, and mode. The 701R's fan is covered by a fine mesh that will prevent fingers or paws from touching the blades. Overall, this model is a safe and well-designed machine that will fulfill the needs of most exercisers.

Specifications: height, 25½"; width, 19½"; depth, 93"; weight, 72 lbs. **Warranty:** structural components, 10 years; other parts, 2 years.

Approx. retail price **$799**
Approx. low price **$733**

TREADMILLS

Treadmills are at the forefront of buyer consciousness, and sales continue to rise steadily. Perhaps because walking and running are so natural, many folks committed to fitness are abandoning steppers, rowers, or stationary bikes in favor of treadmills. If you chose to purchase a powered treadmill, check a few key factors. First, ask your dealer about service history. Treadmills are acknowledged to be the most service-intensive of all fitness products. Some brands, however, have excellent service records. Then look for a motor rated at a minimum of 1½-horsepower continuous duty. Comfortable foot strike is another important feature. More and more manufacturers are introducing platforms that in some way cushion foot strike. Also, listen carefully while testing each machine; the belt should be quiet. Motivational electronic controls can be simple or complex. Their true purpose is to provide an interesting and varied exercise course. Look for big bright numbers and a progressive course/effort display to keep you kicking.

Unpowered treadmills require hand rests, like powered treadmills. Since you must push the belt back with each stride, an upright posture is vital. Smaller flywheels with variable tension permit the belt to minutely vary speed at foot strike for stability. Apply similar considerations of reliability, service, motivational electronics, and belt size to unpowered treadmills that you do to powered models.

Electric Models

PRECOR M9.25

✓ BEST BUY

Precor's latest models include modern technologies such as the company's "Ground Effects" elastomeri suspension system to cushion the bed and "Integrated Footplant," which minutely reduces belt speed as your foot hits th belt, increasing stability. This model includes the Precor Cardiologic System to monitor heart rate and adjust effort accordingly. The 9.25 is smooth and quiet; foot strike is soft. Walking or running is easy because the "floating" platform cushions foot fall. This unit recognizes four users and retain information such as weight and preferred work level for each. Modes include manual; two custom programs; and five pro grammed courses, including two interval courses, Heart Rate, Fitness Test, Weight Loss, and Quick Start (which jumps to the last program used or manual mode). The company's Fitness Test and Weight Loss programs are based on research from the Cooper Institute for Aerobics Research. Much of Precor's technology is hidden under the covers: It's not flashy but contributes to a good exercise experience and injury prevention.

Specifications: height, 43″; width, 28½″; depth, 67″; weight, 192 lbs. **Warranty:** parts, 3 years; labor, 1 year.

Approx. retail price	**Approx. low price**
$2,900	**$2,499**

STAR TRAC 900

✓BEST BUY

Star Trac is a recent player in home treadmills but long a popular fitness club supplier. The model 900 includes a heart-rate monitor and can keep you in your training range by adjusting speed and elevation. The weight loss programs hold the heart rate at 65 to 70 percent, while cardiac improvement programs allow 65 to 80 percent. Heart-rate control may be entered and exited at will; the monitor will override the program to maintain a safe rate. Foot strike is diminished by the running deck's polyethylene cushion. An extra-large surface, 19 by 53 inches, is centered by crowned rollers. This machine is not as quiet as some but not objectionably noisy. Motor speed is monitored at a rate of 430,000 times per minute for precise control. Star Trac places an oval track on its large information display screen. Small triangles note your position on the track. Other indicators show your progress in variable effort programs. Controls include scan, stop/start, speed change, elevation change, heart rate, and program selection. A magnetic key stops the machine should you fall and prevents use if absent. Readouts include speed, distance, elapsed time, and total calories. Star Trac's excellent service record is another big plus.

Specifications: height, 52″; width, 28¼″; depth, 69″; weight, 200 lbs. **Warranty:** parts, 2 years; labor, 1 year.

Approx. retail price	**Approx. low price**
$2,995	**$2,900**

Unpowered Model

PRECOR 903/904

BEST BUY

Precor 903/904 nonpowered treadmills are fundamental machines combining friction, flywheels, and exerciser power to produce solid exercise value. Precor 903 has a front-mounted handlebar; the 904 has two hefty ski-type poles. Both have twin flywheels and a friction band adjustment to vary effort. The friction band is not precise, which is generally not a problem. However, noise is a factor—both models exhibit a modestly high noise level. Either machine occupies the same space as a powered treadmill. Neither model cushions foot strike, making them comparable to outdoor walking or running. The belt is wide and deep. A simple push-off gets you moving as the belt slides on a polished composite surface. Each foot fall minutely slows the surface for a feeling of stability. The 904's poles are side-mounted back-and-forth devices with adjustable friction (poles may be locked into place should you prefer a more stable hand grip) and the right pole carries the friction control; on the 903 it is located on the handlebar. Either model is a good home treadmill.

Specifications: height, 44"; width, 24"; depth, 54"; weight, 82 lbs. **Warranty:** parts, 1 year; labor, 90 days.

Approx. retail price	Approx. low price
$500 (model 904)	**$388**
$430 (model 903)	**$323**

STAIR CLIMBERS

Stair climbers are primarily lower body exercisers unless equipped with upper body resistance devices. These machines focus on the large major muscle groups of the body which consume the most calories when worked to maximum. An all-out workout on a stair climber can consume as much energy as you are capable of producing.

Most experts agree that a machine that keeps the steps parallel to the floor at all times is superior, allowing totally natural

Prices are accurate at time of printing but are subject to manufacturers' changes.

foot articulation. Some machines do not keep their steps completely horizontal but do avoid extreme foot flexion. Look for sturdy hand rests to help you balance (they're not for support). Heavy-gauge steel or aluminum resists stress-related failures. Independent step action, a feature of all machines reviewed, provides a natural stride. While motorized steppers offer more features, hydraulic cylinder machines can offer more bang for the buck. Before you buy any model, be sure to research its service history and reliability.

Electric Models

PRECOR M7.2E/L

✓BEST BUY

Precor's M7.2E/L has 12 courses including manual, two custom programs, and a 30-minute weight loss program to maximize caloric burn. The display is less cluttered than most, including several large buttons and a central display of effort level/progress. A heart-rate transmitter is included. The machine is very quiet, almost silent, due to electromagnetic eddy current resistance. With no friction surfaces to wear, long life and reliability are assured. The pedals change angle during a stroke: Your toes decline at the beginning and elevate at the end. The angular change, however, is modest. At the bottom of the stroke, action changes from independent to dependent to prevent bottoming out. The large handrails are padded with sweat-proof closed cell foam. This quiet, sturdy climber requires minimal floor space and provides a strong workout. The compact M7.2E/L will roll to be stored. Because of the smoothness, quietness, and Precor's reputation for quality, this is a Best Buy.

Specifications: height, 57½"; width, 22"; depth, 35"; weight, 125 lbs. **Warranty**: parts, 3 years; labor, 1 year.

Approx. retail price	**Approx. low price**
$1,400	**$999**

TECTRIX PERSONAL CLIMBER

✓BEST BUY

The Tectrix Personal Climber has features that place it in the forefront of home steppers. Tectrix has considered realistic needs and provides a sturdy Lexan-covered display, wraparound handlebars, easily programmed electronics, and a smooth step action. Quiet, almost silent, the Personal Climber's action has a gentle "whoosh-whoosh" sound. Pedals are hung from high-strength aircraft cable and remain horizontal throughout all phases; pedal surfaces are very large. Cables connect to a chain and sturdy flywheel that is governed by an electronically controlled friction band. No moving parts are exposed. High exercise speeds, up to 150 feet per minute, promise a pace even elite athletes find challenging. Sturdy plastic covers all internal parts and exposed metal surfaces are enameled or covered in cushioned rubber that resists tearing and sweat absorption. A complete display has windows for distance/calories/average speed, effort level (feet per minute)/calories per hour/heart rate (if you have a Polar transmitter), and time remaining/elapsed or intervals. A graduated, stacked LED display shows both progress and level of difficulty. On the panel is a display showing feet per minute climb rate. Training modes include manual, race, and custom. All preprogrammed workouts include a brief warm-up period, the workout phase, and a cooldown. While costly, the Personal Climber is the equal of most club machines and should serve the needs of any family for years to come.

Specifications: height, 58"; width, 31"; depth, 42"; weight, 192 lbs. **Warranty:** parts, 3 years; labor, 1 year.

Approx. retail price	Approx. low price
$3,095	**$2,165**

STAIRMASTER 4000PT

Recommended

StairMaster wrote the book on steppers—all others are compared to it. The 4000PT is a familiar fixture in almost every fitness club in America, with good reason. Its smooth action, minimal noise, and easily controlled workout pace have made it a favorite among users. This model has pedals large enough for every foot and pedal geometry arranged to remain parallel to the ground throughout the stroke, encouraging good form. Stroke length is well beyond the average 8-

Prices are accurate at time of printing but are subject to manufacturers' changes.

inch stair. You can tailor your own step height to vary the muscles challenged from deep strokes for glute work to short uphill running steps targeting the calves. The StairMaster also offers visible progress reports via a large display that charts elapsed time, calories burned, miles traveled, floors climbed, step rate, cumulative work output, and instant/average power. Eight preprogrammed courses and ten customizable programs are available, along with manual control. You can also choose from ten levels of difficulty and set the 4000PT for any duration from 1 to 45 minutes. StairMaster machines are rugged, dependable, and functional. Because of its high price compared to other well-built home machines, this unit is in the Recommended category.

Specifications: height, 58″; width, 32″; depth, 40⅖″; weight, 150 lbs. **Warranty:** parts and labor, 1 year.

Approx. retail price	**Approx. low price**
$2,195	**$2,098**

Hydraulic Models

TUNTURI TRI-STEPPER 700

✓BEST BUY

Featuring independent action and easily adjustable resistance, the Tunturi Tri-Stepper 700 is a low-cost and rugged stepper suitable for under-200-pound exercisers. Large-diameter mandrel-bent steel tubes form this exerciser's frame, insuring strength and longevity. An innovative hand rest covered in closed neoprene permits many different support positions; side-mounted "ski" poles provide the added benefit of upper-body exercise. The Tri-Stepper's pedals are not self-leveling but their angle is close enough to natural to be no problem unless you have limited range of ankle motion. The range of adjustment of the low-noise hydraulic cylinders should be great enough to permit slow movement by heavier exercisers or beginners, a near running pace for all. The "ski" poles provide adjustable resistance and have a large range of motion. Stride can be full-length or short—the machine allows extension all the

Prices are accurate at time of printing but are subject to manufacturers' changes.

way to the floor. A convenient plus, this handsomely designed machine can be rolled into an empty closet or corner.

Specifications: height, 32″; width, 55″; depth, 31″; weight, 77 lbs. **Warranty**: parts, 2 years; structural components, 10 years.

Approx. retail price	**Approx. low price**
$249	**$249**

PRECOR 731E

BEST BUY

Precor says an independent study shows the 731e surpasses most Nordic ski machines for overall muscle involvement, providing the greater range of motion and the best total-body workout among units tested. It certainly is easier to coordinate movement of your arms and legs on this stepper than on a ski machine, especially for beginners. On the Precor 731e, effort is governed by shifting the attachment point of twin hydraulic cylinders to the foot pedals. Adjustment locking knobs are large and easy for most users; folks with finger joint disorders should check the effort before purchase. This unit steps independently, as "strider" handles move back and forth. You may chose to let your arms go along for the ride or add power from your upper body to increase effort and build muscles. This unit is smooth enough to let you read or watch TV while stepping. A small display shows on/off, time, strokes, total strokes, and pace.

Specifications: height, 62″; width, 24″; depth, 34″; weight, 82 lbs. **Warranty**: parts, 1 year; labor, 90 days.

Approx. retail price	**Approx. low price**
$430	**$317**

CROSS-COUNTRY SKI SIMULATORS

If it weren't for NordicTrack we might not have cross-country ski simulators. Twenty years ago, NordicTrack began direct sales to the new at-home exercise market. The company's claim of total-body exercise attracted many dedicated users. NordicTrack's products set the standard, offering independent action and a smooth glide that has minimal impact on joints. The one-way clutch allows independent foot action and a sure "catch" that simulates the feel of skis on snow. Although NordicTrack still claims the most models and the greatest variety, other manufacturers have begun marketing very good cross-country ski simulators of their own.

Important features to consider in these machines are ease of use—ski simulators are notoriously difficult to learn—and joy of use. Independent action (skis sliding independently of each other) is critical; while they make the motion tougher to master, independent skis duplicate the feel of real skiing more effectively. Ease of resistance changes, ski pole vs. rope pull, and electronic displays are matters of taste.

NORDICTRACK PRO

✓BEST BUY

The Pro is NordicTrack's most popular model and, now that NordicTrack has established retail stores in malls nationwide, it's easier to purchase than ever before. First timers will find coordinating movements a challenge, because NordicTrack machines resist only the push phase of the motion, just as if you were really skiing. Once you get the hang of it, however, the rewards are great. You can add further effort by inclining the unit (not all models). Upper- and lower-body resistance is set separately, and the vinyl hip-support pad is easily adjustable for different users. The skis work smoothly on their tracks. The control panel measures speed, time, and distance. A plus for the Pro: Its use of hard rubber rollers on wood makes it quieter than aluminum club models. This model folds for easy storage and has wheels to move it from room to room. Options available are a heart rate monitor and a book rack.

Specifications: height, 20" (folded); width, 26"; depth, 55"; weight, 53 lbs. **Warranty:** parts and labor, 2 years.

Approx. retail price	**Approx. low price**
$600	**$600**

TUNTURI XC560 SKIFIT

Recommended

Tunturi's ski simulator is a solid product; magnetic resistance creates a smooth glide and real-feeling ski poles

Prices are accurate at time of printing but are subject to manufacturers' changes.

promote sport-specific training. The angled foot skates are broad with sizable toe pockets for firm support for any size shoe. Beginners will benefit from an anatomically curved forward lean brace and easy control of effort. Hand grips edging the computer display allow learners to get the hang of the motion before using the ski poles, which pump air to provide adjustable resistance. Poles have molded grips and a "feel" that's similar to real skiing. Arm and foot movements are totally independent and the support mast folds for storage. An easy-to-read display shows time, speed, distance, and calories; time and distance can be counted down. One drawback—an occasionally slightly rough glide—puts the XC560 SkiFit in the Recommended category.

Specifications: height, 44"–52"; width, 25"; depth, 68"; weight, 82 lbs. **Warranty:** structural parts, 10 years; other parts, 2 years.

Approx. retail price	**Approx. low price**
$449	**$449**

STRIDERS

Striders are a recent offshoot of the ski simulator category. They have an action that does not imitate the motions of skiing as well as the ski simulators. Your legs move forward and backward in the familiar scissor movement, but there the similarity ends. One machine uses a semicircular curved track to eliminate learning time and some of the stress. Another holds you back while slightly tipping you forward and offers no incline. Prices are wildly different as well. This is an emerging product category and may point the way to the future of the ski simulator market.

CROSS CONDITIONING SYSTEMS XL 100 CROSS CONDITIONER

✓ BEST BUY

The XL 100 Cross Conditioner "strider" is a unique club-quality machine. A large multiple display fully describes what you must do, with one display tracking progress levels and another offering information on your actual vs. goal speed, distance, time remaining, effort (mets, calories-per-hour, watts), total calories, and current heart rate (optional). Select a course from "walk in the park," Himalayan trek, interval, Vail pass, race course, steady climb, competition, or manual. You can also choose your effort level and time and input your weight and age (for target heart rate calculation). A Polar heart rate monitor is optional. As with ski simulators, the striding action heavily involves every lower body muscle. Poles also allow a rigorous upper-body workout. Because of the slight decline in foot wells (there are no straps) your heel rise is natural and you never fear stepping out. Although the price is very high, the totality of exercise offered makes this a Best Buy.

Specifications: height, 60"; width, 29"; depth, 85"; weight, 305 lbs. **Warranty:** parts and labor, 2 years.

Approx. retail price	Approx. low price
$4,995	$4,698

FITNESS MASTER FM 220

Budget Buy

The Fitness Master FM 220 strider fits into the entrant level of home exercise machines. By utilizing a curved track, the FM 220 provides a zero impact workout that should encourage unfit beginners. A unique "pendulum swing" motion keeps your torso more stable—your pelvis remains in the same plane. By slightly bending your knees a "running skiing" motion becomes possible. Because there is no resistance, exercise speed governs caloric expenditure; a long gentle workout is this machine's forte. The FM 220 offers a small electronic panel that gives you information on elapsed time, speed, distance traveled, and calories consumed. A mutable pacer beeps to keep you at a preset tempo. This unit emphasizes lower-body work. You'll feel stable while you use it, even without holding on to the handlebar. The FM 220's biggest hitch is its hard plastic roller wheels gliding on a plastic track surface to create considerable noise; it would be hard to hear the TV or radio while exercising. Even with the noise and limited resistance, this unit can make a good entry-level fitness solution, especially with its Budget Buy price.

Specifications: height, 52″; width, 20″; depth, 57″; weight, 30 lbs. **Warranty:** parts, 2 years; electronics, 1 year.

Approx. retail price	**Approx. low price**
$299	**$299**

HOME GYMS

Home gyms have made enormous strides in recent years. Affordable multistation units easily surpass the best commercial units of a generation ago. Most use complex pulley arrangements and a single weight stack to provide resistance at a variety of exercise stations. Pulley diameter and bearing type make a difference in smoothness of operation; ball bearings and larger pulleys are better. Cables should be aircraft quality and nylon covered. Tubing thickness is critical, and a lower number (i.e., 10 to 12 gauge) is better. Every multistation gym excels at some exercises, usually major muscle group exercises, with only passing marks for others. Consider purchasing a gym that does essential exercises well and fill in the gaps with free weights.

Most gyms easily fit into a ten- by ten-foot square area, but don't just assume a given model will fit your space. You should make sure you have enough room to walk around the gym. And remember to check the ceiling height of your workout space. Folks with low-ceilinged basements could be in for an annoying surprise if they're not careful about measurements.

TUFF STUFF TG-150

✓BEST BUY

The Tuff Stuff's TG-150 home gym is significant for versatility, strength of construction, and offering lower-body exercise that rivals purpose-built club machines. The high-quality pec deck for chest work converts easily and swiftly to a posterior deltoid exercise station. Both quadriceps extension and hamstring curl are performed in a seated position and offer effort and range of motion that will remind you of Cybex and Nautilus. The chest press is effective, and this station modifies to become a back-supported military or overhead press station. A low cable provides biceps curl and ab/adduction for leg exercises as well as low row or medial deltoid exercises. Another pulley, overhead, provides lat pull-down and triceps extension. If you're willing to spend a little extra, the TG-150 has some very nice options. Consider the leg press station with a tilting foot plate. For the price, this is a great home unit that should fulfill the needs of most athletes and families.

Specifications: height, 83½"; width, 103"; depth, 80"; weight, 800 lbs. **Warranty:** moving parts, 5 years; frame, lifetime.

Approx. retail price	**Approx. low price**
$1,995	**$1,663**

VECTRA ON-LINE 1500

Recommended

Easily the most handsome unit on the market, the On-Line 1500 is also among the largest and most expensive. Vectra's machines provide extremely smooth action with never a hint of cable whip and require minimal changes between exercises. The 4½-inch ball-bearing pulley never gives a "cable" feel. The chest press station easily switches to shoulder, incline, and bench presses. Its wide and comfortably padded bench swivels aside to permit additional exercises. All strokes are ball-bearing guided. The 1500's leg extension station is comfortable and has cam action, but lacks an adjustable back rest. The pec deck ratchets to fit user size. The standard 210-pound weight deck can be expanded to 260 pounds. This beautiful, sturdy, and smooth unit narrowly misses a Best Buy designation because of its higher price and larger space requirement. If you have the space, check it out and decide whether it's worth the money to you.

Specifications: height, 83"; width, 120"; depth, 72"; weight, 677 lbs. **Warranty:** 1 year; frame, 5 years.

Approx. retail price	**Approx. low price**
$3,295	**$2,897**

RIDERS

Born of the infomercial, riders, or gravity dependent bikes, have swept the nation as the hottest fitness machine craze. All

Prices are accurate at time of printing but are subject to manufacturers' changes.

of these machines are not created equal. Some painfully emphasize the upper body and neglect to balance the lower body. There is a potential for lower back stress and pain in poorly designed models. If you are considering such a machine be sure to try it out or receive a money-back guarantee. Look for engineering that emphasizes the power of your legs. Bearings should be used at all pivot points. Tube wall thickness is important for longevity, as is the material of any rollers.

HEALTH RIDER AEROBICRIDER

✓BEST BUY

AeRobicRider from Health Rider is a store model of the popular infomercial product. It lacks Health Rider's removable handlebar, providing instead a revolving, angled and padded handlebar—and a far lower price. The width of the handlebar allows multiple positions to emphasize shoulders and back. By changing foot placement, you can emphasize different lower-body muscle groups. Secondary pedals allow you to concentrate on upper-body development. The small display unit provides time, repetitions per minute, scan, and count. Operation is smooth, natural, intuitive, and nearly silent. AeRobicRider offers balanced operation favoring the lower body where most large muscle groups are concentrated. For low price, excellent ergonomics, and sturdy construction, this is a Best Buy.

Specifications: height, 22½"; width, 19¾"; depth, 41"; weight, 58 lbs. **Warranty:** most parts, 3 years; welded frame, lifetime; electronic timer/counter, 1 year.

Approx. retail price	Approx. low price
$299	$299

LAWN CARE

If you've been shopping for lawn care equipment, you've probably seen a variety of prices for items that look quite similar at first glance. The differences between the Brand X mower selling for $200 at a discount store and a good-quality mower selling for between $300 and $600 at a lawn equipment dealership aren't always obvious. Most of the differences among mowers are found in the engineering, choice of components, warranty, convenience features, comfort, reliability, and power. A $200 mower that's hard to start, cuts poorly, and fails within a few years is no bargain. This holds true whether you're discussing basic walk-behind mowers or full-size lawn tractors—you get what you pay for.

String Trimmers and Blower/Vacs

These two handy tools take care of the touch-up jobs around your lawn. String trimmers use a spinning nylon line to cut grass, weeds, and even light brush. Power usually comes from either an electric motor or a small 2-cycle engine, although 4-cycle engines have recently been introduced by Ryobi. The nylon line must be replaced periodically, since it wears out during operation.

Some string trimmers allow the cutting head to rotate 90 degrees so that the trimmer can also be used as an edger. Larger models can be fitted with brush-cutting blades (similar to the blades on circular saws) to remove heavy brush and shrubs.

Hand-held blower/vacs simplify the cleanup of debris and leaves in yards, driveways, and even gutters, usually by means of a powerful blast of air. Or you can convert them to a vac-and-mulch mode, meaning that leaves are picked up, chewed up, and deposited in a shoulder-hung bag. Most of these tools are intended for soft yard debris, but some will also pick up pieces of wood and metal.

As with other tools, engine-powered blower/vacs are much more powerful and convenient to use than electrics, but since the need for such a tool is infrequent, an electric model is probably a better investment for most consumers.

Best Buys '96

Our Best Buy, Recommended, and Budget Buy lawn care products are listed below. In each category, the item we consider the best of the Best Buys is listed first, followed by our second choice, and so on. Remember that a Best Buy, Recommended, or Budget Buy designation applies only to the model listed; it does not necessarily apply to the other models made by the same manufacturer or to an entire product line.

LAWN MOWERS

Gasoline Walk-Behind Mowers

SEARS CRAFTSMAN ADVANTAGE 37285

✓BEST BUY

Very few mowers in this price range come close to offering so much, which helps explain why the Craftsman Advantage 37285 is a best-seller. This model is front-wheel power propelled, with one-pull starting and an easy-service 5½-horsepower Eager-1 engine. It also features 3-in-1 convertibility: You can select side discharge, bagging, or mulching. The Advantage cuts a 22-inch swath and has a superbly designed 2.4-bushel rear bag. Cutting height is adjustable from 1⅜ to 3⅝ inches. Everything considered, the Advantage 37285 is a very good deal, especially when it's on sale.

Warranty: 2 years, limited.

Approx. retail price	**Approx. low price**
$350	**$325**

LAWN-BOY SILVER SERIES 10201

Recommended

A moderately priced push mower, the 2-cycle Lawn-Boy 10201 is a recommended choice and a solid performer. The commercial-grade, easy-to-start 4½-horsepower engine is a plus. The unique staggered front wheels make for easy and neat mowing under fences and around shrubs. The blades cut a 21-inch swath, and the cutting height range is 1 to 3½ inches. Options available at additional cost are rear bag, side

Prices are accurate at time of printing but are subject to manufacturers' changes.

bag, and leaf shredder kits, plus a "mow-and-feed" fertilizer spreader attachment to fertilize while you mow.

Warranty: 2 years, limited.

Approx. retail price **$270** | **Approx. low price** **$259**

MTD 410A

Budget Buy

Even though it's a bare-bones economy mower, the MTD 410A has a reliable 3½-horsepower Briggs and Stratton 4-cycle engine and is backed by MTD's unique 90-day no-fault guarantee (plus a 2-year limited warranty). The 21-inch deep dome "donut" deck design provides optimum performance whether operating in the standard rear-bagging mode or using optional side discharge or mulcher kits. The 9-position height adjustment (from 1½ to 3½ inches) is standard. The cutting swath is 21 inches.

Warranty: 90 day no-fault; 2 years, limited.

Approx. retail price **$189** | **Approx. low price** **$179**

Electric Walk-Behind Mowers

BLACK & DECKER MM850

✓BEST BUY

Black & Decker has replaced its popular MM450 electric mower with the new MM850, which boosts power from 9 amps to 13 amps, making this model an even better buy for a clean, fairly quiet small-lawn mower. The MM850, like its predecessor, is a mulcher that converts to side discharge or bagging with an optional grass catcher. Height adjustment (ranging from 1½ to 3½ inches) is one-touch. The polymer deck is rust free. The handle folds and swings over the deck for very compact storage.

Warranty: 30-days no-risk; 2 years, full; deck, 5 years.

Approx. retail price **$240** | **Approx. low price** **$194**

Prices are accurate at time of printing but are subject to manufacturers' changes.

RYOBI BMM2400

Recommended

Using a battery-powered mower makes grass cutting about as easy and as pleasant as it can get. These models are very quiet, and there's no fussing with gas or cords. The time-proven Ryobi BMM2400 24-volt mower is a mulcher too, further easing the job. And it will give you 90 minutes of cutting on a single charge of its hefty battery. However, the battery does need 16 hours to fully recharge. The mower cuts an 18-inch swath, and height adjustment (range from 1 to 3½ inches) is one-touch. The handle folds and swings over the deck for easy storage.

Warranty: 2 years.

Approx. retail price	**Approx. low price**
$350	**$298**

Riding Mowers

HONDA HARMONY H1011 RSA

✓BEST BUY

Honda's Harmony H1011 RSA is pure fun to drive, and with its curvy design, it gets a lot of attention. Visibility is superb, and this model practically "turns on a dime." The Honda 11-horsepower engine powers a 30-inch blade and drives the mower through a 6-speed transmission. Control location and ease of operation are among the best around. Electric-start and hydrostatic-transmission models are also available. Double-bagger grass-catcher kits and mulching kits are optional accessories. The Honda engine is known for its overhead-valve design and commercial-duty, long-life quality.

Warranty: 2 years.

Approx. retail price	**Approx. low price**
$1,600	**$1,575**

JOHN DEERE SRX-75

Recommended

Deere's SRX-75 rider is a rock-solid machine with a 30-inch cutting swath and a very capable, electric-start 9-horsepower engine. You really have to drive it to see how nicely the foot-controlled, variable speed drive works. Both hands are on the steering wheel at all times, so your eyes are on the terrain ahead. The high-back seat is particularly comfortable. The optionally available Tricycler mulching attachment is an exceptionally smooth, flat cutter. A rear bagger kit is available for this model.

Warranty: 2 years.

Approx. retail price	Approx. low price
$2,299	$1,950

MTD B560B

Budget Buy

The MTD B560B is a considerably lower-priced rider and an exceptionally good buy. While it doesn't look as stylish as some of the other riders, it still cuts a 30-inch swath and has a 10½-horsepower Briggs and Stratton Industrial/Commercial engine with electric start. This model has a very adequate 6-speed, shift-on-the-go transmission. The optional mulcher kit is very effective. A 6½-bushel twin-bag grass collection system is also optionally available. While the controls are not very stylish, they are comfortably accessible.

Warranty: 2 years, limited; 90 days no-fault.

Approx. retail price	Approx. low price
$899	$775

Mulching Mowers

TROY-BILT 5-HORSEPOWER SELF-PROPELLED 34022

✓BEST BUY

This full-featured, 22-inch mulcher with a high- quality 5-horsepower Briggs & Stratton Quantum engine is a very good deal. The controls are nicely grouped and include Troy-Bilt's great 6-speed self-propelled feature. The single-lever cutting-height adjusting system is excellent. The very rigid cast aluminum deck provides very good mulching performance.

Warranty: parts and labor, 7 years.

Approx. retail price $470 | **Approx. low price** $460

TORO SUPER RECYCLER 20462

Recommended

With 5½ horsepower, a three-speed rear-drive transmission, and "SmartWheel" to select the proper mower height, the Toro 20462 Super Recycler is a user-friendly machine. It earns its name with a very effective mulcher deck and blade design. Options include a dethatcher, rear-bag kit, side discharge, and Toro's popular "Mow & Feed" fertilizer spreader. The operating controls are well organized, and the handle folds for storage. The cutting swath is 21 inches.

Warranty: 2 years, full.

Approx. retail price $500 | **Approx. low price** $436

SNAPPER R21500

Recommended

If you prefer a push-model mulching mower, the Snapper R21500 is a good choice. It features a 5-horsepower Briggs & Stratton engine, Snapper's excellent Ninja mulching blade, and Hi-Vac steel deck design, all of which combine to produce a good mulching cut. The cutting swath is 21 inches, and the handle folds for storage. A side-discharge kit and rear grass catcher are available as accessories.

Warranty: 2 years, limited.

Approx. retail price $425 | **Approx. low price** $379

YARD-MAN 149C

Budget Buy

For the budget price, you're not likely to find a better mulcher than this anywhere. The Yard-Man 149C has a 6-horsepower Briggs & Stratton Industrial/Commercial engine, 6 shift-on-the-go front-drive speeds, and a folding handle for easy storage. The cutting swath is 21 inches. A side discharge kit is included in the price, adding to the budget value. A grass catcher is an available option. Another neat feature: The mower comes fully assembled in the carton.

Warranty: 2 years; 90-day no-fault guarantee.

Approx. retail price **$365**

Approx. low price **$282**

LAWN TRACTORS

14 Horsepower or Less

HONDA HARMONY H2013SDA

✓BEST BUY

This new addition to Honda's Harmony Line is a nicely styled 13-horsepower lawn tractor with an overhead-valve engine. With its 38-inch twin-blade deck, the Harmony H2013SDA is a side-discharge mower that easily converts to mulching or rear bagging. It shares many winning comfort and operational features with the Harmony riding mower, making it a nimble performer. Lights, snow thrower, grass catcher, guard, and hitch are optional. While this model has a 5-speed shift-on-the-fly transmission, a hydrostatic transmission model is also available.

Warranty: parts and labor, 2 years.

Approx. retail price **$2,190**

Approx. low price **$2,048**

More than 14 Horsepower

SEARS 25252

✓BEST BUY

The Sears 25252 is a lot of garden tractor for the money. It has a quiet, 15-horsepower, industrial-quality Briggs & Stratton Gold overhead-valve engine. The 42-inch mulching mower deck is easily converted to side discharge or optional 2-bin or 3-bin rear-mounted bagging containers. Electric start and lights are standard. This model is highly maneuverable, with a 25½-inch turning radius and 68-inch length.

Warranty: 2 years.

Approx. retail price **$1,400**

Approx. low price **$1,399**

TROY-BILT 13040 GARDEN TRACTOR

Recommended

Premium priced and premium quality, this rugged 18-horsepower tractor has a twin-cylinder Briggs & Stratton overhead-valve engine and a hydrostatic transmission. The price below includes a 42-inch mowing deck; other sizes are available, as are a snow thrower, a dozer blade, two grass collection systems, and more. Seating and controls are very convenient and comfortable. Headlights are also included. Visibility is excellent, and turning radius is a tight 22 inches.

Warranty: parts and labor, 7 years.

Approx. retail price	Approx. low price
$4,599	$4,180

STRING TRIMMERS

Gasoline Models

RYOBI 990R

✓ BEST BUY

Ryobi's powerful new 18-inch 990r trimmer uses the company's new 26.2cc, environmentally friendly, 4-stroke "Pro4Mor" engine and comes with a brush-cutting blade accessory. Well-balanced, easy to handle, and easy to start, this model is an excellent performer. To round it out as a lawn-and-garden system, optional "Trimmer-Plus" accessories such as an edger, blower, cultivator, and pruner are available, all powered by the same engine unit.

Warranty: 2 years.

Approx. retail price	Approx. low price
$229	$189

HOMELITE Z725CE

Recommended

The new Homelite z725ce has become a real hit among homeowners. This very good 17-inch, 2-string gas trimmer features push-button electric start, a first for trimmers. Not that Homelite's time-honored 25cc 2-stroke engine wasn't always an easy start (it is), but there's something compelling about being

Prices are accurate at time of printing but are subject to manufacturers' changes.

able to just push a button to start, especially if the neighbors are watching. And the whole works weighs only 12 pounds.

Warranty: 2 years.

Approx. retail price	**Approx. low price**
$170	**$162**

WEED EATER FEATHERLITE

Budget Buy

"FeatherLite" is an accurate description for this 15-inch gas trimmer: It weighs in at a svelte 7¼ pounds. With Weed Eater's easy-to-start 2-cycle engine and quick-change string spool system, the FeatherLite is a very good entry-level gas trimmer choice.

Warranty: 2 years.

Approx. retail price	**Approx. low price**
$75	**$73**

Electric Models

RYOBI 132R TRIMMER PLUS

✓ BEST BUY

Like Ryobi's popular gas version, the electric Ryobi 132R Trimmer Plus can be converted into an edger, blower, vac, or light-duty cultivator with quick-change add-on accessories available as options. As a trimmer, it weighs only 9 pounds, has a gutsy 5.2-amp motor, and cuts a 15-inch swath.

Warranty: 2 years.

Approx. retail price	**Approx. low price**
$64	**$47**

TORO 51326

Recommended

For the average-size yard, this Toro 12-inch electric trimmer is a good choice. It's light, comfortable, and has the manufacturer's solid reputation behind it, as well as Toro's no-tools string spool replacement feature.

Warranty: 2 years.

Approx. retail price	**Approx. low price**
$35	**$30**

Cordless Models

RYOBI 150R

✓BEST BUY

This 12-volt trimmer has a battery in the head with enough juice to trim a mile or so of average after-mowing weeds with its 10-inch swath, which ought to handle most homeowners' needs. At 10 pounds, the Ryobi 150R is quiet and easy to use. It comes with a wall-mount charging bracket.

Warranty: 2 years.

Approx. retail price
$95

Approx. low price
$87

WEED EATER HANDYSTIK

Recommended

"HandyStik" is an apt description for this 9.4-pound, 12-volt trimmer. Its battery holds enough charge to easily trim an average lawn and then some. This 9-inch trimmer is equipped with Weed Eater's Tap-N-Go line advance and includes a wall-mount charger bracket.

Warranty: 2 years, limited.

Approx. retail price
$75

Approx. low price
$73

BLOWER/VACS

Gasoline Models

WEED EATER BARRACUDA SV 30

✓BEST BUY

Barracudas are described as fierce. With a 30cc engine, 180-mph air velocity at 375 cubic feet per minute, and a mulching reduction ratio of a very high 16:1, the Weed Eater Barracuda fits this description. This model also features Weed Eater's exclusive antivibe handle. Optionally available are a cutter cleaning kit and a Flex-Vac kit, which converts the machine to a shop-type vac (because of engine fumes, however, remember not to use the vac in a closed space). The bag holds one bushel.

Prices are accurate at time of printing but are subject to manufacturers' changes.

Warranty: 2 years, limited.

Approx. retail price $139 | **Approx. low price** $139

ECHO SHRED 'N' VAC ES-1000

Recommended

Echo's ES-1000 has a number of nice features to make it a sound buy: a reliable engine, comfortable 9.1-pound weight, 3-speed throttle interlock for excellent blower control, 35-inch long no-stoop vacuum tube, a generous 1¾-bushel vac bag, and an elbowed vac discharge tube that comfortably positions the bag. Echo's 12:1-ratio shredding mechanism is patented.

Warranty: parts and labor, 2 years; electronic ignition, parts and labor, 5 years; electronic parts, lifetime.

Approx. retail price $220 | **Approx. low price** $199

Electric Models

TORO SUPER BLOWER VAC 51582

BEST BUY

With a 12-amp motor and a 190-mph airstream, Toro's new blower/vac is an impressive performer. And it's light and easy to use. Blower velocity is varied with simple movement of a tab. Changing from blowing to vacuuming/mulching is a quick, easy, no-tools task. Blower orientation is such that there is no torque twist when the machine is started. The leaf shredding reduction ratio is 10:1.

Warranty: 2 years.

Approx. retail price $75 | **Approx. low price** $66

WEED EATER GATORVAC

Recommended

The Gatorvac is a handy, lightweight blower and vac with a lot of power and some neat features. A simple

Prices are accurate at time of printing but are subject to manufacturers' changes.

twist of a knob selects one of two levels of vacuuming power or blower mode without tools or additional components. It inhales large leaves and debris, as well as grass clippings, collecting them in a unique near-transparent mesh bag that can hold ⅞ bushel.

Warranty: 2 years.

Approx. retail price
$90

Approx. low price
$81

Prices are accurate at time of printing but are subject to manufacturers' changes.

SNOW REMOVAL

The two critical factors in choosing a snow thrower are the size of the area you want to clear and the average winter snowfall in your part of the country. If you have only a short walk or a few steps to deal with and if your climate is mild (snowfall rarely more than a few inches), then a gas or electric power shovel is a reasonable choice. Toro is the principal manufacturer of these light-duty tools. Because most homeowners will not find them adequate for clearing a large driveway or a long walk, however, such devices are not covered here.

Snow throwers can be divided into three categories, based on size and power:

- Small: Under 5 horsepower, either single- or two-stage
- Medium: 5 to 7 horsepower, all two-stage
- Large: 8 horsepower and above

Small snow throwers are for homeowners with only small spaces to clear and for areas of the country that usually receive only light snowfall (less than 6 inches). They are capable of handling heavier snows, including compacted driveway snow, but they will make you do more of the work and will take much longer. These units typically are not self-propelled, although the biting action of the auger blade helps to propel the machine. You'll find both 2- and 4-cycle engines in this category, and the small engine size means they are usually easy to start. These are also the simplest snow throwers to store because they are light and in many cases can be hung on the garage wall or folded.

If you live in the snowbelt and have an average-size walk or drive, almost any of the medium snow throwers should be adequate for just about anything winter might bring. They're an excellent all-around choice: neither too big nor too expensive. These units have four-cycle engines and can be hard to start under extremely cold conditions. However, the majority of snow throwers now have Tecumseh Snow King engines specially engineered for cold-weather performance, with primers, automatic compression releases for reduced starting effort, shrouding, and moisture-resistant ignition systems. Honda snow thrower engines also have cold-weather starting aids. Electric starters are offered as standard equipment or as options on almost all models, and we recommend them, especially if any concern exists about the user's ability to manage pull-starting. All these models are two-stage, meaning that a slow-speed auger breaks up the snow and feeds it to a high-speed impeller which then throws it up and out through the chute. Most of these units are self-propelled and can take a number of useful accessories, such as drift busters, headlights, tire chains, and even a protective cab for the operator.

If your area of the country measures its winter snowfall in the hundreds of inches, or if you have an especially long walk or driveway to clear, then consider a large snow thrower. In this category, buy as much power as you can afford and be sure to get electric start: You have to be in top shape to pull-start a large snow thrower in frigid weather. An 8-horsepower motor may sound like a lot, but in this situation, more is better. These larger units are self-propelled and they can cut a 28-inch path. Options include tire chains, headlights, heated handgrips, and protective cabs.

Tips on Use and Safety

Snow throwers can be dangerous; the risks are increased by extremely cold and slippery conditions. The first heavy snowfall of the season often brings several unlucky snow thrower operators to hospital emergency rooms because people neglect basic safety considerations. The primary precaution: NEVER, under any circumstances, place your hand or foot into the chute or auger area to clear a jam, even with the engine off. These motors can sometimes be started simply by turning the auger, so always use a broomstick or some similar tool. Snow throwers can throw ice chunks, stones, and debris as well as snow, so never operate around people—especially children—and pets.

At the start of the season and throughout the winter, use only fresh gas—buy only a gallon or two at a time. A new spark plug, fresh oil, and some auto paste wax on the inside of the discharge chute will prepare you for winter. Keep one or two spare shear pins on hand (that's a special fastener designed to break under stress in order to protect the auger if it becomes jammed).

And when spring finally arrives, to prevent varnish formation, either drain the fuel tank and carburetor or add some fuel stabilizer. Change the oil in 4-cycle engines and spray an aerosol lubricant over metal parts that show any bare metal or rust.

Best Buys '96

Our Best Buy, Recommended, and Budget Buy snow removal equipment follows. The item we consider the best of the Best Buys is first, followed by our second choice, and so on. Remember that a Best Buy, Recommended, or Budget Buy designation applies only to the model listed. It does not necessarily apply to other models by the same manufacturer or to an entire product line.

SMALL SNOW THROWERS
(Under 5 Horsepower)

TORO 38185

✓ BEST BUY

The Toro 38185 is the largest of Toro's stable of five small single-stage snow throwers using the company's unique Power Curve rotor. The 38185 has a 4½-horsepower Toro guaranteed-to-start 2-cycle engine, which clears a 20-inch swath of snow very adequately. It is simple, compact, lightweight, easy to store, and a great choice for homeowners with moderate snow removal needs. Electric start is optional.

Warranty: 2 years, full.

Approx. retail price **$760**

Approx. low price **$649**

JOHN DEERE TRS-22

Recommended

If you want a wheel-propelled snow thrower but don't need a big, gutsy engine, consider the John Deere TRS-22. It's a fine performer with lots of big-thrower features, such as a 4-horsepower Tecumseh Snow King 4-cycle engine with six

Prices are accurate at time of printing but are subject to manufacturers' changes.

forward and two reverse travel speeds. This model clears a 21-inch path in pretty serious snow. Controls are nicely grouped.

Warranty: 2 years, limited.

Approx. retail price **$819** | **Approx. low price** **$809**

ARIENS SS322

Budget Buy

New from Ariens this season is the SS322 auger-propelled snow thrower. Its 22-inch clearing width is as large as single-stage snow throwers get. The SS322 is powered with a 3-horsepower Tecumseh Snow King engine with optional electric start. Weighing in at 59 pounds, it's also easy to move and store. The sturdy design of the auger makes this unit a good performer at a budget price.

Warranty: 5 years, limited.

Approx. retail price **$479** | **Approx. low price** **$447**

MEDIUM-SIZE SNOW THROWERS
(5 to 7 Horsepower)

TORO 38072

✓BEST BUY

With a 7-horsepower Tecumseh engine and 24-inch clearing width, the Toro 38072 is an impressive performer in heavy, deep, and wet snow, at least in part because of Toro's husky drum-type augers. This self-propelled unit has three forward speeds and one reverse. Chains, electric start, shield, and drift breakers are optionally available for this great intermediate-size unit.

Warranty: 2 years, full.

Approx. retail price **$1,050** | **Approx. low price** **$899**

ARIENS ST 524

Recommended

The Ariens ST 524 is a good, rugged performer. It has a 5-horsepower Tecumseh Snow King engine with vari

Prices are accurate at time of printing but are subject to manufacturers' changes.

able speed Disc-O-Matic drive, providing six forward and two reverse speeds. The clearing width is 24 inches. Like most wheel-propelled snow throwers these days, it's equipped with fat, decidedly knobby Snow Hog tires that give superior traction in any type of snow no matter how deep or wet. "Mitten Grip" controls are standard; electric start and drift cutters are optional.

Warranty: 5 years, limited.

Approx. retail price **$1,059**

Approx. low price **$826**

SNAPPER I7243

Recommended

The Snapper I7243 is another dependable, medium-size, 24-inch performer with a 7-horsepower Tecumseh engine. However, the Snow Hog tires are a bit smaller than those on other models. The four forward and one reverse speeds can be shifted on the go with a single lever. Electric start is optional; drift cutter is standard.

Warranty: 2 years, limited.

Approx. retail price **$1,025**

Approx. low price **$916**

LARGE SNOW THROWERS

(8 Horsepower and Above)

TROY-BILT 42010

✓BEST BUY

The 8-horsepower Troy-Bilt 42010 just about has it all. A Snow King engine, built-in electric hand warmers on the grips, Snow Hog tires, limited slip differential, five forward and two reverse speeds, 24-inch clearing width, and the best available warranty (seven years) make this one terrific machine for dealing with very serious snowstorms. Electric start is optional, as are chains, cab, and headlight.

Warranty: 7 years.

Approx. retail price **$1,329**

Approx. low price **$1,239**

Prices are accurate at time of printing but are subject to manufacturers' changes.

HONDA HS828K1WAS

Recommended

Honda's top-of-the-line 8-horsepower snow thrower is premium priced but has a lot going for it besides th heralded Honda overhead-valve engine. Electric start is stan dard, as is a very nice hydrostatic drive system that gives infi nitely variable forward and reverse travel speed and precis control. Interconnected drive and auger clutch levers leave on hand free for chute adjustments as you proceed. This unit clear a 28-inch swath. For really tough going, a track-drive versio (HS828K1TAS) is also available.

Warranty: parts and labor, 2 years.

Approx. retail price	**Approx. low price**
$1,824	**$1,788**

TORO 38556

Recommended

Like Toro's other large snow throwers, the 10-horsepower 38556 model has the company's unique Powe Shift system for dealing with deep, hard-packed snow. This sys tem allows the machine to lean into the job; a quick flip of lever shifts the wheels to the rear, doubling the weight on th auger. The Toro 38556 has four forward and two reverse speed and a clearing width of 28 inches. An optional differential ki affords independent wheel traction.

Warranty: 2 years, full.

Approx. retail price	**Approx. low price**
$1,135	**$1,135**

Prices are accurate at time of printing but are subject to manufacturers' changes.

FOOD PREPARATION APPLIANCES

Today, the name of the game in cooking is speed. Few people nowadays can make a habit of spending entire days in the kitchen turning out magnificent meals. But we're not willing to sacrifice quality and good taste in our foods. To respond to this need for efficiency and quality food preparation, manufacturers have created a vast variety of appliances to handle every job, great and small. On the one hand, you'll find machines that can perform the chores formerly done by several. On the other hand, ever more specialized appliances handle very specific jobs, such as making bread or espresso. This section will help you sort through the maze of appliances to find the right products for your specific needs.

Best Buys '96

Our Best Buy, Recommended, and Budget Buy food preparation appliances follow. Products within each category are listed according to quality. The best of the Best Buys is listed first, followed by our second choice, and so on. A Best Buy, Recommended, or Budget Buy designation applies only to the model listed; it does not necessarily apply to other models made by the same manufacturer or to an entire product line.

FOOD PROCESSORS

Today's kitchen is equipped with an array of modern appliances from staples such as a coffeemaker and toaster to the more esoteric pasta and bread makers. In between are the food processors. For years considered nothing more than a trendy toy or culinary fad, the food processor has proven itself to be a reliable, essential addition to the kitchen. Today's food processors do more than ever. Bigger, more powerful machines can knead dough for two loaves of bread, slice and shred a party-size batch of coleslaw, or slice whole fruits or vegetables through an expanded feed tube. Smaller models save work space and are perfect for smaller tasks such as processing a single onion, a handful of herbs, or a cup of mayonnaise. Mini mincers specialize in chopping small items such as garlic cloves, nuts, or coffee beans. These small units also are handy for making single servings of baby food.

Because of the differences between the many types of food processors, you may decide to purchase more than one. And, because some food processors now perform the added functions of a mixer, blender, and citrus juicer, you can combine several appliances into one unit. At the very least, because of their ease of use, versatility, and compact size, no kitchen should be without a mini mincer.

The first-time processor owner may want a machine that's as uncomplicated as possible. The single-button or two-speed models offer the most ease of use. Masters of processor techniques may prefer a variable-speed model. All models share the following features: 1) stainless-steel chopping blade, also called an "S" blade, for chopping, mixing and blending, pureeing, or kneading bread dough (though some machines have separate dough blades or hooks); 2) work bowl, usually transparent (some machines have extra bowls as well as blender carafes for added features and convenience); 3) on/off/pulse, these are the common speeds for a processor—"on" for continuous action, "pulse" for short, consecutive rotations of the blade for more even chopping; 4) motor base—generally speaking, the bigger the machine, the more powerful the motor, but some of the compact models pack a surprising punch.

Large Food Processors

CUISINART PRO FOOD PREP CENTER DLC-7SFP

The Cuisinart DLC-7SFP PRO Food Prep Center ✔**BEST BUY** is designed for the serious cook. It comes with a 14-cup Lexan work bowl—the largest in its class—that can accommodat over two pounds of ground beef, enough dough for two large bread loaves, or about five cups of mashed potatoes in a single batch. An added feature is the whisk attachment, which enables the machine to function as a high-power mixer. The large capacity is great for parties—you can shred an entire head of cabbage without emptying the work bowl. Two fingertip switches, on and pulse/off, are easy to use. The Food Preparation Center comes with a stainless-steel chopping blade, heavy-duty plastic dough blade, medium slicing disc, medium shredding disc, stainless-steel whisk attachment, and plastic spatula. Two covers—one compact cover for use with chopping and mixing and one standard cover with both large and small feed tubes—enable you to slice whole fruits and vegetables in addition to long, thin produce. Also included with the package is a Cuisinart how-to video that shows the proper techniques for achieving perfect results with your processor. Optional attachments include a fine shredding disc; fine and medium julienne discs; French fry disc; ultra-thin, thin, medium, thick, and extra-thick slicing discs; citrus juicer; and power strainer attachments. All parts, except motor base, are dishwasher safe.

Warranty: 3 years, limited; motor, 5 years.

Approx. retail price	**Approx. low price**
$299	**$299**

KITCHENAID 11-CUP ULTRA POWER FOOD PROCESSOR KFP600WH

✓ BEST BUY

The KitchenAid 11-cup Ultra Power Food Processor combines superior performance with incredible ease of use. The unit comes with a clear 11-cup work bowl with chopping blade, reversible thin slicing/shredding disc, medium slicing disc, medium shredding disc, dough blade, plastic spatula, and mini chopping bowl and blade. The multi-purpose chopping blade and mini chopping blade are made by Sabatier, a manufacturer of quality knives. You also get an accessory storage box to house all the blades/discs when not in use. Touchpad controls let you switch from on to off or pulse instantly. Process up to one pound of chopped beef or produce,

Prices are accurate at time of printing but are subject to manufacturers' changes.

three cups of dough, or up to three cups of chopped nuts or peanut butter. A mini bowl can handle up to one cup of semi-liquid ingredients or ½ cup of solids. Unit assembles and disassembles easily for hassle-free operation and wipes clean with a damp cloth. Bowls and blades are dishwasher safe. You'll also save on counter space thanks to a vertical profile (bowl on top of motor) and wraparound cord storage.

Warranty: total replacement, 1 year.

Approx. retail price	Approx. low price
$229	$180

BRAUN FOOD PREPARATION CENTER 5-IN-1 K1000

Recommended

The Braun K1000 Food Preparation Center is an all-in-one appliance, combining the functions of food processor, blender, chopper, and ice crusher. It comes with a clear 11-cup processor work bowl (for slicing, shredding, grating, mixing, and chopping), an opaque 18-cup kitchen machine work bowl (for heavy kneading, beating, mixing, mashing, and whipping), and a 4-cup glass blender carafe (for liquefying, pureeing, chopping, and crushing ice). Other accessories include a stainless-steel chopping blade; slicing, shredding, grating, and French fry discs; two whisks; a dough hook; a disc storage box; and a spatula. The motor is powerful but not excessively noisy, with variable-speed control dial, which may seem a bit complicated, especially to the first-time processor owner. A number of symbols designate the proper speed for different functions. Speeds are also given numerically (from 1 to 5). One dial selects your speed, while another activates the power. A separate pulse button allows manual pulse operation to obtain exact results. Automatic pulse is also provided for convenient hands-free operation. The 5-in-1 is not geared toward the occasional cook, but the avid cook/entertainer will find its many functions and quality parts (blades made by the renowned Sabatier knife company) to be an exceptional value.

Warranty: 1 year.

Prices are accurate at time of printing but are subject to manufacturers' changes.

Approx. retail price
$290

Approx. low price
$270

Mid-size Food Processors

CUISINART PRO CLASSIC FOOD PROCESSOR DLC-10S

✓BEST BUY

The Cuisinart Classic Food Processor boasts all the power of the Cuisinart line but with reduced capacity and price. The smallest of Cuisinart's full-size processors, this machine comes with a seven-cup Lexan work bowl that can process dough for two standard loaves of bread or grind up to 1¼ pounds of meat in a single batch. A three-position lever is easy to use and lets you switch from off to on or pulse in seconds. Standard equipment includes cover with both large and small feed tubes, flat cover for chopping and mixing, stainless-steel chopping/mixing blade, reinforced plastic dough blade, medium shredding disc, and plastic spatula. You also receive a special how-to video that explains the ins and outs of processor operations. Optional attachments include a fine shredding disc, fine and medium julienne discs, French fry disc, a range of slicing discs, whisk, citrus juicer, and power strainer attachments. All parts, except motor base, are dishwasher safe.

Warranty: 3 years, limited; motor, 5 years.

Approx. retail price
$150

Approx. low price
$150

BLACK & DECKER POWERPRO FP1000-04

✓BEST BUY

The Black & Decker PowerPro is an efficient, easy-to-use appliance. While it doesn't come with a lot of extras, such as whisk or specialty disc attachments, it does do an excellent job with basic tasks, such as chopping an onion or slicing apples for a pie. The unit comes with a 6-cup clear work bowl, chopping blade that is straight on one side and curved on the other for better bowl coverage and more thorough processing, two reversible discs for thick or thin slicing and shredding, cover with food chute, and Black & Decker's exclusive "food fingers" (a metal, comblike clip that fits inside the food chute to hold long, thin produce upright for even slicing). The unit is activated by three touchpad buttons: on, off, and pulse. Assembly and disassembly are a snap and cleanup is easy, since bowls and blades go right in the dishwasher.

Warranty: 2 years.

Approx. retail price	Approx. low price
$120	$58

BRAUN MULTIPRACTIC UK100

Recommended

The Braun Multipractic UK100 is a good choice for cooks who want to produce fancy results with a smaller machine. An interchangeable blade system features three inserts (slicing, fine shredding, and French fry) that snap into place. The adjustable dial lets you select from wafer-thin to thick slices. Standard equipment for the UK100 includes a 6½-cup tinted work bowl, adjustable blade system, heavy-duty stainless-steel chopping blade, and plastic spatula. A three-position dial switch lets you select low (I), high (II), or pulse/off. Process up to four cups of liquid or enough dough for one large pizza. The variable slicing takes some practice but yields excellent results. The base wipes clean with a damp cloth and other parts should be hand-washed in warm, sudsy water.

Warranty: parts and labor, 1 year.

Approx. retail price	Approx. low price
$100	$88

Compact Food Processors

CUISINART LITTLE PRO PLUS PROCESSOR/JUICER LPP

✓ BEST BUY

The Cuisinart Little Pro Plus is well suited for singles or small families. It comes with a see-through Lexan work bowl for chopping and mixing, an opaque white bowl with a chute assembly for continuous slicing or shredding di-

Prices are accurate at time of printing but are subject to manufacturers' changes.

rectly into a waiting bowl, a stainless-steel chopping/mixing blade, serrated slicing disc, shredding disc, and spatula. The "Plus" is a citrus juicer attachment with three stackable reamers for juicing lemons/limes, oranges, and grapefruit. The clear work bowl can accommodate up to three cups of sliced or shredded produce, one half pound of chopped meat, or enough dough for a 15-inch pizza. A three-position on/off/pulse lever is easy to use. Don't let the compact size fool you—this unit is powerful and unusually quiet.

Warranty: 3 years, limited.

Approx. retail price	**Approx. low price**
$100	**$95**

SUNBEAM OSKAR 4817

Budget Buy

The Sunbeam Oskar food processor is the original compact food processor. The unit features a tinted 2-cup work bowl and domed cover with drip hole for adding liquids during processing, stainless-steel chopping blade, slicing/shredding disc, and side discharge cover/attachment for continuous slicing and shredding into a separate bowl. Slice or shred 1 to 1½ cups of ingredients directly into the work bowl or use the side discharge attachment to process unlimited quantities for family use or entertaining. Operation is simple—a twist of the lid engages the motor. However, since the bowl has no handle, it can sometimes be awkward to insert, twist, and remove, especially if the bowl is not completely dry. A sleek, vertical profile saves counter space. All parts, except motor base, are dishwasher safe for easy cleanup.

Warranty: 2 years.

Approx. retail price	**Approx. low price**
$40	**$20**

Mini Mincers

CUISINART MINI-PREP PROCESSOR DLC-1

✓BEST BUY

The Cuisinart Mini-Prep Processor DLC-1 is the perfect solution for tedious chores such as chopping onions or

Prices are accurate at time of printing but are subject to manufacturers' changes.

a handful of nuts. This unit features a clear 21-ounce-capacity work bowl—the largest in its class—and a patented reversible chopping blade. It chops and minces onions and garlic, mixes and blends sauces and mayonnaise, purees baby food, grinds coffee beans and spices, and grates chocolate and cheeses. The Mini-Prep has low and high speeds plus pulse control. Use high speed with the blade's blunt edge for grinding and grating hard foods. Use the low speed and sharp edge for soft or watery foods. The Mini-Prep takes up minimal space and the hidden wraparound cord keeps counter clutter to a minimum. The work bowl and lid disassemble easily and are dishwasher safe.

Warranty: 18 months, limited.

Approx. retail price	**Approx. low price**
$30	**$30**

BLACK & DECKER HANDYCHOPPER MINCER/CHOPPER HC2000

✓ BEST BUY

The Black & Decker HandyChopper Mincer/Chopper will quickly become a favorite tool in your kitchen. With its 12-ounce work bowl, single stainless-steel chopping blade, and extra-large on button, it couldn't be easier to use. Most items are processed in seconds. The 12-ounce work bowl is perfect for mincing small amounts of onion, garlic, and fresh herbs; grinding nuts; and pureeing baby food. The unit comes with a curly, telephone-style cord that expands to 3½ feet then retracts to reduce counter clutter, and rubber feet for stability. All parts except base are dishwasher safe for easy cleanup.

Warranty: 2 years.

Approx. retail price	**Approx. low price**
$30	**$26**

ELECTRIC MIXERS

The electric mixer is both familiar and reliable when it comes to mixing batters, whipping cream, and mashing potatoes. Not only does the mixer eliminate much of the drudgery associated with these tasks, but it also does a faster, more thorough job. This machine is unmatched when it comes to aerating mixtures—increasing the volume by incorporating air into creams, batters, egg whites, etc.

Traditional stand mixers, with their supplied work bowls, offer the most power, with the added advantage of hands-free mixing. Portable mixers are less expensive and can be tucked away in a drawer when not in use. Many mixers now come with added attachments, such as dough hooks, whisks, or immersion blender rods, making them even more versatile.

Portable Mixers

CUISINART SMART POWER 7-SPEED ELECTRONIC HAND MIXER HTM-7L

✓ BEST BUY

The Cuisinart Smart Power 7-Speed Electronic Hand Mixer is a powerful, easy-to-grip hand mixer that has electronic touchpad controls and lets you switch between speeds with a gentle touch on the + (increase speed) or – (decrease speed) buttons. Press the power button to activate the mixer on its lowest speed. The mixer starts up slowly to prevent splattering even when working with dry ingredients. The lower speeds are perfect for folding or start-up mixing. Higher speeds are extremely fast for quick whipping and aerating. Sturdy wire beaters have no center posts for dough to climb and clog mixing action. Made of stainless steel, these beaters cut cleanly through even heavy cookie dough. The unit also comes with a stainless-steel whisk attachment for fluffy whipped cream and egg whites. Other features include a rotating cord that's designed to stay out of the way during mixing. Beaters and whisk are dishwasher safe for easy cleanup.

Warranty: 3 years, limited.

Approx. retail price
$50

Approx. low price
$50

Prices are accurate at time of printing but are subject to manufacturers' changes.

BRAUN MULTIMIX 4-IN-1 HANDHELD FOOD PREPARATION SYSTEM M880

Recommended

The Braun Multimix 4-in-1 Handheld Food Preparation System is extremely versatile; it converts from a hand mixer to an immersion blender to a mini mincer. With its two sturdy dough hooks, the unit also tackles bread doughs. Standard accessories include two heavy wire beaters with a unique angled design for more efficient blending of ingredients, immersion blender rod attachment and beaker, chopper attachment with 10-ounce transparent bowl and plastic cover for storing ingredients, and dough hooks. Because of its many attachments, this appliance is a bit more complicated to use. Three speeds provide an adequate range for mixing and blending. The pulse option is great for quick mix-ins and for removing dough clinging to beaters. Pulse is a little too fast for blending dry ingredients, however.

Warranty: 2 years.

Approx. retail price	Approx. low price
$70	$65

SUNBEAM 6-SPEED BURST OF POWER MIXER 2486

Budget Buy

The Sunbeam 6-Speed Burst of Power Mixer may cost less but it doesn't skimp on features. With its many attachments, including dough hooks, whisk, stir paddle, and immersion blending rod, as well as the standard stainless-steel beaters, this unit is an exceptional value. The rounded design means it's easy to grip, well-balanced, and quite powerful. Slide the thumb-operated control switch to any of the six speed settings. Push down on the burst of power button for added power at any speed except top speed; release the button and the mixer returns to its original speed. The plastic stir paddle is ideal for sauces and gravies and can be used directly in nonstick pans. Use the slender immersion blender for mixing frothy drinks or shakes. The mixer is compact enough to store in a drawer when it's not in use.

Warranty: 2 years.

Approx. retail price
$30

Approx. low price
$27

Stand Mixers

KITCHENAID ULTRA POWER STAND MIXER KSM90

✓BEST BUY

For heavy-duty mixing, kneading, and whipping, the KitchenAid KSM90 Ultra Power Stand Mixer is unbeatable. This unit features an extra-powerful 10-speed motor that is well suited for all types of mixing. Standing about 14 inches tall and weighing about 22 pounds, this unit will stay put—even when tackling the most strenuous chores. Standard equipment includes a 4½-quart stainless-steel mixing bowl with handle, flat beater, dough hook, and stainless-steel wire whip. Unique "planetary" mixing action spins the beater and rotates it around the stationary bowl for maximum bowl coverage. The bowl locks onto the mixer base for added stability. The mixer is available in a variety of colors, and, with a number of optional accessories, the KSM90 converts to a food grinder, pasta maker, fruit/vegetable strainer, sausage stuffer, rotor slicer/shredder, grain mill, citrus juicer, and even a can opener. A fabric cover, food tray, and two-piece pouring shield are also sold separately.

Warranty: 1 year.

Approx. retail price
$220

Approx. low price
$220

HAMILTON BEACH 12-SPEED CHEFMIX 60600

Recommended

The Hamilton Beach 12-speed ChefMix stand mixer is an economical choice that offers good performance. The electronic motor has 12 speeds that handle all mixing tasks from folding to whipping and aerating. A dial control operates the machine. The unit comes with two stainless-steel bowls (2-quart and 4-quart), heavy-duty chrome beaters and dough hooks, and a two-position turntable for automatic rotating with

Prices are accurate at time of printing but are subject to manufacturers' changes.

large and small mixing bowls. Other desirable features include built-in cord storage to eliminate counter clutter and automatic shutoff if a spoon or other utensil is accidentally caught in the beaters.

Warranty: 2 years.

Approx. retail price
$130

Approx. low price
$85

BLENDERS

The two types of blender on the market today are as different as they are alike. Traditional carafe blenders are unmatched for performance when it comes to crushing ice or other hard food items. The carafe not only crushes the ice, it also protects the user from flying ice particles and splashes. Carafe blenders vary by model, giving consumers a choice between glass and plastic carafes, push buttons and dial controls, and specialty features, such as ice-crushing and pulse. Immersion blenders, on the other hand, excel over traditional blenders at jobs involving soft food items, such as pureeing cooked vegetables or blending fruit drinks. They also offer the added convenience of being able to go directly into your own drink cup, saucepan, or other container. For added versatility, many immersion blenders also come with chopping or whipping attachments that allow them to function as mini mincers or hand mixers.

Traditional Blenders

KRUPS POWERX PLUS 239

✓BEST BUY

The Krups PowerX Plus blender combines power and performance with a sleek design and sturdy base. Select from any of 14 speeds using the variable speed dial control, then push the on button. The ice crusher and power burst buttons are touch-and-release to afford a pulselike control. The 48-ounce glass jar is extra strong and has angled sides

Prices are accurate at time of printing but are subject to manufacturers' changes.

with interior ribs that create a whirling motion to achieve thorough blending. The base is extra wide with rubber feet and won't rock back and forth on your counter during tough blending jobs. Other features include a quiet motor and hidden cord storage.

Warranty: 1 year.

Approx. retail price
$65

Approx. low price
$55

OSTER 10-SPEED OSTERIZER BLENDER 4108

BEST BUY

The Oster 10-Speed Osterizer Blender is a traditional push-button blender with the advantages of three pulse speeds—chop, grate, and grind—and seven continuous speeds from stir to liquefy, plus an added ice-crushing speed. The Osterizer Blender is perfect for making bread crumbs, pureeing cooked vegetables for soup, or making sauces or dips. An all-metal drive system is built to withstand years of rigorous use. The unit is both powerful and efficient but not especially quiet. The 40-ounce Perma-Glas carafe is marked with measurements in cups and liters and disassembles easily for cleaning. An 8-ounce mini jar is available separately and is the perfect size for smaller portions or grinding single servings of coffee beans. The mini blend jar comes with its own cover for convenient storage.

Warranty: 1 year, limited.

Approx. retail price
$30

Approx. low price
$30

HAMILTON BEACH BLENDMASTER 8-SPEED BLENDER 58122

Recommended

The Hamilton Beach BlendMaster 8-Speed Blender features six continuous speeds from whip to blend, plus hi pulse and lo pulse switches for optimum blending control. Push-button controls are rounded for easy fingertip operation. A separate ice breaker switch also functions in pulse mode and can crush three to five cubes at a time without adding other liquids. The 48-ounce plastic blending carafe is marked in ounces and cups on one side and milliliters and liters on the other. Interior ribs direct solids down toward the blade for thorough blending. The carafe disassembles for easy cleaning.

Warranty: 2 years, limited.

Approx. retail price	Approx. low price
$30	$36

Immersion Blenders

BRAUN HAND BLENDER + CHOPPER MR 380

✓BEST BUY

The Braun Hand Blender + Chopper is an economical and versatile kitchen tool. An immersion blender and mini mincer in one, this unit consists of a slim-design blending rod with powerful motor, stainless-steel blade, whip disk attachment, resealable 1-pint mixing/measuring beaker, mini chopper accessory, and convenient wall bracket. Blend and puree using the standard rod and blade; add the whip disc to mix light batters and cream; and use the mini chopper to chop small amounts of onion, herbs, or spices. Press the thumb-operated control switch to activate the blender. The mini chopper bowl comes with an airtight lid that lets you store unused quantities quickly and easily. To clean, simply rinse the stem under running water.

Warranty: 1 year, limited.

Approx. retail price	Approx. low price
$40	$36

CUISINART QUICK PREP VARI-SPEED HAND BLENDER CSB-1C

✓BEST BUY

The Cuisinart Quick Prep Vari-Speed Hand Blender is a powerful blending tool with more than a dozen variable speed settings to process a variety of food textures

Prices are accurate at time of printing but are subject to manufacturers' changes.

This unit comes with a stainless-steel chopping/mincing blade for pureeing semi-cooked vegetables or making baby food; stainless-steel blending/mixing disc for powdered drinks, sauces, and dressings; and plastic whipping/beating attachment for making milk shakes, whipped cream, and mashed potatoes; plus a 16-ounce Lexan mixing container and a 24-ounce stainless-steel container that retains icy cold temperatures. The whipping attachment can also be used to aerate skim milk to three times its volume for low-fat beverages or desserts. To clean the blender, simply rinse the stem and blades under running water. All parts, except the motor base, are dishwasher safe. The Cuisinart Quick Prep Vari-Speed Hand Blender also features a wall bracket for off-the-counter storage.

Warranty: 18 months, limited.

Approx. retail price	**Approx. low price**
$50	**$45**

TOASTERS AND TOASTER OVENS

Two-Slice Toasters

KRUPS TOASTRONIC DELUXE 118

✓BEST BUY

The Krups Toastronic Deluxe does a superior job of toasting all types of breads and other baked goods. Available in white or black, the unit features one extra-wide long slot to accommodate up to two slices of bread, bagels, English muffins, or frozen waffles. Adjustable bread guides center thick or thin slices for more even toasting. The variable control dial has settings from 1 (light) to 6 (dark). This model also lets you defrost foods before toasting or reheat without drying out. The unit also has a cool-touch exterior that wipes clean with a damp cloth and a removable crumb tray to simplify cleanup.

Warranty: 1 year, limited.

Approx. retail price	**Approx. low price**
$60	**$53**

CUISINART HEAT SURROUND MOTOR RISE ELECTRONIC TOASTER CPT-50

✓BEST BUY

The Cuisinart Heat Surround Motor Rise Electronic Toaster features a motorized carriage that gently lowers and raises foods to be toasted. Unique heating elements move toward the bread to surround even extra-thin or extra-thick slices and ensure even toasting on all sides. Settings along the slide control range from 1 (light) to 5 (dark). The High Rise toast carriage raises slices 1½ inches above the top for easy removal. Other features include a TruThaw variable defrost setting, a slide-out crumb tray, and wraparound cord storage.

Warranty: 3 years, limited.

Approx. retail price	**Approx. low price**
$50	**$50**

Four-Slice Toaster

KRUPS TOASTRONIC ULTRA 4-SLICE TOASTER 119

✓BEST BUY

The Krups Toastronic Ultra features two extra-long wide slots for toasting up to four thick slices of bread or other baked items. A unique energy-saver switch lets the user turn off the rear bread slot when only the front slot is in use. The shade selector dial has six settings. One button defrosts frozen items before toasting them, and another button reheats toast without drying it out. The automatic bread guide centers thick or thin bread items, and a quartz heating element ensures even toasting without overdrying food. The Toastronic Ultra has a cool-touch housing that wipes clean with a damp cloth. Two removable crumb trays make cleanup a breeze.

Warranty: 1 year, limited.

Approx. retail price	**Approx. low price**
$80	**$73**

Prices are accurate at time of printing but are subject to manufacturers' changes.

Toaster Ovens

DELONGHI AIR STREAM CONVECTION TOASTER OVEN AS50

✓BEST BUY

The DeLonghi Air Stream Convection Toaster Oven features an exclusive turbo convection fan that circulates heat throughout the oven for more even cooking. An extra-large interior accommodates oversize roasts, pies, and casseroles, and an extra rack lets you cook on two levels at once. The thermostat adjusts from 140°F to 450°F. Three dial controls set the oven temperature, with settings for keeping warm and dehydrating; oven on and toast color selection; and desired function (toast, broil, bake, and fan bake). The convection fan cooks foods up to 30 percent faster than standard ovens. The unit comes with two baking sheets and two wire racks. Other features include toast cycle bell timer and automatic shutoff, full-view glass door, scratch-resistant easy-care exterior, continuous-cleaning interior, removable crumb tray, cool-touch handles, power light, cord storage, and nonslip rubber feet. A pizza stone is available separately for about $19.

Warranty: parts and labor, 1 year.

Approx. retail price	**Approx. low price**
$160	**$134**

BLACK & DECKER ULTRA OVEN TOAST-R-OVEN BROILER T670

✓BEST BUY

The Black & Decker Ultra Oven combines superior performance with ease of use. A single dial controls bake/broil temperatures and toast color selection. An extra-large interior accommodates up to six slices of bread, three steaks, or a 2½-quart casserole. The multipurpose bake/broil pan can also handle standard box cake mixes. The Ultra Oven toasts, bakes, broils, defrosts, top-browns, and reheats foods. The unit has a chrome top with white and gray end panels, continuous-cleaning interior, wire rack that slides forward as the door is opened, and slide-out crumb tray. Other features include

Prices are accurate at time of printing but are subject to manufacturers' changes.

a separate on/off switch, a bell that signals when toasting is complete, and a power light.

Warranty: 2 years.

Approx. retail price $120 | **Approx. low price** $86

TOASTMASTER COOL WALL TOASTER-OVEN-BROILER 391

Recommended

The Toastmaster Cool Wall Toaster-Oven-Broiler is a four-slice-capacity unit with nonstick interior and cool-touch exterior. It has dial controls: one with oven temperatures from 200°F to 450°F, plus keep warm and broil settings; the other with toast color selections. A separate toast lever activates toasting. Other features include removable crumb tray, chrome bake/broil pan, sliding wire rack, and power light.

Warranty: 1 year.

Approx. retail price $92 | **Approx. low price** $53

BLACK & DECKER TOAST-R-OVEN BROILER TR0515

Budget Buy

The Black & Decker TR0515 Toast-R-Oven Broiler is compact, easy to use, and economical. The interior can handle up to four bread slices, a 1½-pound meat loaf, one frozen dinner, or a 6-cup muffin tin. Two independent dials control toast color selection and bake/broil temperature settings. A separate toast lever activates toasting, and an in-use light signals operation. A signal bell lets you know when toast is ready. This model comes with a multipurpose bake/broil pan, dual-position broiling grid, continuous-cleaning interior, swing-open crumb tray, and easy-care exterior. An under-the-cabinet heat-guard mounting hood is available separately for about $29.

Warranty: 2 years.

Approx. retail price $82 | **Approx. low price** $58

Prices are accurate at time of printing but are subject to manufacturers' changes.

JUICERS

SALTON VITAMIN BAR DELUXE FRUIT AND VEGETABLE JUICER JC-3

✓BEST BUY

The Salton Vitamin Bar Deluxe Fruit and Vegetable Juicer JC-3 is a combination citrus juicer and juice extractor. It comes with a pulp collector, extractor filter, citrus juicer cone, juice cup, splash guard, and food pusher. When the machine is in use, pulp is automatically collected in the pulp container. The unit disassembles and all parts except the motor base rinse clean in warm, soapy water.

Warranty: 1 year, limited.

Approx. retail price **$30** | **Approx. low price** **$25**

TOASTMASTER CITRUS JUICER 1101

Budget Buy

The Toastmaster Citrus Juicer is a compact, economical juicer that does a good job with all types of citrus fruits. This model consists of a motor base, clear 32-ounce juice container with pouring spout, strainer, grooved juice cone, and clear dust cover. Downward pressure on the cone activates the machine. Other features include a pulp collector built into the strainer and rubber feet that provide stability. The pitcher, cone, and strainer disassemble easily for cleaning in warm, sudsy water.

Warranty: 1 year.

Approx. retail price **$19** | **Approx. low price** **$11**

PASTA MAKERS

CUISINART DELUXE PASTA MAKER DPM-3

✓BEST BUY

The Cuisinart Deluxe Pasta Maker makes a 3-pound batch of fresh pasta from start to finish in under 30 min-

Prices are accurate at time of printing but are subject to manufacturers' changes.

utes. You provide the ingredients; the unit's mixing paddles combine them and knead the dough for you. When pasta reaches the desired consistency, attach one of the seven die plates for the desired shape, and extrude. The usual mixing time is between three and nine minutes after liquids have been absorbed. Extrusion time varies depending on the pasta shape and must be monitored so that pasta can be cut to desired lengths. The shapes range from delicate angel hair to broad, flat lasagna noodles. You can also make grissini (thin bread sticks). A set of three extra pasta shape die plates (linguine, macaroni, and shells) is available separately for $30. Since there are several parts to disassemble, cleaning is more difficult than the actual pasta making. The pasta maker is heavy (about 20 pounds), so stays put nicely on a counter.

Warranty: 1 year, limited.

Approx. retail price	**Approx. low price**
$350	**$315**

ATLAS PASTA MAKER 170

Budget Buy

A product of the VillaWare Manufacturing Company, the Atlas Pasta Maker is a manual-crank unit that provides an economical alternative to electric machines. This unit requires a bit more effort but produces superior results with flat-rolled pastas. It comes with a sturdy 6-inch-wide dough roller and cutters for 1/16-inch spaghetti or 1/4-inch fettuccine noodles. A convenient numbered dial lets you determine the thickness to which the dough will be rolled. An extra-large clamp secures the machine to your work table for hassle-free operation. Atlas accessory attachments include angel hair, trenette, 1/8-inch spaghetti, 1/2-inch and 2-inch curly lasagna, ravioli, and canelloni cutters. Because of its flat-rolling system, the Atlas Pasta Maker cannot produce ziti or other tubular-shaped noodles.

Warranty: 1 year.

Approx. retail price	**Approx. low price**
$50	**$34**

Prices are accurate at time of printing but are subject to manufacturers' changes.

BREAD MAKERS

BLACK & DECKER ALL-IN-ONE PLUS AUTOMATIC BREADMAKER B1800

✓BEST BUY

The Black & Decker All-in-One Plus Automatic Breadmaker is the easiest way to enjoy fresh-baked bread anytime. Just add the ingredients and let the machine do the work. Finished bread takes from three to four hours. Or, set the timer for up to a 12-hour delay before breadmaking is completed. The Automatic Breadmaker can be set to make loaves up to two pounds, as well as letting you select light to dark crust color. You can also choose whole-grain or specialty bread settings or make dough for pizza, bagels, croissants, or pretzels. A viewing window at the top of the machine lets you check on the progress of your bread without opening the machine.

Warranty: 2 years.

Approx. retail price	**Approx. low price**
$180	**$165**

OSTER BREADMAKER 4811/4812

✓BEST BUY

The Oster Breadmaker is an easy-to-use, quality bread-making machine. You can select from four different bread types: white, whole wheat, French, or sweet. The machine can also be set to make white, whole wheat, or sweet dough only (without baking the bread). Crust color options are light, medium, and dark. The Oster Breadmaker lets you make either a large (1½-pound) or small (1-pound) loaf. Other features include a viewing window to let you check on your bread, a ten-minute cooldown cycle that removes hot air from the baking chamber and keeps the bread from getting soggy, and a delay-bake option that lets you set the time your bread will be ready—from 3 hours 45 minutes to 13 hours.

Warranty: 2 years, limited.

Prices are accurate at time of printing but are subject to manufacturers' changes.

Approx. retail price | **Approx. low price**
$150 (model 4811) | **$150**
$190 (model 4812) | **$183**

TOASTMASTER BREAD BOX 1195

Recommended

The Toastmaster Bread Box has eight bread settings: basic light, medium, and dark; whole wheat light, medium, and dark; French; and sweet bread. You can also choose a dough-only cycle and a butter cycle that churns fresh butter from cream in 30 minutes. This unit makes a 1- to 2-pound loaf. Cycles take anywhere from just under 3 hours to 4½ hours. Dough can be made in 1½ hours. The mixing steps tend to be a bit noisy but, during rising and baking, the machine is almost silent. Other features include a viewing window that lets you check on bread without opening the lid, digital push-button controls, a bread-warming feature that keeps bread warm for up to one hour after baking, and a nonstick loaf pan.

Warranty: 1 year, limited.

Approx. retail price | **Approx. low price**
$216 | **$185**

COFFEEMAKERS

The variety of coffeemakers available today can be bewildering. No matter which type you decide to purchase, however, a few criteria apply to almost all models.

First, consider the type of filter you prefer to use. Most (but not all) coffeemakers accept either permanent metal filters or disposable paper filters. Permanent filters are costly, but you'll never run out and the cost is often recovered within a year. Paper filters trap more coffee grounds and oils, providing a clearer brew and somewhat different taste.

Next, find out the brewing temperature of any model you're considering. The Specialty Coffee Association of America recommends 200°F plus or minus 5°F. Higher heat tends to extract bitter oils and burn or decompose the complex organic compounds responsible for flavors. Less heat underextracts flavors, resulting in a weak brew and forcing you to use more coffee.

Prices are accurate at time of printing but are subject to manufacturers' changes.

Automatic Drip Coffeemakers

Automatic drip coffeemakers consist of a base, usually with a warmer built in, water reservoir, filter holder, and decanter. From that basic design hundreds of variations have evolved. Select features, such as the ability to sneak a cup or two while brewing continues, based on your needs. If you're forgetful, an automatic warmer shutoff is critical, as is automatic brewing if you simply must have coffee ready the moment you awake. If your needs are simple, consider a less costly model with fewer frills.

Large-Capacity Automatic Drip Coffeemakers

MR. COFFEE ACCEL 12-CUP COFFEEMAKER PRX20

✓BEST BUY

Mr. Coffee's Accel models claim to have "accelerated brewing for better flavor." The PRX20 delivers 12 cups in under eight minutes. A carafe-activated Pause 'n Serve drip-stop valve allows you to remove the carafe to sneak a cup while coffee is brewing. The removable filter basket means an end to carrying dripping coffee filters to the wastebasket. The wide-mouth decanter doesn't drip and has a knuckle-guard handle to prevent burns. The digital clock timer allows programmed brewing and two-hour automatic shutoff. Easily mastered push buttons set the clock and program brewing. The water reservoir opens wide and has easy-to-read internal fill marks. Available in white, black, and green, this unit also has hidden cord storage.

Warranty: parts and labor, 1 year.

Approx. retail price	**Approx. low price**
$50	**$35**

BRAUN FLAVORSELECT COFFEEMAKER 157

✓BEST BUY

If you so choose, Braun's FlavorSelect can adjust the strength of the brew from robust to mild. The main water charge is delivered to the coffee basket at 198°F–205°F. Fully adjustable, the Flavor-Select dial atop the unit lets you decide how strong to make the coffee. The nicely shaped carafe handle is easy on the hand, and the tight lid with small openings keeps flavors in and pours easily. The removable filter holder prevents spilled grounds and dripped coffee. This model has an exterior water level indicator. Front-mounted controls allow you to select 1–3 cups or full delivery. Braun's design is sleek and won't hog counter space. Color selection is limited to black or white.

Warranty: 1 year.

Approx. retail price	**Approx. low price**
$50	**$50**

MELITTA IBS-10CT PERFECT PULSE

✓BEST BUY

In the Melitta Perfect Pulse, water is heated and collected above the coffee cone, then released in timed 195°F "gushes" to saturate and churn the grounds, resulting in rich coffee taste and full extraction from all grounds. The flip-back water reservoir lid fills easily. The front-mounted push-button controls are easy to find and easy to use, including the programmed wake-up feature. A bright red clock display has large numbers and displays hours and minutes until automatic shutoff once you've made coffee. Hidden cord storage keeps your counter free of electrical cord tangle. The unit has two minor drawbacks: Water level markings are internal with no external display to guide water addition, and the Melitta requires paper filters—permanent filter cones produce very weak coffee.

Warranty: repair or replacement, 1 year; 30-day "taste" guarantee.

Approx. retail price	**Approx. low price**
$85	**$50**

BLACK & DECKER OPTIMA SPACEMAKER ODC 350

Recommended

The new all-white Optima Spacemaker ODC 350 is installed under a cabinet. The included mounting tem-plate and brackets fit this model to virtually any cabinet. This model offers prechosen brewing start time, 1–3 or 4-to-maximum cup options, and a bright green digital clock. Most controls are hidden behind a hinged door; only the clock and on-off/auto-off buttons are normally visible. The removable water container permits installation in any location and has a visible water gauge. Brewing time is short and the 193°F brewing temperature is near-optimum for flavorful coffee. The Sneak-a-Cup feature permits pouring a cup or two while brewing continues. The warming plate can be adjusted to shut off after one to four hours, and the machine can be programmed to begin brewing any time within the next 24 hours. Once programmed, the time is held in memory so you don't have to reprogram every day. The unit comes with an adhesive cord hook to keep extra cord out of harm's way and a package of coffee filters to get you started.

Warranty: 2 years.

Approx. retail price	**Approx. low price**
$79	**$76**

Small Automatic Drip Coffeemakers

MR. COFFEE ACCEL 4-CUP COFFEEMAKER PR5

✓ BEST BUY

Mr. Coffee's Accel models speed up the brewing process; the PR5 delivers all four cups in under four minutes. Mr. Coffee claims that accelerated brewing delivers better flavor. The unit's lighted on-off switch indicates power status, and a decanter-activated Pause 'n Serve feature allows you to remove the carafe for up to 30 seconds to sneak a cup while coffee is brewing. The removable inner filter basket is a great convenience. Both decanter and reservoir have easy-to-read fill marks, and the reservoir lid opens wide for easy filling.

Warranty: parts and labor, 1 year.

Approx. retail price	**Approx. low price**
$25	**$22**

KRUPS CAFE PRIMA 105

Recommended

Cafe Prima quickly brews four cups of coffee with available permanent filters or common #2 filters. The unit's stacked design occupies minimal counter space. Controls are few: A lighted on-off switch signals operational status and a front-mounted magnified sight glass tells you how much water you've added. Cafe Prima's lid flips back for easy water addition, and its few corners and Teflon-coated hot plate make cleanup a snap. This model comes with a self-storing cord, coffee scoop, and starter filters. Cafe Prima uses Krups's "Deep Brew" technology of timed pulses, multi-point water distribution (at a modest 185°F), and double-wall filter holder to produce robust coffee. The lower water temperature does require a bit of extra coffee for full flavor.

Warranty: repair or replacement, 1 year.

Approx. retail price	**Approx. low price**
$36	**$30**

PERCOLATORS

Percolators brew coffee by passing heated liquid over coarsely ground coffee. Each coffeemaker is a self-contained carafe with a heater, permanent coffee basket, and lid. Many have detachable cords. Percolators brew quickly (usually a cup per minute), don't take up much counter space, and are available in stainless steel or self-insulating plastic. Cleaning is quick and easy and storage space is minimal. For parties, larger percolator urns brew 12–30 cups, and 100-cup models are available.

Small-Capacity Percolator

FARBERWARE 134B

BEST BUY

Brewing two to four cups with the Farberware 134B is swift, due to its 1,000-watt heater. This model has all stainless steel construction, including the coffee basket and lid,

Prices are accurate at time of printing but are subject to manufacturers' changes.

and stay-cool handles. Once coffee is finished brewing, the 134B resets itself to keep the coffee hot. Cleanup is easy, and the unit's small size makes storage a breeze. Stainless steel coffeemakers from Farberware have earned their reputation for durability, longevity, and ease of use.

Warranty: repair or replacement, 1 year.

Approx. retail price	**Approx. low price**
$60	**$43**

Large-Capacity Percolator

FARBERWARE 142B

✓BEST BUY

The Farberware 142B's powerful 1,000-watt heater quickly brews coffee in less than one minute per cup, then resets itself for keeping the coffee warm. Built of durable stainless steel throughout, it should last for years. Safety features include a snap-in lid and stay-cool handles. One minor drawback is a hard-to-read water level indicator caused by shallow embossing of the numbers and lines on the coffeemaker's surface.

Warranty: repair or replacement, 1 year.

Approx. retail price	**Approx. low price**
$80	**$58**

Party-Size Percolator

FARBERWARE L1200

✓BEST BUY

With its handsome urn, the Farberware L1200 shows off classic styling that's at home at any social gathering. With a 10–22-cup capacity, it requires less than a minute to brew each cup. This model uses a plastic brew basket to contain either regular or percolator grind coffees; raised markings provide visual water level indication. No cover is used for the brew basket, as the lid performs this function. The lid swivels to lock into the handles to prevent spills or accidental scalding. When coffee is ready, a front-mounted indicator light comes on. The stainless steel interior is easy to clean and maintain. The two-position spigot serves single-cup portions or locks open to fill a carafe. The spigot disassembles for cleaning.

Warranty: repair or replacement, 1 year.

Approx. retail price	**Approx. low price**
$125	**$113**

ESPRESSO MACHINES

In recent years, espresso has become familiar to most Americans—and the trend is gaining steam. The mark of true espresso is **crema,** a layer of caramel-colored foam atop the rich coffee essence. Crema is the result of gases and coffee colloids combining under pressure, and it's a standard for judging espresso. Weak or nonexistent crema indicates a steam boiler machine or improper use of a pump machine. Dark crema indicates too fine a grind or overtamping.

If you're thinking of buying an espresso machine, you should be familiar with some terminology. The **portafilter** is the handle and brew basket that holds the coffee. A **group** is the brew head where water exits.

There are three types of espresso machines:

Pump machines: These machines operate by forcing water at a lower temperature (190°F–197°F is recommended by the Specialty Coffee Association of America) through two tablespoons per cup of finely ground coffee in 20 to 30 seconds. Pressures of 9 to 15 bar (about 9 to 15 atmospheres) are common. Thermo bloc units heat water on demand in a tightly coiled pump. Boiler models heat water in a pressurized boiler typically made of stainless steel or brass. Brass retains heat better.

Steam boiler machines: These units develop about 2.5 bar of pressure and will make great strong coffee. But their water temperature is above 200°F, which overextracts the coffee for espresso production, and the pressure is inadequate to totally extract the coffee's essence. For these reasons, no steam boiler machines have been included in this chapter.

Prices are accurate at time of printing but are subject to manufacturers' changes.

Piston/manual machines: To use these units, the operator must pressurize the water after it is heated in a boiler. Manual espresso machines require a much greater amount of skill and patience to operate than the other types.

Pump Espresso Machines (Under $125)

BRIEL LIDO ES-15

✓BEST BUY

Briel's entry-priced Lido rivals machines that cost far more. This unit features a stainless steel boiler, 15-bar self-priming pump with ten-year warranty, and Briel's Crema Master filter basket for rich crema. Quick to reach operating temperature, the Lido pumps water at 188°F–190°F for optimum extraction. Steam production is quick, powerful, and long-lasting. Briel's Aqua-Stop no-drip system prevents most of the mess after brewing. Milk frothing is quick and easy, and the steam wand pops off for easy cleaning. Top-mounted switches govern on-off, pump, and steam. A rotary control modulates steam. The removable water reservoir fills from the top, and there is a built-in water filter.

Warranty: repair or replacement, 1 year; pump, 10 years.

Approx. retail price	**Approx. low price**
$115	**$98**

SALTON CAPPUCCINO DOLCE PE70

Recommended

Salton's Dolce PE70 addresses the problem of crema with a pressure-enhancing rubber disk it calls a crema disk. It works: Dolce produces a respectable crema with ease. The unit uses a thermo bloc heater. Dolce has easily-understood top-mounted switches and pilot lights to indicate on-off, pump ready, and availability of steam for frothing. A long, swiveling steam nozzle permits the use of most frothing pitchers without difficulty or spills. Salton includes a well-produced videotape to explain all facets of operation. Standard accessories also include a tamper and coffee scoop. Unfortunately, the Dolce produces weaker crema and milk foam.

Prices are accurate at time of printing but are subject to manufacturers' changes.

Warranty: repair or replacement, 1 year.

Approx. retail price $100 | **Approx. low price** $70

Pump Espresso Machines ($125–$250)

BRIEL CHAMONIX ES-35

✔ BEST BUY

The Briel Chamonix ES-35 has a 1200-watt stainless steel boiler, dual thermostats (brew and steam), 15-bar pump with ten-year warranty, Crema Master filter for perfect crema with almost any coffee, and turbo-jet frother. Like other Briel machines, this one delivers 190°F–195°F water to the filter basket for optimum flavor extraction. Additional features are the Quick Froth Cappuccino continuous milk frothing device, a built-in tamper, and storage for the coffee scoop under a lid that also hides a water intake. Most appealing is the Auto Espresso Flow, a microchip control device that precisely measures espresso into your cup(s). Auto flow settings can dispense doses as small as 1¾ ounces or as large as 6 ounces, after which it shuts off the pump and Briel's Aqua Stop feature minimizes dripping. Both the turbo-jet frother and Quick Froth Cappuccino produce beautifully steamed and frothed milk quickly, and cleanup is easy. Water capacity is generous and has a visible gauge. Design is smart: There are three ways to add water and three different power cord exits.

Warranty: repair or replacement, 1 year; pump, 10 years.

Approx. retail price $200 | **Approx. low price** $175

KRUPS PRONTO 988

✔ BEST BUY

Easy to use, the Krups Pronto 988's thermo block heating system is quick to deliver the first shot at 190°F. The Krups system heats water up to three times faster than competitors. This model makes exceptional milk foam with its microchip-monitored steam pump delivering "dry" steam to a Perfect Froth attachment. The Pronto produces perfect crema and mounds of milk foam. Its modest size conserves precious space. Operating controls include a front-mounted on-off switch and indicator light, yellow thermostat light, and center-mounted Steam/Off/Espresso switch. Ready light indicates proper water temperature for steam or brew. The Pronto provides an overhead warming plate to prewarm cups as the machine heats. The visible 37-ounce water container is easy to monitor, and the large drip tray collects spills effectively. Krups also includes a tamper and coffee scoop.

Warranty: repair or replacement, 1 year.

Approx. retail price	Approx. low price
$245	**$223**

Piston/Manual Espresso Machine

LA PAVONI EUROPICCOLA (CHROME)

✓BEST BUY

La Pavoni machines are unremittingly old-fashioned—and beautiful. Models are available in combinations of brass, copper, and rosewood. The Europiccola is finely crafted, durable, and requires skill and involvement on the part of the owner. The simple boiler takes minutes to reach operating temperature. Milk frothing is simple—steam production is prodigious and forceful. This machine retains the heart and soul of espresso but requires patience and learning of the operator.

Warranty: 1 year.

Approx. retail price	Approx. low price
$489	**$450**

COFFEE GRINDERS

Flywheel/Blade Coffee Grinder

KRUPS FAST-TOUCH COFFEE MILL 203

✓BEST BUY

Krups Fast-Touch coffee mill grinds three ounces of coffee beans, enough for up to 15 cups of coffee, in seconds. The grinder's oval shape encourages uniform, eve grinding and makes pouring ground coffee straight into you coffeemaker easy. The blades are stainless steel and shouldn require sharpening for years. Cleanup is simple, and th diminutive size is a plus in a crowded kitchen.

Warranty: repair or replacement, 1 year.

Approx. retail price	**Approx. low price**
$28	**$23**

Cone/Burr Coffee Grinders

BRAUN AROMATIC COFFEE MILL KMM 30

✔ BEST BUY

Heavy duty despite the light price, Braun's KMM 30 coffee mill will deliver years of service. The large bea storage container holds approximately ½ pound, easily a week worth for most folks. Rotating the container adjusts millin fineness to 24 levels; the steel milling disks grind coffee fin enough for some espresso machines or coarse enough for French Press coffeemaker or percolator. The clockwork timer/or off switch controls the amount of coffee ground for consister day-to-day results. A cylindrical coffee receptacle holds groun coffee for up to 12 cups and is easily inserted or removed fro the grinder body. Body and container mate well for minimal co fee dust, and the unit easily disassembles for complete cleanin The cord self-stores beneath the housing.

Warranty: 1 year.

Approx. retail price	**Approx. low price**
$55	**$50**

LA PAVONI PGC GRINDER

✔ BEST BUY

A heavy-duty grinder, the La Pavoni PGC features two methods of dispensing coffee ground between tem pered steel disks. You can dispense it directly into a large, tight sealed hopper or remove the hopper to let coffee flow direct into your portafilter handle. Hopper capacity is a quart pound, and you can select nine settings from fine to coarse. This is a relatively quiet grinder. Coffee dispensing, even into an open portafilter handle, is quite direct with little spillover.

Warranty: parts and labor, 1 year.

Approx. retail price	**Approx. low price**
$179	**$170**

BRIEL JAVA GRINDER CG5

Recommended

Briel's Java is a very high-speed, all-purpose grinder with interchangeable coffee receptacles. Small size, good looks, and rapid grinding are features of note. This model will grind exceedingly fine coffee (the first four settings produce flourlike grinds suitable for Turkish coffee) or produce drip or percolator grinds amazingly fast. The Java is louder and messier than the other models tested. In addition, the bean hopper, though of large capacity, has thin walls that might crack easily. This unit is a good budget choice for espresso machines needing very fine coffee or for homes with both coffee machines and espresso makers.

Warranty: 1 year.

Approx. retail price	**Approx. low price**
$100	**$90**

Prices are accurate at time of printing but are subject to manufacturers' changes.

MICROWAVE OVENS

Microwave ovens today can do much more than reheat left-overs, defrost frozen foods, and cook popcorn. With fea-tures such as automatic sensors, browning elements, combi-nation convection cooking, and built-in range hoods, thes appliances are finally taking center stage in the kitchen. Mi-crowave ovens can make short work of many labor-intensiv recipes as easily as they can reheat coffee.

What size microwave do you need? That depends on whethe you plan to cook entire family-size casseroles in your microwav or just heat up meals for one. Most microwave recipes an cookbooks require an oven with at least 650 watts of powe Compact/subcompact ovens have capacities of up to 0.7 cubi foot and usually have 700 watts of power or less. Medium-siz microwaves range from 0.8 to 1.0 cubic foot in capacity an usually have about 800 watts of power. Full-size microwaves recommended for larger families, are over 1.0 cubic foot in ca-pacity and are rated at 900 watts and up.

Features and Terminology

Turntables are revolving platforms that allow microwaves t penetrate food evenly. Many microwave cookbooks recom-mend manually turning foods if the oven does not have turntable. Glass turntables are standard in microwave oven made today; models with convection ovens usually have porce-lain enamel turntables.

Convection ovens are most valuable when the microwav has a combination convection/microwave setting. The mar-riage of the microwave's quick-cooking abilities and the con-vection's browning and crisping abilities is very useful. Con-vection ovens work by circulating air heated by an electri element. Microwave/convection ovens often contain metal in-teriors, which can slow down microwave cooking time an aren't as easy to clean as the traditional plastic-lined microwav interiors. Another disadvantage of metal interiors is that unlik plastic, the metal becomes very hot to the touch.

Browning dishes/trays/elements all help the microwave turn out crispy, browned foods. Browning dishes are special utensils with a metal content on the bottom that allow the microwave to crisp potatoes and other foods. Browning trays generally need to be preheated several minutes before using and do not perform as well as a traditional oven. Browning elements are similar to broilers in traditional ovens and can help the microwave crisp foods better and more evenly.

Automatic sensors determine when the food is heated by the amount of steam in the oven. The oven then shuts off. These sensors are not foolproof, however; it may still be necessary to stop the oven and check the food's temperature.

Temperature probes work continuously to determine when a food reaches a preset temperature. The probe will automatically turn off the microwave oven when the food reaches that temperature.

Demonstration modes use interactive screens to explain the oven's features and familiarize the consumer with using the microwave oven.

One-button cooking allows you to cook popcorn, potatoes, pizza, or beverages by pressing just one button. If you frequently prepare one food, consider this feature when purchasing a microwave. Another one-button feature is something called minute-plus; this gives you the ability to add an extra minute to a food's cooking time without turning the oven off.

Automatic reheat/automatic defrost/automatic start are preprogrammable functions that allow you to reheat or defrost a food, often with a single push of a button. For automatic defrost, you program in the weight of the food, and the oven selects the correct time. Usually the oven works at several different power levels for a length of time based on the weight of the food. Automatic start is a feature that allows you to program the oven up to 12 hours in advance to turn on at a specific time.

Interactive displays or word prompts are available on the higher-end models. These display digital information on a screen to guide you through the microwave's use. Prompts tell you when you need to reset the clock or ask you to specify a weight when defrosting a food.

Language/weight option allows you to view the instructions display in languages other than English (usually Spanish and French) and switch the weight display between ounces and kilograms.

Best Buys '96

Our Best Buy, Recommended, and Budget Buy choices follow. The unit we consider to be the best of the Best Buys is listed first, followed by our second choice, and so on. Remember that a Best Buy, Recommended, or Budget Buy designation applies only to the model listed. It does not necessarily apply to other models made by the same manufacturer.

FULL-SIZE MICROWAVE OVENS

GENERAL ELECTRIC JE1540GV

✓BEST BUY

The JE1540GNV is a full-size, 1.5-cubic-foot microwave oven with some nice features. This model is greystone with a black door, but it is also available in white (JE1540WV) and almond (JE1540AV). It has 900 watts of power and ten power levels. Features include an auto start/reminder, an add-30-seconds pad, two timed cooking settings, and a child lockout feature. This oven has convenience cooking controls with beverage, cook, popcorn, snacks, and reheat pads. A kit to convert it to a built-in oven is available at an additional cost.

Specifications: Overall dimensions: height $13\frac{7}{16}$"; width, $23\frac{9}{16}$"; depth, $15\frac{7}{8}$"; capacity, 1.5 cubic feet. Cavity dimensions: height, $10\frac{11}{16}$"; width, $15\frac{15}{16}$"; depth, $14\frac{13}{16}$". Cooking power: 900 watts. **Warranty:** parts and labor, 1 year; magnetron tube, 10 years.

Approx. retail price	**Approx. low price**
$220	**$220**

SHARP R-4A87

✓BEST BUY

This Sharp family-size model introduces an industry first: a Custom Help key on the control panel, which il-

Prices are accurate at time of printing but are subject to manufacturers' changes.

lustrates this full-featured microwave's little extras—audible signal elimination, language/weight options, automatic start at a later time—and even gives cooking hints. A new "Touch On" feature offers immediate control—it operates the oven while your finger touches the key. This microwave oven has all the standard features: a four-stage programmable memory, automatic defrost, a childproof lock, a 14⅛-inch-diameter turntable, and a minute-plus control. The R-4A87 is stone gray; the same model is available in white as model R-4A97.

Specifications: Overall dimensions: height, 21⅝"; width, 12⅜"; depth, 17⅜"; capacity, 1.2 cubic feet. Cavity dimensions: height, 15"; width, 8½"; depth, 16¾". Cooking power: 900 watts. **Warranty:** parts and labor, 1 year; magnetron tube, 5 years.

Approx. retail price	**Approx. low price**
$250	**$215**

SHARP R-5H16

BEST BUY

The R-5H16 is Sharp's top-of-the-line microwave oven. It is the largest model (1.6 cubic feet) reviewed here, and its 16-inch turntable is the largest on the market. A whopping 1,000 watts of power provides for fast cooking, and an automatic sensor lets you know when the food is heated. This model has four instant-start sensor keys: reheat, frozen entree, popcorn, and baked potato. The audible signal can be eliminated for quieter operation. The R-5H16 is available in white on white; R-5H06 is the same model in stone gray with a clear oven door. An optional kit is available for wall oven installation.

Specifications: Overall dimensions: height, 13¼"; width, 24"; depth, 19"; capacity, 1.6 cubic feet. Cavity dimensions: height, 9¼"; width, 16⅞"; depth, 17⅜". Cooking power: 1,000 watts. **Warranty:** parts and labor, 1 year; magnetron tube, 5 years.

Approx. retail price	**Approx. low price**
$440	**$306**

PANASONIC NN-6605A

BEST BUY

The NN-6605A is a black, 1.2-cubic-foot microwave oven with 925 watts of power. It is available in white

Prices are accurate at time of printing but are subject to manufacturers' changes.

as model NN-6655. Its multilingual menu action screen lets you view the menu in three languages and switch from ounces to kilograms. Other features include demonstration mode, a popcorn key, automatic defrosting, a minute-plus key, and a childproof lock. This model has six categories of sensor cooking and a one-touch sensor reheat button.

Specifications: Overall dimensions: height, 12″; width, 21⅞″; depth, 16¾″; capacity, 1.2 cubic feet. Cavity dimensions: height, 8⅝″; width, 14¾″; depth, 15 9/16″. Cooking power: 925 watts. **Warranty:** parts and labor, 1 year; magnetron tube, 5 years.

Approx. retail price	**Approx. low price**
$230	**$181**

MEDIUM-SIZE MICROWAVE OVENS

SHARP R-3A87

✓BEST BUY

Sharp is quickly becoming the industry leader in providing versatile microwave ovens for a good value. The R-3A87 has the most features for the lowest price of all the medium-size models reviewed here. It has four different popcorn settings: regular, regular light, snack, and snack light. It has a large, 12¾-inch turntable and automatic defrosting. A custom help feature calls attention to "hidden" features. The Sharp Interactive Cooking System provides feedback and guides the user in microwave use. Other features include a seven-digit interactive display to show entire words of instructions, demonstration mode, language/weight options, a minute-plus key to add time while the oven is in use, a childproof lock, audible signal elimination, and programmable four-stage cooking memory. This model is stone gray with 0.9 cubic foot of capacity and 850 watts of power. The R-3A97 is the same model in white.

Specifications: Overall dimensions: height, 12″; width, 20½″; depth, 15⅜″; capacity, 0.9 cubic foot. Cavity dimensions: height, 7¾″; width, 13¾″; depth, 14½″. Cooking power: 850

watts. **Warranty:** parts and labor, 1 year; magnetron tube, 5 years.

Approx. retail price **$230** | **Approx. low price** **$176**

SHARP R-3K97

BEST BUY

This model is similar to the Sharp R-3A87, but it has an automatic sensor—recommended for reheating take-out food, leftovers, and canned or precooked food. The R-3K97 also includes all the features found in the R-3A87. This model is white; the R-3K87 is the same model in stone gray.

Specifications: Overall dimensions: height, 12″; width, 20½″; depth, 15⅜″; capacity, 0.9 cubic foot. Cavity dimensions: height, 7¾″; width, 13¾″; depth, 14½″. Cooking power: 850 watts. **Warranty:** parts and labor, 1 year; magnetron tube, 5 years.

Approx. retail price **$250** | **Approx. low price** **$250**

PANASONIC NN-5655A

BEST BUY

The NN-5655A is an 850-watt microwave with a white exterior; it is available in black as model NN-5605A. With the sensor reheat key, it will automatically reheat a plate of food—meat, poultry, casseroles, side dishes, soups, sauces, or gravy—with one keystroke. It also has a popcorn selection and automatic defrosting. The multilingual menu action screen allows you to view the display in three languages and switch the weight display from ounces to kilograms. A childproof safety lock, interactive word prompts, and a minute-plus key are also included.

Specifications: Overall dimensions: height, 12″; width, 20″; depth, 14 3/16″; capacity, 0.8 cubic foot. Cavity dimensions: height, 7⅞″; width, 13″; depth, 13″. Cooking power: 850 watts. **Warranty:** parts and labor, 1 year; magnetron tube, 5 years.

Approx. retail price **$200** | **Approx. low price** **$180**

Prices are accurate at time of printing but are subject to manufacturers' changes.

COMPACT/SUBCOMPACT MICROWAVE OVENS

GENERAL ELECTRIC JE48A

✓BEST BUY

This 0.4-cubic-foot, 575-watt subcompact model is ideal for reheating leftovers and heating beverages. It has a timed defrost setting, a 99-minute-99-second timer, and ten power levels. The JE48A has a word prompting display and a space-saving design, with a wood-grain exterior and a black oven door. An optional hanging kit can be purchased for an additional cost.

Specifications: Overall dimensions: height, $9\frac{1}{4}$"; width, 18"; depth, $12\frac{5}{16}$"; capacity, 0.4 cubic foot. Cavity dimensions: height, $5\frac{9}{16}$"; width, 11"; depth, 11". Cooking power: 575 watts. **Warranty:** parts and labor, 1 year; magnetron tube, 5 years.

Approx. retail price **$130** | **Approx. low price** **$83**

GENERAL ELECTRIC JE640GV

✓BEST BUY

This compact model has a 0.6-cubic-foot oven capacity and operates at 700 watts. It has several convenience-cooking touchpads including settings for beverage, cook, popcorn, snacks, and reheat. Other features include a kitchen timer, an on/off beeper, and both timed defrosting and automatic defrosting. An under-cabinet hanging kit is available at extra cost. This model is greystone with a black door; it also comes in white as model JE640WV.

Specifications: Overall dimensions: height, $10\frac{3}{8}$"; width, $18\frac{3}{4}$"; depth, $12\frac{1}{2}$"; capacity, 0.6 cubic foot. Cavity dimensions: height, $8\frac{3}{8}$"; width, $11\frac{3}{8}$"; depth, $11\frac{12}{26}$". Cooking power: 700 watts. **Warranty:** parts and labor, 1 year; magnetron tube, 10 years.

Approx. retail price **$180** | **Approx. low price** **$158**

Prices are accurate at time of printing but are subject to manufacturers' changes.

SHARP R-2M56

Budget Buy

Since this 0.7-cubic-foot, 600-watt model has a manual dial rather than the usual digital control panels, it does not have such features as power levels and instant cook pads. It does, however, come with a 10¾-inch-diameter turntable and an easy-to-set timer with automatic shutoff. It has a white cabinet with a black see-through door. Its price makes this model an ideal office microwave for heating liquids and other simple jobs.

Specifications: Overall dimensions: height, 11¼″; width, 19⅞″; depth, 13″; capacity, 0.7 cubic foot. Cavity dimensions: height, 7⅛″; width, 13⅜″; depth, 11⅞″. Cooking power: 600 watts. **Warranty:** parts and labor, 1 year; magnetron tube, 5 years.

Approx. retail price	Approx. low price
$100	$100

OVER-THE-RANGE MICROWAVE OVENS

GENERAL ELECTRIC JVM250AV

✓ BEST BUY

The JVM250AV is a 1.1-cubic-foot, 850-watt over-the-range microwave oven. This model comes in almond; it is also available in black as JVM250BV and white as JVM250WV. The versatile sensor cooking control has separate touchpads for popcorn, beverage, auto reheat, auto cook, and auto roast using the temperature probe provided. It has a five-stage programmable cooking function and a two-speed, high-capacity exhaust fan. Other features include a night-light, a variable-volume beeper, and a removable double-duty shelf that also functions as a turntable.

Specifications: Overall dimensions: height, 16½″; width, 29⅞″; depth, 14″; capacity, 1.1 cubic feet. Cavity dimensions: height, 8⅛″; width, 18″; depth, 12½″. Cooking power: 850 watts. **Warranty:** parts and labor, 1 year; magnetron tube, 10 years.

Approx. retail price	Approx. low price
$480	$448

Prices are accurate at time of printing but are subject to manufacturers' changes.

SHARP R-1440

✓BEST BUY

This 850-watt, 1.1-cubic-foot model has a demonstration mode to introduce you to its many features. It automatically defrosts foods by weight and has a four-stage cooking memory and a minute-plus key. Preprogrammed keys set time and power by serving size. Some of the preprogrammed keys include coffee/tea, fresh roll/muffin, frozen roll/muffin, hot cereal, scrambled eggs, dinner plate, frozen main dish, pasta/casserole, pizza slice, popcorn, and soup. Two cooktop lights, a childproof lock, a 12-inch-diameter glass turntable, and an audible signal eliminator are some of the other features. The R-1440 has a stirrer fan system. The blower fan is rated at 235 cfm (cubic feet per minute) for vertical venting and 230 cfm for horizontal venting. A charcoal filter kit and a filter panel kit are two optional accessories sold separately for nonducted installations. This model is black; it also comes in white as R-1441.

Specifications: Overall dimensions: height, 15¾"; width, 29⅞"; depth, 14"; capacity, 1.1 cubic feet. Cavity dimensions: height, 7¾"; width, 18⅛"; depth, 13¼". Cooking power: 850 watts. **Warranty:** parts and labor, 1 year; magnetron tube, 7 years.

Approx. retail price	**Approx. low price**
$450	**$395**

KITCHENAID KHMS105B

✓BEST BUY

This sleek over-the-range model is a nice full-featured microwave with 1.1 cubic feet of oven space and 850 watts of power. It is available in black or, for an extra $30, white or almond. It has an electronic touch control timer, delay start option, auto sensor, custom defrost, and an electronic temperature probe. The two-speed exhaust system can be installed to be either vented or nonvented.

Specifications: Overall dimensions: height, 16"; width, 29⅞"; depth, 13⅞"; capacity, 1.1 cubic feet. Cavity dimensions: height, 8⅞"; width, 13"; depth, 12 9/16". Cooking power: 850 watts. **Warranty:** parts and labor, 1 year; electronic controls, 5 years; magnetron tube, 10 years.

Approx. retail price
$530

Approx. low price
$500

OVER-THE-RANGE MICROWAVE/CONVECTION OVENS

GENERAL ELECTRIC JVM290

✓ BEST BUY

This 1.0-cubic-foot model has GE's Circuwave system, in which the microwaves work in a circular fashion. It is available in white, almond, or black and has 800 watts of power. Included are a broiler pan and rack; sensor cook pads for popcorn, beverage, and reheat; variable beeper volume; and a two-speed exhaust fan with a cooktop light and night-light. An add-30-seconds pad increases cooking time while the oven is operating. The express cook feature can program ten power levels. The minute pad operates the oven for one minute. This model also has a delayed start feature. The convection oven's selections include combination microwave-convection cooking and combination microwave-convection roasting using a temperature probe.

Specifications: Overall dimensions: height, 15½"; width, 30"; depth, 14¼"; capacity, 1.0 cubic foot. Cavity dimensions: height, 8 1/16"; width, 18"; depth, 12½". Cooking power: 800 watts. **Warranty**: parts and labor, 1 year; magnetron tube, 10 years.

Approx. retail price
$720

Approx. low price
$679

KITCHENAID KHMC107B

✓ BEST BUY

This stylish, 1.1-cubic-foot, 850-watt model comes in black; you can purchase the same model in almond or white for $30 more. It has two convection cycles and three combination microwave-convection cycles. Some of the features are an automatic sensor, custom defrost, and a popcorn cycle. The two-speed exhaust hood can be installed vented or nonvented.

Prices are accurate at time of printing but are subject to manufacturers' changes.

Specifications: Overall dimensions: height, 16″; width, 29⅞″; depth, 13⅞″; capacity, 1.1 cubic feet. Cavity dimensions: height, 8⅞″; width, 13″; depth, $12\frac{9}{16}$″. Cooking power: 850 watts. **Warranty:** parts and labor, 1 year; convection element and electronic controls, 5 years; magnetron tube, 10 years.

Approx. retail price	Approx. low price
$790	$709

MICROWAVE/CONVECTION OVEN

SHARP R-9H66

✓BEST BUY

The R-9H66 offers both convection and microwave cooking for a great price. It comes in white; the R-9H76 is the same model in metallic charcoal with a black door. It can be transformed into a built-in model with an optional trim kit. The oven has a stainless interior and a porcelain enamel turntable with a diameter of 15⅜ inches. Both a broiling trivet and baking rack are included. The four-way cooking system browns, bakes, broils, or crisps. The broil key preheats the oven and signals when ready. This full-featured oven also includes a sensor with eight food choices. Other features are automatic start, minute-plus, a cook-and-simmer level, a slow-cook level, and a programmable four-stage memory.

Specifications: Overall dimensions: height, 14⅞″; width, 24⅝″; depth, 18¾″; capacity, 1.5 cubic feet. Cavity dimensions: height, 9⅝″; width, 16⅛″; depth, 16⅛″. Cooking power: 900 watts. **Warranty:** parts and labor, 1 year; magnetron tube, 5 years.

Approx. retail price	Approx. low price
$550	$550

Prices are accurate at time of printing but are subject to manufacturers' changes.

RANGES

Today's cooking appliances provide more choices than ever before. New technologies offer a greater choice in burner styles and even ranges that can be programmed electronically. Ranges, cooktops, and ovens today are more powerful and easier to clean.

Gas or Electric?

Unless you plan to undertake a costly remodeling job, your choice of a gas or electric range may be dictated by your present kitchen setup. Electric ranges require a 208- or 240-volt line. Gas ranges need to be hooked up to a gas line, as well as a 115-volt outlet for the lights, clock, and burner-ignition system.

People who prefer cooking with gas enjoy its instant response time and the visible flame. Gas ranges are slightly more expensive than electric. A traditional burner on a gas range produces about 9,000 Btu (British thermal units).

People who use electric ranges enjoy the even heat of electric ovens, the slow simmering possible with electric burners, and the variety of burner styles available today. The traditional burner is the electric coil, but radiant smooth-top cooktops—a flat ceramic-glass surface above an electric coil—are quite popular. Smooth-top cooktops are easy to clean, but they can be used only with flat-bottomed metal cookware. Halogen burners, which heat up somewhat faster than the other burners, are often added to smooth-top cooktops. Magnetic induction cooktops heat up instantly and heat only the pot, not the cooktop surface. They require special cookware.

Range Designs

A freestanding range has a cooktop and an oven and can stand on the floor between two base cabinets, at the end of a line of cabinets, or alone. The most common size of freestanding range is 30 inches.

Slide-in and drop-in ranges fit between two cabinets or into a space in a cooking island. The sides of these ranges are usually unfinished. A slide-in range sits on the floor; a drop-in range may hang from the countertop or sit on a low base. The advantages of slide-in and drop-in ranges are that they can be less expensive and they help provide a seamless transition between your cabinets and your range.

Built-in wall ovens and cooktops are ranges divided into separate units for flexibility in kitchen design. A built-in oven may contain one or two ovens and possibly a microwave or electric/convection oven combination.

Cooktops

Traditional cooktops have four cooking elements. On most gas models, the burners are all the same size. Traditional electric coil ranges have two 6-inch and two 8-inch burners. The traditional cooktop design allows for a work space in the center of two rows of burners, but some newer cooktops may have a grill or griddle in the center, additional burners in the center, or even a totally different design with the burners arranged in an inverted U.

Modular or convertible cooktops are the ultimate in flexibility. Each burner is an interchangeable plug-in unit. Some units include a grill or griddle; separate units such as a wok ring, rotisserie, or deep-fat fryer are also available.

Ovens

Separate wall ovens can be found as either conventional electric or gas models. Convection and microwave ovens are also available as built-in wall models. Convection electric ovens bake with a fan that moves heated air throughout the oven. Many convection ovens have a third, separate heating element that surrounds the convection fan to improve performance. Convection ovens are also available in combination with microwave ovens.

Commercial-style Ranges

The hottest trend in kitchen design is the commercial-style range. Stainless steel with an industrial look, these ranges are now specifically engineered for home use. Their advantage over ordinary ranges is that they can produce more heat, almost 15,000 Btu per burner. Because of this extra heat, commercial-style ranges also require high-powered range hoods. Some models include a built-in grill or griddle in the center of the cooktop.

Commercial-style gas ranges manufactured specifically for domestic use generally do not require special clearance or a special gas hookup to operate. However, many manufacturers recommend adding a stainless steel backsplash between the cooktop and the hood.

Cleaning Your Range

A self-cleaning oven is rapidly becoming a standard feature on both gas and electric ranges. In the cleaning cycle, temperatures above 800°F burn spills to a powdery ash that easily wipes clean after the cycle has ended. Continuous-cleaning ovens have a rough-textured interior that absorbs dirt and soils, which gradually burn off with continued use. This cleaning method is not as efficient as the self-cleaning cycle; you will have to do some manual cleaning of the oven's interior. Manual-clean ovens need to be cleaned regularly with abrasive cleaners and/or harsh chemicals.

Smooth-top electric ranges and sealed gas burners are cooktops designed for minimal cleaning. Spills wipe clean, and the design eliminates the need to lift up the entire cooktop surface to clean below the burner trays. Most cooktops today are made from porcelain enamel and have upswept backsplashes and slightly upturned edges to prevent spills from running over them.

Range Hoods

A range hood is a very important item. Using a poor or nonvented range hood can actually be dangerous if you have a gas range. A cooktop burning natural or bottled gas can leave leftover fumes. Both fumes and cooking odors need to be eliminated by a ventilation system. Nonvented range hoods are available for electric coil or smooth-top cooktops, but they are not recommended for gas ranges.

The traditional range hood is either a horizontal model, which vents through a hole in the wall, or a vertical model, which vents through the ceiling. Downdraft or proximity ventilation systems are sometimes included with certain types of modular cooktops. These ventilation systems are recommended only for those who do not use pots or pans taller than 4 inches or for those who do not frequently fry foods.

All ventilation systems have a cfm rating that details the cubic feet per minute moved. Most traditional wall-mounted range hoods are rated from 200 to 300 cfm. Island hoods and hoods over open grills should move a minimum of 600 cfm. Generally, the more cfms, the more sound the hood motor makes. Always check with your cooktop manufacturer for more details before you choose a range hood, and check the hood manufacturer's instructions to determine how high each size hood should be mounted above the cooktop.

Best Buys '96

Our Best Buy, Recommended, and Budget Buy ranges and range hoods follow. They were evaluated on the basis of quality, efficiency, energy use, and overall value. The ranges are divided into the categories of gas and electric, each with several subcategories. Within each subcategory, models are arranged by quality. This means that the best of the Best Buys is listed first, followed by our second choice, and so on. Remember that a Best Buy, Recommended, or Budget Buy designation refers only to the model listed and not necessarily to other models made by the same manufacturer. Approximate prices apply to models in basic white or the finish mentioned in the description.

GAS RANGES

Freestanding Gas Ranges

GENERAL ELECTRIC JGBP24GEV

✓BEST BUY

The GE JGBP24GEV's most notable feature is its large oven, at 4.4 cubic feet the largest oven in any of the standard gas ranges. This model is available in white or in almond

Prices are accurate at time of printing but are subject to manufacturers' changes.

with a black oven door and has four standard 9,000-Btu burners with black porcelain enamel drip pans and porcelain-on-steel grates. The upswept cooktop is porcelain-enameled. Although this model does not have the convenience of sealed burners, the size of the oven and the attractive price make it a Best Buy. The self-cleaning oven has two racks with six rack positions. This model also includes an in-oven broiler, an extra-large broiler pan/grid, and electronic pilotless ignition.

Specifications: Overall dimensions: height, 45¾″; width, 30″; depth, 28¼″. Interior oven dimensions: height, 17″; width, 24″; depth, 19″. **Warranty:** parts and labor, 1 year.

Approx. retail price	**Approx. low price**
$559	**$552**

MAGIC CHEF 3468

✓BEST BUY

This versatile model comes in several color choices: designer white, white with a black glass door, almond with a black glass door, or designer almond. Two of the four sealed burners in this 30-inch gas range are Super Speed burners rated 12,000 Btus. The large self-cleaning oven is 4.0 cubic feet in size, and this model has an electronic thermostat and electronic controls. The 3468 is a good value that also sports a spill-catching porcelain cooktop, waist-high broiler, and electronic pilotless ignition.

Specifications: Overall dimensions: height, 46¼″; width, 30″; depth, 26⅗₂″. Oven dimensions: height, 16½″; width, 23″; depth, 18⅛″. **Warranty:** parts, 2 years; labor, 1 year; sealed burners, 5 years.

Approx. retail price	**Approx. low price**
$775	**$657**

MAYTAG CRG9700

✓BEST BUY

This sleek 30-inch range has all the features recommended in a gas range at a reasonable price. It has a white or almond exterior with a black glass oven door and four sealed surface burners. It has two Power Boost burners; the remaining two burners are normal. The porcelain enamel cooktop has a

Prices are accurate at time of printing but are subject to manufacturers' changes.

drip retainer around the edges to catch spills and drips, and an upsweep design smoothly connects the cooktop to the backsplash. The large, 4.0-cubic-foot oven is self-cleaning and programmable and has a waist-high broiler, an oven light, and two heavy-duty racks. This model also boasts a solid-state pilotless ignition, precision burner controls, a deluxe electronic clock with timer, and a storage drawer.

Specifications: Overall dimensions: height, 44⅞"; width, 29⅞"; depth, 27½". Interior oven dimensions: height, 16½"; width, 23"; depth, 18⅛". **Warranty:** parts, 2 years; labor, 1 year; sealed gas burner replacements, 10 years.

Approx. retail price	**Approx. low price**
$699	**$674**

WHIRLPOOL SF367PEYQ

Recommended

The Whirlpool SF367PEYQ is an attractive white 30-inch gas range with gray burner grates. (The same range is available in black as model SF367PEYB.) The Clean Top cooking system boasts four sealed gas burners and an upswept porcelain spill-guard cooktop. All four burners are rated at 9,000 Btu but can be turned down to 900 Btu for slow simmering. The spacious, 4.1-cubic-foot oven is self-cleaning and has two adjustable oven racks and a waist-high broiler. This model is a Recommended product instead of a Best Buy because it doesn't have the additional high-speed burner capacity or a programmable oven timer. It's also slightly more expensive than others in its category.

Specifications: Overall dimensions: height, 45 13/16"; width, 29⅞"; depth, 25⅜". Interior oven dimensions: height, 15⅞"; width, 23"; depth, 19 3/16". **Warranty:** parts and labor, 1 year.

Approx. retail price	**Approx. low price**
$757	**$709**

Drop-in/Slide-in Gas Ranges

MAYTAG CHG9800

✓BEST BUY

This 30-inch gas slide-in range comes in deco white or black. Though it carries a higher price than some, it offers many extras. The oven measures a large 4.0 cubic feet and includes two heavy-duty racks with five positions. Burners have precision controls; one of the burners is a power burner. The upswept cooktop and sealed-surface burners make the cooktop easy to clean, and the oven is self-cleaning. This range can be adjusted to use LP gas.

Specifications: Overall dimensions: height, 37″; width, 30¾″; depth, 25⅞″. Interior oven dimensions: height, 16½″; width, 23″; depth, 18¼″. **Warranty:** parts, 2 years; labor, 1 year; sealed burners, 10 years.

Approx. retail price	Approx. low price
$875	**$819**

MAGIC CHEF 6498

BEST BUY

This 30-inch slide-in gas range with a one-touch self-cleaning oven is a good value. The 4.0-cubic-foot oven has five rack positions, antitilt oven racks, a lighted oven window, and an electronic thermostat. The waist-high broiler has a porcelainized broiler pan. The front control panel is tilted back to make it easier to see from above. Two of the sealed burners are super-speed burners at 12,000 Btu. This model is available in four color choices: almond (6498VTA), designer white (6498VTV), designer almond (6498VVD), and brushed chrome with a black glass door (6498XTS).

Specifications: Overall dimensions: height, 36″; width, 30″; depth, 23½″. Interior oven dimensions: height, 16½″; width, 23″; depth, 18⅛″. **Warranty:** parts and labor, 1 year; sealed burners, 5 years.

Approx. retail price	Approx. low price
$950	**$798**

Conventional Gas Cooktops

KITCHENAID KGCT305B

BEST BUY

This 30-inch black glass cooktop is very attractive and is also available in white or almond. Four sealed high-efficiency burners are arranged in an inverted U design and two of the burners are power burners. Power track guides from the knobs to the burners let you know you're turning on the right burner. Also included are color-coordinated cast iron grates.

Specifications: width, 30¾"; depth, 21¾". **Warranty:** parts and labor, 1 year; gas burners and ceramic glass cooktop, 5 years.

Approx. retail price	**Approx. low price**
$559	**$559**

GENERAL ELECTRIC JGP640ES

Recommended

A new trend in conventional gas cooktops is a downdraft ventilation system built into the cooktop. For this cooktop, a separate downdraft venting kit including the motor and blower assembly must be purchased; the kit is JXDV66 and costs about $200. The variable-height, retractable downdraft venting system has variable speed control and a variable-speed fan. The combined price of this model makes it a Recommended product rather than a Best Buy. Desirable features of this cooktop include an automatic reignition (if the burner blows out, it will automatically reignite at the same level), higher burner speed at 11,000 Btu, and up-front controls. The JGP640ES is available in black tempered glass; the white version of this model is JGP641ES.

Specifications: width, 36"; depth, 22¼". **Warranty:** parts and labor, 1 year.

Approx. retail price	**Approx. low price**
$1,049	**$1,042**

Modular Gas Cooktops

KITCHENAID KGCT025A

✓BEST BUY

The KitchenAid KGCT025A, which comes in white, almond, or black, includes two raised high-efficiency sealed burners. It has pilotless electric ignition and automatic reignition. The front burner is rated at 6,000 Btu; the rear burner is a more powerful 10,000 Btus. This is one unit in

Prices are accurate at time of printing but are subject to manufacturers' changes.

KitchenAid's Create-A-Cooktop system. Optional units you can add to this cooktop include a downdraft ventilation system, electric grill, halogen and radiant elements, and a module containing two cast iron elements.

Specifications: width, 11$\frac{15}{16}$"; depth, 21¾". **Warranty:** parts and labor, 1 year; gas burners and ceramic glass cooktop, 5 years.

Approx. retail price	**Approx. low price**
$369	**$353**

JENN-AIR CVG4280

Recommended

This 30-inch gas modular cooktop comes in all black or white or with a stainless steel perimeter. This model comes with two gas burners, one 9,000 Btu and one 10,000 Btu, and also has an even-heat grill element. The CVG4280 has electronic pilotless ignition and a downdraft ventilation system with a two-speed fan. It also accepts optional modules for two additional burners and gas grill accessories. Its higher price gives it a Recommended rating rather than a Best Buy.

Specifications: width, 29⅞"; depth, 21½". **Warranty:** parts, 2 years; labor, 1 year.

Approx. retail price	**Approx. low price**
$829	**$726**

Gas Ovens

WHIRLPOOL SB160PEXB

✓BEST BUY

The SB160PEXB is a 24-inch built-in self-cleaning gas oven. Accessories included are two adjustable oven racks, a porcelain broiler pan, and a chrome grid. The door is removable, and the broiler is at waist height. An electronic clock with oven controls and minute timer is also included. The SB160PEXB is black; the same model is available in white as model SB160PEXQ.

Specifications: Overall dimensions: height, 38$\frac{7}{16}$"; width, 23⅞"; depth, 25⅜". Interior oven dimensions: height, 16"; width, 17"; depth, 18½". **Warranty:** parts and labor, 1 year.

Prices are accurate at time of printing but are subject to manufacturers' changes.

Approx. retail price $809 | **Approx. low price** $809

KITCHENAID KGBS276Y

Recommended

The two self-cleaning ovens in this 27-inch unit make it ideal for the home baker. Infrared broiling and pilotless ignition are featured in both ovens. This model comes with a porcelain broiler pan and chrome tray. It is sold in black (KGBS276YBL) or white (KGBS276YWH). It is rated a Recommended product rather than a Best Buy because of its higher price.

Specifications: Overall dimensions: height, 54½"; width, 26½"; depth, 26". Interior oven dimensions: height, 16"; width, 19¼"; depth, 17". **Warranty:** parts and labor, 1 year; gas burners and electronic control, 5 years; oven cavity and inner door, 10 years.

Approx. retail price $1,999 | **Approx. low price** $1,919

Commercial-style Gas Ranges

VIKING VGSS300-4B

✓BEST BUY

Viking was the first manufacturer of commercial-style ranges for home kitchens. These ranges are high-performance kitchen appliances certified by the American Gas Association for residential installation. The VGSS300-4B is a standard 30-inch gas range with versatile burner settings ranging from a low of 1,000 Btus to a high of 15,000 Btus. The infrared broiler reaches broiling temperatures in 30 seconds. The spacious, 4.2-cubic-foot oven has a porcelain interior with removable bottom, sides, and door. Like most commercial-style ranges, the Viking does not have a self-cleaning oven. The large knobs have childproof, push-to-turn safety features. Other features of this attractive range include an oven light, a broiler pan/grid, two heavy-duty oven racks with five position choices, and dishwasher-safe porcelain burner bowls. This range is available with black, white, or almond exteriors, or in stainless steel or five colors for $275 extra. Standard accessories include a 6-inch-high stainless steel back guard, and a curb base front to conceal the range legs. A wok grate, a wok ring, a portable griddle, and a hardwood cover to fit over surface grates are optional.

Specifications: Overall dimensions: height, 35⅞"; width, 29⅞"; depth, 24⁵⁄₁₆". Interior oven dimensions: height, 16⅛"; width, 24"; depth, 18¾". **Warranty:** parts and labor, 1 year; burners, 5 years; porcelain oven and inner door panel, 10 years.

Approx. retail price	Approx. low price
$2,000	$1,960

FIVESTAR TTM325-B

✓BEST BUY

The TTM325-B gives consumers the best of both worlds—it has commercial-style 14,000-Btu gas burners and an electric oven and broiler. With a flip of the switch on the control panel, the oven's convection system turns on, which uses forced air for even baking. The burners have the lowest simmer level available in commercial ranges—400 Btus. Other features include an electronic pilotless ignition, a storage drawer, an exclusive pull-out broiler tray, and a stainless steel back guard. A barbecue grill accessory is available at additional cost.

Specifications: Overall dimensions: height, 47"; width, 36"; depth, 24". Interior oven dimensions: height, 14"; width, 24"; depth, 19". **Warranty:** parts and labor, 1 year; electronic ignition module, 2 years; stainless steel burner, 5 years.

Approx. retail price	Approx. low price
$4,900	$4,055

Commercial-style Gas Cooktops

DYNASTY DCT36-6

✓BEST BUY

The Dynasty DCT36-6 gas cooktop is an attractive addition to a hardworking kitchen. This 36-inch model has six side-by-side gas burners with black heavy-duty cast iron

Prices are accurate at time of printing but are subject to manufacturers' changes.

grates and removable stainless steel drip trays. Each burner is rated at 15,000 Btu. The cooktop is porcelain with a stainless steel front sporting red accents on the stay-cool knobs. Options for this cooktop include an 11-inch back guard, a butcher block cutting board, and a grooved griddle.

Specifications: height, 9½"; width, 36"; depth, 24". **Warranty:** parts and labor, 1 year; burners, 3 years; stainless steel parts, 7 years.

Approx. retail price	**Approx. low price**
$1,870	**$1,460**

FIVESTAR WTM033

✔BEST BUY

This 36-inch gas cooktop is manufactured specifically for home use. It has a front overhang and a backsplash and gives the convenience of pilotless ignition. The WTM033 has six stainless steel burners with porcelain-covered cast iron burner grates, and the white drip pans under each burner are dishwasher safe. This cooktop has the lowest simmering setting available on a commercial-style cooktop—the front burners can go as low as 400 Btu. All the burners can go as high as 14,000 Btu.

Specifications: height, 11"; width, 36"; depth, 24". **Warranty:** parts and labor, 1 year; electronic ignition module, 2 years; stainless steel burners, 5 years.

Approx. retail price	**Approx. low price**
$2,040	**$1,560**

ELECTRIC RANGES

Freestanding Electric Ranges

MAGIC CHEF 3868

✔BEST BUY

The 3868 is a 30-inch smooth-top electric range priced to sell. It is available in white, designer white, or almond, and the smooth top is available in either white stipple or black ceramic glass. This model has a lighted cooktop with two 8-inch burners and two 6-inch burners. Its 4.0-cubic-foot oven comes with a deep, porcelainized broiler pan. The smooth-top elements on this model heat up as fast as electric coil elements. A spill-catching cooktop and a one-touch self-cleaning oven cycle make this range easy to clean. This model also has an electronic thermostat and removable oven door.

Specifications: Overall dimensions: height, 46¼″; width, 30″; depth, 26⁵⁄₃₂″. Interior oven dimensions: height, 16½″; width, 23″; depth, 18⅛″. **Warranty:** parts and labor, 1 year.

Approx. retail price	**Approx. low price**
$825	**$662**

MAYTAG CRE9400

✓ BEST BUY

The CRE9400 is quite a value. This 30-inch free-standing electric range has a 4.0-cubic-foot self-cleaning oven with a black glass front. It comes with a porcelain enamel broiler pan, four removable electric coil elements, a lift-up cooktop with auto-prop rods, a storage drawer, and a deluxe electronic clock with timer and delay-start cooking. The cooktop is upswept and retains drips.

Specifications: Overall dimensions: height, 44⅞″; width, 29⅞″; depth, 27½″. Interior oven dimensions: height, 16½″; width, 23″; depth, 18⅛″. **Warranty:** parts, 2 years; labor, 1 year; surface, oven, and broil elements, 5 years.

Approx. retail price	**Approx. low price**
$514	**$514**

GENERAL ELECTRIC JBP25GV

✓ BEST BUY

This 30-inch electric-coil range has the standard two 6-inch and two 8-inch electric coil elements and removable one-piece chrome drip bowls. The cooktop lifts up for easy cleaning, and the oven is self-cleaning. The oven features touchpad operation for the self-cleaning cycle, the clock, and the timer, with a single control knob for oven temperatures. An audible signal tells you when the oven has reached the desired temperature, and the oven has an automatic shutoff. The unit is available in white.

Specifications: Overall dimensions: height, 45⅛"; width, 29⅞"; depth, 27½". Interior oven dimensions: height, 16"; width, 23"; depth, 17¼". **Warranty:** parts and labor, 1 year.

Approx. retail price	Approx. low price
$549	$508

KITCHENAID KERI500Y

Recommended

The KERI500Y is a 24½-inch-deep electric range designed to be flush with kitchen cabinets. It is available in either white or almond and has four electric coil elements, two of which are power burners. This range includes a self-cleaning oven, an electric clock, and a lift-up cooktop. This model is rated a Recommended product and not a Best Buy because of the higher price.

Specifications: Overall dimensions: height, 46 13/16"; width, 29 15/16"; depth, 24½". Interior oven dimensions: height, 15¾"; width, 23 1/16"; depth, 18¼". **Warranty:** parts and labor, 1 year; electric elements and electronic controls, 5 years; oven cavity and inner door, 10 years.

Approx. retail price	Approx. low price
$739	$689

Drop-in/Slide-in Electric Ranges

GENERAL ELECTRIC JSP28GV

✓BEST BUY

The JSP28GV takes the electric-coil slide-in 30-inch range into the future with a sleek black exterior and a lift-up overhanging porcelain-enameled cooktop. It has two plug-in heating elements and porcelain-enameled one-piece drip bowls. This model's oven has touchpad electronic controls for the oven timer, temperature, and self-cleaning function, and an automatic oven shutoff.

Specifications: Overall dimensions: height, 35⅞"; width, 30"; depth, 28½". Interior oven dimensions: height, 15¾"; width, 22¾"; depth, 17". **Warranty:** parts and labor, 1 year.

Approx. retail price
$739

Approx. low price
$703

JENN-AIR SVE47500

✓BEST BUY

This 30-inch drop-in/slide-in range comes in black or white and has enough versatility for all your cooking needs. The range comes with a downdraft ventilation system that has a two-speed fan and moves air at 300 cubic feet per minute. The self-cleaning bake/broil oven has 3.8 cubic feet of space and includes two heavy-gauge nickel-finish oven racks. Plus, the convection oven has settings for both convection baking and convection roasting and a variable-temperature-control broiler. The cooktop includes a nonstick coated grill along with two elements. These elements can be either smooth-top, electric coil, radiant, or halogen. Other features include an electronic clock with two timers, a child-lockout control, an optional backsplash, an optional color side panel, and an easy-cleaning grease and liquid collection system. Other optional accessories include griddle, wok, cooker-steamer, rotisserie, big-pot element, and an energy-saver grill assembly model.

Specifications: Overall dimensions: height, 35½″; width, 29¹⁵⁄₁₆″; depth, 26⅜″. Interior oven dimensions: height, 15″; width, 23½″; depth, 18⁹⁄₁₆″. **Warranty**: parts and labor, 1 year; electronic control panel and solid elements, 5 years.

Approx. retail price
$999

Approx. low price
$990

Conventional Electric Cooktops

KITCHENAID KECS100S

✓BEST BUY

The KitchenAid KECS100S is a sleek cooktop designed with four electric coil elements arranged in an inverted U shape. It has two 6-inch and two 8-inch high-speed plug-in cooking elements, and the right front 8-inch burner is a power burner. This model is available in black, white, or almond porcelain or with a brushed-chrome finish. The unit is installed with

Prices are accurate at time of printing but are subject to manufacturers' changes.

triple-action concealed hinges, which make this cooktop easy to service.

Specifications: width, 30¾"; depth, 21¾". **Warranty:** parts and labor, 1 year; electric elements, 5 years.

Approx. retail price	Approx. low price
$319	$279

WHIRLPOOL RC8536XTH ✔**BEST BUY**

The RC8536XTH is a 36-inch electric-coil spill-guard cooktop in brushed chrome. It has two 6-inch and two 8-inch plug-in surface elements, and the reflector pans are removable. An 8-inch canning element is sold separately. Indicator lights tell you when an element is turned on. Lift-off control knobs make the unit easy to clean. A nice feature of this cooktop is the built-in griddle with removable cover.

Specifications: width, 36"; depth, 22⅝". **Warranty:** parts and labor, 1 year.

Approx. retail price	Approx. low price
$388	$388

Modular Electric Cooktop

JENN-AIR CVE4270 ✔**BEST BUY**

This 30-inch modular electric cooktop is available in black, white, or stainless steel. It comes with two radiant elements and one grill module, but both bays are convertible. A downdraft vent in the center of the cooktop has a two-speed fan. Many accessories for the two convertible bays are available for an additional cost: an electric coil element, a wok, a griddle, a rotisserie, and a 2,100-watt big-pot canning element.

Specifications: width, 28⅞"; depth, 20¹⁵⁄₁₆". **Warranty:** parts, 2 years; labor, 1 year.

Approx. retail price	Approx. low price
$529	$504

Smooth-top Electric Cooktops

GENERAL ELECTRIC JP350WV

✓BEST BUY

The JP350WV is a white 30-inch smooth-surface ceramic-glass cooktop that is resistant to both fingerprints and scratches. It includes two 8-inch elements, one 6-inch element, and one dual (6- or 9-inch) element. For safety, it has four indicator lights for hot surfaces. It is available in almond as JP350AV and black as JP350BV.

Specifications: width, 28⅛"; depth, 20½". **Warranty:** parts and labor, 1 year.

Approx. retail price
$549

Approx. low price
$549

KITCHENAID KECC501B

✓BEST BUY

The KECC501B is an easy-to-clean black ceramic-glass cooktop; it is also available in white for $50 extra. This model includes four single-circuit radiant elements with heat controls over an infinite range and built-in protection against overheating. The unit has a "power on" light and hot-surface indicators.

Specifications: width, 30"; depth, 21". **Warranty:** parts and labor, 1 year; electric elements and ceramic glass cooktop, 5 years.

Approx. retail price
$529

Approx. low price
$529

Built-in Electric Ovens

KITCHENAID KEBI200B

✓BEST BUY

This 30-inch double oven in white does not require outside venting. It has a graphic display, electronic touchpad controls, two-element balanced baking, and variable-temperature broiling. The only drawback to this full-featured oven is that only the upper oven is self-cleaning. It is available in black for $20 more.

Prices are accurate at time of printing but are subject to manufacturers' changes.

Specifications: Overall dimensions: height, 59⅜"; width, 29⅝"; depth, 25¼". Interior oven dimensions: height, 16¾"; width, 22"; depth, 16½". **Warranty:** parts and labor, 1 year; electronic control, 5 years; oven cavity and inner door, 10 years.

Approx. retail price **$1,129**

Approx. low price **$1,045**

JENN-AIR WW27430

✓BEST BUY

This 27-inch double wall oven has a sleek flush design with a large oven window. Both ovens are self-cleaning with automatic locks. The upper oven has two convection settings, roast and bake, along with a temperature probe. This unit is available in monochromatic black or white and includes a high-grade porcelain oven interior, variable-temperature-controlled broiling, and clock-controlled baking. Both ovens have an extra-large 3.3-cubic-foot capacity, and each is operated by a separate electronic timer.

Specifications: Overall dimensions: height, 49$^{15}/_{16}$"; width, 26¾"; depth, 24$^{7}/_{16}$". Interior oven dimensions: height, 14¾"; width, 21"; depth, 18½". **Warranty:** labor, 1 year; parts, 2 years; electronic control panel, 5 years.

Approx. retail price **$1,530**

Approx. low price **$1,530**

Built-in Electric/Microwave Ovens

TAPPAN TEB794CBS

✓BEST BUY

The Tappan TEB794CBS is a white-on-white 27-inch wall oven for the budget-conscious. It is also available in black (TEB794BBB). The electric wall oven is self-cleaning with electronic touchpad time and temperature controls and an electronic clock/timer. The microwave oven has a 1.6-cubic-foot capacity and 900 watts of cooking power. Other features of the microwave oven include personal and warm-and-hold cycles, automatic defrosting by weight, an add-60-seconds pad, a pause mode, ten power levels, and a door light. Accessories include a broiler pan and grill, two oven racks, and a removable glass turntable.

Specifications: Overall dimensions: height, 49¾″; width, 25⅞″; depth, 26⅛″. **Warranty:** parts and labor, 1 year.

Approx. retail price	**Approx. low price**
$1,200	**$1,038**

GENERAL ELECTRIC JKP76GV

Recommended

This 27-inch microwave/oven model comes in black and has almost every feature available in ovens today. The microwave is a spacious 1.4 cubic feet and has 800 watts of power and ten power levels. GE's Dual Wave system distributes microwave energy from both the top and bottom. The microwave has both a humidity sensor and a temperature probe. The oven has a broiler pan with grid, electronic touchpad controls, and an audible preheat signal to tell you when the oven is up to temperature. This model is rated a Recommended product rather than a Best Buy because of its higher price.

Specifications: Overall dimensions: height, 43″; width, 26¾″; depth, 23½″. Upper oven dimensions: height, 11⅛″; width, 16″; depth, 13⅜″. Lower oven dimensions: height, 15″; width, 19″; depth, 18″. **Warranty:** parts and labor, 1 year; magnetron tube, 5 years.

Approx. retail price	**Approx. low price**
$1,430	**$1,430**

RANGE HOODS

GENERAL ELECTRIC JV376V

✓BEST BUY

The JV376V High-Air-Flow Range Hood is GE's high-performance range hood. It is 30 inches wide to fit over the standard range and comes in white or black. It is designed with an easy-to-clean continuous surface and two large filters that can be cleaned at the sink or in the dishwasher. This product is recommended for use with indoor grills and griddles and has a 410 cfm vertical exhaust rating and a 380 cfm rear exhaus rating. One unique feature of this range hood is the two cook top lights, which can really help illuminate the cooking are A night-light and a variable-speed fan control are also include

Specifications: height, 7″; width, 29⅞″; depth, 21″. **Warrant** parts and labor, 1 year.

Approx. retail price	**Approx. low price**
$250	**$250**

BROAN 412401

Recommendec

This versatile economy-model 24-inch-wide range hood comes in a baked enamel finish in white. Oth model numbers beginning with 4124 are the same model in a mond, harvest, avocado, and coffee, as well as in stainless stee The duct-free, nonvented Microtek system filter has a tw speed fan control and can hold a 75-watt light bulb. An o tional matching backsplash is also available.

Specifications: height, 6″; width, 24″; depth, 17½. **Warrant** parts, 1 year.

Approx. retail price	**Approx. low price**
$92	**$78**

VIKING VRH30

✓BES BUY

If you buy a commercial-style range, you'll need a commercial-style range hood. The VRH30 is a powerf 30-inch-wide wall hood in white or almond with twin high-pe formance squirrel-cage blowers. This hood uses a centrifuga action grease removal system that eliminates the need for fi ters and minimizes fire hazard. The rating on this hood is 6(cfm. It comes with a fluorescent light for even, shadowless i lumination.

Specifications: width, 29⅞″; depth, 24″. **Warranty:** parts ar labor, 1 year; ventilation motor, 2 years.

Approx. retail price	**Approx. low price**
$650	**$650**

Prices are accurate at time of printing but are subject to manufacturers' changes.

REFRIGERATORS AND FREEZERS

Few home appliances last as long or work as reliably as a refrigerator or freezer. With an average life expectancy of 15 to 20 years, the unit bought today will be around well into the future. Consequently, it pays to take the time to be sure that the refrigerator or freezer you buy is really what you need, both now and for some time to come.

Best Buys '96

Our Best Buy, Recommended, and Budget Buy choices follow for refrigerators and freezers. Refrigerators are divided into the following categories: side-by-side, top-freezer, bottom-freezer, built-in, and bar-size. Remember that the cost of deluxe features such as an ice maker and a through-the-door dispenser can boost the cost of models of any given size. Freezers are divided into upright and chest freezers. For both refrigerators and freezers, variations in appearance, such as exterior color, type of door handles, and interior design are typically designated by different model numbers, as noted in the product reviews. Remember that a Best Buy, Recommended, or Budget Buy designation applies only to the model listed, not to other models made by the same manufacturer.

REFRIGERATORS

Because your refrigerator is one of the primary energy-consuming appliances in your home, replacing an old refrigerator can save you money in the long run. Today's refrigerators use half as much energy as refrigerators from ten years ago. The use of chlorofluorocarbons (CFCs) in all newly manufactured refrigerators will be phased out by the end of 1995.

Which Model?

Traditional top-freezer models sport a freezer at eye level so frozen foods are easier to find. Though the shelves are wide, it can be difficult to find foods on the bottom shelves. Side-by-side refrigerators, the most popular refrigerator model sold today, are more expensive and cost more to run than other models. In a side-by-side refrigerator, doors are narrower and the freezer is larger than those in top- or bottom-freezer models. You can store food at eye level in both freezer and refrigerator, and the side-by-side's tall, thin shape makes it easier to locate items. A bottom-freezer refrigerator has wide eye-level refrigerator shelves. The freezer is larger than that in a top-freezer refrigerator with the same overall storage capacity; the pull-out basket in the freezer reduces usable space. In-the-door water dispensers aren't available in this type of refrigerator. The newest trend in refrigerators is built-in models that are flush with your cabinets. These models can be fitted with optional trim kits to match your kitchen cabinets. Bar-size refrigerators are ideal for offices, dorm rooms, and playrooms. They generally need to be manually defrosted and do not include freezer space, although they may have small ice cube trays.

To determine the size refrigerator you need, plan on 13 to 20 cubic feet in a top- or bottom-freezer refrigerator for a small family, 20 to 24 cubic feet for a medium-size family, and 24 or more cubic feet for a large family. In a side-by-side refrigerator, a smaller family will need 19 to 22 cubic feet, a medium-size family will need 22 to 24 cubic feet, and a large family will want more than 26 cubic feet.

Refrigerator Features

Tempered glass refrigerator shelves with spillproof rims contain spills for quick cleaning and are desirable in homes with growing children. Glass drawers help you see foods more easily without having to open the drawers frequently. Sliding shelves also help you find items. Electronic touchpad temperature controls are now available and can tell you when the door is open or when to clean the coils. Ice makers, ice dispensers, and water dispensers will raise the price several hundred dollars. Ice makers take up valuable freezer space and make four to six ice cube trays' worth of ice a day. Cold water dispensers generally hold about 1½ quarts at a time.

Choose your refrigerator by the types of food you always keep on hand. Look for gallon-deep door bins for milk and juice, adjustable-humidity crispers to prolong the life of your fruits and vegetables, an egg bucket that can store up to two dozen eggs, an adjustable-temperature meat drawer to keep meats at lower temperatures, two-liter door racks to store tall bottles or soda pop, and an under-shelf holder for white wine or bottled water.

Side-by-side Refrigerators

WHIRLPOOL ED20TKXD

✓ BEST BUY

The ED20TKXD is a solid compromise between luxury amenities and cost-saving shortcuts. The four adjustable, full-width shelves are glass, a feature rarely seen in this price range. Other extras include a temperature-controlled meat drawer and a see-through crisper with a glass cover. Door storage features four shelves, including storage for gallon-size containers, and compartments for butter and eggs. The freezer has a slide-out freezer bin; the five freezer door shelves are fixed instead of adjustable. This refrigerator is CFC-free and exceeds 1995 federal energy standards by 20 percent.

Specifications: height, 65⅞"; width, 32¾"; depth (including handle), 30⅞"; shelf capacity, 20.5 square feet. **Warranty:** parts and labor, 1 year; sealed system, 5 years.

Approx. retail price	**Approx. low price**
$949	**$894**

MAGIC CHEF RCE244

✓ BEST BUY

This large side-by-side refrigerator has a 23.5-cubic-foot capacity and is available in almond or white. It features three fully adjustable glass shelves and two humidity-controlled see-through crispers for storing fruits and vegetables. The meat drawer has an adjustable temperature control. Deep, adjustable shelves in the door store large items handily, and the door has a snug bottle retainer. Also included in the door is a

Prices are accurate at time of printing but are subject to manufacturers' changes.

lift-out egg tray. The freezer features a specialty storage shelf and an automatic ice maker with a refreshment center water and ice dispenser.

Specifications: height, 67½"; width, 35¾"; depth (including handle), 29¾"; shelf capacity, 26.4 square feet. **Warranty:** parts and labor, 1 year; compressor, evaporator, condenser and connecting tube, 5 years.

Approx. retail price	Approx. low price
$1,350	$1,094

MAYTAG RSD2200D ✔BEST BUY

The RSD2200D is a full-featured, 21.9-cubic-foot side-by-side refrigerator that comes in white or almond. The three adjustable, easy-glide sealed glass shelves have spill-catcher rims. Other features include a meat drawer with temperature adjustment, two sealed vegetable crispers with humidity control, and a wine rack. In the door are a covered dairy compartment, two slidable inserts to help keep packages neat, a removable egg cradle, and four deep gallon-size bins. The refrigerator has an automatic energy saver switch. The freezer has three slide-out wire freezer baskets, six deep fixed door bins, a freezer light, and four ice cube trays. An ice maker is optional.

Specifications: height, 67½"; width, 33"; depth (including handle), 32⅛"; shelf capacity, 24.7 square feet. **Warranty:** parts, 2 years; labor, 1 year; sealed refrigeration system and cabinet liner, 5 years.

Approx. retail price	Approx. low price
$1,469	$1,139

WHIRLPOOL ED25DQXD ✔BEST BUY

Like all the Whirlpool refrigerators reviewed here, the ED25DQXD is CFC-free. It also exceeds the 1995 federal energy standards by 25 percent. This 25.2-cubic-foot model has adjustable slide-out glass shelves with spill-guard rims. It also has a temperature-controlled meat drawer, two humidity-controlled crispers, an egg bin, and a wine rack. In the door are four gallon-size shelves and a retainer for tall items. The freezer has two slide-out wire freezer baskets and a quick-freeze compartment. A through-the-door crushed ice and water dispenser is standard with this model.

Specifications: height, 68⅞"; width, 35½"; depth (including handle), 33⅝"; shelf capacity, 27.3 square feet. **Warranty:** parts and labor, 1 year; sealed system, 5 years.

Approx. retail price	Approx. low price
$1,629	$1,518

GENERAL ELECTRIC TFX24PRX ✓ BEST BUY

The TFX24PRX, a new addition to the GE Profile "P" series, is an excellent example of the versatility of the side-by-side type of refrigerator. The refrigerator has two slide-out spillproof glass shelves; one slides back to allow for storage of tall items. The plastic vegetable/fruit and meat pans are larger than those on many other models, and the 23.6-cubic-foot capacity is ample for most families. Available in black, white, or almond textured steel, this highly energy-efficient model also includes a beverage rack. The freezer includes wire slide-out freezer baskets, five freezer door shelves, and a dispenser for chilled water, ice cubes, and crushed ice.

Specifications: height, 67⅝"; width, 35¾"; depth (excluding handle), 30½"; shelf capacity, 25.2 square feet. **Warranty:** parts and labor, 1 year; sealed refrigerating system, 5 years; Lexan plastic pans, drawers, and bins, lifetime.

Approx. retail price	Approx. low price
$1,649	$1,404

KITCHENAID KSRS25QD ✓ BEST BUY

This top-of-the-line, 25.1-cubic-foot unit is big in every way: size, price, luxury amenities, even energy efficiency. Although the through-the-door ice and water dispenser takes away some shelf space in the freezer—and helps account for the premium price—ample storage space is left over in the three pull-out wire bins, the fixed wire shelf, and the plastic "fast freeze" shelf. In the fresh food compartment, the door contains a pair of adjustable-height shelves designed for beverage cans, plus four adjustable-height, pull-out bins that can hold gallon-size containers. The full-width dairy compartment is another plus. The regular shelving is height-adjustable glass with one shelf that glides out. The temperature-controlled meat drawer and two humidity-controlled fruit and vegetable crispers all glide on rollers. This model comes in white or almond; it is available in black for $200 extra.

Specifications: height, 68⅞"; width, 35½"; depth (excluding handle), 31"; shelf capacity, 29 square feet. **Warranty:** parts and labor, 1 year; sealed system and liner, parts and labor, 5 years; parts only, 10 years.

Approx. retail price	Approx. low price
$1,719	$1,478

Top-freezer Refrigerators

KITCHENAID KTRC18KD

✓BEST BUY

The KTRC18KD is a basic, no-frills model with 18.1 cubic feet of storage space. It has five glass shelves, one of which is adjustable. Other features include two humidity-controlled crispers, a covered in-door dairy compartment and covered egg bin, an easy-to-clean one-piece liner, and white textured-steel doors. Separate, up-front temperature controls for refrigerator and freezer make adjustments easy. An ice maker is optional. The KTRC18KD does not exceed federal energy rating guidelines and thus is not as energy efficient as a model that exceeds the guidelines.

Specifications: height, 65⅞"; width, 29½"; depth (including handle), 30⅛"; shelf capacity, 24.8 square feet. **Warranty:** parts and labor, 1 year; sealed system and liner, parts and labor, 5 years; parts only, 10 years.

Approx. retail price	Approx. low price
$739	$681

MAYTAG RTC1500D

✓BEST BUY

This is Maytag's most compact top-freezer model refrigerator, with only 14.9 cubic feet of interior space

Prices are accurate at time of printing but are subject to manufacturers' changes.

and a total of 22.4 square feet of shelf capacity. The refrigerator has two adjustable wire shelves, a temperature-adjustable meat drawer, and two sealed crisper drawers. In the door are two deep door bins, a covered dairy compartment, and a removable egg bin. The freezer features one adjustable wire shelf, two deep door bins, and two ice cube trays. An ice maker is optional at an extra cost. The refrigerator has reversible doors and an energy saver switch. It comes in deco white or almond.

Specifications: height, 60″; width, 29″; depth (including handle), 30⅓″, shelf capacity, 22.4 square feet. **Warranty:** parts, 2 years; labor, 1 year; sealed refrigeration system and cabinet liner, 5 years.

Approx. retail price	**Approx. low price**
$749	**$658**

MAYTAG RTD1900D

✓ BEST BUY

The RTD1900D is an 18.6-cubic-foot refrigerator that comes in almond, white, or black. The four adjustable split shelves are made of sealed tempered glass with spill-catcher rims. This refrigerator has such desirable new options as a temperature-adjustable meat drawer, two sealed vegetable crispers with moisture control, and an energy saver option. The door has four adjustable gallon-container-size bins, a removable egg bin, and two covered dairy compartments.

Specifications: height, 65½″; width, 31½″; depth (including handle), 30⅓″; shelf capacity, 28.1 square feet. **Warranty:** parts, 2 years; labor, 1 year; entire sealed refrigeration system and cabinet liner, 5 years.

Approx. retail price	**Approx. low price**
$869	**$850**

AMANA TH18S3

✓ BEST BUY

This 17.8-cubic-foot refrigerator has all the features you could want in a contemporary refrigerator, and it exceeds federal energy standards by 25 percent. It has four adjustable half-width glass shelves, a glass-top deli chiller, two glass-top crispers, and a covered egg bin. Storage in the door

Prices are accurate at time of printing but are subject to manufacturers' changes.

will hold gallon-size containers. The 4.8-cubic-foot freezer has an adjustable wire shelf and two full-width door retainers. A trim kit is optional.

Specifications: height, 65⅜"; width, 29⅝"; depth (excluding handle), 31"; shelf capacity, 23.9 square feet. **Warranty:** parts and labor, 1 year; sealed system components and food compartment liner, 5 years.

Approx. retail price	**Approx. low price**
$729	**$689**

GENERAL ELECTRIC TBX21JIX

✔ BEST BUY

This 20.6-cubic-foot model has two nice-size fruit/vegetable crispers, one with adjustable humidity. The covered deli keeper holds meats and cheeses. Door shelves have storage for gallon-size milk or soda containers. The freezer has a wire shelf and two door shelves, and this model comes with an ice maker. Available in white or almond textured steel, it's a good combination of modern features and value.

Specifications: height, 67"; width, 31¼"; depth (excluding handle), 27¾"; shelf capacity, 25.2 square feet. **Warranty:** parts and labor, 1 year; sealed system, 5 years; Lexan plastic pans, drawers, and bins, lifetime.

Approx. retail price	**Approx. low price**
$839	**$766**

KITCHENAID KTRS22KD

✔ BEST BUY

The KTRS22KD, one of KitchenAid's Superba series, has a decent 21.6-cubic-foot capacity. It has three adjustable, roll-out tempered glass shelves. This refrigerator has a meat locker and two humidity-controlled crispers. Door storage includes a can rack and four adjustable gallon-size containers. This model has a pull-out freezer floor. It is available in white, almond, or black; an ice maker is optional. The KTRS22KD does not exceed federal energy rating guidelines, which means that it will be less energy efficient than models exceeding the guidelines.

Specifications: height, 65⅞"; width, 32¾"; depth (excluding handle), 31"; shelf capacity, 34 square feet. **Warranty:** parts and labor, 1 year; sealed system and liner, parts and labor, 5 years; parts only, 10 years.

Approx. retail price	Approx. low price
$1,000	$904

AMANA TR25S5

Recommended

If you're looking for a refrigerator that can handle a crowd, consider the Amana TR25S5 with a giant 24.5 cubic feet of space and 33.2 square feet of total shelf space. This model has four adjustable half-width glass spill-saver shelves, two glass-top humidity-controlled crisper drawers on rollers, and a temperature-adjustable glass-top deli chiller. The door has two gallon-size buckets, an adjustable bottle hugger, a tall package retainer, a covered egg bin, and reversible dairy storage. The freezer has two adjustable half-width shelves. This unit is available in an almond, ebony, or white textured steel exterior. It exceeds federal energy standards by 25 percent. The Amana TR25S5 is rated a Recommended product rather than a Best Buy because of its higher price.

Specifications: height, 68⅜"; width, 35⅝"; depth (excluding handle), 32¾"; shelf capacity, 33.2 square feet. **Warranty:** parts and labor, 1 year; sealed system components and food compartment liner, 5 years.

Approx. retail price	Approx. low price
$1,179	$1,033

GENERAL ELECTRIC TBX25PCX

Recommended

The TBX25PCX, one of GE's Profile "P" series, has three glass shelves, two of them split for custom adjustments. The Quick Space shelf easily retracts so that you can fit tall items on the shelf below. Also included are two adjustable-humidity vegetable/fruit pans, an adjustable-temperature deli keeper, and an under-shelf bottle rack. Storage dishes in the door can go from refrigerator to microwave. Modular, adjustable door storage bins will hold gallon-size containers. The ice maker produces both cubes and crushed ice, and an ingenious tilt-out storage bin holds the ice conveniently. This model is a Recommended product rather than a Best Buy because of its higher price.

Specifications: height, 68″; width, 34½″; depth (excluding handle), 27¾″; shelf capacity, 27 square feet. **Warranty:** parts and labor, 1 year; sealed system, 5 years; Lexan plastic pans, drawers, and bins, lifetime.

Approx. retail price	Approx. low price
$1,449	$1,348

GENERAL ELECTRIC TBX16DAX

Budget Buy

The TBX16DAX, although not a large or feature-laden refrigerator, is a good model for people on a budget. It has 15.6 cubic feet of storage space and is sold in either white or almond textured steel. The two vegetable/fruit bins are not humidity-controlled; it has three wire refrigerator shelves and a deli keeper. The door has fixed storage space for gallon-size containers. The freezer has two door shelves and comes with two ice cube trays (an ice maker is optional). The refrigerator has only two door shelves, which cuts down on available space.

Specifications: height, 64½″; width, 28″; depth (excluding handle), 26″; shelf capacity, 19.6 square feet. **Warranty:** parts and labor, 1 year; sealed refrigerating system, 5 years.

Approx. retail price	Approx. low price
$619	$541

MAGIC CHEF GT17Y7A

Budget Buy

This top-freezer refrigerator model is ideal for anyone concerned about economy. With an 11.7-cubic-foot refrigerator and a 4.8-cubic-foot freezer, this white textured steel model (also available in almond as the GT17Y7V) has a total of 18.5 square feet of shelf capacity. Features include color-coordinated handles, twin see-through crispers, two adjustable full-width glass shelves, storage in the door for gallon-size containers, a large dairy compartment, and two ice cube trays in the freezer. This refrigerator is on easy-roll wheels to facilitate moving it.

Specifications: height, 64½"; width, 29"; depth (including handle), 29⅞"; shelf capacity, 18.5 square feet. **Warranty**: parts and labor, 1 year; compressor, evaporator, condenser, and connecting tubing, 5 years.

Approx. retail price	**Approx. low price**
$650	**$517**

Bottom-freezer Refrigerators

AMANA BH20S5

✓BEST BUY

The Amana BH20S5, a slightly smaller version of the Amana BS22S5, exceeds federal energy standards by 25 percent. This 20.5-cubic-foot bottom-freezer refrigerator is also available in white or almond. The four adjustable half-width glass shelves have spill-saver rims. The temperature of the glass-top deli chiller is adjustable, and the two see-through sealed crispers are humidity-controlled. Removable food storage containers are included. Door storage includes gallon-size shelving, an adjustable bottle hugger, a dairy module, an adjustable utility rack, and an adjustable tall-package retainer. Thermostatic control assures an accurate temperature. The frost-free freezer has an ice bucket, two ice trays, a pull-out freezer basket, and a full-width glass shelf. Door shelving includes two half-shelves for smaller items. An ice maker is available at extra cost.

Specifications: height, 68⅜"; width, 32⅝"; depth (excluding handle), 31½"; shelf capacity, 25.8 square feet. **Warranty**: parts and labor, 1 year; sealed system components and food compartment liner, 5 years.

Approx. retail price	**Approx. low price**
$949	**$801**

AMANA BX22S5

✓BEST BUY

The Amana BX22S5 is a full-featured, 21.7-cubic-foot bottom-freezer refrigerator at a moderate price. It comes in white, almond, or ebony. The refrigerator sports four spill-saver adjustable half-width glass shelves and two food storage containers. The two glass-top crisper drawers are humidity-controlled, and the glass-top deli chiller is temperature-adjustable. In the door is storage for gallon containers and four adjustable half-width shelves whose sides are sealed to the bottoms to prevent spillovers. The frost-free freezer has one full-width glass shelf, two flex-action ice cube trays, one glide-out wire basket, and two half-width door bins. An ice maker and trim kit are optional additions. This model exceeds federal energy standards by 25 percent.

Specifications: height, 68⅜"; width, 32⅝"; depth (excluding handle), 32¾"; shelf capacity, 28.6 square feet. **Warranty:** parts and labor, 1 year; sealed system components and food compartment liner, 5 years.

Approx. retail price	**Approx. low price**
$1,079	**$962**

WHIRLPOOL EB21DKXD

✓BEST BUY

This 21-cubic-foot bottom-freezer refrigerator has an excellent selection of shelving options. The slide-out shelves can be adjusted up or down and have raised edges to catch spills. Bins in the door can be divided. This model has a tall-bottle retainer, a clear wine rack, a three-piece egg bin, and two clear humidity-controlled crispers. The freezer has two full-width freezer door shelves and two slide-out freezer baskets. An ice maker is optional. CFC-free with a standard energy index, this model is available in white, almond, or black and is a great value.

Specifications: height, 65⅞"; width, 32¾"; depth (including handle), 32¾"; shelf capacity, 28.6 square feet. **Warranty:** parts and labor, 1 year; sealed system, 5 years.

Approx. retail price	**Approx. low price**
$1,049	**$969**

GENERAL ELECTRIC TCX22ZAX

✓BEST BUY

Although slightly higher in price than similar models, the TCX22ZAX, the only bottom-freezer model GE

Prices are accurate at time of printing but are subject to manufacturers' changes.

sells, packs a lot of features in its 21.7 cubic feet. Sold in either white or almond textured steel, this refrigerator has spillproof cantilevered glass shelves. One of the two clear fruit/vegetable bins is humidity-adjustable. Door storage includes two covered shelves and storage for gallon-size bottles. The freezer has a sliding freezer basket, two ice cube trays, and an ice storage bin. An ice maker is optional.

Specifications: height, 68⅜"; width, 32¾"; depth (excluding handle), 28½"; shelf capacity, 28.6 square feet. **Warranty:** parts and labor, 1 year; sealed system, 5 years.

Approx. retail price	**Approx. low price**
$1,099	**$964**

KITCHENAID KBRS21KD

BEST BUY

KitchenAid refrigerators have several features designed to catch the eye of the discriminating consumer. The fresh food compartment has four adjustable shelves, three of which glide out on rollers. A covered meat drawer also is on rollers. The two fruit and vegetable crispers have humidity controls. In the door of this 21-cubic-foot model you'll find a variety of fixed and pull-out bins, with plenty of depth for jars and jugs of all descriptions. A wine rack stores bottles horizontally, and the door has a space-saving shelf for beverage cans. An ice maker is optional. This model comes in white or almond; it is available in black for $30 extra.

Specifications: height, 65⅞"; width, 32¾"; depth (excluding handle), 32⅛"; shelf capacity, 27.1 square feet. **Warranty:** parts and labor, 1 year; sealed system and liner, parts and labor, 5 years; parts only, 10 years.

Approx. retail price	**Approx. low price**
$1,149	**$1,078**

Built-in Refrigerators

MAYTAG RCW2000

BEST BUY

The newly introduced RCW2000 is Maytag's attempt to win over the built-in refrigerator market. This side-

Prices are accurate at time of printing but are subject to manufacturers' changes.

by-side, counter-depth, 19.8-cubic-foot model comes in either white or black. Total shelf capacity of the unit is 22.8 square feet. The refrigerator features adjustable easy-glide glass shelves that are sealed to the plastic base piece to contain spills. It has an adjustable-temperature meat and cheese drawer, a wine rack, and two sealed humidity-controlled crispers. The door has deep bins and a covered dairy compartment. All the drawers are on rollers. The freezer has a slide-out basket and an ice and water dispenser with an optional crushed ice dispenser.

Specifications: height, 67¼"; width, 35¾"; depth (including handle), 27⅞"; shelf capacity, 22.8 square feet. **Warranty:** parts, 2 years; labor, 1 year; sealed refrigeration system, 5 years.

Approx. retail price	Approx. low price
$1,675	$1,448

GENERAL ELECTRIC TPX21PRX/TPX21BRX ✔BEST BUY

Two almost identical models from GE, the TPX21PRX and the TPX21BRX, are the next best thing to a true built-in, since they protrude only a door thickness (two inches) from any adjoining counter. The only difference between the two models is that the PRX doors are textured steel, whereas the BRX takes add-on front panels. Choices here include black, almond, or white glass from the factory (add $100), or custom panels to match your decor. Both have a spacious capacity of 20.7 cubic feet. Three fully adjustable glass shelves, two with spill rims, glide out for easy access. One shelf slides back to half-depth for convenient storage of tall containers. The two vegetable and fruit crispers have individual humidity controls; the meat drawer has a control for deeper chilling. The freezer compartment has exceptional versatility. Four slide-out wire bins make finding foods a snap. A dispenser delivers chilled water, cubes, and crushed ice. Another big plus is the unit's extraordinary energy efficiency; energy cost is $66 per year.

Specifications: height, 69¾" (PRX), 70⅛" (BRX); width, 35¾"; depth (including handle), 28⅛" (PRX), 27⅝" (BRX); shelf capacity, 23.3 square feet. **Warranty:** parts and labor, 1 year; sealed system, 5 years.

Approx. retail price
$1,899

Approx. low price
$1,563

KITCHENAID KSSS42QD

Recommended

This extra-wide large side-by-side built-in refrigerator has many great features, but its higher price makes it a Recommended product instead of a Best Buy. It boasts a 24.6-cubic-foot capacity with a total of 26.5 square feet of shelf space. Sleek styling is the result of the extra door panel kits: white, almond, or black; stainless steel; or your own custom trim. The refrigerator has three glass shelves, a meat locker, a wine rack, and humidity-controlled crispers. The door has four storage bins, and the freezer holds two heavy-duty baskets. An ice and water dispenser is included. A power interruption switch lets you know if the power has been turned off. Like all the KitchenAid refrigerators reviewed here, the KSSS42QD meets the 1996 federal standards for CFC elimination.

Specifications: height, 83⅝″; width, 42″; depth (including handle), 25″; shelf capacity, 26.5 square feet. **Warranty:** parts and labor, 2 years; sealed system and ice maker, parts and labor, 16 years; parts only, 12 years.

Approx. retail price
$3,799 (black)

Approx. low price
$3,282

Bar-size Refrigerators

GENERAL ELECTRIC TAX4BNS

✓ **BEST BUY**

This 3.9-cubic-foot Spacemaker refrigerator is a good value and would be a welcome addition to any student's room or family room. It is available only in light brown and has two half-deep door shelves and three wire interior shelves. The frozen food compartment will make ice in two mini ice trays and can store prefrozen foods up to two weeks.

Specifications: height, 33⅛″; width, 18⅝″; depth (excluding handle), 20½″; shelf capacity, 6.5 square feet. **Warranty:** parts and labor, 1 year; compressor, 5 years.

Prices are accurate at time of printing but are subject to manufacturers' changes.

Approx. retail price **$249** | **Approx. low price** **$236**

GENERAL ELECTRIC TAX2BNS

Budget Buy

Where space is at a minimum, the 1.9-cubic-foot GE TAX2BNS can provide refrigeration in a small area. It is available in light brown; the refrigerator has one wire shelf, and the door has one half-deep shelf. The freezer is adequate only for holding the two mini ice cube trays.

Specifications: height, 18⅞″; width, 18⅝″; depth (excluding handle), 21⅛″; shelf capacity, 2.9 square feet. **Warranty:** parts and labor, 1 year; compressor, 5 years.

Approx. retail price **$169** | **Approx. low price** **$160**

U-LINE 15R

Recommended

U-Line makes top-of-the-line built-in and specialty refrigerators. The 15R model can either fit under a kitchen counter or be used as a freestanding model. This model is a slim 15 inches wide and has 3.5 cubic feet of space. It comes in a black or white vinyl exterior with a recessed handle, and it accepts customized decorator door panels. The four shelves are made of adjustable tempered glass. Unlike the other two bar refrigerators reviewed, this model is frost-free. The U-Line 15R has adjustable legs and interior lighting and weighs 87 pounds. It is rated a Recommended product rather than a Best Buy because of its higher price.

Specifications: height, 35″; width, 14¹⁵⁄₁₆″; depth, 23⅛″. **Warranty:** parts and labor, 1 year; compressor, 5 years.

Approx. retail price **$614** | **Approx. low price** **$567**

FREEZERS

Refrigerators just don't provide enough freezer space for many families. If you have a large family, grow your own food, use large amounts of frozen foods, cook in large quantities, or shop infrequently, a stand-alone freezer is a good choice. Home freezers can assist in saving money on groceries because you can buy food in season when it is less expensive and stock up on foods on sale.

Upright or Chest?

The temperature inside a chest freezer is more stable than in an upright, thus cutting down on recrystallization of frozen foods. The disadvantages of chest freezers are that they require manual defrosting and can cause discomfort to your hands while searching for foods. Upright freezers provide greater accessibility to foods but cost more to purchase and to operate. Although pull-out baskets in chest freezers can assist in finding foods, they reduce usable space in the freezer. Chest freezers use less energy than upright freezers, but they take up more floor space than upright freezers. Whichever type of freezer you choose, check the bright yellow Energy Guide labels on each to compare operating costs.

Features and Terminology

Defrosting options: All chest freezers need to be defrosted manually. Upright freezers can be either manual or frost-free. This convenience comes with a higher purchase price and higher operating costs than those for a manual-defrost freezer. Manual-defrost freezers will require a complete defrosting about once a year and include a defrost drain. A new trend in manual defrosting systems is a power defrost mode, which causes heat to circulate through the cooling coils very quickly, thus reducing defrosting time.

Baskets: Both chest and upright freezers often have removable baskets, which are ideal for bulky, large items such as turkeys and hams.

Temperature control: Setting your freezer to its lowest temperature (zero degrees or lower) will aid in keeping foods frozen and in preventing large temperature swings. Many freezers have an adjustable temperature control; a freezer thermometer can also help. Some freezers have a quick-freeze or power-

Prices are accurate at time of printing but are subject to manufacturers' changes.

freeze setting that puts the freezer in a maximum cooling mode for freezing large quantities of food at one time.

Lock: A freezer lock with a pop-out key provides extra safety and security, especially if you have small children or if your freezer is located in the garage.

Other features: An interior light is very useful if your freezer is located in a dark spot. A fast-freezing shelf has an extra cooling coil and is particularly useful for adding new foods to be frozen. An audible temperature alarm can protect you from losing the freezer's contents if the door is not shut properly or if the electricity source is disabled.

Upright Freezers

WHITE-WESTINGHOUSE MFU14M2BW

✓BEST BUY

This white textured steel upright freezer model has 14.0 cubic feet of space with 15.3 square feet of shelf capacity. The MFU14M2BW has three freezer shelves, five door shelves, and one removable basket on the bottom for holding large or unusually shaped objects. This freezer has adjustable temperature controls and needs to be manually defrosted. Other features include a swing-down gate, a defrost drain, power cord retainer, magnetic door seals, and a door closer. The annual average energy cost is $41, and it exceeds Department of Energy standards by 4 percent.

Specifications: height, 59"; width, 28"; depth (excluding handle), 28½". **Warranty:** parts and labor, 1 year; sealed refrigeration system, 5 years.

Approx. retail price
$399

Approx. low price
$300

WHITE-WESTINGHOUSE MFU16F3BW

✓BEST BUY

This 15.7-cubic-foot upright freezer has a white textured steel exterior and is frost free for added convenience. It has five door shelves and four freezer shelves; total shelf capacity is 18.6 square feet. The temperature controls are ad-

Prices are accurate at time of printing but are subject to manufacturers' changes.

justable. Features for the MFU16F3BW include a lock with pop-out key, a power cord retainer, adjustable leveling legs, magnetic door seals, and a door closer. The annual average energy cost is $60, and it exceeds Department of Energy standards by 10 percent.

Specifications: height, 61½"; width, 32"; depth (excluding handle), 26½"; shelf capacity, 18.6 square feet. **Warranty:** parts and labor, 1 year; sealed refrigeration system, 5 years.

Approx. retail price	**Approx. low price**
$549	**$484**

GENERAL ELECTRIC FF16DS

✓BEST BUY

The GE FF16DS is a 15.7-cubic-foot frost-free upright freezer with five door shelves, four cabinet shelves, and one slide-out bulk storage basket. It has a white textured steel case and door. The interior light, adjustable temperature control, the audible temperature alarm, and the lock with self-ejecting key all combine to make this a full-featured freezer.

Specifications: height, 61½"; width, 32"; depth (including handle), 26½". **Warranty:** parts and labor, 1 year; sealed system, 5 years; food spoilage from parts, 1 year; food spoilage from sealed system, 5 years.

Approx. retail price	**Approx. low price**
$629	**$580**

Chest Freezers

WHITE-WESTINGHOUSE MFC09M3BW

✓BEST BUY

This 8.8-cubic-foot freezer is a good size for a small family. The white textured steel exterior of the White-Westinghouse MFC09M3BW is easy to wipe clean. This model boasts 308 pounds of food capacity. It includes a removable basket, defrost drain, lock with pop-out key, a light to indicate that the power is on, and adjustable temperature controls. It needs to be defrosted manually. The annual average energy cost is $25, and it exceeds Department of Energy standards by 7 percent.

Prices are accurate at time of printing but are subject to manufacturers' changes.

Specifications: height, 34¾"; width, 41"; depth, 23". **Warranty:** parts and labor, 1 year; sealed refrigeration system, 5 years.

Approx. retail price $299 | **Approx. low price** $299

GENERAL ELECTRIC FH25DS

✓ BEST BUY

The GE FH25DS is a large, 24.8-cubic-foot white chest freezer ideal for a large family. Its features include adjustable temperature control, an interior light, three removable sliding bulk storage baskets, counterbalanced lid to make opening and closing easier, a built-in lock with self-ejecting key, an audible alarm for temperature monitor, and a defrost water drain to assist in manual defrosting.

Specifications: height, 35"; width, 73¼"; depth, 29½". **Warranty:** parts and labor, 1 year; sealed system, 5 years; food spoilage from parts, 1 year; food spoilage from sealed system, 5 years.

Approx. retail price $569 | **Approx. low price** $502

WHITE-WESTINGHOUSE MFC25M4BW

✓ BEST BUY

With 24.9 cubic feet and 872 pounds of food capacity, this is White-Westinghouse's largest chest freezer model, which makes it suitable for a large family. This manual-defrost model has a white textured steel exterior. Other features include an adjustable temperature control, two removable baskets, a defrost drain, a divider/drain pan, a lock with pop-out key, and a power cord retainer. The average annual energy cost is $47, and the model exceeds Department of Energy standards by 10 percent.

Specifications: height, 35"; width, 73¼"; depth, 29½". **Warranty:** parts and labor, 1 year; sealed refrigeration system, 5 years.

Approx. retail price $529 | **Approx. low price** $521

DISHWASHERS

A dishwasher not only saves time and water, it actually gets dishes cleaner and closer to germ-free than you could by hand. It has been estimated that a dishwasher will save an average of four hours a week in a home situation. One study found that washing a load of eight place settings and serving pieces by hand used an average of 16 gallons of water. The dishwashers listed in this section use from around 7 to 9 gallons of water in the regular cycle.

Dishwashers range in price from about $200 to over $2,000. We believe that to buy a model at the lower end of the range is a mistake because evidence of inferior materials, construction techniques, or engineering design is likely to surface after a few years' use. As for models priced at the higher end of the range, we believe that they are overpriced and few service personnel are experienced in installing and repairing these lesser-known models.

You may be deciding whether to buy a built-in or a portable dishwasher. Built-in units are far more popular than portables. Built-ins are permanently attached to water pipes, drains, and electric lines. The main disadvantage of a built-in is that it deprives you of kitchen cabinet space. However, a few compact built-in models are designed for installation in less space.

Portable dishwashers roll on casters, connect to the sink, and drain through hoses. Most portables have a flow-through valve that lets you draw water from the faucet while the appliance is in operation. Many models can be converted to built-in units. If you are a renter who someday hopes to own a home, you might want to consider a convertible portable model.

Features and Terminology

Controls: Push-button or dial controls are the most economical and reliable. Electronic touch controls add up to $150 to the cost of the machine and give it a high-tech look. Some models have cycle monitor lights and a clean indicator light on the control panel.

Cycles: Three basic cycles handle most loads—normal wash, light wash or water-saver wash, and heavy-duty or pots/pans. Rinse/hold lets you rinse a partial load and wait until you load more dirty dishes before adding detergent and selecting a wash cycle.

Filtration: Up to four stages are used to remove solid materials from the wash water.

Racks: Nylon-coated racks are more durable than vinyl-coated racks. Better racks are also deeper and adjustable.

Sound insulation: The more noise-dampening features, the quieter the operation. Up to three layers of high-density fiberglass and quilted foil around the tub are the most common. Better-quality models also have a quiet-design motor, rubber motor mounts, and high-density padding around the motor.

Time delay: Some models can be set to begin washing up to 12 hours or more after loading. This lets you take advantage of off-peak electric rates.

Tub and inner door materials: Triple-coated porcelain enamel on steel is considered the best, most reasonably priced tub material. Stainless steel is the most durable and expensive. Polypropylene is very durable and inexpensive.

Washing action: The best results are obtained with a three-way mechanism. Good results can also be obtained with two-way action. One-way action may not provide satisfactory cleaning.

Water heating: Many models have an automatic water temperature booster system that ensures consistently hot water of about 140°F for the wash and rinse cycles. This feature lets you reduce the cost of operating your hot water heater by setting the thermostat as low as 120°F. Some models also have an extra-hot rinse option that heats the water to about 160°F. Water at this temperature may be effective in killing germs.

Best Buys '96

Our Best Buy, Recommended, and Budget Buy dishwashers follow. They are divided into categories of built-in and portable models. Within each category, the unit we consider to be the best of the Best Buys is listed first, followed by our second choice, and so on. Remember that a Best Buy, Recommended, or Budget Buy designation applies only to the model listed. It does not necessarily apply to other models made by the same manufacturer.

BUILT-IN MODELS

KITCHENAID SUPERBA KUDS230

✓BEST BUY

The KitchenAid Superba KUDS230 boasts a ½-horsepower motor—the most powerful in its class. It has push-button controls and four cycles: normal, light/china, soak/scrub pots/pans, and rinse/hold. Monitor lights indicate the cycle in progress. This model also features KitchenAid's exclusive TriDura porcelain-on-steel tub and inner door, which resists scratching and stains and aids in the drying process. The Hydro-Flo filtration system combines with a coarse strainer and heavy-duty stainless-steel food grinder to eliminate food particles from water. Other features include a durable stainless-steel upper wash arm, whisper-quiet operation, delay-wash, energy-saver no-heat dry and sani-rinse options, and adjustable nylon racks with a silverware basket that has a covered compartment to keep small items in place during washing.

Specifications: height, 33¹¹⁄₁₆"–35"; width, 24"; depth, 26"; water use, normal cycle, 7.3 gallons. **Warranty:** 1 year, full; motor and racks, parts, 5 years; tub and inner door, 25 years.

Approx. retail price	Approx. low price
$759	$675

GENERAL ELECTRIC PROFILE 4900 SERIES

✓BEST BUY

The GE Profile 4900 series dishwasher is a state-of-the-art machine with electronic touchpad controls and four cycles: normal, pots/pans, china/crystal, and rinse/hold. Features include a SmartWash system with three-level multi-orbital washing, CleanSensor system that adjusts water and water temperatures according to wash load, super quiet performance,

Prices are accurate at time of printing but are subject to manufacturers' changes.

and a flexible rack system with a silverware basket that divides in two and a slotted compartment that can be used as a knife holder or to contain loose items. A normal load takes just under one hour and uses 7.6 gallons of water. The self-cleaning filter traps food particles, then washes them down the drain. A digital systems monitor shows cycle in progress and time remaining. Other features include energy-saver dry, 14-hour delay start, and reset options, as well as a "lockout" touchpad that prevents accidental starting by small children.

Specifications: height, 34"–35"; width, 24"; depth, 24¾"; water use, normal cycle, 7.6 gallons. **Warranty:** 1 year, full; parts, 2 years; electronic controls and racks, 5 years; tub and inner door, 20 years.

Approx. retail price	Approx. low price
$649	$548

FRIGIDAIRE GALLERY FDB878GC ✓BEST BUY

The Frigidaire Gallery FDB878GC dishwasher has a ⅓-horsepower motor. Its Ultra-Power cleaning and solid food disposer eliminate the need to rinse or prewash dishes. A fixed tower wash system circulates water at three levels for maximum efficiency. The normal wash cycle uses only 7.7 gallons of water. The rotary control operates five wash cycles, including normal, heavy, power scrub, water saver, and rinse/hold. Easy-to-use touchpads control start/cancel, 6-hour delay, hi-temp (140°F) wash, and no-heat dry options. Other features include an Ultra-Quiet sound insulation system and easy-to-load extra-deep racks with a standard removable silverware basket, in addition to a separate utensil basket that has a closed compartment to contain small items during washing. This unit also comes with a 30-day money-back satisfaction guarantee.

Specifications: height, 34"–35"; width, 24"; depth, 25¼"; water use, normal cycle, 7.7 gallons. **Warranty:** 2 years, full; electronic controls and racks, 5 years; tub and door, 20 years.

Approx. retail price	Approx. low price
$449	$396

MAYTAG DEPENDABLY QUIET PLUS DWU9200

✓BEST BUY

The Maytag DWU9200 features a ⅓-horsepower motor with both push-button and rotary controls. Cycles include normal, light/china, pots/pans, sani-rinse, rinse/hold, and quick cycle. Other options include no-heat drying, temp-boost sensor water heating, three-level jet-spray wash system for greater scrubbing action, micro-mesh food filter and food disposer to eliminate waste particles, plus sound-absorbing insulation for quiet performance. This unit also has deluxe racks with folding shelves and an extra-large silverware basket, 12-hour delay start option, and indicator lights that tell you what cycle the machine is in.

Specifications: height, 33¾"–35¼"; width, 23⅞"; depth, 23½"; water use, normal cycle, 9 gallons. **Warranty:** 1 year, full; parts, 2 years; wash system, controls, racks, and exterior cabinet, 5 years; tub and door liner, 20 years.

Approx. retail price	Approx. low price
$499	$482

GENERAL ELECTRIC QUIETPOWER GSD1200X

Recommended

The GE Quietpower model GSD 1200X offers electronic touchpad controls with seven cycles: normal, light wash, pot scrubber, rinse/hold, water saver, short wash, and plate warmer. It has a three-level SmartWash system for optimum cleaning using 25 percent less water (9 gallons for a normal load). Other features include a temp-boost for wash water, energy-saver no-heat dry, plus 6-hour delay start options. This unit also has deluxe racks (with a lift-out silverware basket that splits into two sections and has a covered compartment to contain smaller items), self-cleaning filter system to eliminate food particles, and sound-dampening materials and insulation for quiet operation.

Specifications: height, 34"–35"; width, 24"; depth, 25⅛"; water use, normal cycle, 9 gallons. **Warranty:** 1 year, full; parts, 2 years, limited; rack and electronic parts, 5 years, limited; tub and door liner, 20 years.

Approx. retail price
$429

Approx. low price
$380

AMANA ADU6000

Recommended

The Amana ADU6000 has a ⅕-horsepower motor and seven cycle options: normal, pots/pans, light wash, heavy wash, short wash, plate warmer, and rinse/hold. It features the Elipticlean wash system with three wash levels, self-cleaning filter, push-button and rotary controls, 6-hour delay start, water temperature boost, and no-heat dry options. The extra-large lift-out silverware basket has a closed compartment to hold small items in place during washing.

Specifications: height, 34"; width, 24"; depth, 24"; water use normal cycle, 9 gallons. **Warranty:** 1 year, full; water distribution system, 2 years, limited; tub and inner door liner, 20 years.

Approx. retail price
$439

Approx. low price
$439

CALORIC CDU510

Budget Buy

The Caloric CDU510 offers a ⅕-horsepower motor with three-level wash system and five cycles: normal pots/pans, light, rinse/hold, and plate warmer. Controls are push-button and rotary with options that include water temperature boost and no-heat dry. The self-cleaning filter collect and drains food particles, and deluxe sound insulation provide quiet performance. The lift-out silverware basket has a closed compartment for small items.

Specifications: height, 34"; width, 24"; depth, 24"; water use normal cycle, 9 gallons. **Warranty:** 1 year, full; tub and door liner, 20 years.

Approx. retail price
$359

Approx. low price
$355

PORTABLE MODELS

GENERAL ELECTRIC GSC1200X

BEST BUY

The GE GSC1200X has all the features of a built-in unit with the added versatility of a portable. This uni

Prices are accurate at time of printing but are subject to manufacturers' changes.

is 24¾ inches wide, with wheels and a utility work top, and can be converted to built-in use at a later time. Touchpad and rotary controls operate seven cycles: normal, pot scrubber, light wash, short wash, water saver, rinse/hold, and plate warmer, as well as 6-hour delay start, temp-boost, and no-heat dry options. Extra-deep racks accommodate tall items, and the lift-out silverware basket splits into two separate sections with three compartments each and a cover to enclose small items.

Specifications: height, 36¼" (includes top and wheels); width, 24¾"; depth, 27"; water use, normal cycle, 9 gallons. **Warranty:** 1 year, full; parts, 2 years, limited; rack/electronic parts, 5 years, limited; tub/door liner, 20 years.

Approx. retail price	**Approx. low price**
$529	**$458**

FRIGIDAIRE FDP652RBR

✓ BEST BUY

The Frigidaire FDP652RBR is a 24-inch portable unit with wheels and a cherry-wood veneer top. It has a ⅓-horsepower motor and a three-level washing system. The five wash cycles include normal, heavy, power scrub, water saver, and rinse/hold. Other options include a no-heat dry and hi-temp wash. This unit has push-button and rotary controls, a soft food disposer that removes food particles from water, and insulation for quieter operation. Its normal cycle uses 7.6 gallons of water.

Specifications: height, 36"; width, 24½"; depth, 26⅞"; water use, normal cycle, 7.6 gallons. **Warranty:** 1 year, full; poly tub/door liner, 10 years, limited.

Approx. retail price	**Approx. low price**
$419	**$409**

MAYTAG DEPENDABLY QUIET DWU7400

Recommended

The Maytag DWU7400 is a convertible/portable unit that comes with a hardwood top, heavy-duty cabinet, and wheels. Push-button and rotary controls operate four cycles: normal, pots/pans, light/china, and rinse/hold.

Prices are accurate at time of printing but are subject to manufacturers' changes.

Other features include a temp-boost sensor water heating option and an energy-saving no-heat dry option. The normal wash cycle uses about 9 gallons of water. The flexible rack system has a removable extra-large silverware basket.

Specifications: height, 36½"; width, 28¼"; depth, 24¼"; water use, normal cycle, 9 gallons. **Warranty:** 1 year, full; parts, 2 years; wash system parts, computer controls, racks, and exterior cabinet, 5 years; tub and door liner, 20 years.

Approx. retail price	**Approx. low price**
$419	**$415**

FLOOR CARE

The era of the one-vacuum-cleaner household is fast becoming a thing of the past. The reason? Over the years, the vacuum cleaner has been refined and improved, giving rise to a new generation of specialized vacuums.

However, purchasing multiple cleaners doesn't simplify the shopping process. If you have several machines that aren't tailored to your home and habits, you will not get housework done as efficiently as you would with one cleaner that really suits your needs. So before you make any purchases, answer a few questions that will help you pick the right model (or combination of models).

What size is your home? There's no need for a huge model if your closet won't accommodate it or if you have a lot of bare floors. But even a small home with thick carpeting won't be easy to tackle with a mini machine.

What types of flooring do you have? If you have a sea of wall-to-wall carpeting, a powerful upright will probably be most effective. Lots of tile and wood will be maintained well with a suction-type canister or even a mini broom vac. An even mixture of surfaces might be cleaned best with a powerhead canister or possibly an upright and hand-held combination.

What type of vacuum cleaner are you most comfortable using? Logic may lead you to a certain type of cleaner, but if you're most at ease operating an upright and your home is crying out for a canister, it may be best to go with what you know. For some, vacuuming is unpleasant enough. There is no need to choose a machine style that goes against your grain.

The best shopping tip of all is to be educated about the advantages and disadvantages of the various categories of cleaner.

Upright, Canister, or Powerhead Vacuum Cleaner?

As stated previously, an upright is best for rug and carpet cleaning. Its agitator, which is essentially a beater bar outfitted with bristles, digs up embedded dirt and grit from even high-pile carpeting. Currently available uprights are more lightweight than other models. This makes them easier to handle on stairs, but they still do not boast the maneuverability of a canister. The upright also usually loses to the canister in above-the-floor cleaning (upholstery, windowsills, and draperies, for example) since the attachments needed to tackle these jobs are not always as accessible, and the upright doesn't roll along with the job as easily. A new generation of upright cleaners store above-the-floor tools on the unit, and some even have a permanently attached hose, which greatly increases convenience.

Canister vacuum cleaners are designed to make up for the shortcomings of uprights. The canister is usually quieter than the upright and does a fine job of cleaning bare floors and low-pile carpets. The nozzle's low profile permits better access under furniture, into tight spaces, and on stair treads, while its easy-to-change attachments allow it to be used effectively to remove dust from walls, curtains, and lamp shades. Because it lacks the upright's agitator, the canister does not remove dirt that has sifted down into the carpet pile as well as an upright. Most new canister models are extremely lightweight and maneuverable, but they are generally less powerful (in terms of suction).

A strong canister vacuum cleaner with a powerhead combines the best of the upright and the standard canister. It has a rolling tank (usually with a tool caddy), a hose, and a nozzle just like a canister, but it also has a powerhead, which is outfitted with an agitator similar to those on uprights. When you shop for a powerhead, examine the brush roll carefully. Some units of this type have an independent motor that allows them to dig deeper into thick-pile carpet. Others have a turbo- or suction-driven brush roll that has less strength, but may still be adequate for your needs. Remember, try it out before you buy.

Mini Vacuum Cleaners

Compact vacuum cleaners are available in many shapes and sizes. They are designed for quick spot cleanups or dry spills. These scaled-down units can be a great convenience, as long as you remember that they are intended for smaller jobs. The motors on minis have less power, and the dust bag or cup must be emptied often. Cordless minis are supremely portable and ideal for room-to-room touch-ups and car care. Corded models have greater strength and won't run out of juice, but you'll have to work with the same outlet limitations as with a regular vacuum cleaner.

Steam Cleaners

Once only available through rental, carpet steam cleaners now have a significant presence at retail outlets. These vacs typically are a bigger-ticket item than their conventional counterparts, but offer added cleaning capability. Also known as spray extraction machines, these units work by dispensing a cleaning solution into the carpet. A brush connected to the head of the nozzle helps agitate dirt before the dirty water is sucked back into the machine.

Wet/Dry Vacuum Cleaners

Wet/dry vacuum cleaners handle messes indoors and out. Full-size models quickly clean up a muddy garage or soapy washing machine overflow. Some units feature a blower for added versatility.

Best Buys '96

Our Best Buy, Recommended, and Budget Buy floor-care appliances follow. These appliances have been selected on the basis of convenience, performance, and overall value. Within each category, the item we consider the best of the Best Buys is listed first, followed by our second choice, and so on. Remember that a Best Buy, Recommended, or Budget Buy designation applies only to the model listed; it does not necessarily apply to other models made by the same manufacturer or to an entire product line.

UPRIGHT VACUUM CLEANERS

EUREKA VICTORY THE BOSS 4335 ✓BEST BUY

The Boss Upright is part of the innovative new Victory series from Eureka, which is designed with increased filtration and noise reduction systems, as well as consumer friendly features such as ergonomic handles. Its powerful 10 amp motor, which has a high-efficiency bypass air system fo deep carpet cleaning, is very effective and relatively quiet, whil the ergonomic handle, which tilts forward to reduce bending truly makes vacuuming easier on the back. Other factors tha contribute to this model's ease of use and maneuverability in clude its light weight for an upright (less than 15 pounds), a automatic conversion system to switch over from carpet t above-the-floor cleaning, a convenient on-board tool storag system (with a built-in hose, nested wands, a combination up holstery nozzle/dusting brush, and a crevice tool), a seven-po sition carpet height adjustment, and a wraparound furnitur guard. High performance and a reasonable price combine t make this unit a terrific buy.

Warranty: 1 year, limited.

Approx. retail price	**Approx. low price**
$160	**$100**

HOOVER POWER DRIVE U6311-930

BEST BUY

The Hoover Power Drive does a remarkable job of picking up dust and dirt thanks to its motor, which uses onl 7.8 amps of power but is extremely efficient. The unit merit its price, which is higher than other upright models, becaus of its superior cleaning capacity, loads of special features, an solid construction. "Power Drive" refers to the fact that the uni is self-propelled for effortless vacuuming (despite its 21. pounds), which makes the unit very easy to maneuver. Its spe cial features are also well thought out and sensibly designec with an on/off switch in the hand grip (to avoid bending), tool kit (including a built-in hose, crevice tool, dusting brush extension wand, and furniture nozzle) placed at the top of th unit in an on-board storage box covered with clear plastic, ur complicated slide-button controls located on the unit's base, durable easy-change bag compartment, and a powerful "dir finding" headlight. The unit also has a built-in handle to faci itate carrying it between floors, an extra-long 31-foot powe

Prices are accurate at time of printing but are subject to manufacturers' changes.

cord for added flexibility, and on-board storage for an extra dust bag and motor belt. Made of high-impact ABS thermoplastic, this unit is extremely sturdy and a great performer.

Warranty: 1 year, full.

Approx. retail price $370 | **Approx. low price** $270

HOOVER ELITE SUPREME U5071-930

Recommended

The Hoover Elite Supreme offers many of the special features this brand is known for at a more moderate price, including outstanding cleaning capabilities and a solid, sensible design. The 7.2-amp motor is very efficient and does an admirable job on dust and dirt, while the special features make cleaning easy. The front of the unit snaps wide open for easy dust bag changes. A tool kit (with a built-in hose, crevice tool, dusting brush, extension wand, and upholstery nozzle) is stored on board, the unit has a headlight for working under furniture, uncomplicated slide-button controls are located at the base, and a three-position handle allows the unit to lie flat for low-clearance furnishings. A nice touch is a special grip located on the front of the vacuum, to facilitate the chore of cleaning stairs.

Warranty: 1 year, full.

Approx. retail price $200 | **Approx. low price** $137

ROYAL DIRT DEVIL MVP 088305

Recommended

With its sleek design and stunning bright red hue to match its name, the Royal Dirt Devil is one of the best-looking vacuums around. But it has more than just its great looks to make it a good performer. MVP stands for maximum vacuum power, and the 12-amp motor does a good job of earning that title. The unit also has a "dirt-finding" headlight and can be laid flat for cleaning under low-slung furnishings such as coffee tables and beds. Other handy features include an extra-long 32-foot cord, easy-to-reach on-board tools (including a built-in hose, telescopic wand, crevice and upholstery

Prices are accurate at time of printing but are subject to manufacturers' changes.

tools, and dusting brush), and a motor-guard system to prevent damage to the fan and motor from hidden debris in sofas and chairs. The sensible price and stylish design, coupled with a few more nice touches (such as a carrying handle and quick-cord release) make the unit a good all-around cleaning tool.

Warranty: 1 year, full; motor, 2 years.

Approx. retail price $170 | **Approx. low price** $133

EUREKA BRAVO! BOSS 9334

Budget Buy

If you can live without the solid construction of a sturdier vacuum (more expensive models have hard plastic casings covering the dust bags, while this one has a cloth bag), Eureka's Bravo! Boss is a superb choice. Considering the efficiency and efficacy of the 9-amp motor, which picks up dust and dirt almost as well as units listed as Best Buys, Bravo is an apt name. This no-frills vac does a great job and sports an on-board assortment of tools that includes two extension wands, a crevice tool, and a combination dusting brush/upholstery tool. It also has a seven-position carpet height adjustment, and it can be made to lie flat for cleaning under coffee tables and beds. Plus it only weighs 13 pounds. You can't go wrong with this vac, especially considering its price.

Warranty: 1 year, limited.

Approx. retail price $150 | **Approx. low price** $93

CANISTER VACUUM CLEANERS

EUREKA THE BOSS MIGHTY MITE II 3621A

✓ BEST BUY

The name Mighty Mite fits this unit, which looks like a sturdy little creature ready to pounce on dirt. Thanks to its low weight (just over 10 pounds) and clever design (with oversized wheels and a large handle right on it

Prices are accurate at time of printing but are subject to manufacturers' changes.

back), you can lift it just like a small suitcase and use it right where it's needed. The Mighty Mite has relatively good suction—it works much better on bare floors. Its ingeniously concealed on-board attachments include a crevice tool, dusting brush, and upholstery tool designed to work on a variety of household surfaces. The dust bag is very easy to change. Other nice touches include a triple filtration bag system and oversized wheels, which help make this a great multipurpose vacuum that can complement an upright for carpets or go on its own if a residence has mostly bare floors.

Warranty: 1 year, limited.

Approx. retail price **$120** | **Approx. low price** **$80**

HOOVER FUTURA S3523

✓BEST BUY

This sleek, all-tools-on-board canister from Hoover merits the name Futura. It is also moderately priced but offers many of the same features as more expensive models. The efficient 7.6-amp motor does a relatively good job of picking up dust and dirt—it works better on bare floors. The unit has great maneuverability thanks to its 20-foot cord, low weight (just under 12 pounds), easy-roll wheels, and six-foot hose with swivel joint, which is an especially nice feature, as it can be pulled from any direction. The on-board tool set includes two extension wands, furniture and rug/floor nozzles, a crevice tool, and a dusting brush.

Warranty: 1 year, full.

Approx. retail price **$290** | **Approx. low price** **$103**

ROYAL DIRT DEVIL CAN VAC 082023

Recommended

This bright red compact canister has more than just its chunky good looks to make it a decent can vac. With a 9.2-amp motor, it also offers good cleaning power on bare floors and moderate suction on carpets. Its best points include its small size (the canister weighs only 9.5 pounds), an on-board tool set (including a hose, carpet and crevice tools,

Prices are accurate at time of printing but are subject to manufacturers' changes.

bare floor and dusting brushes, two locking extension wands, and a shoulder strap), and an optional (separately purchased) power nozzle that can improve its performance on carpets. Easy-roll wheels and a good-size handle smack on its back make this unit extremely maneuverable and round out its appeal.

Warranty: 1 year.

Approx. retail price	**Approx. low price**
$100	**$82**

POWERHEAD CANISTERS

EUREKA WORLD VAC HOME CLEANING SYSTEM 6865

✔BEST BUY

Don't be fooled by the cute appearance of this powerhead vac: It delivers superior performance. The powerful 12-amp motor supplies optimum suction strength for cleaning both carpets and bare floors, while the Filteraire bag system retains 99 percent of the dirt, dust, and pollen it picks up, according to the manufacturer's claims. The motorized carpet nozzle, complete with headlight for working under furniture, has a double-sweep bristle brush roll that provides dual-edge cleaning and is easy to maneuver, thanks to a swivel joint at the base of its hose. Large easy-glide wheels, a 7-foot hose and 25-foot power cord, and a comprehensive tool set conveniently stored on top of the unit (with two chrome steel wands, an upholstery nozzle, dusting and bare floor brushes, and a crevice tool) also contribute to its ease of use. Touches such as a bag-full indicator, automatic carpet height adjustment, and a sturdy carrying handle make this a premium unit. And it weighs in at only 12 pounds. While the World Vac has a premium price, the superior performance and outstanding features can be worth it.

Warranty: 1 year, limited.

Approx. retail price	**Approx. low price**
$320	**$210**

Prices are accurate at time of printing but are subject to manufacturers' changes.

HOOVER FUTURA S3567

Recommended

The Hoover Futura is a well-priced, efficient new entry into the powerhead canister vac market, with sleek styling that gives it an aerodynamic look. The Futura has an efficient 9.8-amp motor that does a superior job picking up dust and dirt, and it's loaded with all the features of more expensive models. These include a 6-foot swivel hose, a 25-foot retractable cord, a full-bag indicator, a carrying handle, and on-board molded storage for its tool set (which includes two chrome extension wands, a crevice tool, dusting brush, furniture nozzle, and wall/floor brush), as well as two chrome extension wands. The motorized power nozzle has a two-brush agitator, brushed edge cleaning on both sides, and a powerful headlight. Although it's not cheap, the price is fair for all the features packed on this vac.

Warranty: 1 year, full.

Approx. retail price	Approx. low price
$290	$219

ROYAL DIRT DEVIL POWER PAK 082123

Budget Buy

This compact powerhead canister, which is very similar to its "sister" can vac, has chunky good looks, weighs in at 9 pounds without its power nozzle, and has a 10-amp motor. While it offers decent cleaning power on bare floors and very moderate suction on carpets, its low price and weight make it a good option for small jobs. The Power Pak's best points include its small size (the main body is only 13 inches long) and an on-board tool set (including a hose, crevice tool, dusting brush, two extension wands, and a shoulder strap). Easy-roll wheels and a good-size handle on its back make the unit extremely maneuverable and round out its appeal.

Warranty: 1 year.

Approx. retail price	Approx. low price
$150	$123

Prices are accurate at time of printing but are subject to manufacturers' changes.

MINI VACUUM CLEANERS

BLACK & DECKER COLLECTOR AC8000

✓BEST BUY

Black & Decker originated the Dustbuster 15 years ago, and the Collector, their entry in the mini-vac market, was the first (and still may be the only) hand-held vac to have its tools and attachments on board. And it's a great idea, since it gives this little unit maximum flexibility. The power brush seems exceptionally sturdy, and it automatically disengages when the 32-inch extendable hose and crevice tool attachment are used. This system allows the 2-amp motor to provide maximum air flow for peak performance to whichever air suction device is being used. The unit weighs 4.5 pounds and has an extra-long 25-foot cord, as well as a large-capacity dirt bag (2.5 quarts) that's easy to empty. A disposable paper filter bag can also be used with the unit, which is an exceptional performer for a hand vac. For added versatility, a four-piece accessory kit can be purchased for about $20.

Warranty: 2 years.

Approx. retail price	**Approx. low price**
$50	**$45**

EUREKA CORVETTE VAC 52A

✓BEST BUY

Even though the Eureka Corvette Vac sports the same slick styling as its namesake, it's a real workhorse. The 2-amp motor, which directly drives the brush roll, is efficient and really sucks up dirt and dust. The Riser Visor—the company's name for the front visor of the unit that houses the brush roll—can be placed in a horizontal or vertical position to reach into nooks, crannies, and crevices. A long cord (25 feet) and low weight (4 pounds) give the unit maximum mobility, but one of its most appealing features is that it uses no dust bags—you just empty the clear plastic dust cup when it's filled. The bright red unit comes with no additional tools, but two different accessory sets are available: the Corvette Attachment Set with three tools for cars and the Mini-Tool Attachment Set with seven tools for

Prices are accurate at time of printing but are subject to manufacturers' changes.

the home and electronic equipment. These greatly increase the Corvette Vac's versatility and make it an ideal unit for every kind of task.

Warranty: 1 year, limited.

Approx. retail price
$50

Approx. low price
$34

STEAM CLEANER/EXTRACTOR

HOOVER STEAMVAC F5815

✓BEST BUY

The Hoover SteamVac not only brings the ease and convenience of upright floor vacuuming to deep steam cleaning for carpets and upholstery (these units have traditionally resembled canister vacs), it features a unique configuration that enables the machine to clean in forward and reverse motion. A two-tank design, with the upper tank for cleaning solution and the bottom tank for dirty water recovery, eliminates the need for faucet hookups, while a handle with a trigger controls how much hot cleaning solution is sprayed into the carpet. At 17.9 pounds, it's also light enough to carry and has several outstanding ease-of-use features, such as large, simple latches to empty the recovery tank, easy-roll wheels for increased maneuverability, and a 10-foot hose and nozzle attachment that quickly converts the unit for cleaning carpeted stairs and upholstery. Given the cost of renting a steam cleaner, the SteamVac F5815 can be an economical addition to a home that has lots of carpeting and upholstered pieces.

Warranty: 1 year, full.

Approx. retail price
$210

Approx. low price
$180

WET/DRY VACUUM CLEANERS

BISSELL BIG GREEN CLEAN MACHINE 1671

✓BEST BUY

Bissell calls its Big Green Clean Machine "the one for all," which it very well may be. This three-function

Prices are accurate at time of printing but are subject to manufacturers' changes.

cleaning system takes the wet/dry vac to new heights: Use it for both wet and dry vacuuming, as well as heavy-duty deep cleaning. It has a state-of-the-art dual filtration system for dry vacuuming that requires no bags and has a washable, reusable dry filter. It also has a high-pressure pump for deep cleaning. A built-in brush can be used to tackle stubborn stains, and a whole range of tools are included with the machine for cleaning upholstery, stairs, and crevices (and supposedly even unclogging sinks). The extra-long cord (18 feet) and flex hose (8 feet) are a big bonus. But perhaps its biggest advantage is an included videotape that explains the unit's assembly and use.

Warranty: 2 years, full.

Approx. retail price **$190** | **Approx. low price** **$190**

HOOVER WET/DRY VAC SUPREME S6751

✓BEST BUY

Hoover's Wet/Dry Vac Supreme is a fully loaded, top-of-the-line model that performs superbly thanks to its two-tank construction, large 12.5-gallon capacity, and efficient 9.5-amp motor. Its built-in tool storage system includes a 12-piece set, complete with nozzles and wands for every conceivable cleaning task, and a detachable blower that snaps out easily. The two-tank system provides instant changeover from wet to dry without emptying the tank or changing the filter—you just flip a big red selector button and insert the hose into the opening for the wet or dry tank. The drainage system is cleverly placed at the bottom of the unit, so it just needs to be uncapped to be emptied. The cartridge filter is easy to install. The Wet/Dry Vac Supreme also has a low center of gravity and wide wheel base, which makes it tip-resistant and easy to maneuver. It has a 6-foot hose, a 12-foot cord, and a dark gray body with red and black trim.

Warranty: 2 years, limited.

Approx. retail price **$130** | **Approx. low price** **$114**

Prices are accurate at time of printing but are subject to manufacturers' changes.

EUREKA SHOP BOSS WET/DRY 2818

Recommended

The Shop Boss is a good performer in this category, with its 9.5-amp motor, 9-gallon capacity, and WideTrack five-wheel caster system to prevent tipping. It comes with an eight-piece accessory kit that is stored on-board, including a detachable blower and 6-foot hose. This model has a six-foot cord. The sturdy design has a low center of gravity. You can use the Shop Boss indoors or out for liquid spills and debris that is heavier than the usual dust or dirt. It's a good buy for the price.

Warranty: 1 year, limited.

Approx. retail price	Approx. low price
$120	$120

ELECTRIC BROOM

EUREKA POWERLINE SUPERBROOM 296

✓BEST BUY

In general, electric brooms are not very powerful, but the Powerline Superbroom packs more power, and operates more quietly, than most. It has an efficient 6-amp motor that can be used for light tasks and electronic speed control dials to adjust the power on various settings. A floor nozzle with a two-position adjustable brush and an Edge Kleener are other nice features, especially since they make it easier to use the unit on carpet or bare floors. But the 1.8-quart dust cup is this unit's best feature, since it eliminates the necessity for frequent bag changes (although you do have to empty the cup regularly).

Warranty: 1 year, limited.

Approx. retail price	Approx. low price
$80	$60

LAUNDRY CARE

As with so many other industries, the laundry care business changes quickly. In 1996, energy savings is a major issue. One of the most important pieces of information on a washer or dryer is how much energy it uses. Look closely at any machine and you'll quickly discover its energy-saving features, which are usually built around an eye-catching name or phrase.

Energy savings is not the only issue, however. Another particularly significant trend in this area is toward large-capacity washing machines. Industry experts predict that the number of available standard-size washers will continue to decline as manufacturers focus on making extra-large-capacity machines. The change, experts say, is in response to consumer demands for larger-size washers.

Which machine is right for you? There is no scientific way to determine the answer to that question. Price point and personal needs are the key issues. Prices range from $200 for a low-end machine to $1,800 for a designer-style washer with every conceivable feature. Besides price, consider the type of clothing you own. If you favor permanent press fabrics, buy a dryer with a permanent press cycle. If you have a preference for delicate materials, consider a washer with a hand wash option.

Gas or Electric Machines

In general, gas dryers cost up to $50 more than electric models. Whether you buy an electric or gas unit depends on which energy source you have in your home. Both gas and electric dryers come in full-size and compact models. Small-capacity portable electric units are also available. Gas dryers must be permanently installed because they require attachment to a gas line and must be vented to the outside. Most gas models include an energy-saving electronic ignition system.

Washer Features and Terminology

Capacity: Tub sizes range from 1.5 to 3.5 cubic feet. Machines with extra-large capacity boast 3.0 or more cubic feet; large capacity, 2.5 cubic feet; regular or standard, 2.0 cubic feet; and compact, 1.5 cubic feet.

Controls: The new wave in appliances is digital controls. You'll find them on radios, televisions, and washers and dryers. While the appearance is upscale, the performance can be below that of push-button or rotary dial units. The best advice is to ask your appliance repair service. Most agree that push-button or rotary dial machines are still more reliable than those with electronic controls.

Cycles: Commonly found cycles are regular, permanent press, delicate, and a soak setting. Cycles can be automatic or set prior to wash.

Lint filter: All units have a lint filter. Its primary purpose is to strain lint out of the rinse water and keep it off your clothes. Many machines have self-cleaning filters. Others catch lint in a basket, which must be cleaned manually. Both work well. To decide which system is best for you, consider whether your wash water empties into a home septic system or a sewer system. If it's a septic system, you may not want the extra material flowing into it.

Load-balance stabilizer: When a load becomes unbalanced, some washers sound a warning, others shut off, and still others slow down and automatically correct the problem. A buzzer is generally most effective, provided you are able to hear the warning.

Speed: Most washers have two speeds, high and low. Others offer combinations such as normal agitate/normal spin and slow agitate/slow spin.

Water temperature: All machines carry a number of wash-rinse water temperature settings based on combining hot, warm, and cold. The most energy efficient is a cold-water cycle. Warm-water rinse is better for clothes than hot water, which is best for soaking heavily soiled white clothes.

Dryer Features and Terminology

Air fluff: This feature tumbles the load without heat to make items soft. It is commonly used for pillows, blankets, and even towels.

Controls: Timed control permits you to run the machine for an hour or longer. Automatic control can be set for the desired degree of dryness. Electronic control senses when the load is dry and shuts off the unit.

Drying cycles: The three basic cycles are regular, permanent press, and delicate. Permanent press has a cooldown period of about five minutes—the drum rotates with the heat off. This cycle minimizes wrinkles and brings the load to room temperature. The delicate cycle runs on low heat and is easy on clothes.

Drying sensor: This feature prevents overdrying. The sensor also detects clothing's moisture content or the dryer's exhaust and shuts off the unit when the humidity reaches a specific level.

Lint filter: This feature catches lint as the load is drying. The filter should be accessible and easy to clean. Some filters signal when they need cleaning. The lint filter is generally located up front around the dryer opening.

Drying rack: This feature has limited uses, but you'll be glad to have one when drying sneakers. Dry these items without a rack and you risk damage to the inside of your machine.

Wrinkle prevention: Ever unload your dryer long after it stops, only to find wrinkles in the clothes? If so, then you may want to invest in this feature, which continues to tumble the load intermittently without heat for up to 2½ hours. On some models, a buzzer sounds at intervals during this period.

Best Buys '96

Our Best Buy, Recommended, and Budget Buy clothes washer and dryer choices follow. In each category, the unit we consider the best of the Best Buys is first, followed by our second choice, and so on. A Best Buy, Recommended, or Budget Buy designation refers only to the model listed and not necessarily to other models by the same manufacturer or to an entire product line.

EXTRA-LARGE-CAPACITY WASHERS

WHIRLPOOL LSE9355B

✓BEST BUY

The Whirlpool LSE9355B is a high-quality extra-large-capacity clothes washer. This model has three wash/spin

Prices are accurate at time of printing but are subject to manufacturers' changes.

speeds, five water level settings, and five wash/rinse/spray temperature combinations. The automatic cycles include super wash, heavy wash, normal regular, permanent press–regular, delicate, hand wash (Ultimate Care), soak, and delay wash. Other notable features include automatic load balance compensation; self-cleaning lint filter; child lockout; on/off end-of-cycle signal; dispensers for detergent, bleach, and fabric softener; an extra rinse option; and a porcelain-coated steel wash tub. This model is available in white-on-white or almond-on-almond.

Specifications: height, 42⅜″; width, 26⅞″; depth, 25½″; volts/amps, not avaliable. **Warranty:** 1 year, full; replacement parts related to gear-case assembly, 5 years; outer tub, parts, 10 years.

Approx. retail price **$629** | **Approx. low price** **$585**

GENERAL ELECTRIC WWSR3090T

✓BEST BUY

The General Electric WWSR3090T extra-large-capacity washer is a new addition to GE's line for the 1996 model year. This roomy machine has three wash/spin speed combinations, four water level settings, and four wash/rinse temperature combinations. The nine automatic cycles are power wash, heavy soil, medium soil, light soil, extra rinse, permanent press, knits, delicates, and auto soak. Other useful features include automatic load-balance compensation, self-cleaning lint filter, dispensers for bleach and fabric softener, an extra-rinse option, and a durable tub and basket. This model is available in either white-on-white or almond-on-almond.

Specifications: height, 42″; width, 27″; depth, 25½″; volts/amps, 115/9.5. **Warranty:** 1 year, full; Auto Balance Suspension System, transmission, ArmorGuard lid, and cover protection, 5 years; outer tub, 10 years, limited; PermaTuf II basket, 20 years, limited.

Approx. retail price **$489** | **Approx. low price** **$439**

Prices are accurate at time of printing but are subject to manufacturers' changes.

LARGE-CAPACITY WASHERS

AMANA LW8203W2

✓BEST BUY

Available in white or almond, the Amana LW8203W2 is a reliable large-capacity washer. This model has two wash/spin speeds, variable water-level settings, and three wash/rinse temperature combinations. It also features seven automatic cycles: regular-heavy, regular-normal, regular-light, permanent press–normal, permanent press–light, delicate-normal, and delicate-light. Additional handy features are gentle cycle; automatic shutoff for unbalanced loads; self-cleaning lint filter; self-adjusting rear leveling legs; dispensers for detergent, bleach, and fabric softener; and a stainless steel wash tub.

Specifications: height, 43¼″; width, 25⅝″; depth, 28″; volts/amps, 120/15. **Warranty:** 2 years, full; transmission, 5 years, full; rust on cabinet, 5 years, limited; transmission, 10 years, limited; tub, 20 years, limited.

Approx. retail price	Approx. low price
$449	$414

MAYTAG LAT9304

✓BEST BUY

The Maytag LAT9304 is a high-quality large-capacity washer. This Fabric-Matic model has a two-speed ½-horsepower motor. The Fabric-Matic delicate cycle uses alternating periods of agitation and soaking to produce an effect similar to hand washing. This model has four water level settings, three wash/rinse temperature combinations, and seven automatic cycles: regular-heavy, regular-normal, regular-light, permanent press–heavy, permanent press–normal, permanent press–light, and delicate. Other notable features include self-cleaning lint filter, dispenser for fabric softener, and a white porcelain-coated steel wash tub. This model comes in white or almond.

Specifications: height, 43⅝″; width, 25½″; depth, 26¾″; volts/amps, 120/15. **Warranty:** parts and labor, 1 year; parts, 2 years; replacement parts related to cabinet rust and washer motor, 5 years; transmission, parts, 10 years.

Approx. retail price
$500

Approx. low price
$492

SEARS KENMORE 25882

Recommended

The Sears Kenmore 25882 is a good, reliable machine with a four-position speed switch, variable water-level settings, and an automatic temperature control. The eight automatic cycles are heavy duty, regular, gentle, normal, permanent press, second rinse, prewash (manual), and soak (manual). Other nice features include a self-cleaning lint filter, dispensers for bleach and fabric softener, and a double-coated porcelain steel wash tub. This model is available in white-on-white or almond-on-almond.

Specifications: height, 43⅛"; width, 27"; depth, 25½"; volts/amps, 120/15. **Warranty:** parts and labor, 1 year; gear case, parts only, 5 years.

Approx. retail price
$500

Approx. low price
$500

STANDARD-CAPACITY WASHERS

ADMIRAL LATA200AAW

✓BEST BUY

The Admiral LATA200AAW is an excellent standard-capacity washer. This two-speed unit has a ¾-horsepower motor. It has variable water-level settings and four wash/rinse temperature combinations. The three automatic cycles are cotton/linen, permanent press, and knits/delicates. Other convenient features include self-cleaning lint filter, bleach dispenser, and a molded polymer wash tub. This model is available in white or almond.

Specifications: height, 44"; width, 27"; depth, 27"; volts/amps, 120/11.5. **Warranty:** parts and labor, 1 year; transmission, parts, 10 years; inner wash basket and outer tub, parts, 20 years.

Approx. retail price
$415

Approx. low price
$379

Prices are accurate at time of printing but are subject to manufacturers' changes.

MAYTAG LAT7304

✓BEST BUY

The Maytag LAT7304 is a solid, reliable machine. This Fabric-Matic model has a two-speed ½-horsepower motor. The Fabric-Matic delicate cycle uses alternating periods of agitation and soak for an effect similar to hand washing. It has variable water-level settings and three wash/rinse temperature combinations. This model offers seven automatic cycles: regular-heavy, regular-normal, regular-light, permanent press–heavy, permanent press–normal, permanent press–light, and delicate. A self-cleaning lint filter, dispenser for fabric softener, and white porcelain-coated steel wash tub are additional convenient features. You can choose white or almond.

Specifications: height, 43⅝"; width, 25½"; depth, 26¾"; volts/amps, 120/15. **Warranty:** parts and labor, 1 year; parts, 2 years; replacement parts related to cabinet rust and washer motor, 5 years; transmission, parts, 10 years.

Approx. retail price	Approx. low price
$479	$467

ASKO PREMIER 10504

Recommended

The Asko Premier 10504 is a front-loading washer built with European technology. A quiet-running machine, it's also energy and water efficient. This model has two wash/spin speeds, a variable water level, and a variable wash/rinse temperature range (68°F–194°F). This model offers 11 automatic cycles: prewash, long main wash, short main wash, wool wash, five rinse cycles, short spin, and final spin. In addition to these basic cycles, there are several program options that allow the user to custom-adjust the automatic cycles. Program options include gentle wash, fast wash, economy program, delay spin, and high rinse level. Other notable features include automatic load-balance compensation, child safety lock, a trap to catch buttons and pins, lint filter, internal water heater (this unit requires only a cold water line for hookup), dispenser for detergent and fabric softener, and a stainless steel wash tub. This unit uses only 11 to 17 gallons of water per load (verses 41 to 49 gallons for a conventional clothes washer) and spins up to 1,000 rpm to get as much moisture out of the wash as possible, thus cutting down on dryer time. The Asko Premier is available only in white.

Specifications: height, 33¼"–33½"; width, 23½"; depth, 34⅜" (with door open); volts/amps, 208–230/15. **Warranty:** parts and labor, 1 year; solid state controls, pumps, and motors, parts, 5 years; stainless steel tank from rust, parts, 25 years.

Approx. retail price	**Approx. low price**
$999	**$941**

MAGIC CHEF W225

Budget Buy

If you're looking for a good buy on a standard-capacity washer, check out the Magic Chef W225. This model has three wash/spin speeds, four water-level settings, and three wash/rinse temperature combinations. The eight automatic cycles are cotton/linen–heavy, normal, and light; permanent press–heavy, normal, and light; and delicate–normal and light. Other handy extras include automatic load balance compensation, self-cleaning lint filter, dispenser for bleach, and a poly wash tub. This model is available in white or almond.

Specifications: height, 44"; width, 27"; depth, 27"; volts/amps, 120/15. **Warranty:** parts and labor, 1 year; transmission, 10 years, limited; tub, parts, 22 years, limited.

Approx. retail price	**Approx. low price**
$399	**$373**

COMPACT WASHER

SANYO ASW36NP

✓BEST BUY

The Sanyo ASW36NP is a well-built compact washer. This model has two wash/spin speeds—normal and gentle. It has four water-level settings and two wash/rinse temperature combinations. Fully automatic, drip dry, and wash only are this unit's three automatic cycles. Other notable features include automatic load-balance compensation, lint filter, dispenser for fabric softener, and a poly wash tub. The Sanyo ASW36NP does

Prices are accurate at time of printing but are subject to manufacturers' changes.

not require plumbing; attach the water supply line to a sink faucet and drain waste water into a sink. It is available only in white.

Specifications: height, 37"; width, 21¼"; depth, 21 7/16"; volts/amps, 120/30. **Warranty:** parts and labor, 1 year.

Approx. retail price	**Approx. low price**
$460	**$390**

OVER/UNDER COMBINATIONS

FRIGIDAIRE FLSG72GCS (GAS)/ FLSE72GCS (ELECTRIC)

✓BEST BUY

The Frigidaire FLSG72GCS/FLSE72GCS is a high-quality clothes washer/dryer system. The washer has a ¾-horsepower, 2-speed motor offering three wash/spin speed combinations. It has four wash/rinse temperature combinations and variable water-level settings. The ten automatic wash cycles are four regular cycles, three permanent press cycles, knits/delicate cycle, soak cycle, and prewash cycle. Other notable features include automatic load-balance compensation, self-cleaning lint filter, dispensers for bleach and fabric softener, safety lid lock, and a poly tub and basket. The dryer features four timed dry cycles, three auto dry cycles, and four temperature settings. The dryer also has an interior drum light, drying rack, and end-of-cycle signal. This system is available in white or almond.

Specifications: height, 75½"; width, 27"; depth, 33 13/16"; volts/amps (gas dryer), 120/20; watts/volts/amps (electric dryer), 4,500/240/30; gas heating element, 20,000 Btu. **Warranty:** 2 years, full; tub, 25 years.

Approx. retail price	**Approx. low price**
$1,030 (gas)	**$939**
$1,030 (electric)	**$903**

MAYTAG LSG9904 (GAS)/ LSE9904 (ELECTRIC)

✓BEST BUY

The Maytag LSG9904/LSE9904 is an excellent laundry care system. The washer has a ½-horsepower motor and two wash/spin speed combinations. It has four wash/rinse temperature combinations and three water-level settings. You can do your wash with six automatic wash cycles: soak only, regular, permanent press, delicates/knits, rinse, and spin. Other electronic options include small, medium, and large loads; pause/resume; automatic presoak; and warm rinse. You'll also find conveniences such as automatic load-balance compensation, self-cleaning lint filter, dispensers for bleach and fabric softener, cycle sequence lights, self-diagnostics, and white porcelain on a steel tub. Electronic controls for both the washer and dryer are centrally located on the bottom of the dryer. The dryer features three timed dry cycles and three temperature selections with options for delicate, timed dry, air fluff, and wrinkle prevention. The dryer also has an end-of-cycle signal. A cooldown indicator light is also on the control panel. The filter is located in the front of the unit. This system is available in white or almond.

Specifications: height, 73″; width, 27½″; depth, 27½″; volts/amps (gas dryer), 120/15; watts/volts/amps (electric dryer), 4,600/240/30; gas heating element, 18,000 Btu. **Warranty:** parts and labor, 1 year; parts, 2 years; replacement parts related to cabinet rust, washer motor, computer touch controls, and dryer drum, 5 years; transmission, parts, 10 years.

Approx. retail price	Approx. low price
$1,345 (gas)	**$1,099**
$1,299 (electric)	**$1,069**

WHIRLPOOL LTG5243D (GAS)/LTE5243D (ELECTRIC)

✓ BEST BUY

The Whirlpool LTG5243D/LTE5243D is a solid washer/dryer system. The washer offers two wash/spin speed combinations, four wash/rinse temperature combinations, and three water-level settings. This model offers five automatic wash cycles: super wash, regular/heavy, permanent press, delicate, and soak. Additional conveniences include automatic load-balance compensation, easy-clean lint filter, and a poly tub. The clothes dryer features five timed dry cycles and an on/off end-

Prices are accurate at time of printing but are subject to manufacturers' changes.

of-cycle signal. The dryer also has an interior drum light and an easy-to-clean lint screen. Choose from white or almond.

Specifications: height, 71¾"; width, 23⅞"; depth, 27⅝"; volts/amps (gas), 120/20; watts/volts/amps (electric), 3,600/240/30; gas heating element, 10,500 Btu. **Warranty:** 1 year.

Approx. retail price	**Approx. low price**
$949 (gas)	**$854**
$899 (electric)	**$816**

LARGE-CAPACITY DRYERS

SEARS KENMORE 75882 (GAS)/ 65882 (ELECTRIC)

BEST BUY

The Sears Kenmore 75882/65882 is a good dryer with a very nice wrinkle prevention feature. Its ten cycles are timed, normal, cotton, permanent press, air only, delicate/knit, auto dry II, touch-up, soft heat, and Wrinkle Guard I. This model has five temperature settings, including air only. An end-of-cycle alarm with variable volume alerts you when the cycle is done. The lint filter has an audible alarm that alerts you when the front-mounted screen requires cleaning. The interior drum light and nonheated drying rack are handy extras. This unit features four-way rear venting. Available colors are white-on-white and almond-on-almond.

Specifications: height, 43⅛"; width, 27"; depth, 27½"; volts/amps (gas), 120/15; watts/volts/amps (electric), 5,400/240/30; gas heating element, 22,000 Btu. **Warranty:** parts and labor, 1 year; extended warranty available at extra cost.

Approx. retail price	**Approx. low price**
$520 (gas)	**$480**
$470 (electric)	**$430**

FRIGIDAIRE FDG847GC (GAS)/ FDE847GC (ELECTRIC)

BEST BUY

The Frigidaire FDG847GC/FDE847GC is a high-quality large capacity dryer featuring two-way tumble drying and extended cooldown (Press Saver). It has six auto cycles (regular, permanent press, knits/delicate, cooldown, extended cooldown, and refresher) and four timed drying cycles (regular, permanent press, knits/delicate, and air fluff). The four temperature options are high, medium, low, and air fluff/no heat. Other appealing features include a drying rack, adjustable-volume end-of-cycle signal, internal drum light, quick-clean lint screen, and safety start button. There are three venting options for the gas model and four for the electric unit. This unit is available in white-on-white or almond-on-almond.

Specifications: height, 44″; width, 26⅞″; depth, 27″; volts/amps (gas), 120/30; watts/volts/amps (electric), 4,500/240/30; gas heating element, 25,500 Btu. **Warranty:** parts and labor, 2 years.

Approx. retail price	Approx. low price
$440 (gas)	**$406**
$400 (electric)	**$363**

KITCHENAID KGYW770B (GAS)/ KEYW770B (ELECTRIC)

✓BEST BUY

The KitchenAid KGYW770B/KEYW770B is a reliable large-capacity clothes dryer featuring the company's Smooth Guard system for extended tumbling. This model has five automatic cycles: regular, heavy, permanent press (with cooldown), air tumble, and quick press. Also available is time dry (0–70 minutes). There are five temperature selections. Other useful features include a drying rack, adjustable-volume end-of-cycle signal, internal drum light, top-mounted lint screen (with audible signal), and door window. The gas model has three venting options and the electric model has four. An optional fabric-softener-sheet dispenser is available as an accessory. This unit comes in white-on-white, black-on-white, and almond-on-almond.

Specifications: height, 35″; width, 29″; depth, 28″; volts/amps (gas), 120/6; watts/volts/amps (electric), 5,400/240/30; gas heating element, 22,000 Btu. **Warranty:** 1 year, full; parts, 2 years; cabinet (rust), heating element, electronic controls, and motor, 5 years; drum, 10 years.

Approx. retail price	**Approx. low price**
$549 (gas)	**$512**
$499 (electric)	**$469**

WHIRLPOOL LGR7848D (GAS)/ LER7848D (ELECTRIC)

✓BEST BUY

The Whirlpool LGR7848D/ LER7848D is a reliable clothes dryer with the company's Dry-Miser feature, which senses the amount of moisture in the clothes and shuts the dryer down when the preset level of moisture is reached. There are seven drying cycles: Dry-Miser, timed drying, damp dry, Tumble Press, Finish Guard, heavy dry (80 minutes), and fluff air. The four temperature settings are high, medium, low, and air dry. Other nice features include on/off end-of-cycle signal, large top-mounted lint screen, and rotary controls. You can choose from white-on-white or almond-on-almond.

Specifications: height, 42⅜″; width, 29″; depth, 28³⁄₁₆″ (gas), 27¹³⁄₁₆″ (electric); volts/amps (gas), 110/20; watts/volts/amps (electric), 5,400/240/30; gas heating element, 22,000 Btu. **Warranty:** 1 year.

Approx. retail price	**Approx. low price**
$479 (gas)	**$422**
$419 (electric)	**$376**

STANDARD-CAPACITY DRYERS

ASKO EXCELLENCE 7704

Recommended

The Asko Excellence 7704 is a high-quality standard-capacity electric dryer featuring a condenser to collect moisture (thus conventional venting is not required). This well-made machine has moisture sensor-controlled drying cycles (extra dry, dry, damp dry, and iron dry). Anti-crease, low heat, and timed drying (5–90 minutes) programs are also available. Other features include nonvariable-volume end-of-cycle signal, large door-mounted lint screen, lint screen cleaning alert, wrinkle prevention, air fluff drying, delay start (up to 12 hours), and stainless steel drum. It is available in white. Vented units are also available (7004 and 7304) at lower cost.

Specifications: height, 32¼"–33½"; width, 23½"; depth, 46½" (door open); watts/volts/amps, 3,000/230/15. **Warranty:** parts and labor, 1 year; all solid state controls and motors, 5 years; stainless steel drum from rust, 25 years.

Approx. retail price	**Approx. low price**
$1,049	**$1,036**

HOTPOINT NJLR473GT (GAS)/ NJLR473ET (ELECTRIC)

BEST BUY

The Hotpoint NJLR473GT/NJLR473ET is an excellent dryer with automatic dry control, which monitors the moisture level and ends the cycle when clothes are properly dried. An optional press guard feature helps prevent wrinkles. This model has six automatic cycles: cotton, optional press guard, permanent press, timed dry (up to 80 minutes), damp dry, and de-wrinkle. It has four temperature selections. Other notable features include a porcelain-coated drum, interior light, and removable front lint screen. There are three venting options for the gas model and four for the electric unit. This unit is available in white or almond with a black backsplash.

Specifications: height, 42"; width, 27"; depth, 25½"; volts/amps (gas), 120/15; watts/volts/amps (electric), 5,600/240/30; gas heating element, 22,000 Btu. **Warranty:** 1 year, full.

Approx. retail price	**Approx. low price**
$349 (gas)	**$349**
$299 (electric)	**$299**

WHIRLPOOL LGR5624D (GAS)/ LER5624D (ELECTRIC)

BEST BUY

The Whirlpool LGR5624D/LER5624D is a high-quality dryer with the company's Dry-Miser feature, which senses the amount of moisture in the clothes and shuts the

Prices are accurate at time of printing but are subject to manufacturers' changes.

dryer down when the preset moisture level is reached. There are five drying cycles: Dry-Miser, timed drying, damp dry, Tumble Press, and fluff air. There are two in-timer temperature settings. Other notable features include a top-mounted lint screen and rotary controls. This model is available only in white-on-white.

Specifications: height, $42\frac{3}{8}$"; width, 29"; depth, $26\frac{3}{16}$" (gas), $25\frac{13}{16}$" (electric); volts/amps (gas), 110/20; watts/volts/amps (electric), 5,400/240/30; gas heating element, 22,000 Btu. **Warranty:** 1 year.

Approx. retail price	Approx. low price
$389 (gas)	**$389**
$339 (electric)	**$339**

FRIGIDAIRE FDG336RB (GAS)/ FDE336RB (ELECTRIC)

Budget Buy

The Frigidaire FDG336RB/FDE336RB is a reliable machine. It has fewer features than the more deluxe models but offers good value for the money. This model has one automatic cycle and features a delicate timed dry cycle. The four temperature options are high, medium, low, and air fluff/no heat. Convenient features include quick-clean lint screen and safety start button. There are three venting options for the gas model and four for the electric unit. You can choose from white-on-white and almond-on-almond.

Specifications: height, 44"; width, $26\frac{7}{8}$"; depth, 27"; volts/amps (gas), 120/30; watts/volts/amps (electric), 4,500/240/30; gas heating element, 20,000 Btu. **Warranty:** 2 years, full.

Approx. retail price	Approx. low price
$360 (gas)	**$353**
$320 (electric)	**$309**

COMPACT DRYERS

WHIRLPOOL LGR3622D (GAS)/ LER3622D (ELECTRIC)

✓BEST BUY

The Whirlpool LGR3622D/LER3622D is an excellent compact dryer featuring Dry-Miser, which senses the

Prices are accurate at time of printing but are subject to manufacturers' changes.

amount of moisture in the clothes and shuts the dryer down when the preset moisture level is reached. This model has three drying cycles and two temperature settings. An internal lint screen, end-of-cycle signal, and rotary controls are other nice features. You can choose white-on-white or almond-on-almond.

Specifications: height, 32"; width, $23\frac{7}{8}$"; depth, $22\frac{15}{16}$" (gas), $21\frac{15}{16}$" (electric); volts/amps (gas), 120/20; watts/volts/amps (electric), 5,400/120/30; gas heating element, 10,500 Btu. **Warranty:** parts and labor, 1 year.

Approx. retail price	Approx. low price
$419 (gas)	**$419**
$369 (electric)	**$369**

SANYO CD25OUT

Budget Buy

The Sanyo CD25OUT is a dependable, duct-free electric compact dryer that's well suited for locations where venting is not possible. It features semiconductor-controlled heating with automatic temperature control. A post-cycle automatic cooldown feature minimizes wrinkles. Other notable features include a removable sneaker drying rack, door-mounted lint filter, adjustable (forward/reverse) 2-hour timer, air fluff drying, and a poly drum. This unit can be stacked on top of a Sanyo washer with an accessory steel rack.

Specifications: height, $25\frac{3}{16}$"; width, $25\frac{3}{16}$"; depth, $13\frac{11}{16}$"; watts/volts/amps, 1,450/120/12. **Warranty:** parts and labor, 1 year.

Approx. retail price	Approx. low price
$300	**$290**

Prices are accurate at time of printing but are subject to manufacturers' changes.

ENVIRONMENTAL CONTROL APPLIANCES

Best Buys '96

Our Best Buy, Recommended, and Budget Buy environmental control products follow. In each category, units are listed according to quality. The best of the Best Buys is listed first, followed by our second choice, and so on. Remember that a Best Buy, Recommended, or Budget Buy designation applies only to the model listed; it does not apply to other models made by the same manufacturer or to an entire product line.

ROOM AIR CONDITIONERS

What's an easy way to keep your cool during the dog days of summer? Install a room air conditioner. It can take some of the heat out of the muggy season, help you get a good night's sleep, and increase your comfort level throughout the day.

If you shop in early spring before you actually need the air conditioner, you'll find the widest selection in stores. You'll also save money on the purchase price during preseason sales. If you shop in the fall, prices may be even lower, because the stores will want to clear out any remaining stock. Don't worry about getting an outdated model. There will be some changes in the models from year to year, but the end-of-the-year closeouts generally offer a quality product at a good price.

Energy Efficiency

When shopping for a room air conditioner, don't forget to take the cost of operation into consideration as you compare prices. Today's air conditioners are designed to be extremely energy efficient because of energy standards mandated by the federal government. All room—also called window—air conditioners manufactured after January 1, 1990, must have an

Energy Efficiency Rating (EER) of at least 8.0. (The EER is computed by dividing cooling capacity, measured in British thermal units per hour, or Btu, by the watts of electricity used.) All the models listed here have high ratings, making them particularly energy efficient for their size.

The government requires that all room air conditioners carry a bright yellow energy label that gives cost-of-operation information, including the EER. The higher the EER, the more efficient the unit and the lower the operating cost.

When you shop, remember that a model with a low EER may carry a lower price tag, but its operating costs will be higher over the years of its use. Even though a room air conditioner with a high EER may cost more to purchase, you'll save money in the long run with lower electricity bills.

Your Cooling Needs

Purchase an air conditioner with enough cooling capacity for your needs without getting one that is too big. If a unit is too small, your room will not be sufficiently cooled. If a unit is too large, it will not dehumidify properly, and the room will be uncomfortable and clammy. Large units tend to be noisier than small ones. It is sometimes better to buy two or three small units than one large one. This also allows you to cool only the rooms you use the most.

Areas to be cooled (in square feet)	**Cooling capacity needed (in Btu)**
up to 150	4,000–5,000
150–250	5,000–6,000
250–450	6,000–8,500
450–600	8,500–11,000
600–900	11,000–14,000
900–1,200	14,000–19,000

Most models are designed for double-hung (opening up and down) windows, though models are also available for sliding windows. Be sure to take your window opening measurements with you when you shop.

Instead of installing the air conditioner in a window, you might want to consider through-the-wall installation. In a room with only one window, this might be the only way you can retain the use of the window. Through-the-wall installation means cutting a hole in the wall and siding. It's a lot of trouble, but it provides a much quieter, much more secure installation. You'll also have less air leakage in a through-the-wall installation, making your unit more effective in the summertime and keeping the warm air in during the winter. Most units provide instructions for this type of installation. Be sure to check for any additional hardware requirements.

Features and Terminology

When purchasing an air conditioner, your primary concern should be efficiency in both performance and energy. The following are key items to keep in mind:

Air movement: Look for fully adjustable louvers and vents that let you adjust air movement in different directions.

Design: The latest trend in room air conditioner design is smaller, lighter models with plastic housings instead of metal. This makes them easier to install in the window at the beginning of summer and to remove in the fall.

Filters: The filter should be cleaned and reinstalled at the start of the cooling season and then cleaned each month during the season.

Thermostatic controls: This numbered dial or series of buttons alters the frequency with which the compressor turns on and off. Some thermostatic controls have one or more fan-only settings that run without the compressor operating.

Air Conditioners from 5,000 to 8,000 Btu

WHITE WESTINGHOUSE WAC086T/W7A

✓ BEST BUY

This model is one of White Westinghouse's Custom series of compact air conditioners. Its EER is 9.2. The WAC086T/W7A features grooved copper tubing for fast, effi-

Prices are accurate at time of printing but are subject to manufacturers' changes.

cient heat transfer. The staggered coil arrangement allows for maximum air flow. The coils are also self-cleaning, so you have one less system to maintain. This unit is very quiet when running. It has a high-speed fan that moves 250 cubic feet of air per minute, three cooling speeds, and three fan-only settings for maximum comfort. The louvers are adjustable four ways. The rigid frame filter is easy to remove and easy to clean. Controls are located on top of the unit to make them very visible and accessible, with little bending or stooping required. The dehumidification rate of 2.3 pints per hour makes this model a good choice for a small to mid-size room with high humidity.

Specifications: height, 12 7/16"; width, 19 1/8"; depth, 18 1/2"; weight, 74 lbs.; maximum window width, 38"; minimum window width, 22"; watts, 870; volts, 115; amps, 7.5; moisture removal rate, 2.3 pints per hour; air delivery, 250 cu. ft. per minute. **Warranty:** parts, 1 year; sealed refrigerant system, 5 years.

Approx. retail price	Approx. low price
$399	$349

FRIEDRICH QSTAR SQ05H10D

Recommended

The Friedrich Qstar series of room air conditioners is designed to be extra quiet when running. Model SQ05H10D is the smallest of the four SQ models. Choose the model size that matches the size of the room you want to cool. The cabinet slides off the chassis, making window installation very simple. Even the packaging was designed to make it easy to remove. The package also includes hardware for through-the-wall mounting as well as for window installation. Wall installation is more secure and will allow the air conditioner to run much more quietly. The filter on this unit is simple to remove and easy to clean—just tilt the louvers down, put your thumbs on the lifts, and pull out. The indoor air coils can be cleaned by snapping off the front cover and dusting or vacuuming them.

Specifications: height, 14"; width, 19 3/4"; depth, 21 3/8"; weight, 76 lbs.; maximum window width, 42"; minimum window

Prices are accurate at time of printing but are subject to manufacturers' changes.

width, 26″; watts, 560; volts, 115; amps, 5.1; moisture removal rate, 1.5 pints per hour; air delivery, 160 cu. ft. per minute. **Warranty:** all parts, 1 year; sealed refrigerant system, 5 years.

Approx. retail price	**Approx. low price**
$399	**$399**

FRIGIDAIRE FAC063T7A

Budget Buy

The Frigidaire FAC063T7A (EER 8.2) is great for cooling small rooms (up to 340 square feet) without putting a strain on your budget. With a dehumidification rate of 1.7 pints per hour, it can make a room feel a lot more comfortable without using up the extra power required by larger models. This model has a quality cooling system with self-cleaning, grooved copper tubing for maximum heat exchange. The inside air filter is easy to remove and clean by pulling up on the handle just below the louvers. This unit's chassis and frame are one piece—instead of installing a lightweight cabinet, then sliding in the heavier chassis, you install the unit all at once. This makes installation harder but does bring down the price. If you plan to leave the air conditioner in year-round or don't mind the slightly more difficult installation, this model could be for you.

Specifications: height, 12⅞″; width, 19⅛″; depth, 18″; weight, 67 lbs.; maximum window width, 38″; minimum window width, 22″; watts, 725; volts, 115; amps, 6.6; moisture removal rate, 1.7 pints per hour; air delivery, 175 cu. ft. per minute. **Warranty**: parts, 1 year; sealed refrigerant system, 5 years.

Approx. retail price	**Approx. low price**
$319	**$319**

Air Conditioners from 8,000 to 10,000 Btu

PANASONIC CW-1005FU

✓BEST BUY

The Panasonic CW-1005FU (EER 9.5) is a 10,000-Btu air conditioner that features a three-speed fan and

3.2 pints per hour dehumidification for excellent performance. Other features include air-swing air circulation vents that constantly swing from side to side, spreading cool air across the room (the air-swing feature can also be turned off for fixed air direction); a 12-hour automatic on/off timer; a time-delay safety circuit to avoid a quick restarting of the unit (quick restarting can cause damage to the compressor); and four-way deflection louvers. There's also an exhaust feature to discharge stale room air. The one-touch filter slides in and out easily. The unit has a slide-out chassis for easier installation.

Specifications: height, 14¾″; width, 22″; depth, 23⅝″; weight, 88 lbs.; maximum window width, 42⅛″; minimum window width, 25¹³⁄₁₆″; watts, 1,050; volts, 115; amps, 9.3; moisture removal rate, 3.2 pints per hour; air delivery, 310 cu. ft. per minute. **Warranty:** parts and labor, 1 year; sealed system, 5 years.

Approx. retail price	Approx. low price
$550	$460

GENERAL ELECTRIC AMD10AB

Recommended

Wouldn't it be nice to come home to a cool, comfortable room after a long, hot day? With the GE AMD10AB, you can do that and still save money! The GE premium air conditioners come standard with a built-in 12-hour timer. Not only can you have your air conditioner start an hour before you get home, you can set it to stop after you go to bed. This model is designed for medium- to large-size rooms needing the full 10,000 Btu of cooling power. Even with its large capacity, this model has an EER rating of 10, making it a very efficient air conditioner. An energy-saver switch turns off the fan when the compressor is not running. With a slide-in chassis, installation is easy, and the expanding side panels adjust easily for a tight fit. The inside filter slips out sideways through the front panel, making it easy to clean and replace. This unit also features electrically driven oscillating louvers to circulate the air evenly throughout the room.

Specifications: height, 14¾″; width, 22⅙″; depth, 23⅝″; weight, 88 lbs.; maximum window width, 41″; minimum window width, 31¼"; watts, 1,000; volts, 115; amps, 8.9; moisture removal rate, 3.2 pints per hour; air delivery, 310 cu. ft. per minute. **Warranty:** all parts, 1 year; sealed refrigerant system, 5 years.

Approx. retail price **$550** | **Approx. low price** **$483**

FEDDERS A2Q10F2BG

Recommended

Designed for modest to mid-size rooms and with an EER of 9.2, this model is the largest of the Fedders portable series of air conditioners. It is designed to keep on cooling even during low-power brownout periods. The painted galvanized steel cabinet will hold up against extreme weather conditions without extra protection. Installation is fairly easy with simple, flexible side curtains to adjust to the correct width. The narrow opening requirement (20½ inches) makes this model a good choice for many windows. The air exchanger is especially helpful, as it reduces the stale air, dust, and dirt in the room without much adjustment. With three cooling speeds, two fan speeds, and a cross ambient thermostat, the Fedders A2Q10F2BG makes it easy to get the room just the way you want it.

Specifications: height, 12½"; width, 20"; depth, 19⅛"; weight, 74 lbs.; maximum window width, 39"; minimum window width, 20½"; watts, 1,090; volts, 115; amps, 9.5; moisture removal rate, 3.3 pints per hour; air delivery, 160 cu. ft. per minute. **Warranty:** parts, 1 year; sealed refrigerant system, 5 years.

Approx. retail price **$600** | **Approx. low price** **$354**

Air Conditioners Over 10,000 Btu

AMANA 12C2MY

✓BEST BUY

The Amana 12C2MY (EER 9.5) is a compact air conditioner that delivers 11,800 Btu of cooling capacity with

Prices are accurate at time of printing but are subject to manufacturers' changes.

very good energy efficiency. It has a three-speed fan, air exhaust to get rid of stale room air, multidirectional air flow, and an easy-access filter. The rotary controls are easy to operate. This model is competitively priced, delivering powerful cooling and very good dehumidification at 3.3 pints per hour.

Specifications: height, 15⅞"; width, 24½"; depth, 23⅞"; weight, 118 lbs.; maximum window width, 42"; minimum window width, 28"; watts, 1,240; volts, 115; amps, 10.5; moisture removal rate, 3.3 pints per hour; air delivery, 340 cu. ft. per minute. **Warranty:** 1 year, full; sealed system, 5 years.

Approx. retail price	**Approx. low price**
$550	**$439**

AIR CLEANERS

Air cleaners are the latest weapon in the battle for clean indoor air. City dwellers often invest in an air cleaner to get rid of pollutants. Allergic people in both city and country use them to remove pollen and other allergens from the air. As well as freestanding units, you can also purchase inexpensive air-cleaning filters for your furnace.

Two critical considerations in shopping for an air cleaner are the size of your space and how much noise you can tolerate. Make sure you select an air cleaner that's the right size for the room you plan to put it in. A unit installed in a too-large space won't do a good job of producing breathable air. Also make sure you listen to the machine operating before you buy it. Most air cleaners are very quiet, producing a gentle "white noise," but people have different levels of tolerance for this type of background noise.

HONEYWELL/ENVIRACAIRE PORTABLE AIR CLEANER 13520

✓BEST BUY

The Honeywell/Enviracaire Portable Air Cleaner is an effective, easy-to-use High Efficiency Particulate Air (HEPA) cleaner. Its capacity is 20,000 cubic feet per hour at

Prices are accurate at time of printing but are subject to manufacturers' changes.

high speed. The circular design blows in all directions, producing a gentle, even distribution of air throughout the room. The 13520 model is lightweight and relatively quiet. Running at the highest speed, it produces a gentle, even "white noise." Some users may wish to lower the speed during the night to reduce the sound, while others may find it restful. This model has three speeds and an "off" setting. For the best effect this model should be kept on, even when you are not in the room. The charcoal prefilters are available in two packs and should be replaced every three months. The main HEPA filter should last three to five years. The filters are simple to replace and the manual directions are clear and easy to follow. You can get replacement filters either from the store where you bought the air cleaner or by calling Honeywell's toll-free number.

Warranty: 2 years, limited.

Approx. retail price
$230

Approx. low price
$196

3M FILTRETE CLEAN AIR FILTERS

✓BEST BUY

You don't have to own a separate air cleaner if you want to filter pollen and other fine particles out of the air. 3M's Filtrete Clean Air Filters can turn your central heating system or room air conditioner into a more efficient air filter. They simply replace the existing air filters in your furnace or air conditioner. Made of electrostatically charged polyolefin fiber, Filtrete filters are not coated or treated with any chemicals. No respirable fibers are released during use. The filters are one inch thick and come in a variety of sizes, as well as 26 × 58-inch "hammock" type filters. For room air conditioners, they come in a 15 × 24-inch sheet you cut to fit your particular model. In one pass, these filters are capable or removing over 97 percent of air pollen and over 35 percent of dust and fine particles. Humidity does not affect filter performance. These filters are recommended for use with furnaces that have an air velocity of less than 450 feet per minute.

Approx. retail price
$5–20 (depending on size)

Approx. low price
$5–20

Prices are accurate at time of printing but are subject to manufacturers' changes.

HUMIDIFIERS

A humidifier replaces moisture in a room that has been parched by an active heating system and low humidity levels in the outdoor air. By adding moisture to the room air, you not only relieve physical discomfort but you keep your plants, furniture, and other room furnishings from becoming too dry.

It is essential that humidifiers be cleaned scrupulously in order for them to function at peak efficiency. For this reason, you should choose a model that's designed for easy cleaning. For example, look for a unit with a tank in which the filler hole is large enough to allow a hand to maneuver around inside. Also look for a model with demineralizing features. Finally, check to see that the mist nozzle rotates 360 degrees. A carrying handle is a plus.

DURACRAFT WARM MOISTURE DH-904

✓BEST BUY

The Duracraft Warm Moisture humidifier is a tabletop room humidifier that's easy to use and maintain. It runs very quietly. The unit consists of three main pieces: a Rinse-to-Clean base, a water supply tank, and a control panel with humidity nozzle. There is also a dishwasher-safe medicine dispenser. The removable, wide-mouth, leakproof tank is easy to fill and has a two-gallon capacity. A safety system automatically shuts off the humidifier when the tank is empty or is removed. With two moisture settings and an adjustable humidistat, you'll find it effortless to keep the moisture level just where you want it. No filter is required because the system does not produce any white dust. Any accumulated residue is collected in the base unit, which can then be rinsed clean. For nighttime functioning, the illuminated on/off switch is a nice feature. Customer service is excellent with a seven-day, toll-free consumer hot line.

Warranty: 3 years.

Approx. retail price **$68**

Approx. low price **$68**

Prices are accurate at time of printing but are subject to manufacturers' changes.

TOASTMASTER 3435

Recommended

The Toastmaster 3435 Comfort Conditioner is a console model that can put out 12 gallons of water per day. It is a quiet unit with three speeds and an automatic humidistat. The two-tone gray cabinet fully conceals all controls and the water tanks. A refill signal light shows when more water is needed. If it does run out of water, the unit automatically turns off. Because of the unit's large capacity, there are two separate water tanks. Each has a carrying handle and a narrow mouth. The unit is shallow, only 13⅖ inches deep, so that it fits smoothly against a wall, a plus where space saving is a concern. The humidifier has a cotton-fibered filter to remove mineral deposits. This prevents them from clogging the unit or causing indoor air pollution. Replacement filters can be purchased where you bought the humidifier or through the company's toll-free number.

Warranty: 1 year.

Approx. retail price
$167

Approx. low price
$167

BABY EQUIPMENT

Choosing the best baby products can be overwhelming for new parents. These days, the industry is more innovative than ever, with companies racing one another to develop the most advanced products at the most competitive prices. That's great news, but it means the market can be quite confusing for the inexperienced shopper. In shopping for baby equipment, keep in mind that your first considerations are safety and comfort; looks are secondary.

Safety Tips

Several organizations monitor juvenile products. The Juvenile Products Manufacturers Association (JPMA) rigorously tests and certifies products in categories not covered by government regulations. Products that pass the test may state this on their label, so look for the JPMA seal of approval.

Here are a few more tips to help you choose safe products for your baby:

• Make sure all hinges and rough parts are covered so that they don't pinch your baby's fingers or toes. Look for baby-safe materials such as plastic and rubber; avoid metals that can heat up in the sun. Also look for soft, comfortable fabrics, such as cotton.

• Make sure all small parts are firmly secured. Small objects that come loose could present a choking hazard for your baby.

• All products that hold your baby should have a sturdy frame that won't tip. Look for high chairs with a wide base and strollers with large wheels and a substantial frame that won't tip when you hang your bag on the handlebar.

• Straps on car seats, changing tables, and high chairs should hold your baby securely.

Once you've made your purchase, it's important to stay on top of recall information, in case the product turns out to be faulty. The U.S. Consumer Product Safety Commission keeps track of most children's products that have been recalled. The National Highway Traffic Safety Administration tracks recalls of car seats.

Best Buys '96

Our Best Buy, Recommended, and Budget Buy baby equipment follows. Within each category, products are rated according to quality and safety. The item we consider the best of the Best Buys is listed first, followed by our second choice, and so on. Remember that a Best Buy, Recommended, or Budget Buy designation applies only to the model listed. It does not necessarily apply to other models produced by the same manufacturer or to an entire product line.

PORTABLE CRIBS AND PLAY YARDS

Play yards and portable cribs are similar and are often considered the same thing. While they can be used for the same activities at times, it is better to use each of these products exactly as specified by its manufacturer. A piece of equipment intended only for use as a portable crib should not be used as a play yard, and vice versa. And stop using these units when the baby outgrows them; for the most part, they are intended for children who are less than 34 inches tall or weigh under 30 pounds.

A portable crib is a handy piece of equipment to own for travel or overnight visits to friends and relatives. But it should never be used on a permanent basis in place of a full-size crib. Most portable cribs are shaped rectangularly and have a sturdy metal or plastic frame, a hard bottom with some kind of padding, and fabric sides with mesh panels. Generally, they fold down to a compact piece that can fit inside a carrying case.

Some play yards are made in similar configurations to portable cribs, while others are a bit roomier and have mesh sides that allow parents total view of the child inside. Some also have sides that drop down for the folding-away process. These should always be raised while the child is in the unit.

When purchasing either a portable crib or a play yard, make sure it's sturdy. Give it a shake to make certain it can't tip over or collapse accidentally. Look for mesh that is tightly woven (so small fingers or buttons on clothing can't get caught) and securely attached to the top rail and floor of the unit. Make sure any vinyl on the unit is thick enough to withstand sucking or teething (so small pieces don't get stuck in a child's throat), and make sure no foam is exposed so the child could pick at it and potentially swallow it. Also watch for sharp points or edges, exposed seams or hardware, and the potential for the unit to fold up accidentally. Finally, in addition to your baby's comfort and safety, consider your own convenience: Avoid models that are bulky, heavy, and difficult to set up or take down.

Portable Cribs

EVENFLO HAPPY CABANA 346138

✓BEST BUY

The clean-lined good looks of this nautical-striped travel crib (which can double as a smaller play yard) make it appealing, while its clever design and reasonable price make it a sensible choice for traveling with a baby. The sturdy unit is well constructed, with smooth corners and padded rails, and very easy to use. It can be set up in less than a minute without the cabana, which is a separate cover to shield your baby from the elements; with the cabana, it takes another minute or so. The cabana also features shades that can be rolled down the sides of the crib to cover see-through mesh panels when the baby naps or to act as a draft guard. It matches a removable toy bag included with the crib—both pieces can be washed. The Happy Cabana is extremely mobile, with its lightweight, zippered carry bag (about a foot high and wide and a yard long), and large wheels on two legs to move the crib when it's assembled.

Warranty: 1 year, limited.

Approx. retail price	**Approx. low price**
$100	**$100**

GRACO PACK 'N' PLAY WITH BASSINET 9045

Recommended

All the standard features of a good travel crib are included on this model, plus an innovative extra. Its construction is sturdy but lightweight and features smooth corners. It can be assembled in less than a minute, features strong nylon mesh on two panels with a roll-down flap on one side, and is made of attractive nylon that can be easily cleaned. The Pack 'N' Play 9045's most outstanding feature is a bassinet attachment that elevates the mattress and support board to a position suitable for newborns. This model also features a unique "attached" carrying case: The support board actually becomes the unit's case. This is an ideal crib for traveling with an infant. Graco does not publish a warranty but claims to stand behind its products and provides a toll-free number for consumers to call in case of problems.

Warranty: Not available.

Approx. retail price **$110** — **Approx. low price** **$100**

EVENFLO HAPPY CAMPER TRAVEL CRIB & PLAY YARD 344170

Budget Buy

You'll find many of the same superb features of the Evenflo Happy Cabana (above) in this unit, which sells for about $20 less. The size is the same, but the unit lacks the cabana attachment with the roll-down sides. The Happy Camper has the same easy-to-set-up design and sturdy construction as the plusher model. Features include smooth corners and padded rails, see-through mesh panels on two sides, and a matching removable toy bag. A zippered carry bag about a foot high and wide and a yard long makes it easy to transport the crib when it's disassembled; casters on two legs move the assembled crib. This unit is a good value for the price.

Warranty: 1 year, limited.

Approx. retail price **$80** — **Approx. low price** **$80**

Play Yards

CENTURY FOLD 'N' GO 10-807

✓BEST BUY

Everything about this play yard makes it a superb choice. It's considered a portable model but is actually the ideal size for any house or apartment. All corners are covered with sturdy plastic, the strong steel frame and floorboard are covered with padded nylon that comes in a variety of patterns, and mesh panels are inset in all four sides of the unit to keep your child visible at all times. But the easy-to-use "micro-fold" system, with a Posi-Lock mechanism on the top rail, is what truly makes this unit special. The Fold 'N' Go 10-807 is so simple to set up and take down, and so compact in its closed position, it's great for a residence where space is a problem. The unit comes with a comfort pad to enclose it and a shoulder-bag tote that measures 11 by 11 by 32 inches. The play yard measures 28 inches wide by 41 inches long; at 25 pounds, it's also lightweight.

Warranty: 1 year.

Approx. retail price	Approx. low price
$90	$70

KOLCRAFT OCTAGON PLAYARD 18503

✓BEST BUY

This is one of the roomiest play yards around, but it's still lightweight and relatively easy to set up and take down. The double-drop sides have sturdy Stay-Loc hinges. One of the nicest features about this unit is the visibility it allows parents. While the strong steel frame and floorboard are covered with padded nylon casings and mats (in a variety of patterns and colors), the sides of the unit are made of a strong mesh that is easy to see through. Coupled with the unusual design of the frame, which features center support legs that extend diagonally to the unit's outside edges (instead of posts at each corner), this unit allows parents to view a child from every angle.

Warranty: 1 year.

Approx. retail price	Approx. low price
$80	$65

CENTURY FOLD 'N' GO 10-707

Budget Buy

All the plush features of the higher-priced Fold 'N' Go 10-807 are present in this model, minus a few

Prices are accurate at time of printing but are subject to manufacturers' changes.

inches off each side. While the other unit is 28 inches wide, 41 inches long, and weighs 25 pounds, the 10-707 measures 26 inches wide and 38 inches long and weighs 24 pounds. It's identical to the larger model in every other respect, with covered plastic corners, a padded nylon covered steel frame and floorboard, mesh panels on all four sides for high visibility, and the easy-to-use "micro-fold" system with a Posi-Lock mechanism on the top rail. Also included are the carrying case with shoulder straps and a pad to encase the folded unit. The smaller size can be a definite plus if you're short on space.

Warranty: 1 year.

Approx. retail price
$80

Approx. low price
$60

ELECTRIC SWINGS

COSCO DREAM RIDE PLUS 08-980

BEST BUY

It's refreshing to find an old-fashioned idea with innovative new twists, and this classic windup swing from Cosco is the perfect example of an exceptional product with remarkable upgrades. To begin with, the swing seat is also a combination (rear-facing) car seat or (side-facing) car bed that can be used in a sideways cradle position in either the swing or car. Once on the swing, it can also be switched from a sideways position to a conventional forward-facing position with a rotating motion without removing the whole seat. Unlike most of the deluxe models on the market, the Dream Ride Plus operates on a winding mechanism instead of batteries, but the crank is unusually quiet, the swing runs for a full 30 minutes, and the unit features a "Minute-Minder" to time the mechanism as it winds down. Overall, the Dream Ride Plus offers outstanding flexibility for a very fair price.

Warranty: 1 year, limited.

Approx. retail price
$100

Approx. low price
$100

Prices are accurate at time of printing but are subject to manufacturers' changes.

CENTURY 2-IN-1 FREEDOM SWING 12-565

✓BEST BUY

The name says it all for this outstanding electronic swing. It has a two-in-one seat that is actually the award-winning removable Century Infant Car Seat/Carrier (you can use it in the swing or as a car seat/carrier), plus a unique "Freedom" configuration that departs radically from the classic models. Instead of hanging from a top bar, this swing has a base in which the seat sits, while a patented mechanism that creates a natural arc motion causes it to rock back and forth. This gives parents access to the unit from above and all sides, making it very easy to put the baby into the seat and take him or her out. The setup also takes up less space than a conventional swing. It operates on four "D" alkaline batteries.

Warranty: 1 year.

Approx. retail price
$110

Approx. low price
$100

GRACO ADVANTAGE SWING 1452

Recommended

An innovative design, plus an advanced electronic drive, make the Advantage an excellent swing despite the fact that the seat can't be used for other functions (such as a car seat or carrier). A unique A-shaped frame makes the unit easy to set up and allows the seat, which can be set in four positions that range from sitting to reclining, to be suspended from the sides of the swing. It also eliminates the need for a bar across the top, which makes it easier to get the baby in and out of the seat and gives the unit a streamlined appearance. The simple, push-button control panel is located on the unit's side, and is one of the few motors to feature three speed variations and a low battery indicator. The motor should run for up to 200 hours on four "D" alkaline batteries. Graco does not offer a published warranty but claims to stand behind its products and offers a toll-free number for customers to call in case of problems.

Warranty: Not available.

Approx. retail price
$85

Approx. low price
$77

Prices are accurate at time of printing but are subject to manufacturers' changes.

NURSERY MONITORS

Nursery monitors help keep your mind at ease when you're not able to be in the same room as your baby. The monitor's transmitter stays in the baby's room and relays any noise your baby might make—from soft cooing sounds to loud crying—to your receiver. Most transmitters are able to pick up sounds within a six-foot to ten-foot radius and can relay them up to 150–200 feet, depending on the environment. Modern monitors come with extra features. Some transmitters also double as a night-light. Others come with built-in antennas so they're more portable and look nicer. There's even a new model that beeps to let you know you are within range, so there is no more guessing in the backyard. Keep in mind that because monitor systems are sensitive to interference from other environmental sources (such as physical obstructions or cordless phones), it's important to periodically check in on your baby in person.

GERRY RANGE CHECK NURSERY MONITOR 610

✓BEST BUY

The Gerry Range Check 610 truly meets parents' needs. Instead of posting a maximum operating range, which is often inaccurate due to site-specific local interference, this monitor has an exclusive "Range Check" device that lets parents make sure they are within range of the transmitter and the monitor is working. Other features include adapters for outlet use, a built-in night-light, and two channels to ensure clear reception. Another nice extra touch is the sleekly styled, innovative design. The baby's unit folds to enclose the parent's unit, making the Gerry Range Check a compact, portable unit. The transmitter and receiver each use four "AAA" batteries; an adapter is included.

Warranty: 1 year.

Approx. retail price
$35

Approx. low price
$35

Prices are accurate at time of printing but are subject to manufacturers' changes.

FISHER PRICE SOUND 'N LIGHTS MONITOR 1550

✓BEST BUY

Loads of extra features make this an outstanding monitor, including an out-of-range indicator, a variable light display (to help distinguish between a yawn and a cry), a low battery indicator, adapters for outlet use, two channels to insure clear reception, and range selectors for added privacy. Both the receiver and transmitter sport durable, flexible antennas and easy-to-use controls on the fronts of the units. The transmitter uses four "C" batteries; the receiver uses one "D" battery.

Warranty: parts, 1 year.

Approx. retail price	Approx. low price
$52	$40

FISHER PRICE SUPER-SENSITIVE NURSERY MONITOR 1555

Budget Buy

This basic unit is sensitive enough to do a fine job monitoring a baby but lacks the frills of more expensive models. The easy-to-use controls are self-explanatory. This unit has two channels to minimize interference and flexible antennas on both transmitter and receiver. It lacks light displays and a low battery indicator. The receiver can work on a nine-volt battery or line power (an adaptor is included), but the transmitter must be plugged in.

Warranty: parts, 1 year.

Approx. retail price	Approx. low price
$33	$30

CAR SEATS

Car seats for infants and young children are mandatory in all states, and newborns are often not released from hospitals unless a parent has an appropriate restraint system to use immediately. All car seats are required to conform to Federal Motor Vehicle Safety Standards, but this does not mean that all seats are suitable for all children: There are many varieties on the market, and it is important to choose the appropriate car seat for each child. Options include infant-only, convertible, and booster car seats.

Infant Car Seats

Infant car seats, which can also be put to good use outside the car, are intended for newborn babies up to infants weighing about 20 pounds (around nine months to one year of age). They are used only in a rear-facing position in the car, but can also become carriers, feeding seats, or even rockers in the home. This type of seat is also the best choice for low-birth-weight babies, since convertible car seats, which can also accommodate older infants or toddlers, can be too large in the infant position for smaller newborns. If the child does not fit correctly in the seat, the seat's ability to provide optimum protection is decreased.

Convertible Car Seats

Designed for children from birth to 40 pounds, these seats are used in a rear-facing position for newborns or infants under 20 pounds and in a forward-facing position for children who weigh from 20 to 40 pounds. Consequently, it is important that these units have adjustable harness systems that can accommodate very small babies (if the seat is to be used instead of an infant model) and still grow with a child. Five-point harness systems are ideal for use with infants, since the T-shaped shields can be too large for smaller newborns and fit them incorrectly. This can result in a child's discomfort and the possibility that the rest of the harness system is not secured snugly enough. For parents buying only this sort of seat, be careful to choose a product that suits your child.

Booster Car Seats

While the current rule of thumb regarding car seats seems to be "four years and 40 pounds," many children don't fit into this neat game plan. Some four-year-olds weigh far less than 40 pounds and would be best served by remaining in a car seat, while others reach 40 pounds long before the age of four. And some children spurn the car seat long before it is safe to sit in a car's regular harness system. Booster seats can pick up the slack in many situations and are intended for children who weigh between 30 and 60 pounds. Opt for a model that utilizes some sort of shoulder restraint system (either its own or the three-point system in newer-model cars); this type of system provides maximum restraint.

Infant Car Seats

COSCO ULTRA DREAM RIDE 719

✓BEST BUY

You can transport newborns lying down or sitting up with this innovative car seat, which can also be used as a carrier, feeding seat, or rocker. The car bed configuration is recognized as a good option for transporting preemies and low-birth-weight infants and was developed by the company with this in mind. In this position, the infant lies flat in the unit, which straps into a front or back seat in a side-facing position (it can also be used with an air bag, while rear-facing car seats cannot). This model converts easily to a rear-facing position for older infants (up to 20 pounds). Or you might prefer to use it in other capacities (the rocking feature is especially nice). The three-point harness system is adjustable and easy to use. The cotton cover is removable and washable and comes in several patterns.

Warranty: 1 year, limited.

Approx. retail price
$59

Approx. low price
$59

CENTURY 565 SERIES

Budget Buy

This car seat and carrier for newborns and babies up to 20 pounds is the best all-around basic for the price, especially since it's loaded with features and comes in a wide range of fabrics and patterns. The well-designed three-point harness system sports a push-button clasp and quick-thread buckle to hold straps in place; the four-position handle can be adjusted so the seat can be used to carry, feed, or rock an in-

Prices are accurate at time of printing but are subject to manufacturers' changes.

fant; and the fabric pads and canopy (in most models) are removable and washable. The position indicator on the seat is an especially useful feature, since it confirms whether or not the unit is correctly installed in the car.

Warranty: 1 year, limited.

Approx. retail price	**Approx. low price**
$40	**$40**

Convertible Car Seats

CENTURY 2000 SERIES

✓BEST BUY

For those who can only afford one car seat, the Century 2000 series offers outstanding options. A soft polyurethane shield in a bulky T shape makes this convertible car seat very easy to use, since you can strap a baby in with one quick step. It accommodates children from birth to 40 pounds—it can be used in a rear-facing position for infants and it has a six-position growth harness (which is also a plus for winter's bulky clothing). With a contoured seat and a Posi-Lock reclining system that adjusts to two positions, the Century 2000's comfort level for the child is high. With its removable, washable fabric pads and convenient front strap that can be pulled to tighten the whole harness system, it's a great choice for parents, too. This seat offers outstanding protection and convenience at a reasonable price.

Warranty: 1 year, limited.

Approx. retail price	**Approx. low price**
$70	**$60**

EVENFLO ULTARA V PREMIER 234186

✓BEST BUY

Pillowlike removable pads and a three-position recline make this car seat uncommonly comfortable. A five-point harness system that can be adjusted to accommodate a growing child makes it practical and safe. Use the seat in a rear-facing position for infants from 5 to 20 pounds (thanks to the removable pads, this is one of the few convertible car seats that truly offers adequate support for the smallest babies) and forward-facing for toddlers up to 43 pounds. The seat also features a front strap that can be pulled to tighten the harness system, and the luxurious wraparound pad system (made of a plush material) is removable and washable. This is another option for parents who can only consider one car seat, although it is more expensive than other available models.

Warranty: 1 year, limited.

Approx. retail price	Approx. low price
$100	$100

Booster Car Seat

CENTURY BREVERRA SPORT 4890

✓BEST BUY

At last, here is a booster seat that makes sense. While the typical booster seat consists of a raised bottom with a bar across the front, which may not offer adequate protection should a child be thrown forward in a crash, this seat takes advantage of the three-point harness systems (shoulder and lap belts) already required in newer-model cars. The Century Breverra Sport consists of a thick, seat-shaped pad (with a back and bottom) that surrounds the child's body and lifts him or her several inches off the seat of the car, thus reaching the perfect height for the car's own three-point harness system. This seat will not work with older-model cars that have only lap seat belts. Use this booster seat for children who weigh from 30 to 60 pounds. Since it looks like a bucket seat to begin with and comes in a variety of colorful patterns, it may make a good alternative for a child who objects to the typical car seat.

Warranty: 1 year, limited.

Approx. retail price	Approx. low price
$45	$45

CONVERTIBLE INFANT CAR SEAT/STROLLERS

These products can come in mighty handy, serving as car seats, strollers, and infant carriers. Many parents enjoy the convenience of being able to take the baby from the car to the stroller without undoing and refastening complicated harnesses. If you're shopping for a convertible infant car seat/stroller, read the introductions on infant car seats and strollers—you'll want to make sure the model you're considering has all the safety and comfort features of an individual car seat or stroller. In addition, check the fasteners that hold the car seat to the stroller—they should be sturdy and secure—and make sure the conversion from car seat to stroller and back is quick and easy enough to suit your needs.

KOLCRAFT PLUS 4

✓BEST BUY

Kolcraft's Plus 4 offers the same kind of versatility and convenience as Century's 4-in-1 System (below). It combines an infant car seat/carrier with a lightweight stroller, which is easy to fold and comes with an adjustable sunshade and a large storage bin. The seat locks easily into the stroller. This model sports more features than the Century model (such as the two-position reclining stroller seat with a hard back and a washable extra seat pad) and is easier to use.

Warranty: 1 year.

Approx. retail price	Approx. low price
$129	$100

CENTURY 4-IN-1 SYSTEM DELUXE 11-597

Recommended

It is possible to move a sleeping baby from a car seat to a stroller with this combination unit, which offers four functions in one by teaming up a great infant car seat (Century's 565 or 590 series unit) with a lightweight stroller. You can use this model as a car seat or a carrier, attach it to the stroller for an infant stroller, or use the stroller alone for a toddler. The seat locks easily into the stroller, which is lightweight, easy to fold in one step, features an adjustable canopy that can also be used with the carrier, and has a large storage bin. All this adds up to an extraordinary piece of equipment for the price. One small drawback: The stroller features a "sling" seat that lacks a firm back and doesn't recline. Important safety note: There is a lot of debate about whether Century's 590 model car seat meets safety standards. Just to be on the safe side, choose this unit with the Century 565 car seat.

Warranty: 1 year.

Approx. retail price	**Approx. low price**
$130	**$125**

STROLLERS

Many parents tend to buy an infant carriage or a standard stroller, in addition to an umbrella stroller, to carry around easily in the car. Today, the best strollers grow with your baby, combining the luxury of a carriage and the practicality of an umbrella stroller.

Look for a lightweight, easy-to-fold stroller that still offers removable, padded seats; reversible handles; and large, durable wheels. Extra features are important, too. Many strollers come with seat inserts to keep a tiny baby's head secure, two shopping baskets instead of only one, and removable canopies with a sun strip.

Safe strollers have wide bases to prevent tipping; wide wheels and shock absorbers for smooth, straight steering; seat and crotch belts securely attached to the frame; straps that are easy to fasten and unfasten; and secure brakes. It is important to test the brakes first. Shopping baskets should be located directly over or in front of rear wheels. Make sure that you always fasten the seat belt, and keep your child's hands away when folding or unfolding the stroller.

GRACO BROUGHAM SL2 7525

✓BEST BUY

The Brougham is a good option for parents who can afford only one stroller, because it's loaded with all sorts of practical features at a sensible price. It has a well-engineered easy-fold mechanism that collapses the stroller in one step, a three-position reclining seat, dual parking brakes, a reversible handle, a pad that offers infant head support, a canopy with a peekaboo window, a padded guard rail, and a footrest. It also features an extra-large storage basket on the bottom of the stroller, and a storage bag built into the canopy. Steering is relatively effortless, the suspension system is good, and balloon tires ensure a smooth ride. This unit is substantial enough to be a principal piece of equipment for daily use, but light enough to stash in a car trunk and use on the go. Graco does not offer a published warranty but claims to stand behind its products and provides a toll-free number for customers to call in case of problems.

Warranty: Not available.

Approx. retail price
$110

Approx. low price
$105

COMBI SAVVY-Z

✓ BEST BUY

A hefty price is the only drawback to this outstanding Japanese unit, which is so versatile and well engineered it can work well for parents who intend to purchase only one stroller. Thanks to the use of aircraft aluminum for the frame, it weighs only 7.7 pounds and is exceptionally sturdy. It's also extremely easy to collapse with one movement, and it reclines to any position up to a 140-degree angle. Other features include an adjustable and removable canopy, a storage bin under the unit, a footrest, a cushion that's easy to remove for washing, and a shoulder strap attached to the unit for carrying in its collapsed position. Steering this lightweight stroller—which is surprisingly "solid" on the road—is smooth, easy, and even fun. It is not certified by JPMA because the harness system, which consists of a seat belt with a crotch system, comes around the side of the unit instead of through the back, which means a child can fall out if (and only if) the stroller is turned upside down. (It does meet all certification standards for other countries where it is sold.)

Warranty: parts and labor, 1 year.

Approx. retail price
$199

Approx. low price
$199

Prices are accurate at time of printing but are subject to manufacturers' changes.

KOLCRAFT TECHRIDER 46123

✓BEST BUY

Reversible handles, which can be a real plus on a stroller, depending on the nature of a baby, are usually found only on full-featured strollers. However, the lightweight TechRider from Kolcraft sports this attribute, which won Kolcraft an industry award for innovative design. But the TechRider has many more features, including a two-position reclining seat back, an extra-large storage basket, an adjustable sun canopy with a see-through panel, a padded comfort handle, dual rear brakes, removable self-leveling front swivel wheels, and an extra seat pad that's washable. It's also extremely easy to collapse and steer. With its reasonable price, this is a good all-around piece of equipment.

Warranty: 1 year.

Approx. retail price	Approx. low price
$90	$75

GRACO STEALTH LITERIDER 6973

✓BEST BUY

Full-featured strollers are getting lighter, as evidenced by this Graco LiteRider. This model also sports everything you need in a stroller, such as a quick and easily adjustable recline feature (including one setting at full recline for infants); a thickly padded, removable and washable pad; a full-size seating area; a canopy with a window; an ergonomically designed handle that, at 40 inches, is a bit taller than those of other strollers; a large storage bin; and a one-step "collapse" system that's extremely easy to use. It also boasts sturdy balloon wheels that ensure a smooth ride, and it's easy to steer. All this adds up to a lightweight piece of equipment that can easily last over the long haul for parents who plan to purchase only one stroller. Graco does not offer a published warranty but claims to stand behind its products and provides a toll-free number for customers to call in case of problems.

Warranty: Not available.

Approx. retail price	Approx. low price
$80	$80

Prices are accurate at time of printing but are subject to manufacturers' changes.

CENTURY TRAVELITE SPORT SERIES 11-171

Budget Buy

You'll find many of the conveniences of more expensive strollers on this Century TraveLite, which is lightweight, extremely easy to collapse, and sports a new handle design that's higher than other strollers, padded with foam, and designed so it can be pushed with just one hand. The storage bin is roomy, the wheels are sturdy, and the whole unit rolls smoothly. Two special new features are a "cab-forward" seating design that positions the seat to give baby a better view, and a longer canopy with a peekaboo window in the back. It's a great choice for the price.

Warranty: 1 year.

Approx. retail price	Approx. low price
$60	$60